International Law and Business

A global introduction

Bart Wernaart

First edition

Noordhoff Uitgevers Groningen | Houten

Cover design: G2K (Groningen-Amsterdam)
Cover illustration: Stocksy
Cartoons: Sandor Paulus, Son en Breugel (the Netherlands)

If you have any comments or queries about this or any other publication, please contact Noordhoff Uitgevers BV, Afdeling Hoger Onderwijs, Antwoordnummer 13, 9700 VB Groningen, The Netherlands, e-mail: info@noordhoff.nl

MIX
Papier van verantwoorde herkomst
FSC® C118189

1 / 17

ISBN 978-90-01-87157-4
NUR 820

Contents

Foreword

The idea to write this book evolved during the years in which I was simultaneously conducting my Phd research and lecturing my IBMS students. What I've noticed is that there are many books entitled 'introduction to international law' or 'international business law'. However, none of the existing titles were eagerly read by my students. I missed several elements that I tried to include in this book.

The first thing is a chapter about methods. This is quite unheard of in law, especially in the international context. However, I do believe that comparative methods can and should be used by business students when they take decisions in the sphere of export and international contracts. In fact, such methods seem to linger somewhere in academic circles and are quite endlessly debated. Instead, I think such methods deserve to be used in practice, and applied by business students all around the world.

Second, many books introduce law on a global level, and do not go any further than discussing international organizations that harmonize international law, such as the UN, the Bretton Woods Institutions, and the EU. What is missing, is a broader perspective in which there is not only room for other forms of economic integration next to the EU, but also a rich and colourful reference to national concepts of law. After all, the origin of most legal concepts can be found in national law, not in international law.

Third, I wanted to shift the European/American focus to a truly worldwide focus. There is more than just U.S., French, German and UK law, which are the usual countries that are discussed in the context of business law. It is true that these are the countries that have set the example in many was in developing legal solutions to problems. However, it would not do justice to the particularities of other legal systems, including Islamic, Asian, African, Latin-American and Australian law. There is much to learn there as well.

So, what I've tried to do is to give some real insight in how law works around the globe in the context of international business. I did so by discussing different solutions in law using examples from many different regions and countries, using colourful, funny, and I hope inspiring examples. Furthermore, I tried to do this in using understandable, clear language that can be read by business students who do not necessarily have a legal background. The book is set up rather broadly, so that it can be used by teachers through their entire curriculum.

Each chapter ends with a clear summary, and practice questions. I used three different kinds of questions, to make sure the student applies different aspects of his skills: open questions, essay questions and multiple choice questions. On the website www.internationallawandbusiness.noordhoff.nl the author will frequently post blogs, vlogs and other materials to keep this book as up to date as possible. Furthermore, extensive case studies that would be too voluminous to include in the main text are published on this site (and referred to in this book).

Please accept that each time when I use 'he', it might as well be a 'she'. However, it would make the book less readable if I would use both.

Writing is a lonely occupation, but I am lucky with so many great and warm people around me. First of all, I would like to thank all my wonderful students. They 'sharpen my knives' every day when we engage in fruitful and inspiring discussions about international business law. Without them, this book would not exist.
Next to that, I would like to thank my colleague Therese van Oosterhout, my 'partner in crime' at our department. She read my draft chapters, gave here comments and gave me very useful feedback during the process.
Also, I would like to thank the management of Fontys IBMS (department Marketing and Management) and the Lectorate for facilitating my writing career in terms of time and genuine interest. A special thank you goes to Anthony Murphy, my team leader, for strongly supporting my writing career.

On a more personal note I would like to thank my parents and brothers for their ongoing support. And last, and most of all, a warm thank you to my beautiful wife, who is a shining star in my life and who gave birth to the most beautiful son in the world during the period this book was written. If you really want to know, our son was born halfway chapter 7, right before the section about the free movement of services.

Therefore, I would like to dedicate this book to our son Vik, who sat on my lap during the other half of the writing process. I hope you will become a man with a nuanced and respectful sense of justice. The world may be dark sometimes, but when one tries to understand one another, it is the most powerful key to justice and peace.

Bart Wernaart
Valkenswaard (the Netherlands), November 2016

PART 1
Introduction and methods

In this part, we will introduce international law as well as comparative methods in law in an international business context.
In chapter one, we will introduce the main characteristics of law and explain the main features of legal terminology. Also, we will portray the origin and sources of law.
In chapter two, we will explore comparative methods which can be used to compare different legal systems. This is done on a macro level, in which the legal families of the world are discussed, and on a micro level, in which particular phenomenon in law are compared.

I LOVE KNITTING!
156-2
Sandor

1 What is law and where can we find it?

In this chapter, we will discuss how law is used in the organization of just behaviour. To this end, we will focus on the relations that are regulated by law, and the different branches of law. Also the meaning of just behaviour will be explained. We will discuss the three elements of 'just', that is: justice, opportuneness and legal certainty. Furthermore, the origin of law will be explored. In this light, two views on law are explained: natural law and positivist law. Last, the sources of law that are generally used around the world are discussed.

1.1 The organization of just behaviour

In everyday life we are engaged in legal issues and act in compliance with many legally binding rules, as we might see in example 1.1. Such rules are necessary to organize just behaviour in a given society. Or in other words: to regulate what is just to avoid chaos. Law is a tool to create such rules.

| Law organizes just behaviour in a society. **Law**

Imagine a country in which people could choose randomly their side of the road: one would risk his life when participating in traffic, and probably the one with the biggest or strongest cars will dictate what happens on the road. To avoid traffic chaos, law defines how traffic participants should use the roads. One of these legal rules is the obligation to use a particular side of the rode. Usually, such rules are applicable in a given society. Such a society may have many different shapes and sizes. In the example, the society is a state. However, there are also other forms, such as a small group of people, a city, a state, a region, or sometimes even the entire world. On all these levels, law can be used to organize just behaviour.

EXAMPLE 1.1

Driving on the right side of the road

Article 13 of the Malaysian Highway Code (LN 165/1959) stipulates that: 'Vehicles should at all times be driven on the left-hand lane of the road, the slower the speed the further left the lane of the road.' The Malaysian Highway Code stipulates that all traffic participants have to use the left side of the road. This is historically determined due to the fact that Malaysia was a former colony of Great Britain. In Great Britain, people traditionally use the left side of the road. This can be traced back to practical considerations in medieval times: a majority of people is right handed, and when driving your horse using the left side of the road, one can easily draw a sword with their sword arm, or – in more peaceful tidings – offer a greeting to passengers with the 'right' hand. In Canada, also a former British colony, the left side of the road was originally used as well. However, the Canadian changed their laws to facilitate smooth traffic flow (and trading) between Canada and the U.S.A., for in the latter country, the right side of the road is used.

To further clarify the concept of law, it is important to explain in what manner law organizes just behaviour, what relations are organized by law, and what different kind of branches of law we distinguish. This is done in the remainder of this section below.

1.1.1 Substantive law and formal law

Law organizes just behaviour by applying two different kinds of rules: rules on content (substantive law) and rules to maintain this content (formal law).

Substantive law

To organize just behaviour in a society we first need standards that define the 'rules of the game' that people are required to obey. These rules are about the content of what people are supposed to do, or not to do, such as driving on the right side of the road (and not on the wrong side of the road). In legal terms, we refer to these rules as substantive law.

Substantive law

> Substantive law is composed of legal rules that define the content of just behaviour.

Formal law

However, such substantive rules in itself are rather pointless when there are no means to maintain these rules. If there are no consequences when substantive law is violated, a society is depending on the good will of the people to obey the law. As lovely as that may seem, there will always be people who will challenge the substantive rules one way or another for various reasons. Therefore, a legislator will need to adopt different kinds of rules next to the substantive rules: formal rules.

Formal law

> Formal law is composed of legal rules that maintain substantive law.

In example 1.2, we see an attempt of the Moroccan legislature to introduce a penalty system that aims to better maintain the substantive traffic rules. When a traffic participant risks losing his points when they break a speed limit, there is a stronger urge for this person to obey speed rules compared to the situation in which there are no legal consequences when driving too fast. This urge is probably even more instant when they risk losing their driving licence, paying a fine or ending up in jail. On top of that, the required traffic education when losing a certain amount of points is designed to make people aware of the need to obey traffic rules. The idea is that the speed limits and other traffic rules are better maintained by this penal system. In other words: the penal system includes formal rules in order to maintain the substantive traffic rules.

EXAMPLE 1.2

The Moroccan highway penalty system
In Morocco, traffic incidents are a major problem. To stimulate safer traffic with fewer casualties, the Moroccan legislature adopted a new Highway Code in 2010, with a refined penalty system (Le Nouveau Code de la Route au Maroc, 2010). Each driving licence holds 30 points (or 20, in case of a new licence). One can lose points when offending the traffic laws and regain points in case of good behaviour, such as following education sessions to improve traffic behaviour. Full credits are regained when traffic laws are not offending in 3 years time. Through this system, one might lose the ability to drive. Besides this approach, the more traditional fines and sanctions exist, and in case of grave violations of traffic law, one might even me imprisoned.

FIGURE 1.1 Substantive and formal law

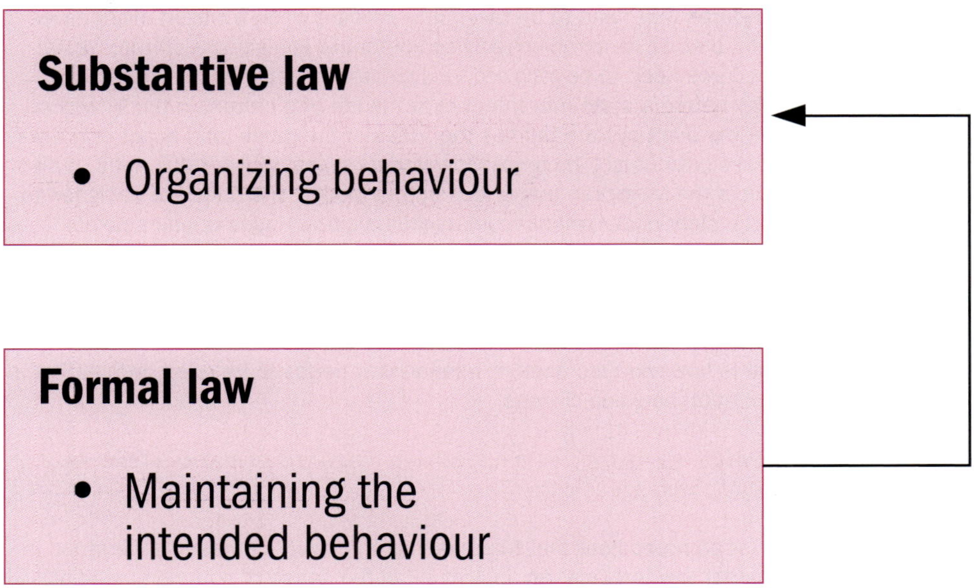

1

1.1.2 Public law and private law

In this section we discuss which relations are organized by law. Substantive and formal rules are both created to regulate two particular relations within societies: the relation between the government and its citizens, and the relation between citizens. In legal terminology, the law that organizes these relations is called public law and private law respectively.

Public law

Public law

> Public law is the law that regulates the relation between a government and its citizens.

Public substantive law

In many societies it is usually the state that oversees the enforcement of the law, and decides when a citizen needs to be punished for not behaving according to its laws. On the one hand, these legal rules authorize a state to interfere when people are misbehaving. Simultaneously, these rules also restrict the power of a state: the state has to act in accordance with its competences laid down in these rules. In public law, we find both substantive and formal rules as we can see in the 'Moroccan highway penalty system' example.
In the first place, there are substantive rules in society everyone should comply with (traffic rules). They are adopted for the public wellbeing/good. When one offends such a substantive traffic rule, the state interferes, and punishes the citizen accordingly, in line with the appropriate formal rules. Regulating this relationship between the state and its citizens is one of the purposes of law, and is referred to as public law. The state adopts the substantive law for the benefit of society in general, and acts when one misbehaves, for the sake of society. This means that traffic rules, from a legal perspective, are rules between the individual and society.

Public formal law

In the second place, there are formal rules that regulate the legal procedures that need to be taken into account when a citizen misbehaves. Mostly, a state is not unlimitedly competent in punishing a citizen: formal procedures need to be followed, and evidence should be of a particular quality before a state may interfere in the life of a citizen. In the Moroccan case, the point system defines the 'rules of the game' and is not only a way to make citizens act in compliance with the substantive traffic rules. It also restricts the Moroccan authorities in their power: the rules are designed to make it clear under what circumstances a citizen loses or gains points. When these rules are taken into account by the Moroccan authorities, a citizen cannot not be punished randomly.

Private law

There is however also another relation that needs to be ruled by law. That is the relation between citizens.

Private law

> Private law is the law that regulates the relation between citizen or those who act as citizens.

It must be noted here that the meaning of 'citizen' is mostly understood in a broader way than just an 'individual' in the sense of a human being of flesh and blood.

In most legal systems, a company is considered to be an equivalent to an individual in terms of its capacity to legally act. After all, a company is not a government that acts on behalf of the public good. Therefore, private law also regulates the relation between an individual and a company, or between companies.
Occasionally, a government institution may also be considered acting as a citizen. This could be when a parliament orders food for their lunch break. In such cases, they do not act in their capacity as a government institution, but participate in business just as an individual would. The relationship between the parliament ordering food and the caterer is therefore also governed by private legal rules.

As stated above, one should obey traffic rules on behalf of the society in general. The idea is that when everyone acts in accordance with traffic rules, we could have safe traffic within society without too many problems. However, when someone breaks such a traffic rule, and as a result damages the property of someone else, the victim would want this damage to be compensated. In the newspaper article, there are several victims: the injured people, the owner of the house and the lawful owner of the car. The driver breaks several rules of public law that apply in Washington D.C. It will be no surprise that in the State of Columbia stealing is forbidden as well as driving your car into someone's house. For instance, the Code of Columbia (§22-3211) stipulates that:

'A person commits the offense of theft if that person wrongfully obtains or uses the property of another with the intent:
(1) To deprive the other of a right to the property or a benefit of the property; or
(2) To appropriate the property to his or her own use or to the use of a third person.'

The penalty for first degree theft (in case the stolen property exceeds a value of $1.000) is a maximum fine of $5.000, and imprisonment for no more than ten years (Code of Columbia, §22-3212).
The victims however would probably be not too impressed by the fact that the driver is fined by the authorities for breaking several rules, or even ends up in jail. This punishment for the illegal behaviour is after all on behalf of the society, and not on behalf of the victims: it is based on public law. However, it is in the interest of the victims to seek legal remedies against the driver directly in order to claim damage compensation. For this, we need private legal rules that enable a victim to make such claims. Not on behalf of society, but on his own behalf since he – and no one else – suffered the damage.

1

THE WASHINGTON POST, 10 MAY 2011

Car crashes into D.C. house, driver flees

BY: THEOLA LABBÉ-DEBOSE

D.C. police are looking for a driver who crashed a car into a North-East home Wednesday morning and then fled the scene.

The accident took place in the 2600 block of 24th St. NE., near Douglas St. NE. Shortly before 10 a.m., police say, officers responded to a 911 call of a hit and run accident.

When they arrived, they found the car – which has Maryland license plates – crashed into the house but the driver was nowhere to be found, said Officer Anthony Clay, a police spokesman.

There were three people in the house at the time of the crash, but they were not seriously injured, said D.C. Fire/EMS spokesman Pete Piringer.

One of the occupants, described as an elderly female, was taken to a hospital for further evaluation; the other two were examined at the scene but were not treated for any injuries, Piringer said.

Police are investigating whether the car was stolen, possibly from Prince George's County, Clay said.

In the example 1.3, two legal issues are at stake. In the first place, the shop delivered the wrong product to Miranda. This legal issue is between the company and Miranda. In the second place, Miranda causes injuries to the shop employee. This legal issue is between two individuals: the employee and Miranda, although perhaps the company might also be involved because the employee was hurt while performing his job for the record shop.

Private substantive law

We need some substantive rules that regulate the relation between the quarrelling parties to solve these issues. When considering the Sales of Goods Act of Ontario (Ontario Sales of Goods Act, R.S.O. 1990, Chapter S.1.), Article 29 (3) stipulates that:

> 'Where the seller delivers to the buyer the goods contracted to be sold mixed with goods of a different description not included in the contract, the buyer may accept the goods that are in accordance with the contract and reject the rest, or may reject the whole.'

Besides, Miranda could have invoked Article 33 of the same Act, which emphasizes that:

> 'Where goods are delivered to the buyer that the buyer has not previously examined, the buyer shall be deemed not to have accepted them until there has been a reasonable opportunity of examining them for the purpose of ascertaining whether they are in conformity with the contract.'

In other words, Miranda did not have to accept the delivery of the wrong product, and could easily claim her money back and/or buy the right product. Regarding the injury and damage of the shop employee, the Canadian courts have developed the construction of 'tort' in their case law throughout the years, in which rules are developed for compensating damage to the victim of a wrongful act. In this case, the employee will probably claim compensation damage from Miranda, based on the particular form of tort that is defined as 'battery', meaning that someone intentionally made unwanted contact with another person, such as a punch in the face, and from this, damage resulted.

Private formal law

And also here, rules to maintain the law are necessary. To this end, in Ontario, there are several legal standards that regulate the proceedings when one individual seeks legal remedies against the other in court. For instance, 'Ontario Regulation 258/98,' regulates the procedure for small claims, while the 'Rules of Civil Procedure. O. Reg. 575/07, s. 6 (1),' regulate procedures before the higher courts (the Court of Appeal and Superior Court of Justice).

EXAMPLE 1.3

Justin Bieber v. the Foo Fighters

Miranda (Ontario, Canada) is a big Justin Bieber fan. As a true 'Belieber', she sleeps in front of the closest record shop on the eve of the release of Bieber's newest record: a real music fan still wants the real 'physical' record after all. When the shop opens at 9 AM, she – amongst many other Beliebers – risks her life in the crowd to get the newest record as soon as possible. She pays 30 U.S. dollars, and is the happiest person on earth when she holds her own copy of the record. The shop employee shouts at Miranda to leave quickly, because there are many more girls waiting in line that want to purchase the record. Miranda therefore leaves the place without opening the CD box. At home however, her euphoric feeling radically changes when she discovers that the shop employee accidentally put the wrong record in the box. Miranda now owns a Justin Bieber CD box, with a record of the latest Foo Fighters album. Of course, she is extremely upset and wants the record shop to provide her with the correct disk: the one she actually paid for. However, when she returns to the shop, it is so busy with screaming Bieber fans that she is unable to discuss the problem properly. She therefore cannot constrain her anger anymore, and punches one of the shop employees in the face. The employee needs medical treatment as a result of Miranda's outburst.

FIGURE 1.2 Public law and private law

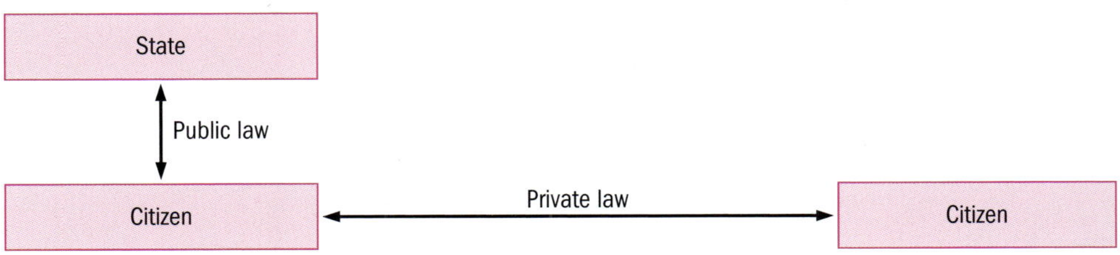

1.1.3 The branches of law

So, we need substantive law to define the content of just behaviour, and formal law to maintain this just behaviour in society. Both types of law are necessary in regulating the relation between a government and its citizens (public law) and between citizens (private law). In legal sciences we usually further subdivide law in more detailed categories. This subdivision is based on the topic or issue that is dealt with by this particular branch of law. In this book, the chapters are similarly categorized. In this section, the branches are briefly touched upon, while in the following chapters their meaning will be further explored.

On an international level there is an increasing international economic cooperation. While this is in the first place an affair for states among themselves, the effects of this cooperation has profound impact on citizens and companies. While the form is that of public law – states engage in these kinds of cooperation on behalf of the public good within their society – the effects are sometimes also noticeable in the relation between citizens. Therefore, it is not easy to categorize this particular branch of law in either public or private law.

Furthermore, there is a law that is designed to regulate the affairs of a state and its relation with citizens: pubic law. In each state laws are adopted that regulate the way a state is governed and the fundamental rights their citizens are entitled to. This is referred to as constitutional and administrational law.

Then, there are several branches of private law that relate to doing business. There are laws that deal with contracts, liability, labour contracts, the legal form of a company, privacy, and intellectual property.

FIGURE 1.3 Branches of law

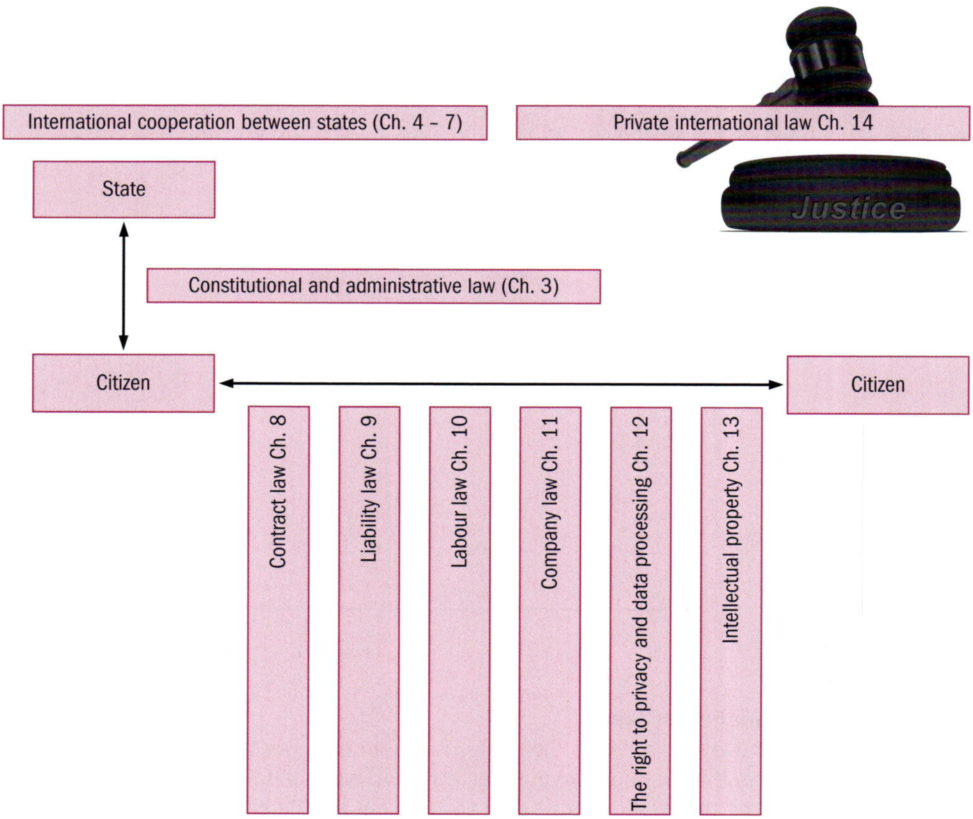

Also, there are legal rules that define how to settle a dispute between citizens in both public and private law. Such rules are of course formal rules, because they facilitate maintaining substantive rules in cases where substantive law is violated. For instance, there are rules that regulate where to settle a dispute (jurisdiction) under which law and how to execute a verdict. We call these rules private international law.

Please note that there are more branches of law that are not discussed here because they are not that relevant for this book. Take for instance criminal law, or the law that regulates court proceedings.

1.2 The meaning of just behaviour

We now know how law regulates just behaviour in society. What remains unclear so far is the meaning of the concept 'just'. To start with, there is no specific answer to that question, because the perception of what just is will differ per society. However, in general one could say that 'just' is defined by three basic values that are commonly shared in every society: justice, opportuness and legal certainty (Habermas, 1992), see figure 1.4. The exact way this balance is designed greatly determines the characteristics of the society's legal system.

Just

> Just implies a balance between the values 'justice', 'opportuness', and 'legal certainty'.

FIGURE 1.4 The functions of law

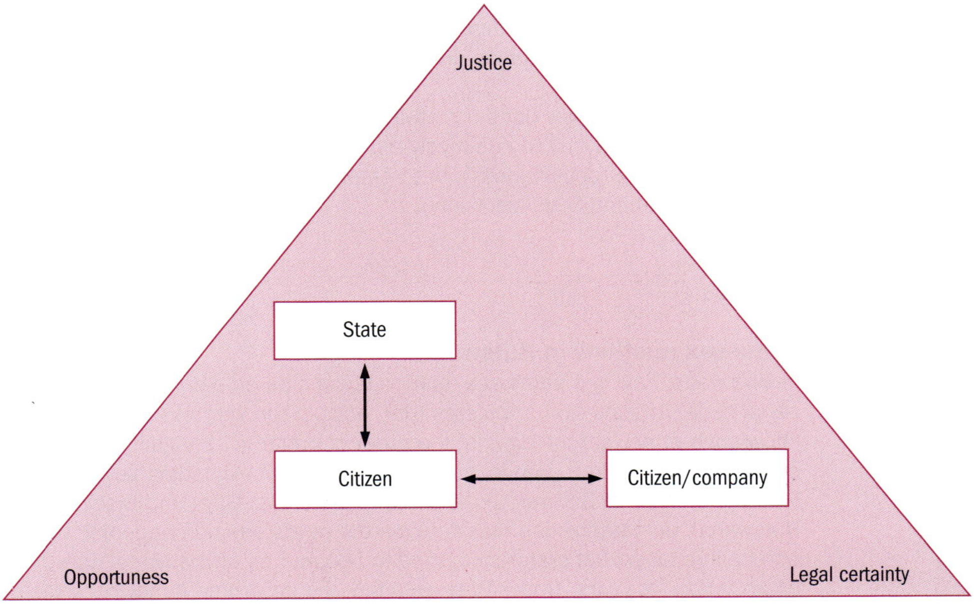

1.2.1 Justice

The first element of 'just' is the idea of 'justice'.

Justice

Justice is the moral conviction of a given society expressed in law.

1

In many cases, the law expresses a certain moral conviction that is supported in a society. Considering the Ontario legal standards from the case 'Justin Bieber v. the Foo Fighters', we can observe that there is a moral conviction behind the applicable rules. For instance, when you buy something, and the product does not match the criterion you could reasonably expect, you do not have to accept the product; and when you deliberately cause damage to someone, you have to pay compensation damage. While such moral convictions are widely shared and appear in some shape or form in almost all legal systems around the world, there are other moral convictions expressed by law that are highly controversial. For example, the justice in the death penalty is a fiercely debated topic around the world, and there are very different views on the morality this penalty expresses, as you can see in case study 1.1 on the website.

One should however be careful in identifying law with justice as a synonym. In the first place, law usually expresses the moral conviction of the legislature. This does not mean however that this moral conviction is shared with all the citizens of that particular society. As we see in the case example 1.4, the legality of a same-sex relation is under dispute in Botswana. While the law forbids having a same-sex relation, a lobby group supporting those with lesbian, gay and bisexual preferences fights for its right of existence. Eventually, the high Court of Botswana had to balance different opposing fundamental rights in order to reach a verdict, allowing this organization to legally exist. As it seems, not everyone in Botswana agrees with the prohibition of same sex relations. On the other hand, the government sustains that such a relation is unnatural and should therefore be classified as a crime.

In the second place, law does not always express a moral conviction: sometimes law is a tool to effectively regulate something in society that needs to be done (opportuness), or to establish clarity on someone's legal position beforehand (legal certainty).

EXAMPLE 1.4

Same-sex relations in Botswana

In Botswana, having a same-sex relation is considered a crime under their penal code. Articles 164 stipulates that 'any person who has carnal knowledge of any person against the order of nature (...) is guilty of an offence and is liable to imprisonment for a term not exceeding seven years' (The Penal Code of Botswana). LeGaBiBo, (Lesbians, Gays and Bisexuals of Botswana), an organization that defends the rights position of people with a non-traditional sexual preference, tried to become an officially registered organization for years. Under Botswana law, the government may deny the registering of an organization when it is allegedly used for illegal purposes (Art. 7. Societies Act of Botswana). Based on this provision, the registering of LeGaBiBo had been denied several times due to the fact that this organization supported and promoted illegal sexual relations.

Simultaneously however, the Constitution of Botswana recognizes the right of freedom of expression, association and assembly (Art. 3, 12 and 13, Constitution of Botswana). LeGaBiBo appealed against the decision of the government to deny their status as a lawful organization within Botswana. Eventually, the High Court of Botswana ruled that 'the objects of LeGaGiBo as reflected in the societies' Constitution are all ex facie lawful. They include carrying out political lobbying for equal rights and decriminalization of same sex relationships. Lobbying for legislative reforms is not per se a crime. It is also not a crime to be homosexual. Refusal to register LeGaBiBo was not reasonably justifiable under the Constitution of Botswana nor under section 7(2)(a) of the Societies Act (...). It violated the applicant's rights to freedom of expression, freedom of association and freedom of assembly (...)' (High Court of Botswana, 14 November 2014).

1.2.2 Opportuness

Opportuness

Opportuness is the expression of effectiveness by a given society in law.

Sometimes, law is not used as a tool to express a moral conviction but rather a tool to effectively regulate something in society. For instance, the choice to drive a car on either the left side or the right side of the road seems a random choice, usually influenced by coincidental historical factors. The choice in itself is not an expression of morality or justice. It is simply something that needs to be organized from a practical point of view. It is an opportune way to effectively regulate traffic.
In most situations, justice and opportuness go very well hand in hand with one another. However, sometimes in a given society, something needs to be regulated by law from an effective or practical point of view while it is perceived to be an unjust legal standard. For instance, when states adopt laws that lead to downsizing and reforms during economic hardship, a majority of the population will probably disagree because they strongly feel that injustice is inflicted on them, as we can see in example 1.5. However, the legislature will most likely argue that there is no other way to effectively organize the addressed issues without the new approach.

EXAMPLE 1.5

The Greek economic and financial reforms

As a result of a financial crisis, the Greek authorities had to adopt severe laws and policies in the period 2009-2012 to improve their economy in compliance with European and IMF standards. During this period, the average retirement age was raised from 61 to 65, and later even to 65, while salaries went down drastically, up to 30 per cent (Greek Law 4093/2012). It will need no further elaboration that the average Greek citizen, to put it mildly, was unpleasantly surprised. This was expressed in a massive demonstration against these economic and financial reforms, and resulted in a dramatic loss of the elections of the then-government in 2014 and 2015. The radical left party Syriza won the parliamentary elections in

2015. It was generally believed that this victory was due to the fact that the electorate was very dissatisfied with the economic and financial reforms that were adopted by the previous government. While Syriza promised radical changes regarding these reforms, it soon became apparent that also the radical left party had to pursue most of the reforms, because it was economically simply impossible not to downsize drastically. Doing something else would result in a bankruptcy of Greece, and possibly their exit from the European Union. The consequences of such events would have unthinkable effects for the Greek society.

1.2.3 Legal certainty

Legal certainty

Legal certainty is the expression of legality in a given society.

A last function of law is that of legal certainty. The idea is that every citizen and the relevant government should be able to know the legal consequences of their actions beforehand, and not afterwards. This is also defined as the principle of legality. In order words: law should – to a certain extent – be predictable. This means for instance that a citizen cannot be punished for something that was not forbidden at the time of his actions. This also means that a government may not interfere in the life of its citizens without a valid legal ground that is applicable at that time.

This principle was the main cause for debate in the case of Amanda Knox, an American student accused of murder in Italy. As you can see in the newspaper article, Amanda Knox was sentenced to prison by an Italian court for murdering her roommate in 2009. However, in appeal, she was released of all charges due to invalid evidence in 2011, and she could as a result leave the country and go home to the U.S.A. However, in Italian society her name will probably always be linked to the murder of Meredith Kercher. It appears that the Italian crowd waiting outside the courtroom was not convinced that Amanda and her former boyfriend were innocent in this murder case. In the media at that time it was rumoured that she was involved in a rather extreme sex-game, that led to the death of Kercher (Malone, 2007). However, there was only circumstantial evidence, which was considered to be unreliable. Therefore, the Appellate Court held that it could not lawfully imprison someone based on this evidence alone (Court of Assizes of Appeal of Perugia, 3 October 2011). However, in cassation, the Supreme Court in Italy ruled that Knox was guilty nevertheless, and sentenced her to prison for 28 years and six months (Italian Supreme Court of Cassation, 30 January 2014). The new theory was that there was no extreme sex-game, but an argument over money. According to the Supreme Court, Amanda even delivered the final blow that caused the death of Kercher. Luckily for Amanda, the sentence was ruled in her absence, because she lived in the U.S.A. at the time the verdict was reached. Knox in turn, claimed that the evidence was suggestive, incomplete, and the court completed the picture of the crime scene with rumours and questionable testimonies of a co-defendant (Cuomo, C & Ford, D, 2014). Finally, on 27 March 2015, the Italian Supreme Court of last instance ruled that Amanda was innocent, and thereby gave a final legally binding interpretation to the case.

NEW YORK TIMES, 3 OCTOBER 2011

Amanda Knox Freed After Appeal in Italian Court

BY: ELISABETTA LEDO

With a rapt worldwide television audience looking on, an Italian court on Monday reversed the murder conviction of 24-year-old Amanda Knox, the American student whose sensational murder trial had reverberated on both sides of the Atlantic. The decision was read out a little before 10 p.m. to a courtroom heavy with tensions and emotions built up over the four years since the arrest of Ms. Knox and her boyfriend at the time, Raffaele Sollecito, for the killing of her roommate, Meredith Kercher. Mr. Sollecito's conviction was also overturned Monday.

As it became evident that she was being cleared of all charges, save one of defamation, a deeply stressed Ms. Knox slumped back in her chair and began to sob, before falling into the arms of one of her lawyers, Maria Del Grosso.

(...)

The joyful reaction of the defendants contrasted sharply with the looks of ashen disappointment by prosecutors and relatives of Ms. Kercher. They had flown to Perugia on Monday.

(...)

Lyle Kercher, the brother of the slain woman, said he was 'very disappointed.' He added, 'In any case, no one will give us Meredith back, but we are very upset.'

1.3 The origin of law

One could endlessly debate the ultimate source of law. However, two approaches in legal philosophy are traditionally distinguished regarding the origin of law: the natural law approach, which assumes that law emerges from nature, and the positivist approach, which assumes that law emerges from codified standards.

1.3.1 Natural law

Natural law

In a natural law approach it is assumed that laws emerge from nature.

This means that a law does not need to be codified (written down) first to be a law, but already exists regardless its appearances.

An example of this is the concept of human rights. Two of the most important international human rights treaties are the International Covenant on Civil and Political Rights (ICCPR) and the International Covenant on Economic, Social and Cultural Rights (ICESCR). In these treaties human rights are recognized for each individual. In their preambles, it is stipulated that: 'these rights derive from the inherent dignity of the human person' (ICCPR and ICESCR, Preamble). In the covenants, it is therefore assumed that people have human rights simply because they were born. In other words: human rights are inherent to mankind, also when they have not been written down and recognized on a piece of paper somewhere.

The advantage of a natural law approach is that law (and justice) is not depending on any formalization, and therefore can be applied because it is only reasonable to do so. The disadvantage is that natural law can be subdue to many different forms of understanding, leading to legal uncertainty. In this light, there is always the pitfall that someone believes to have a monopoly on the correct understanding of natural law and as a result imposes this particular understanding of law on others. Simply because he assumes that this particular understanding follows from the nature of things and is therefore the only reasonable explanation of law. One rather extreme example was the German concept of law during their Third Empire, where – amongst others – Jewish people were considered to be inferior to German people, as we can see in the example 'the racial laws in the Third Empire'. This alleged inferiority did not emerge from a written code but was rather assumed to be the truth due to the fact that German people were naturally superior to others. From this belief the so-called 'Nuremberg laws' arose that marked the start of the legal prosecution of the Jews (Reichsgesetzblatt I, 1935, pp. 1146-7).

1.3.2 Positivist law

Positivist law

In a positivist law approach, it is assumed that law comes forth from codification.

This means that law is only law when it has been written down first. The advantage of such an approach is that people know beforehand what the rules of the game are (in line with the principle of legality). Next to that, in most legal systems the forming of written codes is subdue to strict rules in which a certain degree of quality and consent of the people that are bound by this law is guaranteed. This is exactly what legal positivism stands for: to protect people against extreme understandings of natural law. However, the disadvantage of a positivist law approach is that written law is always two steps behind reality, because one cannot create rules beforehand that flawlessly provide solutions to every possible case. Usually, some flexibility is required, as we can see in example 1.6. Furthermore, it might lead to over-formalizing relations in society, when only written standards can be applied. This is also referred to as bureaucracy.

EXAMPLE 1.6

Theft of electricity in the Netherlands

In the Netherlands, 1921, a clever dentist found a way to manipulate the meter reading in his dental office: he used a knitting needle to block the disk that would rotate in case of energy consumption. As a result, the electricity bills were much lower compared to the actual energy that was used. The dentist was tried for theft, stipulated in Article 310 of the Dutch Penal Code:
'The person who takes any good which belongs completely or partly to another person, with the objective of unlawful appropriation of the good, shall be sentenced, as guilty of theft, to a prison sentence not exceeding four years or a fine of the fourth category'.
However, there was a problem, because electricity does not fall under the category of 'any goods', since electricity are mere moving electrodes, and

not tangible things. Here, the legislature that adopted the Penal Code, dating back to 1881, could not reasonably foresee that it would be possible to 'steal' non-tangible things such as electricity.
Now, the Dutch Supreme Court was in a difficult position. On the one hand, it was obvious that it was the intention of the original legislature to penalize theft in general, not necessarily restricting this to tangible items only. Besides that, not penalizing this behaviour would give all energy consumers a carte blanche to manipulate energy bills. On the other hand, widening the scope of an existing law beyond the rather clear content would violate the principle of legality, and would conflict with the role of a court in the Dutch trias politica, that is to apply law, and not create (new) laws.

Eventually, the Dutch Supreme Court considered that it was the clear purpose of the Penal Code to protect assets, and the code did not specify the concept 'any goods'. Especially the first argument demonstrates that the Court applies a principle (you do not take away what belongs to someone else) that transcends the content of the written standard and stems from a general sense of what should be right. As a result, the dentist was sentenced to three months in prison (the Supreme Court of the Netherlands, 1921). This case demonstrates that positivist law cannot per definition provide for legal solutions in each case, and the Supreme Court had to widen the scope of the article by applying a more general concept of theft that is reasonably assumed to be law, and can be applied in line with the more current technological developments. It must be noted here that in the Netherlands, this ruling was not received without concern, especially due to the fact that from a positivist point of view, the Court exceeded its authority and violated the principle of legality.

1.3.3 Between legal positivism and natural law

Natural law and positivist law are two opposing extremes in elucidating the origin of law, as you can see in figure 1.5. In most legal systems, one needs a bit of both to function properly in a balance that suits the involved society. This balance is not only different per legal system, but may also shift over time, as we can see in example 1.7. Somewhere between the two opposite origins of law, we can find the most used sources of law around the globe. These sources usually have features of both positivist and natural law, although the emphasis differs. In the next paragraph, these sources of law will be further explored.

FIGURE 1.5 Positivist law and natural law

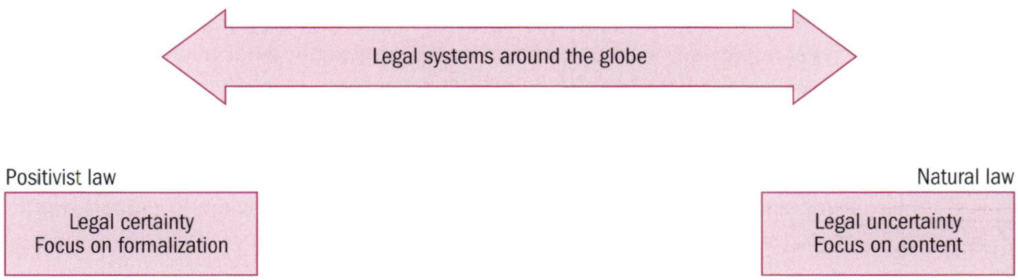

1

EXAMPLE 1.7

The struggle of China

The Chinese legal system – one of the oldest in the world – is a complex merge of two opposing legal philosophies that were, to put it mildly, at odds for centuries. Both seem to lead to a radically different solution to achieve social order. On the one hand, there is Confucianism, emphasizing Chinese tradition, consisting of (in order of importance) the nature of things, moral precepts, rites, custom and (least preferably) law. When a society is organized according to these concepts, people will be able to experience shame, and as a consequence intrinsically do the right thing, which then leads to a community in harmony. It is the duty of a ruler to lead by example. From the perspective of Confucianism, law as in written standards lead to a hollow application of rules without any notion of what is right and wrong, and therefore can only lead to chaos. On the other hand, there is legal Positivism, or Legalism, advocating the adoption of written codes, to achieve order. Legal positivists of China have always been cautious in assuming that people are capable of acting in accordance with the principles of Confucianism. Instead, strong legislation is proposed to force people to behave properly, and put consequences on misbehaving. Also, the exercise of power should not be unlimited and therefore legislation is required to restrict the power of public authorities. Chinese law is a result of centuries of discourse between these two major legal philosophies, and therefore rather unique, especially compared to Western legal systems, with a focus on legal positivism (Lefande, 2000).

1.4 Legal sources

While any categorization of legal sources might be arbitrary, and perhaps do no justice to the rich variety of legal sources, the following sources are generally used: codified standards, the application of law, legal writings and teachings, religious writings and teachings, customary law and legal principles. It will come to no surprise that in each legal system there are differences in the usage and hierarchy of legal sources. It is impossible to discuss this in a general sense. To understand the exact usage of legal sources and the hierarchy between these sources, one would have to study this on the level of states, which we will do in this book in chapter 3. For now, we will focus on explaining the meaning of the legal sources in itself.

All sources have elements of both positivist law and natural within them, however the balance is different, as you see visualized in figure 1.6.

Let's take a closer look at the two extremes: codified standards and legal principles. In codified standards there is naturally a strong emphasis on legal positivism, because written codes are exactly what positivist consider to be the source of law. In legal principles, there is a strong emphasis on natural law, because a principle is usually an abstract value that represents a foundation in law, which naturally applies without the need to be codified. However, one might argue that a codified standard needs a bit of natural law, and a legal principle might need some legal positivism to actually work.

FIGURE 1.6 Sources of Law

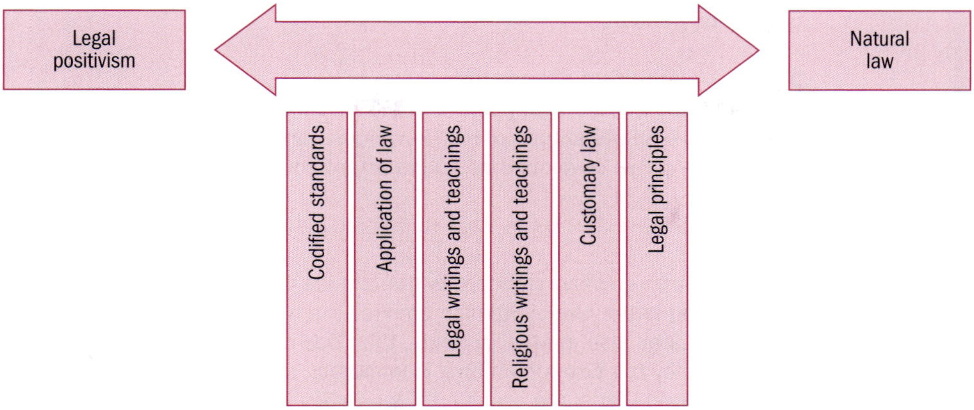

A codified standard can never be fully comprehensive and offer a clear solution to each individual legal conflict. There is always a need for a certain room for interpretation, as we saw in the case 'Theft of electricity in the Netherlands'. This means that written standards always need a certain flexibility, so that they can be applied in various cases. In other words, the written text needs to leave some room for elements of natural law that create this flexibility that is necessary to apply the law on various – differing – cases.
On the other hand, a legal principle is sometimes considered to be too vague and imprecise to apply to a real case, and in the eyes of a positivist may not be legitimately applied without the consent of a legislature. Therefore, a legal principle might need some support in written standards in order to be specific enough to be effectively used.
These two sources of law seem to unite in Article 307 of the German Civil Code, that stipulates:

'(1) Provisions in standard business terms are ineffective if, contrary to the requirement of good faith, they unreasonably disadvantage the other party to the contract with the user. An unreasonable disadvantage may also arise from the provision not being clear and comprehensible.

(2) An unreasonable disadvantage is, in case of doubt, to be assumed to exist if a provision
   1 is not compatible with essential principles of the statutory provision from which it deviates, or
   2 limits essential rights or duties inherent in the nature of the contract to such an extent that attainment of the purpose of the contract is jeopardised.'

In fact, the legal principles of reasonableness and good fate are now codified in the German Civil Code for the specific context of a business contract. On the one hand, these codified standards are rather flexible due to their general wordings as principles. Therefore, the provision can be used in a wide range of cases. On the other hand, the principles – that come forth from natural law – are now formalized in the legitimate form of a written law, and fine-tuned on the particular situation of a business contract and its scope is narrowed down a bit. This example shows that in a way, positivist law and natural law approaches may also complement rather than oppose one another.

1

1.4.1 Codified standards

As considered above, legal positivists assume that the codification of legal rules is the ultimate source of law. In various parts of the world, the codification of law developed as an important source of law.

Codified standards

I Codified standards are written rules produced by a legislator.

The first known codified standard is the famous Code of Ur-Nammu, a penal code applied in the Mesopotamian empire. The code was written around 2100 BC. Later, also in Mesopotamia, the Code of Hammurabi was enacted in 1754 BC by the Babylonian King Hammurabi, stipulating crimes and their punishment. In China, the so-called 'Tang Code' was one of the first known penal codes and dates back to 624 AD (Gernet, 1972), establishing a more consistent judicial system with clear punishments to certain crimes.

On the European mainland, especially private law gradually developed through history with a starting point in the Roman Empire. Arising from unrest between the social classes in ancient Rome, the Twelve Tables of Rome mainly provided for procedural law to settle a conflict between citizens, as you can see in case study 1.2. on the website. Where this was sometimes still a rather bloody occasion (most procedures were founded on the 'eye for an eye' principle), the area of private law evolved gradually during the Roman period as a distinct and codified legal subject, apart from public law (Stein, 1999). For instance, in the earliest days of the Roman empire, concepts of law were developed that could be classified as family law (Lex Canuleia), the ownership of land (Lex Licinia Sextia), and tort law (Lex Aquilla). Where such laws were rather casuistic in their approach in the early days, a more coherent and systematic approach in law emerged especially in the East Roman Empire (Byzantium), through famous codes enacted by emperors, such as the Corpus Iuris of Emperor Justinianus, adopted around 530 AD. The influence of the Roman concepts of codified standards in private law cannot be underestimated.
After the collapse of the Roman empire, the Roman laws were carefully studied by legal scholars and rulers who wanted to draft their own legislation.

During the enlightenment in the 19th century, a so-called codification movement spread through Europe. Enlightened thinkers no longer accepted the totalitarian reign of kings and emperors, or the divine power of God. Instead, they assumed that through reason a society could be based on a 'social contract', in which people willingly gave up power to a ruler in order to establish a peaceful and secure society in which they all could co-exist, but also had the right to rebel against this ruler when he abused his power. Law was a means to organize such a society. During that period, Roman law greatly influenced the Civil Codes of Germany, Austria, Italy and England and France. Especially the private law of the French empire under the reign of Napoleon Bonaparte is noteworthy here. A civil code was adopted in 1804 that regulated the settlement of legal conflict between citizens, which included rules on liability, commerce, property and civil procedures. While the French empire eventually collapsed the influence of their private legal rules is still noticeable in the civil codes of most Western-European countries.

International codified standards

On the international level, written standards are usually created in the form of a contract between states. Such a contract is often referred to as a treaty.

Treaties

A treaty is a written contract between two or more states who consider themselves bound to its content relative to each other.

Next to the word treaty, other words are randomly used to address a contract between states such as covenant, convention, pact, agreement and protocol. In this section, we need to address what type of treaties exist, how states express their consent to be bound by a treaty and how the content of a treaty has legal effect in the domestic legal order of a state.

In legal terminology a distinction is made between a treaty between two countries, and a treaty between more than two countries. The first is named a bilateral treaty, while the latter is called a multilateral treaty.

Bilateral treaty

A bilateral treaty is a treaty to which two states are party.

Such treaties deal with matters that primarily relate to the interest of the two involved countries only.
For instance, a bilateral treaty could regulate certain aspects of trade between the involved countries. One example of this is the 'Agreement Between the government of Canada and the government of the Republic of Côte D'Ivoire for the Promotion and Protection of Investments'. The purpose of this treaty, signed in 2014, is to provide greater predictability and certainty for Canadian investors in Côte D'Ivoire. Amongst others, the two countries agreed that a favourable climate should be created for Canadian investors in Côte D'Ivoire. To this end, investors should be treated equally compared to national investors in Côte D'Ivoire (Art. 4). Also, a dispute settlement procedure was adopted (Section C).

Another matter that might be dealt with in a bilateral treaty is for example the usage and maintenance of a river that flows through the territory of both countries, such as the Columbia River Treaty between the U.S.A. and Canada, signed in 1964. In this treaty the building of energy dams and flood control is regulated for both countries.

Sometimes, a bilateral treaty is used to determine the exact state boundaries. For instance, Mexico and the U.S.A. agreed in the 'Treaty to resolve the pending boundary differences and maintain the Rio Grande and Colorado as the international boundary' that the two said rivers determine the exact international boundaries between the countries.

Multilateral treaty

A multilateral treaty is a treaty to which more than two states are party.

Such treaties deal with matters that relate to the interest of more than two countries. The scope can range from a handful of countries only to a near-global level when most countries in the world are a Member State. Multilateral treaties may deal with varying topics that need to be dealt with on an international level.

For instance, also here aspects of trade can be regulated through a multilateral treaty. Several forms of free trade have been established in regions around the world. Amongst many others, a free trade zone is established between Canada, the U.S. and Mexico (NAFTA), an economic and monetary Union in Europe (European Union), and a customs union in the Caribbean (CARICOM). Also the world's most important financial institutions are established by multilateral treaties, such as the World Trade Organization (WTO), the International Monetary Fund (IMF) and the World Bank (WB).
Furthermore, treaties are adopted that recognize and clarify human rights, such as the International Convention on Civil and Political Rights (ICCPR), the International Covenant on Economic, Social and Cultural Rights (ICESCR), the International Covenant on the Rights of the Child (ICRC) and many others.

Also, boundaries and the access of territory are regulated by multilateral treaties. For example, 'the Convention on International Civil Aviation' regulates amongst others the access of civil flights in the territory of the Member States. The 'Treaty on Principles Governing the Activities of States in the Exploration and Use of Outer Space, Including the Moon and Other Celestial Bodies' regulates that space cannot be claimed as national territory, and cannot be used for military purposes.

While the approach differs per country, the state's consent to be bound by a treaty is usually expressed in two steps: the signature and the ratification of the treaty.

Signature

> The signature of a treaty implies the consent of the responsible negotiator on behalf of the state to the treaty.

A treaty is drafted during a negotiation process of the involved states. These states are represented by an authorised negotiator. This could be – depending on the significance of the treaty – a high official, or a member of the government such as a minister or a head of state. In most legal systems, the signature on behalf of the state must be approved by a legislative body, to guarantee some political control over the performance of the negotiator.

Ratification

> The ratification of a treaty implies the consent of the responsible Legislator on behalf of the state to the treaty.

Usually, when the legislature consents to the signing of the treaty, the state expresses the final approval, and considers itself bound to the treaty. As you can see the example 1.8, the Danish Constitution is a good example in which the two steps are separated: the government has the authority to negotiate and sign treaties and the parliament needs to ratify them.

EXAMPLE 1.8

Denmark and the signature and ratification of treaties
Article 19 of the Danish Constitution stipulates that the King – in practice always represented by the government – has the authority to 'act on behalf of the Realm in international affairs'. This means that the government will be responsible for participating in the negotiations and sign the treaty on behalf of Denmark. However, the same Article underlines that the King 'shall not undertake any act whereby the territory of the Realm shall be increased or reduced, nor shall he enter into any obligation the fulfilment of which requires the concurrence of the Folketing or which is otherwise of major importance; nor shall the King, except with the consent of the Folketing, denounce any international treaty entered into with the consent of the Folketing.' This means that the Folketing – the Parliament – needs to approve in a majority of the cases whether they agree with the signature of a treaty. Only then, Denmark will consider itself to be bound by the signed treaty. Ratification therefore follows in most cases from the consent of the parliament (Harhoff, 1996).

Once a treaty is signed and ratified, the content of this treaty somehow needs to become a part of the domestic legal order. In essence, there are two approaches in law regarding the effect of international law in the domestic legal order: monism and dualism. The main question in this context is whether or not international law, once it has been ratified, is considered to be a part of the domestic legal system, or needs to be transformed first.

Monism

Monism is an approach in law in which it is assumed that the content of a signed and ratified treaty is automatically part of the domestic legal order.

In a monistic legal system, the international law is automatically a part of the national legal order, and any contradicting national rules will – from that moment on – not apply. For instance, Japan, Mexico, Portugal, Spain and Switzerland are predominantly monistic states (UNIDROIT, 2006).

Dualism

Dualism is an approach in law in which it is assumed that a signed and ratified treaty needs to be transformed into domestic law first before it forms part of the domestic legal order.

In a dualistic system, a transformation is required in which the national legislature usually adopts the content of the treaty and simultaneously alters any contradicting domestic legal standards in line with the treaty. For instance, Canada, Italy, the Russian Federation and Great Britain are predominantly dualistic countries (UNIDROIT, 2006).

Monism and Dualism in its purest form will hardly appear. They are rather two extremes on a sliding scale. Mostly, the constitutional system of a country has elements of both but the focus tends towards monism or dualism (Wernaart, 2013 1). A clear example of this is the situation of

Brazil, which might seem a dualistic country at first glance, but certainly shows elements of monism as well (example 1.9).

EXAMPLE 1.9

Brazil and international law

The Constitution of Brazil stipulates that the President is authorized to sign international treaties (Art. 84), while the Parliament needs to ratify them before Brazil is bound to them (Art. 49). So, once again a clear distinction between the signature and ratification. However, before the treaty becomes part of the domestic legal system, it is required that the president incorporates this treaty into the domestic legal order through a presidential decree.
The Supreme Federal Court of Brazil ruled that without this incorporation the treaty will have no effect in the domestic legal order, even if it has been signed and ratified in accordance with the Constitution (Supreme Federal Court, 1998). However, it would be incorrect in categorizing Brazil as a purely dualistic country: the decree of the President is usually nothing more than a short foreword followed by the exact text of the ratified treaty. In practice therefore, the purpose of this presidential decree is to merely publish the content, rather than actually transforming the content in the domestic legal system by altering contradicting national law.
In answer to the question whether Brazil was monistic or dualistic, the Supreme Federal Court replied that 'it is the Brazilian Constitution – and not in the doctrinal controversy that agonizes monists and dualists – that one should search for the normative solution for the question of incorporation of international Acts in the Brazilian internal positive law system (Supreme Federal Court, 1997; Santa Cruz Oliveira & Angela, 2015).

Domestic codified standards

In the domestic legal order of a state, the authorized legislature will adopt written codes in various levels. Usually, written standards appear from a centralized level, adopted for a nationwide use, to a decentralized level, adopted for more local use. The exact type of rules and its scope will differ per state and greatly depend on its constitutional organization. A state with a very clear hierarchy in written legal standards is Belgium, as you may see in example 1.10.

EXAMPLE 1.10

The complexity of Belgium

Belgium is a federation, with a central federal government. However, due to differences in language area's and economics, Belgium is subdivided in federated areas, each with their unique and exclusive authorities: three Communities were established to preserve the cultural identity of the language groups, and three Regions were established that reflect the different economical area's within the country. The Federal Government, Communities and Regions have exclusive legal competencies on different areas and their legislation is equally important. The laws of the Federal Government are named 'statues', the Communities adopt 'decrees', and the Regions enact 'ordinances'. Next to that, on a lower level, Belgium is subdivided in Provinces and Municipalities, who also adopt their own lower legislation.

Due to this complexity in legislative competencies, Belgium has a very specific legal order of written standards. Overall, the principle is applied that a lower written standard may not contradict a higher legal standard. The judiciary therefore is not allowed to apply lower legislation that contradicts higher legislation.
In Belgium, a predominantly monistic country, international standards are considered to be the highest written standards. Second in this hierarchy, there are the statues, decrees and ordinances adopted with a 2/3rd majority are the highest in hierarchy. Third comes the statues, decrees and ordinances adopted with a normal majority. Fourth, there are the Royal Decisions (executive decisions from the Federal Government) and executive decisions from the Communities and Regions. On the fifth place, we have the Provincial Regulations. Lowest in hierarchy are municipal regulations (Wernaart, 2013 2).

1.4.2 Application of law

A second source of law is the application of law. In the end, a legal standard – either codified or not – needs to be applied in specific cases. Usually, the application is not an automatic process in which the legal standard can be applied just like that. After all, a legal standard will always be some sort of a generalization of the context in which a case appears that needs to be concretized in a specific case. The applicator of the legal standard will then always provide a certain interpretation of that standard. In doing so, the legal standard is further nuanced and specified. This interpretation in itself can be a source of law when it is accepted as a valid legal reasoning.
On a worldwide scale most law application is performed by courts and tribunals, the administration, and the military.

Courts and tribunals

In most countries, the judiciary is responsible for applying the law in cases of dispute regarding its specific meaning. The particular way a court understands and applies the law can be a legal source in its own right. Other courts – or even the same court – may consider a previous court ruling when they are confronted with a similar type of case. This way, established reasoning patterns may evolve that can be qualified as 'case law'.

Case law

> Case law is a chain of authoritative legal rulings in which the same reasoning pattern of the court is applied in similar cases.

In some legal systems, such a chain of rulings is called a precedent. When courts apply the same legal reasoning in similar legal issues, the unity of the judiciary is preserved, and it serves legal certainty.
Especially in Anglo/American legal systems, where case law is a very important source of law, the principle of *stare decisis* applies.

Stare decisis

Stare decisisis a legal principle in which courts have to follow the legal reasoning as applied in previous cases.

1

This usually means that lower courts may not rule in contradiction with the legal reasoning of a higher court in a similar legal matter. Besides that, it is assumed that in case of equal courts, the precedent of a previous ruling should be respected. This way, case law is a consistent source of law. Take for instance Example 1.11: the precedent that a therapists – under circumstances – has a duty to warn a possible victim of one of his patients is a legal norm that has been applied ever since in the State of California (Smith, 2010). The rule is considered to be a permanent part of the tort-law regime, and is now even codified by the legislature of California (California Code § 43.92).

EXAMPLE 1.11

'Crime passionel' in California

Prosenjit Poddar, a student from India, studied at the University of California in 1967. During his stay he met a girl named Tatiana Tarasoff during folk dancing classes. They spent some time together, and on one night even kissed one another. Because of this, Poddar believed that Tarasoff was interested in a relationship with him. However, Tarasoff had to admit that this was not her intention, and even was with other men from time to time. Poddar was extremely disappointed, and fell into a depression. He even sought professional psychological help from Dr. Moore, who diagnosed him with paranoid schizophrenia. Poddar confessed to Dr. Moore that he wanted to kill Tarasoff. Promptly, Dr. Moore requested that Poddar would be detained because he was a dangerous person. However, during the short detention, Poddar seemed to act normally, and was set free on behalf of the superior of Dr. Moore. From that moment on, Poddar stopped seeing his psychologist. A few months later, on the 27th of October 1967, he killed Tarasoff. Due to a procedural error, Poddar was set free and returned to India, out of reach for the relatives of Poddar. Instead, these relatives sued the hospital, for failing to warn Tarasoff and her relatives of the possible danger.

In example 1.11, the main legal question that needed to be settled in court was whether or not the therapists, being public employees, were immune from liability for failure to warn. After all, Article 820.2 of the Governmental Code of California stipulates that: 'Except as otherwise provided by statute, a public employee is not liable for an injury resulting from his act or omission where the act or omission was the result of the exercise of the discretion vested in him, whether or not such discretion be abused.' In casu however, the Supreme Court of California ruled that the defendant therapists could not invoke this protection. Referring to a previous case, Johnson v. State of California, the Court had ruled before that this immunity for tort for public employees should be restrictively understood, and the 'immunity's scope should be no greater than is required to give legislature and executive policymakers sufficient breathing space in which to perform their vital policymaking functions.'

In the same court ruling, a parole's officer failed to warn foster parents that their child had a background of violence. According to the court, not informing the parents could hardly be characterized as a policy decision. A parallel was found with the case of Tarasoff, in which the failure to warn could not be considered as a policy decision for which a public employee should enjoy adequate freedom to make a decision without the risk to be held liable for its policy. Therefore, the Court ruled that the therapists were not immune from the protection stipulated in Article 820.2 of the Governmental Code of California. As a result, the therapist had a duty to warn the possible victim.

The Administration

Administration

> The administration is the branch in the public sector that executes the law within the boundaries of its competences.

For instance, in some countries a minister on education may decide on new policy rules in bachelor education programmes, a town council may grant permission to build a new hospital, or a tax agency decides the exact amount of tax a citizen should pay. The administration is organized rather differently around the globe. However, members of the administration all have in common that they are in the service of the public sector and are entrusted with the power to execute the law in given situations.

In some countries, entrusting power to the administration is formalized in written standards while in other countries such power arises from established practices. Whatever the source may be of this entrusted power, there will always be a certain margin in which the administration may operate to execute the law at their own discretion.

Margin of discretion

> The margin of discretion is the room allowed to the administration to execute the law at their own discretion.

This margin can be larger or smaller, depending on the context. When the administration uses this margin of discretion to realize their policy goals, this is a source of law in itself. It is assumed that administrative powers must be used in line with principles of good governance. For example, the law should be executed for the benefit of the common good, instead of private gain of the administrator. The latter would come down to corruption. Another example is that the law should be executed without arbitrariness and with respect for equality, or that a law should be executed consistently. To guarantee equal and consistent law execution, the administration may adopt policy rules to make sure that all their agents approach the execution of law in a similar way.
An example of this is the Dutch drugs policy (example 1.12.): these policy rules set clear guidelines on the prosecution of hard drugs, and the tolerance of small amounts of soft drugs in order to separate both worlds. The Dutch citizens may have the reasonable expectation that the Public Prosecution Service – which is part of the Dutch administration – will apply these policy rules in a consistent way without randomness. This way, the application of law is predictable. The policy document that is used by the Public Prosecution Service when they apply the Opium Law is thereby a legal source in itself.

EXAMPLE 1.12

The Dutch drugs policy

In the Netherlands, the Public Prosecution Service has a margin of discretion in the prosecution of persons suspected of a crime. This means that the Service may choose to intensify the prosecution of certain crimes, or instead deliberately tolerate crimes by not prosecuting people for certain crimes. In the Netherlands, a toleration policy is adopted regarding the use and sales of soft drugs (note to the Opium Law, 2011). This means that while using or selling soft drugs is still considered a crime, soft drugs users or sellers may have the reasonable expectation not to be prosecuted for this crime. Soft drugs users are not prosecuted when they possess no more than 5 gram of marijuana, and coffee-shops will not be prosecuted when they possess no more than 500 gram of marijuana.

The main motivation for this policy is pragmatic: according to the Dutch government it is unrealistic to expect that all soft drugs use can be successfully banned. Also, the usage of soft drugs is not by far as damaging to health compared to hard drugs. Furthermore, criminality related to hard drugs is usually better organized and of a more serious nature compared to criminality related to soft drugs. Simultaneously, it appears that when both the soft drug and the hard drug world operate in the underworld, it is easy for soft drug users and sellers to end up in the hard drug circuit. In that case, the long-term consequences for health and safety are much worse compared with the situation in which they would remain in the soft drug scene. All the more reasons to separate those worlds. This is done by tolerating the usage and sales of a small amount of soft drugs while intensifying the prosecution of hard drug criminals. In applying their margin of discretion this way, the worlds are artificially separated. Soft drugs usage and sales are now not part of an obscure underworld scene, but rather tolerated and controlled. The Public Prosecution Service now instead allocates its resources to seriously prosecute hard drug criminals (www.government.nl, 2015).

The Military

In some countries, the military is authorized to apply the law, or parts of the law. In some countries this is institutionalized and regulated in their constitutional laws. The military is then a political power with constitutional competencies. For instance, in China, the military is considered to be one of the four constitutional powers in the country. In other countries, the military rules after a military coup. This means that the military simply took power by using its armed force, and since then rules the country. For instance, since 2014, the Thai Armed Forces are in effective control of the legislature, administration and judiciary of Thailand. The military took power after six months of political instability in the country (General Prayut Chan-O-Cha, 2014). One can have different opinions about the legitimacy of political power by the military. However, it is a fact that the military in some countries is involved with law application. For instance, in Egypt, the military has always been a significant power that is deeply involved with governing the country, including the creation and application of law, as you may see in example 1.13.

EXAMPLE 1.13

The Egyptian Armed Forces

Since the Egyptian revolution in 1952, it has been a tradition that the presidents of Egypt were all former officers with a significant career in the military. However, during the Arabian Spring in 2013, military backed Hosni Mubarak had to step down as president. He was replaced by a civilian president: Muhammad Morsi. However, the unrest in Egypt remained and his reign was only a short one. In the same year, after large protests of the Egypt people, the military intervened and forced him to step down. He was replaced by former general Abdel Fattahel-Sisi, and therefore military backed.

A new constitution was adopted, that considerably broadened the political powers of the military. For instance, since 2014, 'The Minister of Defence is the Commander in Chief of the Armed Forces, and shall be appointed from among its officers' (Article 201 Constitution of the Arab Republic of Egypt). In fact, this constitutional standard prevents any civilians to become the head of the army. It furthermore guarantees that the appointment of the Chief of the Armed Forces comes from within the military, taking this power away from the legislature, administration or the courts.

Civilians and the military courts

Another provision in the new Constitution stipulates that: 'No civilian shall face trial before the Military Court, except for crimes that constitute a direct assault against military facilities or camps of the Armed Forces, or their equivalents, against military zones or border zones determined as military zones, against the Armed Forces' equipment, vehicles, weapons, ammunition, documents, military secrets, or its public funds, or against military factories; crimes pertaining to military service; or crimes that constitute a direct assault against the officers or personnel of the Armed Forces by reason of performing their duties' (Article 204 Constitution of the Arab Republic of Egypt). This means that civilians can be tried in a military court when their alleged crime affects the said issues. It is believed that this competency of the military courts has been widely used ever since (Elmenshawy, 2014).

1.4.3 Legal writings and teachings

Legal writings and teachings can be a legal source in its own right. Scholars who are experts in law will regularly comment on legal developments, or collect and structuralize legal information. Such works and teachings can be used as a source of law.

For instance, in Bhasin v. Hrynew (2014) the Supreme Court of Canada consulted several books to find inspiration for their decision. This case will be discussed into more detail below, in the context of the legal principle of good faith.

In this case, one of the Judges considered:

'However, these broad pronouncements have been, for the most part, restricted by subsequent jurisprudence to specific types of contracts and relationships, such as insurance contracts, leaving unclear the role of the broader principle of good faith in the modern Anglo-Canadian law of contracts: *Chitty on Contracts* (31st ed. 2012), vol. I, *General Principles*, at para. 1-039; W. P. Yee, "Protecting Parties' Reasonable Expectations: A General Principle of Good Faith" (2001), 1 *O.U.C.L.J.* 195, at p. 195; E. P. Belobaba, "Good Faith in Canadian Contract Law", in *Special Lectures of the Law Society of Upper Canada 1985 – Commercial Law: Recent Developments and Emerging Trends* (1985), 73, at p. 75. One leading Canadian contracts scholar went so far as to say that the common law has taken a "kind of perverted pride" in the absence of any general notion of good faith, as if accepting that notion "would be admitting to the presence of some kind of embarrassing social disease": J. Swan, "Whither Contracts: A Retrospective and Prospective Overview", in *Special Lectures of the Law Society of Upper Canada 1984 – Law in Transition: Contracts* (1984), 125, at p. 148.'

1.4.4. Religious writings and teachings

In some countries, religious writings and teachings are accepted as a source of law. These counties are non-secular states.

Non-secular state

A non-secular state is a state in which governance and religion are mixed.

For instance, in the Cairo declaration on human rights in Islam, Shari'ah law (given by God) is recognized as ultimate legal source: 'In contribution to the efforts of mankind to assert human rights, to protect man from exploitation and persecution, and to affirm his freedom and right to a dignified life in accordance with the Islamic Shari'ah'. This means that the writings and teachings of the Islam are considered to be the source of law.

A similar consideration can be found in the Constitution of Saudi-Arabia (Art. 1):

> 'The Kingdom of Saudi Arabia is a sovereign Arab Islamic state with Islam as its religion; God's Book and the Sunnah of His Prophet, God's prayers and peace be upon him, are its Constitution, Arabic is its language and Riyadh is its capital.'

Another example, but now involving Christianity, is the Preamble of the Constitution of Argentina, 'invoking the protection of God, source of all reason and justice.'

In some countries, religious sources are explicitly excluded as a legal source. In that case, religion is not involved in the governance of a state (including its laws). These countries are secular states.

Secular state

A secular state is a state in which governance and religion are separated.

For instance, Article 4 of the Constitution of the Republic of Fuji explicitly recognizes that:
'Religion and the state are separate, which means:
(a) the state and all persons holding public office must treat all religions equally;
(b) the state and all persons holding public office must not dictate any religious belief;

(c) the state and all persons holding public office must not prefer or advance, by any means, any particular religion, religious denomination, religious belief, or religious practice over another, or over any non-religious belief; and
(d) no person shall assert any religious belief as a legal reason to disregard this Constitution or any other law.'

1.4.5 Customary law

A custom is an established and accepted legal practice.

Custom

From this definition we can learn three things.
First, a custom is a legal practice. This means that this source of law finds its origin in the interaction between people, and not in a written standard. The correlation between a written standard and legal custom is that a written standard is sometimes legal custom first, and is, after a while, formalized in the form of a written standard.
Second, a custom must be an established practice. This means that the practice must last for a while in a consistent way. This way, people can reasonably expect the application of this legal practice, for it has become a sort of a tradition. We use the Latin word *usus* to refer to this element of legal custom.

Usus

Third, a custom must be an accepted practice by its users. The mere fact that a legal custom is applied for a long time does not necessarily mean that those who are involved with the application agree with it. Therefore, it is generally accepted that a legal custom can only be a valid source of law when those who are involved with its application are of the opinion that the custom should indeed be a legal rule. In legal terminology, we use the Latin words *opinio iuris sive necessitates* to refer to this element.

Opinio iuris sive necessitates

In some legal systems, the use of customary law is not unlimited. Usually, customary law may not be in contradiction with certain applicable written standards and other sources of law. For instance, Article 2 (4) of the Constitution of Kenya stipulates that: 'Any law, including customary law, that is inconsistent with this Constitution is void to the extent of the inconsistency, and any act or omission in contravention of this Constitution is invalid.' In Nigeria, before applying a customary rule in court, the judge(s) will have to perform a validity test to establish whether or not the custom is in contradiction with other elements of applicable law. Example 1.14 shows into more detail how the elements of the definition of customary law appear in the Nigerian legal system.

EXAMPLE 1.14

Killing twins in Nigeria
Before Nigeria was colonized by the British, the domestic legal system consisted mostly of customary rules. These rules where orally transmitted from generation to generation, and could differ per region or tribe. However, during their colonial rule, the British established their own legal system in Nigeria based on the common law tradition. This included written standards and a legal doctrine established by court rulings (the application of law).

1

This does not mean that the traditional customary rules were now banned: they could still apply as long as they would not be contrary to rules that came forth from the British system. This explains why in Nigeria, since the departure of the British, customary laws still play a profound role in the domestic legal system (Asiedu-Akrofi, 1989). In the Nigerian Evidence Act, the law that regulates what evidence is valid in court proceedings, the effect of customary law is recognized. Article 18 stipulates that: 'A custom may be adopted as part of the law governing a particular set of circumstances if it can be judicially noticed or can be proved to exist by evidence.' This means first that custom can be used as evidence in a case when it has been accepted before in equal or higher courts. The more a custom has been applied in the courts, the stronger the effect of the rule can be. This principle was introduced by the commonwealth Privy Council in 1916 (Angu v. Attah). This pretty much reflects the idea of *usus*. Second, it means that if there is no established jurisprudence on the matter, evidence must be found from within the community that usually applies the custom. This means that chiefs or others who are knowledgeable about the customary laws may testify in court that the custom is indeed considered to be a part of the local legal system. This reflects the idea of *opinio iure sive necessitates*.

Customary law?

The principle that customary laws may not contradict with the British legal system that was established in Nigeria still applies. Article 18 (3) of the Nigerian Evidence Act stipulates: 'In any judicial proceeding where any custom is relied upon, it shall not be enforced as law if it is contrary to public policy, or is not in accordance with natural justice, equity and good conscience.' In fact, this rule does not necessarily aim at maintaining the heritage of the British law system, but rather prevent the application of rather barbarian customs (as ruled in Laoye v. Oyetunde, 1944). For instance, in some parts of eastern Nigeria, it was a custom to kill newly born twins. They were believed to bring bad luck to the community where they were born, for the birth of twins was considered to be an unnatural phenomenon. Igbo tribes in south-east Nigeria would bring newly born twins to an 'evil forest' and leave them there to die (Adewumi, 2014). While this custom seems to gradually disappear, the rejection of twins still composes a social problem in the south-east of Nigeria today (Asindi et al., 1993; Taiwo-Obalonye, 2013). Application of this custom would contradict with concepts as 'public policy' and 'natural justice' and would therefore not be legally applicable.

1.4.6 Legal principles

A legal principle is considered to be a founding principle in law that may not be violated.

Legal principle

| A legal principle is a general value that applies in law.

Such principles can be found in all fields of law. For instance, in penal law, the principle of legality may apply. This means that someone may not be condemned for something he could not be aware of, for instance due to the

fact that a law is applied in retro-perspective, or was formulated unclear. For example, the Constitution of South Africa stipulates that: 'Every accused person has a right to a fair trial, which includes the right (...) not to be convicted for an act or omission that was not an offence under either national or international law at the time it was committed or omitted.' Also in private law, legal principles may apply, such as the principles of reasonableness and fairness, or the principle of good faith as you can see in case study 1.3 on the website.
From this case study we can learn that the same legal principle may apply in more than one legal system. As a matter of fact, the principle of good faith in contract law is applied in a wide range of countries. One might even argue that such a principle has a universal scope. In law, we call this phenomenon *ius cogens*.

Ius Cogens

Ius Cogens are universally binding legal principles.

In some cases, a principle is considered to have a universal scope. Although opinions on the exact meaning of *ius cogens* are very different, some legal principles seem to be widely accepted. For instance, the prohibition to genocide, slavery and torture are in most countries – at least in theory – accepted principles. Furthermore, concepts as equality, respect and freedom are universally proclaimed. Also in private law, the notion that trade should be fair, reasonable and with integrity is widely accepted, and could therefore be considered as universally applicable.
In this light, one needs to be cautious however. The legal principles that are said to have a universal scope are usually rather vague and understood differently around the world. It will at all times depend on the actual application of these principles in a given context to find out what their exact meaning is in that particular legal system.

Summary

1

The organization of just behaviour

- Law organizes just behaviour in a society using two types of legal rules: substantive and formal legal rules.
  - Substantive law is composed of legal rules that define the content of just behaviour;
  - Formal law is composed of legal rules that maintain substantive law.

- Substantive and formal legal rules are necessary to regulate two types of relations: public and private relations.
  - Public law is the law that regulates the relation between a government and its citizens.
  - Private law is the law that regulates the relation between citizen or those who act as citizens.

- For the purpose of this book we further subcategorize different legal branches.
  - At international level: economic cooperation;
  - At national public law level: constitutional and administrative law, and criminal law;
  - At national private law level we categorize law that deals with contracts, liability, labour contracts, the legal form of a company, privacy, and intellectual property.

- 'Just' implies a balance between the values 'justice', 'opportuness', and 'legal certainty'.
  - Justice is the moral conviction of a given society expressed in law;
  - Opportuness is the expression of effectiveness by a given society in law;
  - Legal certainty is the expression of legality in a given society.

The origin of law

- There are two opposing views regarding the origin of law: natural law and positivist law. They are two extremes, and are usually both apparent in legal systems.
  - In a Natural law approach it is assumed that law comes fort from nature;
  - In a positivist law approach, it is assumed that law comes forth from codification.

The sources of law

- The following sources are generally used: codified standards, the application of law, legal writings and teachings, religious writings and teachings, customary law and legal principles.

- Codified standards are written rules produced by a legislator;
  - At international level, written standards are usually created in the form of a contract between states: a treaty.
    - A bilateral treaty is a treaty to which two states are party.
    - A multilateral treaty is a treaty to which more than two states are party.
  - A state expresses the will to be bound by a treaty by signing and ratifying the treaty.
    - The signature of a treaty implies the consent of the responsible negotiator on behalf of the state to the treaty.
    - The ratification of a treaty implies the consent of the responsible Legislator on behalf of the state to the treaty.
  - There are two approaches in how international written standards have effect in the domestic legal order of state parties to a treaty: monism and dualism.
    - Monism is an approach in law in which it is assumed that the content of a signed and ratified treaty is automatically part of the domestic legal order.
    - Dualism is an approach in law in which it is assumed that a signed and ratified treaty needs to be transformed into domestic law first before it forms part of the domestic legal order.

- Law application is performed by courts and tribunals, the administration, and the military.
  - Case law is a chain of authoritative legal rulings in which the same reasoning pattern of the court is applied in similar cases. In some countries, the principle of *stare decisis* applies.
    - *Stare decisis* is a legal principle in which courts have to follow the legal reasoning as applied in previous cases.
  - The administration is the branch in the public sector that executes the law within the boundaries of its competences.
    - The margin of discretion is the room allowed to the administration to execute the law at their own discretion.
  - In some countries, the military is authorized to apply the law, or parts of the law.

- Legal writings and teachings can be a legal source in its own right.

- In some countries, religious writings and teachings are accepted as a source of law.
  - A non-secular state is a state in which governance and religion are mixed;
  - A secular state is a state in which governance and religion are separated.

- A custom is an established and accepted legal practice.

- A legal principle is a general value that applies in law.
  - *Ius Cogens* are universally binding legal principles.

Practice questions

Open questions

1.1 Please read the following consideration of the Supreme Court of Appeal of South Africa (Renasa Insurance Company Limited v. Watson (32/2014) [2016] ZASCA 13 (11 March 2016).

In casu, a certain payment from an insurer in a case of fire was disputed: the insurer refused to pay since the claimant was believed to have caused the fire by negligent acting. The reference made to clause 5 is an Article derived from the general terms, used by the insurance company.
'In view of the conclusion that I have reached on the alternative defence, it is not necessary to consider whether or not the full court in Santam Limited v. CC Designing CC, and accordingly the court a quo too, correctly interpreted clause 5. Having regard to the wording of clause 5, it is at the very least clear that to require an insured to take steps to prevent a loss, proof of foreseeability of loss eventuating is required. This would require proof that the reasonable person in the position of the insured would have foreseen the reasonable possibility of the loss eventuating and would therefore have taken reasonable steps to prevent same.'

What kind of legal sources is the Court referring to (one could distinguish at least two)? Please explain thoroughly.

1.2 Please, read Article 8 of the Vietnamese Civil Code:

'The establishment and implementation of civil rights and obligations must ensure preservation of ethnic identity and shall respect and promote the good customs, practices and traditions, solidarity, mutual support, [the tradition of] 1 each person2 for the community and the community for each person, and the high moral values of the various ethnic groups living in Vietnam. Ethnic minorities shall enjoy favourable conditions in their civil relations in order to improve steadily their physical and spiritual life. Assistance to elderly persons, young children and disabled persons in the implementation of civil rights and obligations shall be encouraged.'

As we have seen, there are three purposes of law: justice, opportuness and legal certainty. Which of these three are served best by this Article, and which is not so much guaranteed here? Please explain thoroughly.

1.3 Gerry bribes a government official. He claims that he has the right to do so, because this has been going on for ages, and is simply the way things work. He claims that this matter of affairs can be justified under customary law. However, the victims of the bribery who bear the consequences are not so happy with this.

What element of customary law is Gerry overlooking here, which would make this course of affairs invalid?

1.4 The King of Norway orders a Pizza at a Restaurant. He leaves without paying, claiming that since he is the King, and therefore a public legal institution, private legal rules are not applicable to him or his actions.

Could you kindly tell the King why he is mistaken?

Essay question

Please, reflect on the pros and cons of natural law and positivist law. Conclude with your own opinion on the matter: which approach do you prefer and why?

Multiple choice questions

1.1 *Opinio iure sive necessitas* is a prerequisite for

a a legal principle
b a legal custom
c law application

1.2 In the UK, an international treaty is only internally binding when the national Parliament adopts a national law with the same content.
The UK has a

a monistic system
b dualistic system
c tripartite system

1.3 Article 81 of the Argentine Constitution reads: ‘No bill wholly rejected by either House shall be reintroduced in the legislative session of the same year. No House shall totally reject a bill originated in it and later added or amended by the revising House. If the bill were subject to additions and amendments by the revising House, the result of the voting shall be made known in order to state if such additions or amendments were made by the absolute majority or by two-thirds of the members present…’

This is predominantly an example of
a public substantive law
b private formal law
c public formal law

1.4 The International Covenant on Economic Social and Cultural Rights (164 ratifications) is an example of
a a bilateral treaty
b a universal treaty
c a multilateral treaty

SORRY, CAN'T HELP YOU!
FOOD!
Sandor

2 Comparative law and legal systems

In this chapter, the method of comparative law is explored. First, we discuss the purpose of comparative law and how it can be applied. Next, on a macro level, the legal families of the world are introduced. Finally, on a micro level, the functional method in law comparison is explained, and rules of thump are given for functional comparative research.

2.1 The purpose of comparative law

Comparative law is an important element of legal methodology, as will be demonstrated below. While the comparing of law probably dates back to ancient Greek societies (Donahue, 2006), it only recently found its way in the academic circuit. Since the 1900 Congress for Comparative Law, held in Paris, the subject plays an active role within the walls of universities. Unfortunately, it seems that the subject stayed there and is now more a subject of extensive academic discourse rather than a widely applied science (Wernaart, 2013). Therefore, during my PhD-defence, I made a promise to the academic world to design a more practical methodology that is useable and accessible in applied sciences. May this chapter be part of the fulfilment of that promise.

According to Zweigert & Kötz (1998), comparative law has five main purposes:
1 Gaining of knowledge.
2 Evaluating the better law.
3 Substantiate the application of law.
4 Improve legal education.
5 Unification of law.

2.1.1 Gaining of knowledge

It is the simple assumption that if someone looks further than their own legal system, that person will learn more. In other legal systems, one may organize just behaviour in a different way. When comparing this with your own or another alien legal system, one simply gains more insight in how law works.

2

Take for instance the case study 2.1.'Searching a dustbin for food?' on the website. The case law in two neighbouring countries – the Netherlands and Belgium – about a similar case seems to look quite the same at first glance. However, if one would conduct an in-depth research to clarify the reasoning patterns of the courts, one would have to reassess that conclusion.
As it seems in the Netherlands, the tensed relation between the judiciary and the legislature on the application of international law seems to explain the verdicts of the courts: the judiciary simply follows the viewpoints of the legislature and merely applies that view. In Belgium, the historical language struggle explains the existence of the Constitutional Court, and its relatively powerful position. It also explains why the Court is, on the one hand, not that much involved with the particularities of cases, but dares to, on the other hand, oppose the legislature when it adopts legislation that is too harsh.
Comparing the two approaches leads to much more detailed insight compared to the situation in which one would study only the legal practice in one country. Compared to the Belgian Constitutional Court, the Dutch Central Court of Appeal has a rather weak position towards the legislature. On the other hand, in the Netherlands, one apparently has more faith in the legislature when assessing the application of international law. Furthermore, this also explains why the Constitutional Court of Belgium is not too worried to nullify legislation when the legislature crosses the line of being inhuman (in the view of the court, of course).
Such constitutional differences have a profound impact on the way courts approach similar cases. And even when the verdicts appear to be similar, the way towards this conclusion as well as the broader context of the case is different.

2.1.2 Evaluating the better law

A second purpose of comparative law is evaluating the better law. Where in gaining knowledge the researcher has a neutral attitude towards the data he finds, in evaluating, the researcher concludes which law is best in a particular situation.
This function of comparative law is not uncontested, because in the end the researcher will decide that one legal solution is better (and therefore superior) compared to another (Glenn, 2007 1), which may leave a bad taste considering that all societies are equal. On the other hand, one could argue that it is the job of a researcher to have an opinion about the data he finds, and advise on which option is the best (Zweigert & Kötz, 1998).

For instance, evaluating has been done on a frequent basis by legislators all over the world who want to adopt a new law on a given topic. It is not uncommon that a legislator looks at its neighbours for inspiration for new laws, as you can see in the example 2.1.

Also in business, especially in the context of export, a careful evaluation of the legal regime in potential partner countries is essential (Cahn & Donald, 2010). A well known methodological approach in an export-plan is performing a DESTEP analysis. The last P stands for 'political and legal aspects'. In this analysis it is useful to evaluate what country has the best legal climate to offer your products or services. It is the opinion of the author that in a decent external analysis, a legal comparison should be included as a standard element of the research.

EXAMPLE 2.1

The Hungarian Civil Code

Hungary used to be quite autonomous in adopting their own private legal rules before they came under the political sphere of influence of the Soviet regime after the Second World War. Before that time, Hungarian private law was usually regulated by customary law and case law. The only exception was a short period in which Hungary was occupied by Austria. During that time, the Austrian Civil Code of 1811 applied in Hungary.
However, after the Austrian reign, Hungary quickly moved back to its old approach in private law (Grzybowsk, 1961). The only remnant of this period seems to be the adoption of a Hungarian Commercial Code, in 1875. A more comprehensive civil code that would regulate private relations was drafted ever since, but never adopted: besides commercial law, the major part of private law was still governed by case law and customary law.

Soviet period

This all changed during the Soviet period, in which a socialist civil code was adopted. However, this Civil Code had only a limited meaning, because in a socialist state, property and companies are state owned, and trade is regulated by authorised state institutions. In such a society there is a limited need for the further regulation of private relations. It is therefore surprising that the Civil Code adopted during the Soviet period served for such a long time afterwards, because it was only since 2013 that a fully renewed Hungarian Civil Code entered into force (Act V of 2013 on the Civil Code of Hungary).

Evaluating the most suitable law

The drafters of this code had the unique situation in which they were not restrained by any laws from the past. After all, in Hungary there was no long tradition in the application of a civil code, and the country left the political influence sphere of the Soviet Union. Therefore, the legislature used several international sources for inspiration before they presented their final draft. First of all, the harmonized law of the European Union was studied into detail. That is not really surprising, for the European Union demanded conformity with their laws when Hungary accessed the Union in 2004. Furthermore, the legislator carefully studied uniform laws adopted within the context of the United Nations International Institute for the Unification of Private Law. This institution adopted for instance the Convention relating to a Uniform Law on the International Sale of Goods. The result was a careful mix of international standards in private law that were most suitable for the Hungarian situation (Kisfaludi, 2008).

2.1.3 Substantiate the application of law

Before applying the law, the courts, administration or even the military might compare law first to make sure they apply the law correctly. This is especially done in legal systems that have a strong link with the legal systems of other countries, for instance because they share the same legal history. This is in particular the case in courts from (former) States of the Commonwealth of Nations, mostly consisting of former British colonies. They have been part of the British legal tradition for a long time, and are not hesitant in studying the legal reasoning of their colleague courts abroad.

For instance, you may remember the Bhasin v. Hrynew case (2014) from the previous chapter. In its ruling, the Supreme Court of Canada considered the development of the principle of good faith in several countries, including the UK and Australia:

> 'Developments in the United Kingdom and Australia point to enhanced attention to the notion of good faith, mitigated by reluctance to embrace it as a standalone doctrine. Good faith in contract performance has received increasing prominence in English law, despite its "traditional ... hostility" to the concept. (...) Australian courts have also moved towards a greater role for good faith in contract performance. (...) There is no generally applicable duty of good faith, but one will be implied into contracts in certain circumstances. The duty of good faith can be implied as a matter of law or as a matter of fact, although the cases are not always clear on the basis on which the term is being implied. (...) The law of good faith performance in Australia is still developing and remains unsettled.'

2.1.4 Improve legal education

A fourth purpose of comparative law is to improve legal education. May this chapter be an attempt to realize this. Comparative methods have an added value in legal education. Not only in universities of science, where comparative law is traditionally taught, also in applied sciences, comparative law is of the utmost importance. In the first place, it broadens the view of students on law. By comparing legal systems, the student crawls out of his own shell and discovers alternate ideas on the organization of just behaviour. In the second place, as already stated, comparative law can be widely used in various forms of applied research. Especially in international business, the comparing of legal solutions may be an essential step in taking strategic decisions in export.

2.1.5 The unification of law

A last function of comparative law is the unification of law. When countries want to stimulate cross-border trade, it is usually the approach to start lowering trade barriers. However, lowering trade barriers alone is not enough to establish a healthy trade climate that is profitable for all the involved countries. In addition, one also needs to level the rules of the game. In this context, we often see attempts to harmonize or unify law, so that market players are not confronted with too many legal differences within the same trade area.

Legal differences in a free market economy have two side effects that distort the proper functioning of the market. First, companies may have to adjust their products or services to each legal system separately, which is a time consuming and costly affair. Second, as a result, companies will probably use the legal system with the most flexible rules to bring their product or service to the market. Since there is free trade, these products or services are sold throughout the entire zone. The result is that in the end the lowest standards, or most flexible rules, will eventually become the norm.

To tackle these problems, international legislators often seek to unify the law, so that the rules of the game are equal to all market participants within the zone in which trade barriers are lowered. In order to be able to unify law, the legislator will have to compare the involved legal systems and create uniform rules that are more or less acceptable in all these systems.

An example is the European Union Regulation on Cosmetics (example 2.2). In this regulation, the European Union legislature unified the law that relates to the manufacturing and retail of cosmetics. Amongst others, similar rules apply to the composition of cosmetics (the same ingredients are forbidden), the labelling of cosmetics, the responsibility for cosmetic products, risk assessment, and the administration of information regarding cosmetic products.

EXAMPLE 2.2

Cosmetics in the European Union

In the European Union, the selling of cosmetics falls under the regime of EU Regulation 1223/2009. In this regulation, the European legislator attempts to make sure that a high level of consumer protection is guaranteed, the principles of a free market economy are implemented, and the companies have legal certainty regarding the sales of cosmetics (section 29, preamble). To this end, several aspects of the law that relate to the sales of cosmetics are now unified within the European Union. For instance, the definition of what a cosmetic product is, is now the same everywhere:

'Article 1 (a) "cosmetic product" means any substance or mixture intended to be placed in contact with the external parts of the human body (epidermis, hair system, nails, lips and external genital organs) or with the teeth and the mucous membranes of the oral cavity with a view exclusively or mainly to cleaning them, perfuming them, changing their appearance, protecting them, keeping them in good condition or correcting body odours.'

The responsible person

Furthermore, rules on the safety of cosmetics are now unified. This means, amongst others, that the legal responsibility regarding cosmetics is clearly defined. Only cosmetics for which a legal or natural person is designated within the EU as a 'responsible person' can be sold on the European markets (Article 4 (1)). This means that it cannot occur that cosmetics are in circulation without a person who is responsible for them. Such a 'responsible person' is the manufacturer if established within the Union, the importer who imports the product from outside the Union, or the retailer who puts its own trademark on the product (Article 4 (3-6)). An example of the latter could be a cosmetics retailer selling products as a house brand, sing his own trademark.

When you are considered responsible for a cosmetic product, you have the obligation to guarantee that the product is produced and sold in accordance with the regulation. This includes for instance compliance with the list of forbidden substances (Article 14 and Annex II): cosmetics may not contain any of the listed ingredients. This includes also compliance with the labelling rules (Article 19), in which one communicates to the consumer what the main characteristics and effects of the product are. Furthermore, the responsible person may not mislead the consumer regarding the effects of the product by using misleading advertisements (Article 20). Other responsibilities of the responsible person are to keep track of and document the entire supply chain (Article 7), perform a sound safety assessment (Article 10) and create a product information file in which amongst others the details of manufacturing methods, the proof of the effect, and possible information on animal testing is included (Article 11) (COLIPA, 2011).

2.2 Macro comparison: legal families

There are different levels at which law may be compared. Legal comparison is done at macro level.

Macro comparison

Macro comparison is the activity in which the main characteristics of legal systems are compared.

Comparing law at macro level leads to insight into how legal systems work, and to what extent they are similar/different from one another. This is a good starting point if a researcher wants to become knowledgeable of a particular legal system in which he has to operate. Comparing legal systems therefore gives you an idea of the broad context in which a certain legal rule or issue is apparent.

Legal systems

A legal system is a coherent collective of legal rules in which the same hierarchy of legal sources applies, mostly determined by the boundaries of a state.

In fact, there are good arguments to assume that a legal system overlaps with the territory of a state. After all, within the boundaries of a state, people usually share the same history, economy, linguistic background, political and judicial organization. It therefore makes sense to assume that a legal system is usually a legal system of a particular state (Wernaart, 2013).
However, this assumption is not uncontested (Twining, 2007; Cotterrell, 2007), for there are various examples of states in which its citizens no not share such common backgrounds, such as the citizens of Hong Kong in China (see example 2.3). Also, increasingly, on the meta-country level, legislation is adopted. For instance, this is done in the sphere of economic cooperation on a regional level and in the context of the United Nations on an international level: these international laws may have a significant effect on the domestic legal order of states (Nelken, 2007 1). Considering a state as a legal system in itself may therefore prove to be inaccurate.

In this book, we start from the assumption that a state equals a legal system, but will deviate from that principle when necessary.

EXAMPLE 2.3

The one country, two systems principle in Chinese law

While Hong Kong has technically been under the wings of China since 1997, it was under British rule since 1841. This means that the general background of Hong Kong, including its legal development, is very far from that of China. Where Hong Kong was founded on the basis of a capitalist system, China has a predominantly socialist system. This is exactly why in China today, one works with the so-called 'one country, two systems' – principle. This means that Hong Kong law may differ from Chinese law, considering the differences in (legal) background, and peacefully may co-exist within the boundaries of one state (Tiexun, 2009). This is explicitly recognized in the Basic Law of Hong Kong (1990).

Article 2 stipulates that:
'The National People's Congress authorizes the Hong Kong Special Administrative Region to exercise a high degree of autonomy and enjoy executive, legislative and independent judicial power, including that of final adjudication, in accordance with the provisions of this Law.'

Furthermore, Article 5 states that:
'The socialist system and policies shall not be practised in the Hong Kong Special Administrative Region, and the previous capitalist system and way of life shall remain unchanged for 50 years.'

Of course, it is to be expected that Hong Kong law in the end will gradually merge with Chinese law and vise versa (Minkang, 2006).

In comparative law, comparists have been attempting to subdivide the legal systems in the world into a limited amount of categories. These categories are based on apparent common features, most importantly the hierarchy of legal sources. Such a category is often referred to as a legal family.

Legal families

> A legal family is a group of legal systems that share the same basic characteristics in law, including at similar hierarchy of legal rules.

Also here, it needs to be noted that the usage of the words 'legal family' is not uncontested. It is criticized that the word 'family' suggests that law is a rigid phenomenon, because it is almost exclusively used to address a group of states at a certain time in history. However, as we have seen above, a legal system is not necessarily restricted to the boundaries of a state and, also changes over time. Law is therefore a flexible study object. Some authors therefore prefer using concepts such as 'legal culture' (Mattei, 1997) or 'legal tradition' (Glenn, 2007 2) because such concepts do not restrict law to the boundaries of a state, nor do they limit the concept to a given time in history.

This being said, the author suggests that the words 'legal system' as well as 'legal families' can reasonably be used, when taken into consideration the limits of these concepts.

There is no general consensus on how this division should be made exactly (for those who are really interested: compare for instance David, 1988; Zweigert & Kötz, 1998 and Glenn, 2007). The author chose the following legal families, which are more or less accepted in comparative law literature: common law, civil law, socialist law, religious law, traditional law and mixed systems. The selection is based on the differences between the highest legal source of law, because this predominantly defines the main characteristics of legal systems.

TABLE 2.1 Legal families and their highest source of law

Legal family	Highest source of law	Example
Common law	Case law	England
Civil law	Codified standards	France
Socialist law	The administration	Cuba
Religious law	Religious writings	Saudi-Arabia
Traditional law	Custom	The natives of Malaysia
Mixed systems	Combination	Japan

2.2.1 Common law systems

A common law system is case law driven. The law is therefore predominantly developed by judges, rather than a legislator or academics (David, 1988). This does not mean that written standards play no role of significance. However, the draft of written standards is mostly a recognition or summary of permanent precedents in case law (see figure 2.1).
For instance, it was the deliberate aim of the draftsmen of an early version of the English Sales of Goods Act 'to reproduce as exactly as possible the statutory and common law rules relating to the sale of goods, leaving any amendments that may seem desirable to be introduced at a later stage' (Chalmers, 1889). The content of the Act was largely inspired by the status quo in case law (Mitchell, 2001).

Of course, this does not mean that a legislature has no influence on the direction of court rulings. However, in general, it can be concluded that case law is primarily leading in the development of law in a common law system.

FIGURE 2.1 The correlation between case law and codified standards in common law systems

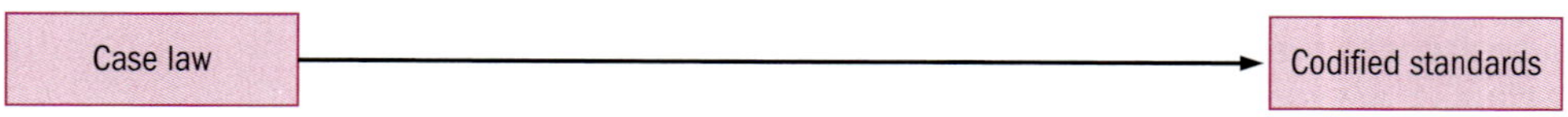

The focus on case law consequentially means that in common law systems there is a great emphasis on the procedural matters of law. After all, the

proceedings in court define the course of law. Therefore, traditionally, formal law has always played an important role in common law systems (Zweigert & Kötz, 1998).

Formal law

The concept of a common law system was developed in England first, and later spread during the worldwide expansion of the British empire. This explains why in most cases the law of the former parts of the Commonwealth of Nations are founded on a common wealth system. Such countries includes the U.S.A., Canada (except Quebec), Australia, Wales, Ireland, former Hong Kong, Singapore, Pakistan, Uganda, Myanmar, Tuvalu, Trinidad and Tobago, Palau, Liberia, Jamaica and many more countries. The origin of the system however must be found in England.

The development of common law in England
Historically, there are several reasons why in England law has always been produced and developed by the courts in the first place. The most important historical factors are the autonomous development of English law, and the introduction of a feudal system (Zweigert & Kötz, 1998). Understanding these developments may help to understand the nature and characteristics of a common law system.

Autonomous development

First of all, England was not as influenced by the legal doctrine of the Roman Empire compared to most countries on the European mainland. The Roman occupation was relatively short, and its laws were never really 'incubated' in the English legal system. This explains why the legal developments in England could take place rather autonomously.

Feudal system

Furthermore, the origin of common law can be found in the feudal system, introduced by King William I in 1066. This means that the King alone was the ultimate possessor of all land, while citizens might hold parts of the lands in exchange for loyalty to the crown, and – of course – tax. A result of this system was that the tax-collecting institutes in the country gradually started to function as courts when there was a dispute regarding the payment of the taxes. Next to that, the King observed that he could only benefit from a regular tax income when peace prevailed in England. Therefore, the King would appoint courts to rule in matters of criminal cases. Gradually, a court system was established in which the royal courts had a wide jurisdiction on all kind of disputes, under the supervision of the Crown. This system replaced all kinds of different local legal systems, and was therefore called 'common law', because it applied to the entire English community. The main purpose of this common law was to provide for practical solutions in actual cases. Gradually, a system of permanent solutions to similar cases began to emerge: the precedents in case law.

English legal professionals

As a result of the developments described above, lawyers or judges were never truly academically oriented: law is considered as an applied tool rather than an academic subject (Zweigert & Kötz, 1998). Legal professionals therefore have always been united in various societies rather than in universities.
In England, the job of a lawyer can, traditionally, either be a solicitor or a barrister. A solicitor advises clients on legal matters in general, and represents them in the lower courts. A barrister is specialised in appeal cases or cases that are dealt with in the higher courts. The exchange of

Solicitor

knowledge, or 'craftsmanship', and education of legal professionals occurs in the Law Society (for solicitors) or the General Council of the Bar (barristers). This does not mean that there are no academic courses at English universities. However, the professional associations play a more important role for the legal professional.
Judges are also not necessarily academically oriented. In the magistrates' court, the court of first instance in small criminal cases and certain matters of family law, the judge is in most cases not even a legal professional. Instead, the judge – called a Justice of Peace – is an honorary job, usually performed by retired people. In other courts, such as the Country Courts (that deals in private law matters) or the higher courts, the Judges are in fact legal professionals, with a background as solicitor or barrister.

2.2.2 Civil law systems

A civil law system is driven by codified standards.
The idea behind a civil law system is that a society can be organized in a coherent way by adopting written codified standards. This idea is greatly influenced by the Enlightenment, a philosophical approach that evolved in Europe in the late 17th century. Law therefore emerges from these codified standards, and is applied in court when necessary. Consequently, the correlation between codified standards and case law is that in case law, the written law is 'merely' applied: the court rulings are firmly based on written laws (see figure 2.2). For instance, the original function of the French Court of Cassation was to make sure that the French judiciary would not contradict the codified standards (and therefore the will of the legislator).

However, this notion would oversimplify matters: a legislature is never able to create specific rules that are applicable in all possible future cases. The role for the Courts is then to apply the spirit of the codified standards to the underlying case. This requires a great deal of creativity, which may result in a doctrine of precedents in case law as well. Sometimes, a legislator may even deliberately include vague terms in codified standards, to allow the judiciary some room for interpretation.
For instance, the French rules on liability for damage is for the greater part regulated in Article 1382 of the Civil Code, that stipulates:

> 'Any act whatever of man, which causes damage to another, obliges the one by whose fault it occurred, to compensate it.'

This is a remarkably broad definition that allows the courts to further fine-tune its exact meaning in an extensive doctrine of precedents in case law (Tomlinson, 1988).

FIGURE 2.2 The correlation between codified standards and case law in civil law systems

Unlike the practice in common law systems, the legal professional in a civil law system is academically oriented. Legal training and research starts at the Universities. Law is therefore a subject of academic discourse, which is

considerably different compared to the common law systems, where law is more an applied science.

The development of civil law in France
The civil law system was first heavily influenced by the codification movement in the Roman empire. The idea to regulate private relations by written codes was spread by the Romans in the major part of the European mainland.

Later, in France, the French Revolution played an important part in revisiting the law. As a direct result of the Revolution in 1789, the French Civil Code was drafted, which would later be one of the most influential laws governing private relations in the world.

French Civil Code

The feudal system was abandoned, and the ideas of freedom, equality and brotherhood (liberté, égalité et fraternité) were implemented. For instance, principles as the protection of private property, contractual freedom and liability for damages were introduced (Zweigert & Kötz, 1998). Furthermore, the Civil Code was a compromise between including private rules derived from Roman law, and codifying the different costmary rules that applied informally in France.

Under the reign of Napoleon, the Civil Code was imposed on the French citizens, practically unifying the various customary rules that applied throughout the country. Also, the French law was exported to the occupied areas under the French expansion. This explains why European countries such as Spain, Portugal, Italy, Belgium and the Netherlands were greatly influenced by the French Civil Code. Furthermore, through colonizing countries all over the world, the French exported their Civil Code to other countries, such as Quebec in Canada, and Louisiana in the U.S.A., and countries in Africa, such as Algeria, Tunisia, Morocco and Senegal. And, the French Civil Code was used by many Latin-American countries as a model for law reforms after the Spanish decolonized these territories. Also Scotland, due to their historical collaboration with the French against the English, has adopted many principles set out in the French Civil Code.

2.2.3 Socialist law systems

While socialist systems gradually disappear since the dissolution of the Soviet Union in 1991, some countries remained socialist, and the effect of former socialist systems are still noticeable in other states. Therefore, the choice was made to include socialist legal system as a separate type of legal systems. Some may also use the term 'communism' to categorize the particular political system that is created based on socialist ideas.

A socialist system is driven by the administration.

In essence, the law is produced by the state (the administration) on behalf of all its citizens to create a society based on socialist principles. Law is therefore a tool to construct such a society. The state, with a political system of one official party, has a firm grip on the construction of this society. Therefore, we see that in the end, the administration, through this political party, is the main source of law.

A socialist system could be categorized as follows (Brown, 2009; Quigley, 1989):

- There is no role for private law. This is a result of the fact that all means of production are owned by the state.
- The country is governed by one powerful political (communist) party, and this party has a monopoly on decision making (so called 'democratic centralism').
- Law is predominantly used to realise a political agenda, founded on socialist ideology.
- Court rulings hardly settle disputes in private relations, and have a limited role in public law.

One of the principles of socialism is that all means are collectivized. This practically means that all properties, including companies, are state owned. Therefore, all issues that would in other legal systems fall under private law, such as employment, ownership, contracts and liability is governed by the state. The state is usually then the equivalent of the only official political party in a socialist country. Law in a socialist system is consequentially limited to public law. Since all is state owned, disputes over private relations will seldom occur. And if they occur, then law is not the appropriate means to settle this.
This means that a court system needs to contribute to the general aim of realizing a socialist state, and therefore mostly applies the law in line with the ideas of the communist party. It would be imprecise to conclude that courts in socialist systems therefore per definition have a limited role in creating law. However, it is the general tendency (Brown, 2009).
The purpose of law is therefore different from that in a civil or common law system: it is not necessarily the intention to offer protection to the individual against other individuals or the state, but rather to set up an ideological agenda that benefits the community.

This approach is clearly reflected in the then Constitution of the Soviet Union, of 1977. Article 39 stipulated that:

> 'Citizens of the USSR enjoy in full the social, economic, political and personal rights and freedoms proclaimed and guaranteed by the Constitution of the USSR and by Soviet laws. The socialist system ensures enlargement of the rights and freedoms of citizens and continuous improvement of their living standards as social, economic, and cultural development programmes are fulfilled.
> Enjoyment by citizens of their rights and freedoms must not be to the detriment of the interests of society or the state, or infringe the rights of other citizens.'

This last principle demonstrates more or less that the wellbeing of the collective prevails over the wellbeing of the individual.
Socialist law systems emerged after the Russian Revolution of 1917, after which the Russian Soviet Federative Socialist Republic was installed. Under the political influence of Russia, Eastern European countries became socialist satellite states. Later, also in Eastern Asia socialist countries emerged, such as China, Vietnam, Laos, North-Korea, Mongolia, and Cambodia. In Latin America, Cuba became a socialist country in 1959. Also in Africa, countries were at some point in the 20th century led by socialist idea's, such as Mozambique, Angola, and Ethiopia. However, at that time it

was debated whether such countries were truly socialist, or mere 'states of socialist orientation' (Brown, 2009).

Currently, only few full socialist legal systems remain. One could call Vietnam, Laos, North Korea and Cuba the remaining socialist legal systems.

Current socialist law systems

Although China has more or less a one-party political system and many socialist characteristics, some consider China a socialist system as well. However, there is enough reason to assume that China is a mixed system, gradually moving away from a strict application of socialism, with recognizable influences of customary law and civil law (Zhang, 2010).

Socialist law in Cuba

Currently, Cuba is one of the remaining socialist legal systems. In Cuba, the socialist principle that the state is organized to create a society in which the wellbeing of the community is most important is reflected in Article 62 of the Cuban Constitution. There is a striking similarity with the previous quote of the then-Constitution of the Soviet Union:

> 'None of the freedoms which are recognized for citizens can be exercised contrary to what is established in the Constitution and the law, or contrary to the existence and objectives of the socialist state, or contrary to the decision of the Cuban people to build socialism and communism. Violations of this principle can be punished by law.'

In Cuba, the Communist Party is the driving force in law creation and application. Article 5 of the Cuban Constitution stipulates that:

> 'The Communist Party of Cuba, Martian and of Marxist-Leninist, the organized vanguard of the Cuban nation, is the superior leading force of the society and the state, organizing and guiding the common efforts aimed at the highest goals of the construction of socialism and advancement toward the communist society.'

The legislature and the administration are closely interrelated. Where the legislator in practice consists of the Council of State (appointed by the National Assembly of the People's Power), the administration consists of the Council of Ministers. The president is the head of both councils, and is therefore relatively powerful (Sánchez, 2003). This explains why the Castro-family can lead Cuba for such a long time.

Furthermore, there is a court system in Cuba, including a supreme court of last instance, to settle legal conflicts. However, in line with Article 10 of the Cuban Constitution, it is the main function of all public institutions to 'strictly observe socialist legality, and to ensure respect for it in the life of the entire society.' This means that court rulings do not necessarily have as their main goal to settle a particular dispute, but rather to contribute to the 'bigger picture' of creating a socialist state.

2.2.4 Religious law systems

A religious system is driven by religious rules. This means per definition that a religious legal system is non-scalar. After all, in the organization of just behaviour, religion and state affairs are clearly not separated.

In some countries, religious law only plays a role in certain legal areas. For example, in Israel, family law is predominantly governed by religious law. Officially, Israel is considered to be a Jewish and democratic state. The word 'Jewish' suggests the existence of religious law, whereas the word 'democratic' suggests the existence of secular rules. Both are true. Matters of commerce for instance are governed by secular rules, whereas matters of family law are traditionally governed by religious rules. Instead, for the Jewish population, Jewish law (Halacha) is applicable, where for Muslims and Christians rules derived from their religion apply (S. Horowitz & Co.,2011; Rataj, 2013).
A system in which a particular legal field is regulated by religious law for the members of that religious society only is not uncommon. For instance, in Malaysia, matters of family law, and a small part of criminal law are regulated by Shari'a law, but only for those who profess the Islam (Federal Constitution of Malaysia, Article 76). Therefore secular and non-secular law co-exist in both Israel and Malaysia.

Shari'a law
In some countries, religious law is the primary legal source. Since the Iranian Revolution, in 1979, Islamic law plays an important role in several Islamic countries, especially in the Middle East. To grasp the idea of Islamic law – hereinafter referred to as Shari'a law – one needs to understand its function in society. Shari'a law reflects the will of Allah. This has several consequences. First of all, since the will of Allah is not restricted to particular topics, Shari'a law is about all aspects of life. This includes the issues that are covered in other legal systems too, such as trade law, but also aspects that are not always regulated by law, such as praying methods. Second, the will of Allah is not flexible. This means that Shari'a law does not necessarily change when societies progress. Instead, the idea is that a society should progress in in accordance with Shari'a law (Zweigert & Kötz, 1998). This notion explains why Islamic lawyers are at some level so much involved with the study of historic interpretative texts and precedents from ages ago: the law after all does not change. It also may explain the mind-set in which Islamic legal punishments are applied in some states. These punishments are considered to be very harsh by others.
In Shari'a law, there are four main legal sources (Zweigert & Kötz, 1998).
- the holy Qu'ran;
- the interpretation of the Qu'ran given by the Prophet Muhammed (Sunna);
- the interpretation of the Qu'ran given by the Islamic people (Igma);
- the interpretation of the Qu'ran given by individual judges or scholars (Fatwa), applied analogously to a case (Giyas).

The first and highest legal source is the holy Qur'an, in which the most important Islamic laws are stipulated. The second source is the writings that come forth from the interpretation to the Qur'an given by Prophet Muhammad. Those are the Sunna, which include different sources, depending on the exact type of Islam one professes. In this light, most Muslims do consider the 'hadiths', the earliest books describing the life and deeds of Muhammad, an important source. The third source relates to the interpretation to the Qur'an as given by humans. This is when the Islamic world reaches a consensus on he interpretation of the Qur'an. This is called Igma. However, there are several groups in Islam that have a different opinion about the importance and exact meaning of this source.

Last, the application of Shari'a law is an important source. A Muslim Judge, when the previous sources do not provide for a clear solution, will try to find analogous cases in the past, and solve the matter in line with that case. This is analogous application of the law is called qiyas. For this, the judge might have to trace back the opinion of other judges or legal scholars in other cases. The individual opinion or decision of a judge or legal scholar is called a fatwa (Mallat, 2006). Such legal opinions are found on various matters, including a broad range of advises. Some of them have been world news, such as the Fatwa against the author Salmon Rushdie, although this Fatwa may not be the most peaceful one, nor represent the average tone of a Fatwa (see the newspaper article).

THE DAILY MAIL (UK) 16 FEBRUARY 2014

Iranian mullah revives death fatwa against Salman Rushdie over Satanic Verses 25 years after it was issued.

BY: MIA DE GRAAF

The Iranian clergy has revived Salman Rushdie's death fatwa 25 years after it was issued over his 'blasphemous' Satanic Verses. On February 14, 1989, Ayatollah Ruhollah Khomeini called on all Muslims to murder the award-winning author and anyone involved in the publication of his work.

This Friday, senior cleric Ahmad Khatami reminded worshippers at the Tehran Friday prayer that the 'historical fatwa' is 'as fresh as ever'.

He added that even if Rushdie repents, it will not affect the sentence.

The religious ruling forced the award-winning writer into hiding, and Britain's ties with the Islamic republic were severely damaged just a few years after collaborating on a UN resolution between Iraq and Iran.

Hitoshi Igarashi, the Japanese translator, was stabbed to death in the face at work, a Norwegian publisher shot and an Italian publisher knifed.

Saudi Arabia

Saudi Arabia is an example of where Shari'a law is the main legal source. As already quoted in Chapter 1, the Basic Law of Saudi-Arabia stipulates in Article 1:

> 'The Kingdom of Saudi Arabia is a sovereign Arab Islamic state with Islam as its religion; God's Book and the Sunnah of His Prophet, God's prayers and peace be upon him, are its Constitution, Arabic is its language and Riyadh is its capital.'

Therefore, the Qu'ran and the Sunnah are the Constitution of Saudi-Arabia. They are also the legal sources for court rulings: the Fatwas (Art. 45 Basic Law). Furthermore, the courts may consider legislation created by the King, as long is this does not contradict the Shari'a law (Art. 48 Basic Law). For instance, the legislature of Saudi Arabia adopted several rules on trade to facilitate trade with business partners from other countries, such as the Foreign Investment Law (2000), regulating the licensing of foreign investments in Saudi Arabia.

The Saudi government 'derives its authority from the Book of God and the Sunna of the Prophet' (Art. 7 Basic Law). In the government, the King has a very powerful position, since the country is officially declared a monarchy (Art. 5 Basic Law). Therefore, the King is the head of the executive branch, the legislative branch and is very influential in the judiciary. After all, the King is ultimately responsible for implementing Shari'a law, as recognized in Art. 50 Basic Law (Ansary, 2008).

2.2.5 Traditional law systems

A traditional law system is driven by customary law.
We have seen several examples of fragments of a traditional law system, such as the customary law of Nigeria, and the Chinese use of customary law in their complex legal system. Nowadays, it must be said that full traditional law systems hardly exist: the export of civil and common law systems by European countries greatly influenced the existing traditional law systems (such as Nigeria), and now mostly the traditional law that is left is complementary to other legal systems (Bennet, 2006).
However, in some communities within states, traditional law is still broadly applied within indigenous communities. In some countries, the traditional law system of these people are protected and preserved, such as the traditional law of the Maori's in New Zealand, the Aboriginals in Australia, and the Orang Asli in Malaysia.

The Natives of Malaysia

Malaysia has a complex history whereby parts of the county were colonized by Dutch and English rulers. Currently, the population consists of a vivid mixture of different ethnic groups, including Muslims, Chines, and Indian people. Due to the historic background of Malaysia, the legal system is a true 'mixed system'. Malaysian law encompasses an interesting cocktail with influences of common law and religious law. As we have seen before, in Malaysia the Shari'a law may be applied in several legal matters, when the people involved profess the Islam. However, this is not the only recognition of the use of particular laws belonging to a particular group. However, there is a third branch of law: the law of the natives of Malaysia.
To protect their way of life, including their legal custom, the Constitution stipulates that it is the responsibility of the Yang di-Pertuan Agong (the elected Monarch of Malaysia) to:

> 'safeguard the special position of the Malays and natives of any of the States of Sabah and Sarawak and the legitimate interests of other communities in accordance with the provisions of this Article (Art.153, Federal Constitution of Malaysia).'

On the peninsula of the country, the indigenous people are named the Orang Asli. The Aboriginal Peoples Act aims to protect the traditional customs of the Orang Asli (Nah, 2008), since Article 4 reads:

> 'Provided that nothing in this section shall be deemed to preclude any aboriginal headman from exercising his authority in matters of aboriginal custom and belief in any aboriginal community or any aboriginal ethnic group.'

Sarawak Court system

On the Island of Borneo, there are even separate Court systems for the Sarawak and Sabah, that – amongst others – are established to rule on matters of traditional customary law of the indigenous people (Ahmad, 2001). For instance, considering the Sarawak, the Native Courts Enactment installs a refined system of native courts and tribunals. Those courts have jurisdiction regarding matters of 'cases arising from breach of native law or custom in which all the parties are natives' (Article 6 (a)). Usually, the courts have no jurisdiction on matters that are governed by federal state laws, such as the penal code.
In Sarawak, the lowest courts are headmen's courts, while the chain of courts moves upwards via the chief's courts, the chief's superior courts, up to the native court of appeal. There are separate tribunals for matters on land disputes: the District Native Court.

2.2.6 Mixed systems
It will come as no surprise that legal systems do not necessarily belong to one particular type only. A legal system may be influenced by several types of legal systems, and may have embraced various such elements. When there is such a mixture of legal approaches in one legal system, we call this a 'mixed system'. The forming of such systems can usually be explained by historic events that caused influences of various approaches in law. Such events are for instance colonization, trade, or war.

Japan
The earliest evidence of the existence of a more or less coherent law system goes back to the year 5 AD. The legal system of Japan was heavily influenced by Chinese legal principles in these days, derived from mostly a Confusian point of view. Under the reign of the Shoguns, Japan remained a closed society. Only the Chinese, and later to a certain extent the Dutch, had access to Japanese soil in order to establish trade relations. Later, the rule of the Shogun came to an end, and the Japanese Emperors took power. Under the supervision of the Emperors, Japan opened its markets to the rest of the world, and trade with mostly European nations emerged. Soon however, the Japanese realised that trade disputes with European parties could hardly be governed by the Chinese-oriented concepts of customary law. Therefore, in the second half of the 19th century, they imported concepts of French and German law that could be applied to trade disputes in which foreign parties were involved. For instance, a criminal code was written based on the French model, and a commercial code and civil code were drafted based on the German model. It can be said that in general, regarding trade law, the Japanese implemented the legal structure and forms of the German model, and the legal substance of a mixed French/ German approach. However, these rules were hardly applied to local trade disputes involving only Japanese, since traditionally, the Japanese prefer to settle disputes outside the courtroom by peaceful mediation.

After the Second World War, the Japanese legal system was heavily influenced by legal concepts of the U.S.A. Especially constitutional and criminal law was reformed in accordance with the American model. This also

means that the Japanese judiciary, true to the Common Law legal tradition, played a role of more importance.
So, in fact, the Japanese legal system could be considered a mixture of Chinese customary law, French and German civil law, and American Common law. Of course, the Japanese have their own style in applying this wonderful mixture, which adds a true Japanese legal identity to this mixed system (Kitagawa, 2006).
Later, the Japanese legal system heavily influenced the (south) Korean legal system, and – believe it or not – the Chinese legal system (see figure 2.3).

FIGURE 2.3 Japanese law

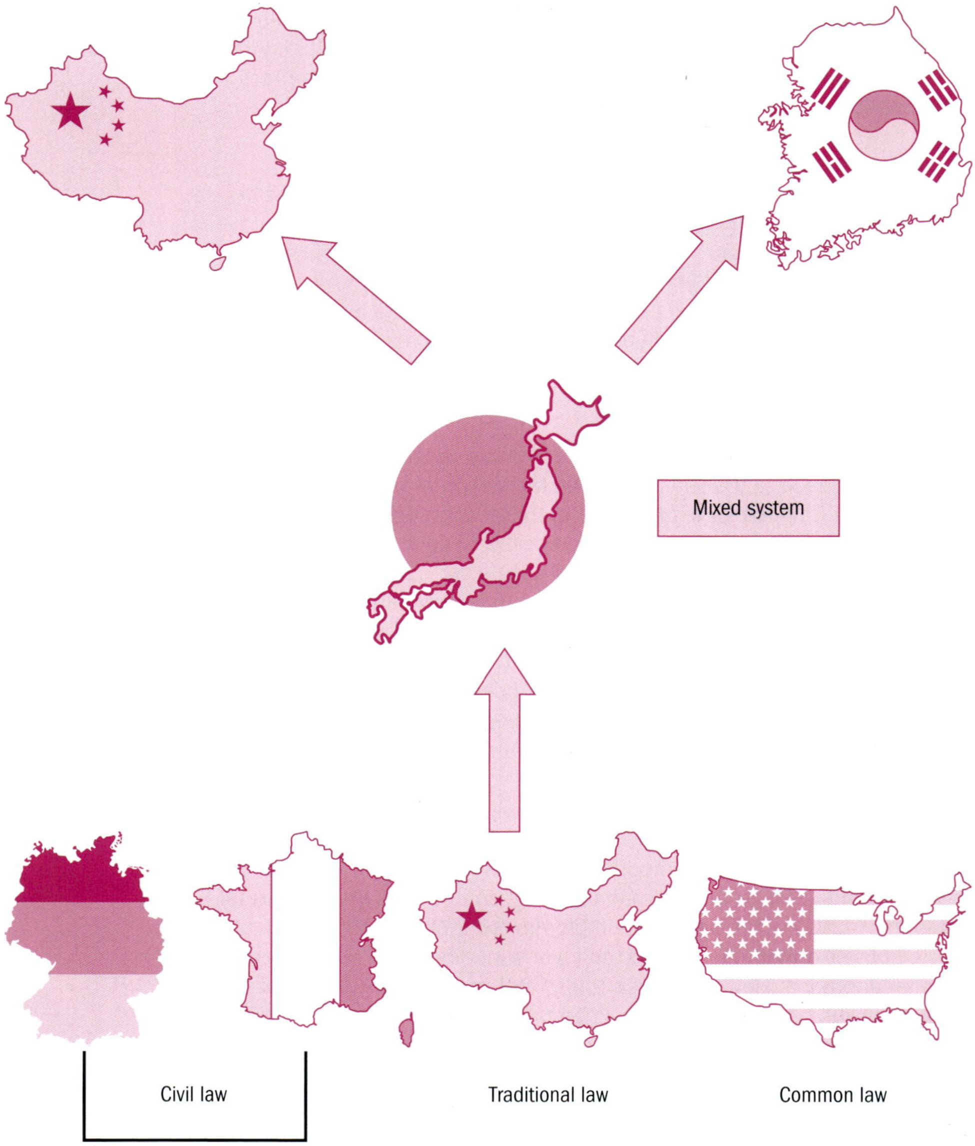

2.3 Micro comparison: a functional method

Where macro comparison gives us insight in entire legal systems, micro comparison is focussed on a particular legal solution to a problem within different legal systems.

Micro comparison

> Micro comparison is the activity in which the legal solution to a social problem in legal systems are compared.

To this end, a functional method is used. This method consists of several elements that need to be clarified. First of all, the comparison starts with a social problem that needs to be solved by law. This social problem could be anything, depending on the researcher's motives. It is the assumption that in each legal system more or less the same kind of problems need to be tackled by law. For instance, a social problem could be: 'it is unclear who the owner is of a copyright when an employee creates artistic work for an employer' In the terminology of legal comparison, we call this social problem a 'tertium comparationis'.

Tertium comparationis

> The tertium comparationis is the shared social problem to which the compared legal solutions answer.

The assumption that more or less the same social problems exist in each legal system is not uncontested, since societies differ greatly (Nelken, 2007 2). However, one simply needs to start somewhere in comparing law, and a shared social problem is usually a useful starting point (Michaels, 2006), or even the reason why a researcher starts comparing law in the first place. In the terminology of legal comparison, the assumption that each society faces the same social problem is called the 'praseumptio similtudinis', a term introduced by Zweigert & Kötz (1998).

Praesumptio similtudinis

> The praesumptio similtudinis is the assumption that in essence each society faces the same social problems

In a majority of the legal systems, there will probably be some kind of a legal solution to solve the social problem 'it is unclear who the owner is of a copyright when an employee creates artistic work for an employer'. It is now the task of the researcher to find the exact legal solution to the shared social problem in different legal systems.

Legal solution to a social problem

> The legal solution to a social problem is the particular legal concept within a given legal system that solves the involved social problem

It is important to realise that while the legal solutions to the social problem found in the legal systems may be different, they are equal in their functional relation. After all they have the same function in society: providing an answer to the same social problem. When we consider the example 2.4., Article 6 of the Copyright Code of Nepal, Article 11 of the UK Copyright, Designs and Patents Act, and the legal custom of Finland have the same function in society. While their content, effect and form may be different, they are equivalent as to their function. Therefore, legal solutions to a similar social problem are 'functionally equivalent'.

Functional equivalent legal solutions

A schematic overview of the functional method, including the used terminology, can be found in figure 2.4.

FIGURE 2.4 Functional method in comparative law

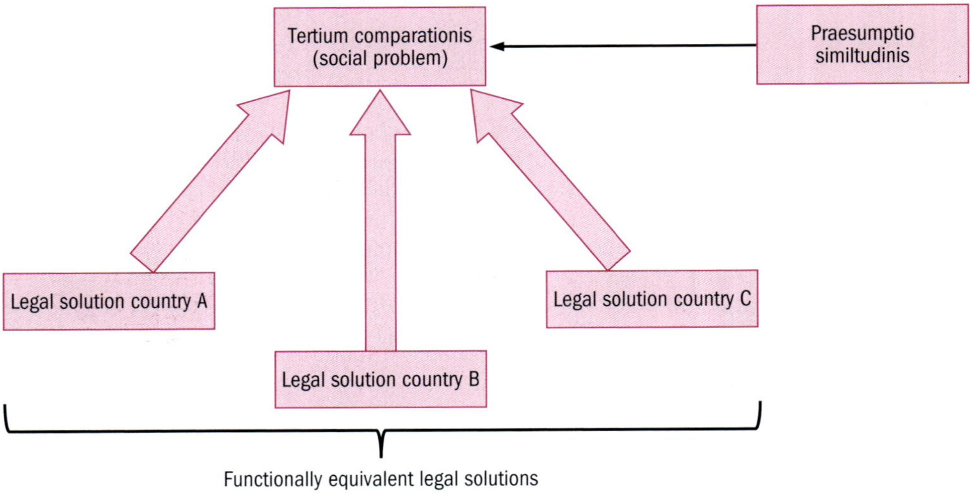

Choice of legal systems

The choice of the legal systems that are compared greatly depends on the agenda of the researcher. For instance, if the researcher writes an export plan, the choice of law depends on the ambition of the company involved, or the market opportunities in certain countries that are suitable for export. The researcher will then probably take a closer look at the legal solutions to several social problems in the selected countries, and compare those.

EXAMPLE 2.4

Copyrights and employment

As already stated in the main text, a social problem could be: 'it is unclear who is the owner of a copyright when an employee creates artistic work for an employer.' When we would compare for whatever reason Finland, the UK and Nepal, we would find the following legal solutions to this problem.

In Nepal, Article 6 of the Copyright Act stipulates:

'the economic right of a work shall vest in the following person or organization in the following circumstances:'(…) 'In case where a work is prepared on payment of remuneration by any person or organization, that person or organization who has paid such remuneration.'

This means that this codified standard provides for a solution to the social problem. The Article clarifies that it is the employer who possesses the economic rights when an employee creates work while he receives payment for this. This means in essence that the employer may use the work publicly for his own benefit. However, the creator of the work will still hold the moral rights to the work (Article 8), meaning above all that his name is mentioned when the work is used in public, and may object to alterations to his work.

The UK Copyright, Designs and Patents Act , Article 11, reads:

'Where a literary, dramatic, musical or artistic work or a film, is made by an employee in the course of his employment, his employer is the first owner of any copyright in the work subject to any agreement to the contrary.'

Also here, a codified standard provides an answer to the social problem. The employer holds the full copyright, including the moral rights. The work may therefore be used publicly for the benefit of the employer, and the name of the author does not necessarily need to be mentioned when the work is used in public. Also, the employer may alter and adapt the work later when necessary, without the consent of the original author. On the other hand, the UK law emphasizes that the employer and employee may deviate from this Article in the labour contract.

However, when we read the Finn legislation on the matter, the Copyright Act remains silent. The law only deals with employment relations when a very particular type of a copyright is concerned: a computer programme. Article 40 of the Copyright Act states that:

'If a computer program and a work directly associated with it has been created in the scope of duties in an employment relation, the copyright in the computer program and the work shall pass to the employer.'

For all other work, there are no codified standards that answer to the social problem. Does this mean that the social problem is not solved by law? The answer is no. Similar to many other countries, there is contractual freedom in Finland. For labour contracts, this is recognized in the Employment Contracts Act (Section 3). In Finland, it is a common practice that employees sign a contract in which they transfer (parts of) their copyrights to the employer when the creation of that work was part of the job. In a way, legal custom, provides an answer to the social problem.

2.3.1 Some rules of thumb

It is not easy to find the 'real' legal solution to the social problem, especially when the researcher is not familiar with the legal system that is under investigation. Things are not always what they seem. A very simple example of this can be found in the 'copyrights and employment' case (example 2.4). Nepal is a relatively new democracy in Asia, experimenting with the implementation of legal concepts from elsewhere in the world. The status of the Copyright Act is therefore until now unknown, and its actual effect is new and uncertain. The Copyright Act in the UK stems from the implementation of a European Directive, rather than that the UK legislature felt the need to create new law. Besides that, the precedents on copyright law provided for the courts may not be overlooked and are relatively powerful. Then, the Finn Act, which is an implementation of the same European Directive, remains silent on the matter. The researcher will instead find the legal solution to the problem in legal practice (custom) rather than in codified standards.

There are so many different legal systems with so many different legal constructions, that it is difficult to provide clear practical guidelines on how to find such legal solutions. In all honesty, and with deep respect, the most important scholars in the field of comparative law have their own handful of practical advises, while actually the general advise comes down to this: use your common sense. Nevertheless, below, some rules of thumb are given that may help the researcher to find the right sources, and understand them correctly.

'Advise 1: determine to which legal family the legal system belongs, and what particular characteristics are important in this legal system.'

When a legal system belongs to a legal family, or is a mixture of different families, the general context of the law in that legal system is more visible to the researcher.
For instance, the fact that a country is predominantly a common law system tells you something of the role of the courts. In a mixed system, one has to be mindful of the interaction between the different legal families that are apparent. Nepal, for instance, could be considered a mixed system in which religious law (hindu law) and common law interact. It is important for the researcher to get a clear idea on what law is influenced by religious elements, and to what extent law is borrowed from other common law systems, such as India and the UK (Urscheler, 2012). The Copyright Act is one of those borrowed elements.

'Advise 2: determine how the legal sources are used by those who live in that legal system.'

The fact that a legal source exists does not automatically mean that it is also effectively used. Therefore, it is important to study the sources you find 'from within'. This means that the researcher tries to determine how the inhabitants of the legal system use the source. For instance, in Nepal, there has been a Copyright Act since 1965. However, the law had several technical defects and lacked any litigation rules. As a result, copyright laws were never applied nor contested in court until the Copyright Act of 2002 came into force. This Act provided for significantly better rules and enforcement procedures. In Nepal, However, piracy is still a major problem, and hardly disputed in the courts, despite these legal improvements: people are simply not aware of Intellectual Property protection, and not used to the fact that it is (in theory) possible to enforce copyrights by law (Upreti, 2013). If you are a publisher, music agency or an artist looking for export opportunities in Nepal, it is important to consider this relevant information.

'Advise 3: do not study the law in the books only, but also the law in practice.'

Under advise 2 we saw that when a legal source exists, this does not automatically imply that this source actually provides for a legal solution in practice. It also works the other way around: the fact that there is no legal source in the form of a codified standard does not automatically mean that there is no legal solution. For instance, in Finland, the law remains silent regarding the social problem 'it is unclear who is the owner of a copyright when an employee creates artistic work for an employer'. However, there is a certain legal practice (custom) in Finland that most certainly responds to the social problem. This example demonstrates that comparing copyright Acts only will probably not give you the right information. The comparing of the acts may be a good starting point, but the researcher should be aware of the fact that it is just a starting point, and not the entire research.

'Advise 4: study the sources in the original form, preferably in the original language.'

In most legal systems, the communication of legislation and court rulings is organized centrally. It might be important to figure out the (online) environment first, before – at random – making use of general search engines. For instance, the UK legislation can be found on: http://www.legislation.gov.uk, while most case law can be found on: http://www.commonlii.org/uk/cases.

'Advise 5: be mindful that a legal solution may respond to more than one social problem.'

It is important to understand that a legal solution is never a separate solution to one particular problem, but rather a legal concept that answers to more than one social problem. To gain a better understanding of the legal concept that is being studied, it might be relevant to also determine the broader context of this legal solution. For instance, Nepal and India have an open boarder since 1950 after signing and ratifying the 'Treaty of Peace and Friendship Between The government of India and The government of Nepal'. This means that products and people can cross the border of Nepal and India freely. For this reason, especially in the context of widespread piracy, it makes sense to harmonize the legislation in that field between India and Nepal. Since Nepal had no effective copyright legislation yet, the model of India served as an important source of inspiration for the Copyright Act of Nepal. Another purpose of the Copyright Act of Nepal is therefore to facilitate free trade between the two countries by harmonizing the rules of the game concerning copyrights. This information gives even more insight in the nature of the Copyright Act of Nepal. It is therefore to be expected that in the near future, the Copyright Act will develop according to the Indian model, including its enforcement.

Summary

- Comparative law has five main purposes:
  - The gaining of knowledge;
  - Evaluating the better law;
  - Substantiate the application of law;
  - Improve legal education;
  - The unification of law.

There are two levels of legal comparison: micro- and macro comparison.

- Macro comparison:
  - Macro comparison is the activity in which the main characteristics of legal systems are compared.
  - A legal system is a coherent collective of legal rules in which the same hierarchy of legal sources applies, mostly determined by the boundaries of a state.
  - A legal family is a group of legal systems that share the same basic characteristics in law, including at similar hierarchy of legal rules.

- There are 6 types of legal families:
  - A common law system is case law driven, for instance England.
  - A civil law system is driven by codified standards, for instance France.
  - A socialist system is driven by the administration, for instance Cuba.
  - A religious system is driven by religious rules, for instance Saudi-Arabia.
  - A traditional law system is driven by customary law, for instance the natives in Malaysia.
  - A mixed system contains two or more elements of the other families, for instance Japan.

- Micro comparison:
  - Micro comparison is the activity in which the legal solution to a social problem in legal systems are compared.
  - In micro comparison, a functional method is used. This encompasses the following elements:
    - The tertium comparationis is the shared social problem to which the compared legal solutions answer.
    - The praesumptio similtudinis is the assumption that in essence each society faces the same social problems.
    - The legal solution to a social problem is the particular legal concept within a given legal system that solves the involved social problem.
    - Legal solutions to a similar social problem are functionally equivalent.

- Rules of thumb in micro-comparison are the following:
  - Determine to which legal family the legal system belongs, and what particular characteristics are important in this legal system.
  - Determine how the legal sources are used by those who live in that legal system.
  - Do not study the law in the books only, but also the law in practice.
  - Study the sources in the original form, preferably in the original language.
  - Be mindful that a legal solution may respond to more than one social problem.

Practice questions

Open questions

2.1 Maud, a French entrepreneur, wants to explore business opportunities in South Korea and Japan. Her business is specialized in the production of fibre plastic. However, before she acts, she wants to perform a proper law comparison. She is aware of the fact that plastic may be harmful for the environment, and is therefore interested in the legal aspects in both countries regarding the production and sales of fibre plastic.

Create a short methodological overview on how to approach this comparison using the functional method terminology. Use in your design at least the terms 'praesumptio similtudinis', 'tertium comparationis' and 'functionally equivalent'.

2.2 Considering question 2.1, what legal sources would you expect to find, if you were Maud, considering the legal families both countries belong to?

2.3 Describe the function of a court in a socialist legal system.

2.4 Describe the function of a court in a civil law legal system.

Essay question

Write an essay in which you explore how patents are protected and filed in South Africa and Nigeria. Compare the two approaches and conclude what the main similarities and differences are.

Multiple choice questions

2.1 In comparative law, the praesumptio similtudinis means:
- **a** The neutral point with which one compares
- **b** The notion that each country faces similar social problems
- **c** The idea that legal solutions to social problems are functionally equivalent

2.2 In comparative law, the tertium comparationis means:
- **a** The neutral point with which one compares
- **b** The notion that each country faces similar social problems
- **c** The idea that legal solutions to social problems are functionally equivalent

2.3 When a court uses comparative law in their verdict, the purpose of the comparison is usually:
a To find the better law
b To substantiate the verdict
c To unify law

2.4 When a legislature uses comparative law during the draft of new legislation, the purpose of the comparison is usually:
a To find the better law
b To substantiate the new law
c To unify law

PART 2
International public law

In international business it is helpful to understand how foreign countries generally work. Therefore, we will explore the main elements of constitutional law in chapter 3. In this chapter, we will discuss how states are organized in general, and what the main issues are in constitutional law. Furthermore, there are various grades of international economic cooperation, realized by internationals public institutions. In chapter 4 we will discuss the most important institutions of the United Nations and how they contribute to economic development. In chapter 5 we will explain the functioning of the so-called Bretton Woods institutions: the IMF, the World bank and the WTO. These organizations have a profound impact on the organization of global economic cooperation.
On a regional level, there is also economic cooperation in various degrees of intensity. Therefore, in chapter 6, we will discuss the NAFTA (a free trade zone), the SACU (a Custon Union) and the MERCOSUR (a common market). In chapter 7, we will discuss the European Union (an Economic and monetary union).

HEY!! BAD GUY!
NO! ...You're the bad guy!
Sandor

3 Constitutional law

Constitutional law primarily regulates the power of state institutions and the freedom of its citizens. In this chapter we explore the characteristics of constitutional law into more detail. We will discuss the concept of dividing power (trias politica), and introduce the vocabulary that is necessary to understand constitutional law

3.1 Trias politica and the struggle for power

In this section we will explore the main characteristics of constitutional law. In short, we will discuss the purpose of constitutional law, which is to regulate and restrict the attribution of power. Then, we will discuss the meaning of freedom. After all, the way states allocate and use power defines the interpretation of freedom within that state. Finally, we will discuss the way power is attributed in states. In some states a separation of powers is established based on the trias politica model, to avoid the exceeding or abuse of power.

3.1.1 The purpose of constitutional law

As we have seen in chapter one, public law regulates the relation between the state and its citizens. The institutions of a state are attributed a certain power towards their citizens, while citizens may invoke rights that restrict and control this power. Such rules are usually regulated by the constitutional law of a state.

Constitutional law

> Constitutional law regulates and restricts the attribution of power within a state.

In most countries this is done by three type of rules.

- The first type defines the state. This is done by defining matters as state boundaries, the political system, the historical or religious background, the national anthem and flag, and state nationality.
- The second type attribute powers to state institutions, and limits these powers to a certain margin.
- The third type recognizes rights of the citizens of that state, that can be invoked when power is abused.

A clear example in which those types of rules appear is the 'Constitution of Chile', as you can see in example 3.1.

While the Constitution of Chile appears in the form of codified standards, one must however be careful in interpreting such written texts (Harding & Leyland).
First of all, a constitution does not necessarily consist of codified standards only. For instance, the constitutional law of the UK does not consist of a single unified constitutional text, but is rather composed of several sources, such as parliamentary acts, case law, custom and international law.
Second, it is always important to explore to what extent the constitution also works according to plan. The law in action therefore needs to be taken into consideration as well, next to the written texts. For instance, Chile developed itself from a dictatorial regime to a more democratic state (Ortega, 2010). The Constitution has been altered several times to facilitate this process. However, the legal reality did not always match the written text of the Constitution (Human Rights Watch, 2004).

EXAMPLE 3.1

The Constitution of Chile
The three types of rules are clearly apparent in the Constitution of Chile.

In the first two chapters, the State of Chile is defined. For instance, Article 4 stipulates that 'Chile is a democratic republic'. Furthermore, chapter two defines the citizenship of Chile: Article 10 defines when an individual has the Chilean nationality, while Article 11 regulates when this nationality is lost. While most 'undemocratic' elements of the constitution have been removed since the end of the Junta reign in 1990 by several constitutional reforms, the historical heritage of this regime is still visible in the constitution (The Economist, 2004). This is mostly noticeable in the preamble, in which until today 'the Hon. Government Junta approved a new Political Constitution of the Republic of Chile, submitting its text to ratification by plebiscite.' Also Article 9 reminds us of the Junta days, because this article forbids terrorism, a provision that may easily be abused to get rid of political opponents by the government and impose stricter sanctions than would be allowed by normal criminal proceedings (Human Rights Watch, 2004).

Chapter 4-7 organizes the Chilean public institutions. In Chile, the administration consists of the President and his Ministers of State. The legislature is the Congress consisting of the Chamber of Deputies and the

Senate. The judiciary consists of several specialized courts of first instance, courts of appeal and a supreme court. Furthermore, Chile has a Constitutional Court that is authorized to review legislation against the constitution, a special court that reviews the legality of elections, and a supervisory body that reviews the legality of administrational acts.

In Chapter 3, all constitutional rights and obligations are stipulated. For instance, the chapter recognizes the right to life, the principle of equality, the right to privacy, the principle of legality, the freedom of conscience, the freedom of speech, the right to education, the right to healthcare, the right to social security, the right to assemble and associate, the freedom to work and the right to property.

3.1.2 State power and freedom

In the context of constitutional law, there is always a certain struggle between the authority and the individual. When power is wielded by the institution of a state, one almost per definition interferes in the life of citizens. For instance, the obligation to pay a certain amount of tax interferes in the life of a citizen. The tax agency of that state will decide on the exact amount per citizen. The question then is to what extent this interference is desirable, and to what extent it is not. In other words: what kind of freedom should the citizen enjoy, and what kind of freedom should the citizen give up when living in that particular state.
European philosophers, such as Thomas Hobbes, Charles de Montesquieu and Jean-Jacques Rousseau, argued that in a society, citizens willingly gave up part of their sovereignty to the authority of the state. In exchange for that, the citizens could benefit from a safe and secure society, in which people could peacefully co-exist. It is the job of the states authorities to guard and maintain this safe and secure society. When authorities would exceed or abuse their powers, the citizens would have the right to stand up against their rulers. This so-called 'social contract' has been an example for organizing states in most European countries.

Social contract

The way power is exercised relates to what concept of 'freedom' is advocated in a society. In this light, Isaiah Berlin defines two – opposing – concepts of freedom: negative and positive freedom. They are two extremes on a gliding scale.

> Negative freedom means that one is free to do whatever he wants, without any interference.

Negative freedom

> Positive freedom means that as a result of interference one has the opportunity to better give direction to his life.

Positive freedom

Please note that the words 'negative' and 'positive' are not an expression of something that is unpleasant or pleasant. It rather expresses the absence (negative) or existence (positive) of interference in the life of a citizen as you may see visualized in figure 3.1.

FIGURE 3.1 Positive and negative freedom

In each state, elements of both negative and positive freedom are apparent. The question is what the mix between the two extremes looks like. The way a state uses the concepts of negative and positive freedom mostly defines the main characteristics of how a state is governed. As we can see in example 3.2, there are different political ideas on how to tackle a social problem such as a school shooting. Where the Republicans want government abstaining (negative freedom), the Democrats advocate government interference (positive freedom) to solve the matter.

EXAMPLE 3.2

The only way to stop a bad guy with a gun is with a good guy with a gun

In the United States, the main political difference between Republicans and Democrats relates to the two concepts of freedom: the Republicans have a stronger focus on negative freedom, while the Democrats usually emphasize the benefits of positive freedom. This is clearly visible in the discussion on the right to bear arms: after each of the notorious 'school shootings', there is an emotional political debate about the matter.
The right to bear arms is recognized in the famous 'second Amendment' of the U.S. Constitution: 'a well regulated Militia, being necessary to the security of a free state, the right of the people to keep and bear Arms, shall not be infringed.'

The Democrats

Democrats usually want to alter the scope of this right, to prevent the wide spread of weapon possession in the United States of America. The remedy to avoid these school shootings is therefore to interfere in the life of citizens by restricting their right to bear arms. The idea is that in a society with fewer guns, the chance that a school shooting occurs is reduced. As a result, people live in a safer state and are better able to give direction to their lives.

The Republicans

This approach is opposed by the Republicans, who consider the right to bear arms a fundamental freedom. According to them, it should be the choice of a citizen whether or not to bear arms, and the right of a citizen to be able to defend himself or loved ones when attacked. The remedy to stop a school shooting is therefore not to interfere in the lives of people, and allow them the freedom to do something about it. Wayne LaPierre, executive vice president of the National Rifel Association, used the following infamous wordings after a school shooting in Newton in 2012: 'The only way to stop a bad guy with a gun is with a good guy with a gun' (LaPierre, 2012).

3.1.3 Trias politica

In most states, the power lies in the hands of different state institutions. The constitutional law of each state usually regulates how the power is distributed amongst the state institutions. The French philosopher Charles de Montesquieu argued that the best way to avoid power abuse is to separate the powers in three branches: the legislature, the executive branch and the judiciary. In short, it comes down to this: the legislature is responsible for law making, the executive branch is responsible for executing the law in practice, while the judiciary is responsible in settling legal disputes. According to Montesquieu, these powers should be attributed to separate institutions. When this is not done accordingly, there would be an end to freedom or a safe and secure state (Gordon, 1999). This concept is named trias politica.

> Trias politica is the organization of a state by separating legislative, executive and judicial powers.

Trias politica

As we can see in case study 3.1 on the website, there are various (modern) interpretations of separating powers in a trias politica model. It needs to be noted here that the idea of separating powers in three branches is an idea with a strong European background. The concept rules out state forms that are governed by one central institution only, including religious institutes, or including the military as a branch of power. It will come as no surprise that European influenced countries usually implemented a system that is more or less based on a trias politica model, but that other countries do not necessarily share this enthusiasm for separating powers this way.

3.2 The language of constitutional law

When discussing constitutional law, and the way powers are separated in societies, we need to familiarize ourselves with certain terminology and phenomena first. The following matters closely relate to constitutional law.

3.2.1 The state structure

In order to rule a state, one needs to organize the structure of the state.

> The state structure is the way power is distributed amongst the entities of a state.

State structure

Two state forms are most used in the world: the federation and the unity state.

> A federation is a state that unites federated areas that are self-governing within the boundaries set by the federation.

Federation

Federations come in a great deal of variety. In case study 3.1, we will see that Brazil, Germany, India, the Russian Federation and the United States of America all have a federal state structure. What they have in common is that the federated entities within that state enjoy a certain level of autonomy in legislation and government. Such entities can be provinces, states, cities, regions, etc. This autonomy differs per federation, and is mostly determined in the constitution of the federation. This structure may lead to tensions between legislators of the federated entities and the federal legislation, especially when there is uncertainty about the exact limits of their jurisdiction. As a solution, some kind of a Constitutional Court may be installed, that settles – amongst others – disputes between these different legislators.

Unitary state

A unitary state is a centrally organized state in which all power is vested in national political institutions.

This means that in a unitary state, the legislature, executive branch and judiciary are centrally focussed and have exclusive power to ultimately deal with the adoption, execution and interpretation of the law. This does not mean that in a unitary state power may not be delegated. As a matter of fact, this usually happens. However, this delegation of power is at the discretion of the highest authority in the country, and does not emerge from a constitution. This means that any decentralization of power may be reorganized at any time, and centralized again whenever the highest institutes of the country desire. In case study 3.1, the People's Republic of China and the Republic of South Africa are unitary states.

3.2.2 The government system

Next to the structure of a state, one needs a way to rule a state in that structure. To this end, each state has entrusted power to political institutions. Mostly, these political institutions can be categorized in the three branches of power.

Government system

A government system is the way in which power is distributed amongst the political institutions of a state.

There are many different government systems, but two systems are most frequently used: a monarchy and a republic. However, it must be noted here that these concepts are used in various meanings and contexts. In the choice of defining these concepts, we considered its practical application rather than the academic discourse regarding its meaning that emerges from time to time. The word 'democracy' is deliberately omitted, because we will deal with that concept later, as a gliding scale that can be applied to both a monarchy and a republic.

Monarchy

A monarchy is a state in which the highest power is vested in and distributed from one person or a group of persons.

Monarchies come in many forms, but have in common that they are led by a head of state that is a person, or group of persons, who is/are appointed based on tradition. Most traditions are based on family ties, in which power is vested within one family, and is transferred from generation to generation. Currently, more than 40 states consider themselves a monarchy.

Republic

> A republic is a state in which the highest power is attributed to political bodies that rule within the boundaries of a constitution and is headed by a president.

In the 19th century, the word republic was mostly used as a concept opposite to a monarchy. Therefore, a republic is not led by a monarch, but by a president. Gradually, many forms of republics appeared in the world. Currently, more than 145 countries consider themselves a republic. The highest legislative power is authorized by the constitution and consists of a body that represents the people. This representation of the people may occur in different shapes or forms, and some republics are more democratic than other republics.

The choice of a governmental system may, but does not necessarily, say something about its democratic nature.

Democracy

> Democracy is a form of government in which the highest power is vested in the people that are governed.

This means in practice that the people decide who represents them in decision-making processes. These representatives could be politicians, united in a parliament, or an individual, such as a president or prime minister. In most democratic countries, people elect the members of the legislature, and sometimes the head and/or members of the executive branch. Mostly, the judiciary is appointed by either the legislature or the executive branch, but not elected by the people. There are, of course, exceptions to this.
In this book, we do not consider a democracy as being a particular governmental system but rather a form that can be applied to both a monarchy and a republic, as we can see in figure 3.2. Although from an academic perspective, this approach could meet some resistance, we believe it is an accurate reflection on reality.

FIGURE 3.2 Government systems and democracy

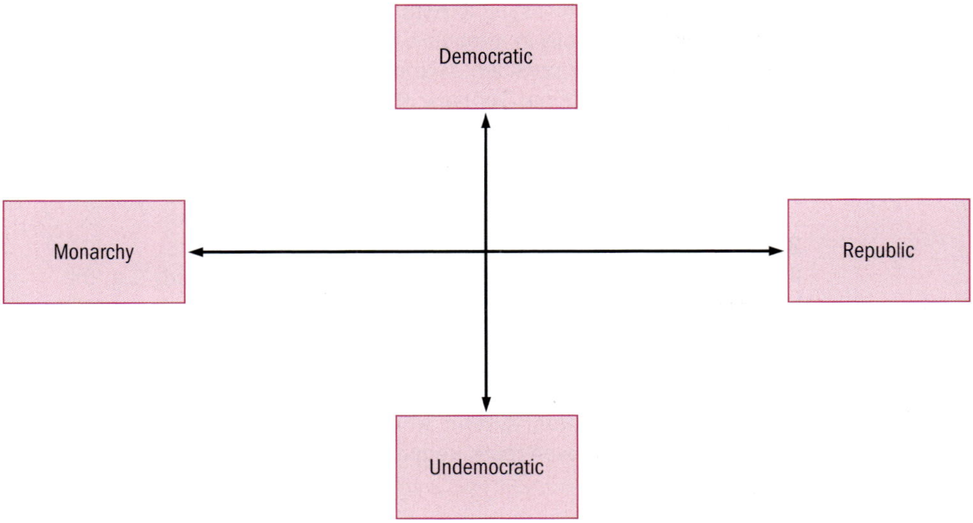

In essence, one would expect a monarchy, in which reign is based on tradition and centralized in one or a handful of people, to be undemocratic. Furthermore, a republic in which a president is appointed to rule on behalf of the people can be expected to be democratic. However, there is a thin line between those concepts. Some republics are not so democratic, where some monarchies are, and vice versa.
For instance, the military regimes in Latin America that emerged in the 60ies-70ies were often referred to as a republic, but were not very democratic. After all, power was practically vested in a handful of military officers. A more recent example would be the Republic Union of Myanmar that had a military government in the period 2007-2011. Also states that are governed from the perspective of one political belief, such as a socialist state, have restricted democracy to that political approach. Examples are countries as China, Laos, Congo, Cuba and Vietnam.

Of course, there are monarchies in which the monarch indeed wields most of the power and are therefore rather undemocratic. Saudi Arabia or North Korea (while the latter is actually called a democratic republic) would be examples in which power is vested in respectively a royal house and a political leader. Such a monarchy is also named an absolute monarchy. However, there are also monarchies in which the head of state is a monarch, although this position is merely a ceremonial function. Most monarchies in Europe for instance are so-called constitutional monarchies, in which there is a monarch, although he has no or very limited political powers. Instead, political power is vested in democratically elected bodies. Examples are the United Kingdom, the Kingdoms of Andorra, Belgium, the Netherlands, Belgium, Norway, Spain, Sweden, the principalities of Luxemburg and Monaco, and the Grand Duchy of Luxembourg.

3.2.3 About the head of state

Mostly, the government system is decisive in determining who the head of state is. In a monarchy, this is the monarch, and in a republic this is the president. However, as we have seen above, the exact power vested in the head of state is rather different per country, and mostly regulated into detail in the constitution.
In this context, it is interesting to note to what branch of power the head of state belongs. Especially in a republic, the role of the president may differ. In some republics, the president is considered to stand above the branches of power, such as in China, Germany and the Russian Federation. In other countries, the president is considered to be the head of the executive branch, with several powers in the field of the legislature and judiciary. Examples are Brazil, India, the U.S.A. and the Republic of South Africa.

3.2.4 About the legislature

Bi-cameral system

Unicameral systems

In a majority of the countries that are discussed in case study 3.1, the legislative branch is composed of two houses: an upper house and a lower house. This is called a bi-cameral system. However, unicameral legislatures do exist as well, such as Andorra, Angola, China, Finland, Israel, Nebraska in the U.S.A. and South Korea. In fact, almost 50 per cent of the world's nations have a unicameral system, while the existence of such a system in local governments is even more frequent.

In a bicameral system, the relation between both houses is usually regulated in the constitution. Mostly, the upper house, or senate, represents the federated areas, regions, or provinces where the lower house, or the House of Representatives, represents the people. Examples are Brazil, Germany, India, the Russian Federation, the U.S.A. and the Republic of South Africa.

3.2.5 About the executive branch

Usually, the executive branch is the government. This branch is mostly led by a president or a prime minister. Although exact names may differ, in some countries both positions exist, such as China, Germany, India and the Russian Federation. In other countries, the position of a prime minister is deleted, merged with that of the president, or simply never existed. Examples are Brazil, the U.S.A. and the Republic of South Africa.

It is always interesting to consider the relation between the executive branch and the legislature. The executive branch has to act in compliance with the laws of the legislature, but usually has a certain margin of discretion in how to execute these laws. Usually, there are some 'rules of the game' to which the executive should commit. These are mostly open norms in the form of 'principles of good governance' the executive should comply with. They vary per legal system, although principles as legitimacy, accountability and fairness (Graham et al, 2003) are commonly used. When the legislature is of the opinion that the executive branch is overreaching its competencies, and pushes the boundaries of their margin of discretion too far, they may interfere. This is sometimes easily done by not approving the budget laws that are necessary to fund the operations of the executive branch. On the other hand, in quite a few systems, the executive branch and/or the head of state may have a veto power over the adoption of law. This might cause serious stalemates when the legislature and executive are dominated by different political majorities, as you can see in the newspaper item.

Principles of good governance

CNN POLITICS, 14 JULY 2015

Now that he has a deal with Iran, Obama must face Congress

BY: KEVIN LIPTAK

With a historic deal meant to curb Iran's nuclear ambitions in place, President Barack Obama has ticked off another legacy-making item on his checklist – as long as Congress doesn't get in his way. Early Tuesday, Obama launched a sales pitch to lawmakers who remain deeply sceptical of the nuclear deal. But while Congress retains the ability to nullify Obama's accord with Tehran, the high bar for action on Capitol Hill – including building veto-proof majorities in just over two months – will make it difficult for opponents to block the President.

(...)

The Republican controlled House has the votes to pass a resolution, but in the Senate Republicans would need to attract support from a half a dozen Democrats.

Because President Obama has already pledged to veto any bill to block the deal GOP leaders would need to convince enough Democrats to join with them to override his veto – a heavy lift.

3.2.6 About the judiciary

In most countries, the judiciary is organized in several layers. Usually, there are district courts at the lowest level: courts of first instance that rule on most civil and criminal law cases. Then, there is usually a middle layer of intermediate courts, or appellate courts that serve as a court of appeal against decisions of the district courts. Lastly, there is usually some kind of a Supreme Court that functions as a court of last instance. There may be some political influence in appointing the highest judges in a country, which is then usually regulated by constitution. Furthermore, most countries have next to their courts of general jurisdiction specialized courts for particular issues, such as labour courts, administrative law courts, military courts and/or tax courts.

Especially in federations, the concept of a Constitutional Court is known. This court primarily deals with disputes between the federation and/or federated areas. The primary competence of such a court is to review legislation against the constitution. In some countries, such as the People's Republic of China, Germany, the Russian Federation and the Republic of South Africa, a separate Constitutional Court is installed. In some other countries, the supreme court functions both as a court of last instance, and as a Constitutional Court. Examples are Brazil, India and the U.S.A.

Summary

- Constitutional law regulates and restricts the attribution of power within a state.
  This is done by three types of rules:
  - Rules that define the state.
  - Rules that attribute power to state institutions.
  - Rules that recognize fundamental rights of citizens.

- The way power is exercised relates to what concept of freedom is supported in a society.
  - Negative freedom means that one is free to do whatever he wants, without any interference.
  - Positive freedom means that as a result of interference one has the opportunity to better provide direction to his life.

- In most states, power within a state is distributed according to the trias politica model that was introduced by Charles de Montesquieu:
  - Trias politica is the organization of a state by separating legislative, executive and judicial powers.

- States are organized in a state structure: The state structure is the way power is distributed amongst the entities of a state. These are the two common state forms: the federation and the unitary state.
  - A federation is a state that unites federated areas that are self-governing within the boundaries set by the federation.
  - A unitary state is a centrally organized state in which al power is vested in national political institutions.

- States are ruled according to a government system: a government system is the way in which power is distributed amongst the political institutions of a state. Two systems are most frequently used: a monarchy and a republic.
  - A monarchy is a state in which the highest power is vested in and distributed from one person or a group of persons.
  - A republic is a state in which the highest power is attributed to political bodies that rule within the boundaries of a constitution and is headed by a president.
  - A monarchy and a republic may have incorporated principles of democracy.
  - Democracy is a form of government in which the highest power is vested in the people that are governed.

- The legislature may be composed of one or two chambers. This is called a unicameral and a bicameral system.

- The executive branch is the government of a country.

- The judiciary is mostly composed of several layers, including:
  - District courts: courts of first instance.
  - Appellate courts: intermediate courts.
  - A supreme court: a court of last instance.

- Next to these courts of general jurisdiction, most countries have specialized courts for particular disputes.

- Some federations have a separate Constitutional Court that is competent to review law against the constitution.

Practice questions

Open questions

Please read the following sample of the Japanese Constitution (and please note that Diet is a term which is not related to food).

'We, the Japanese people, acting through our duly elected representatives in the National Diet, determined that we shall secure for ourselves and our posterity the fruits of peaceful cooperation with all nations and the blessings of liberty throughout this land, and resolved that never again shall we be visited with the horrors of war through the action of government, do proclaim that sovereign power resides with the people and do firmly establish this Constitution. Government is a sacred trust of the people, the authority for which is derived from the people, the powers of which are exercised by the representatives of the people, and the benefits of which are enjoyed by the people. This is a universal principle of mankind upon which this Constitution is founded. We reject and revoke all constitutions, laws, ordinances, and rescripts in conflict herewith.
Article 1. The Emperor shall be the symbol of the State and of the unity of the People, deriving his position from the will of the people with whom resides sovereign power.
Article 41. The Diet shall be the highest organ of state power, and shall be the sole law-making organ of the State.
Article 42. The Diet shall consist of two Houses, namely the House of Representatives and the House of Councillors.'

3.1 How would you classify the state form of Japan? Please, explain.

3.2 How would you classify the government form of Japan? Please, explain.

3.3 Would you consider Japan a democratic country, based on these constitutional articles?

3.4 Please, explain the concept of trias politica.

Essay question

In some republics, the president is head of the executive power (for instance in the U.S.A.) In some, the president stands above the powers in trias politica (for instance in the Russian Federation). Write an essay in which you critically reflect on the pros and cons of these two approaches, and conclude with your own opinion on the matter.

Multiple choice questions

3.1 Considering open question 1, we have to conclude that Japan has a:
a unicameral parliament
b bicameral parliament
c no parliament at all

3.2 The primary function of a Constitutional Court is:
a to review lower legislation against higher legislation
b to review legislation against the constitution
c to review the constitution against international law

3.3 Please, consider the following Article of the Argentinian Constitution:

'Section 19. – The private actions of men which in no way offend public order or morality, nor injure a third party, are only reserved to God and are exempted from the authority of judges. No inhabitant of the Nation shall be obliged to perform what the law does not demand nor deprived of what it does not prohibit.'

In essence, this is a:
a rule that defines the state
b rule that attributes power to state institutions
c rule that recognizes fundamental rights of citizens

3.4 The Russian participant of the Eurovision Song contest (2015) was completely stressed out. Very high results were expected, and she was wondering whether or not she could meet those expectations, especially because she had to perform in a dress she did not really like. However, the programmer of the Eurovision Song contest obliged her to wear this dress, stating that 'it is for the best, now she only enlarges het chances to be victorious.'

This is a clear example of:
a positive freedom
b negative freedom
c conative freedom

RACIST!!
Sandor

4 International cooperation: the United Nations

Around the world, various international organizations were founded to encourage economic cooperation between countries. On a global level, this is mostly done in the context of the United Nations as a result of the Bretton Woods Conference in 1944. In this chapter, we will explore the institutions of the United Nations.

4.1 The United Nations and Bretton Woods

Cooperation between countries on a global level is usually based on multilateral treaties. Based on such treaties, global institutions can be installed. For instance, the Charter of the United Nations is the multilateral treaty signed and ratified by almost all states in the world. This charter is the legal basis for the foundation of the United Nations:

> 'Accordingly, our respective governments, through representatives assembled in the city of San Francisco, who have exhibited their full powers found to be in good and due form, have agreed to the present Charter of the United Nations and do hereby establish an international organization to be known as the United Nations.' (UN Charter, 1945)

The league of nations

Worldwide, the United Nations is the primary organization in which global cooperation takes place in numerous areas. The organization was established in the aftermath of the Second World War. It's predecessor, the league of nations, was a dramatic failure, as you may see in example 4.1. Learning from that experience, the focus was different. Where the League of Nations merely focussed on establishing international agreements on peace and security, the founders of the UN realized that this was not enough.

Interdependency on trade and the progressive realisation of human rights were now profoundly on the agenda, and were believed to be the key to worldwide peace.

EXAMPLE 4.1

The failure of the League of Nations

A call to arms

When the First World War was over, the League of nations was installed in 1920. Its main purpose was to maintain global peace and security, and restore the friendly relations between the former enemies. Unfortunately, the League did not last very long. Its rather narrow approach to focus on peace and security that should be enforced by binding laws did not seem to work (Fenwick, 1936). It appeared that a struggling economy was more powerful than international binding laws. In both Europe and Asia, a bad economy led to tensions between countries, and in the end, The Second World War erupted.

Europe

In Europe, Germany had lost the First World War, and was forced to live up to the Treaty of Versailles (1919). The treaty forced Germany to cede significant territories of land, give up its colonies, and pay damage compensation to several countries that had suffered from German aggression. Whether or not such measures were justified, it caused a situation in which Germany could barely recover from the war. A growing anger amongst the German people emerged, resulting in a distaste for all that was foreign. These sentiments led to the success of the National Socialist Labour Party (Nationalsozialistische Deutsche Arbeiterpartei, NSDAP), led by Adolf Hitler. Hitler took power in 1933, and slowly directed his country into yet another war.

Asia

Also on the other side of the world, poor economic prospects seemed to be a call to arms. Japan used to strive for progressive policies in international trade. However, when in the '20ies and '30ies the world economy stagnated, this attitude changed profoundly. Japan found itself in trouble when especially the U.S.A. and Western European countries protected their domestic markets by adopting barriers to trade. After all, Japan itself did not possess adequate sources for basic materials, and therefore greatly depended on foreign trade to access such resources. The combination of an ever growing population and an impending shortage of essential basic materials proved to be an unfortunate one. Japan felt the need to solve their problems in expanding their territory, and invaded the territories of several countries and colonies (Sagan, 1988). This slowly escalated in a full scaled war in Asia.

Due to the past experiences that led to the Second World War, barriers to trade were considered to be counterproductive and an eventual cause for aggression. Instead, the global economy should have been founded on open borders and free trade. Driven by this realization, a conference was organized in 1944 in Bretton Woods, U.S.A.: the United Nations Monetary and Financial Conference. Representatives of the allied countries gathered to agree on how the world's economy should be organized. As a result of this conference, two important organizations were founded with the aim to encourage a global economy that is based on free trade: the International Monetary Fund, the World Bank. Later, a treaty to lower trade barriers was added: the General Agreement on Tariffs and Trade (GATT). This treaty would later evolve into the World Trade Organisation. While these three bodies are institutions within the UN system, they have mandates that allow them to operate rather autonomously.

In figure 4.1 you see a schematic overview of these so-called Bretton Woods institutions.

FIGURE 4.1 The Bretton Woods institutions

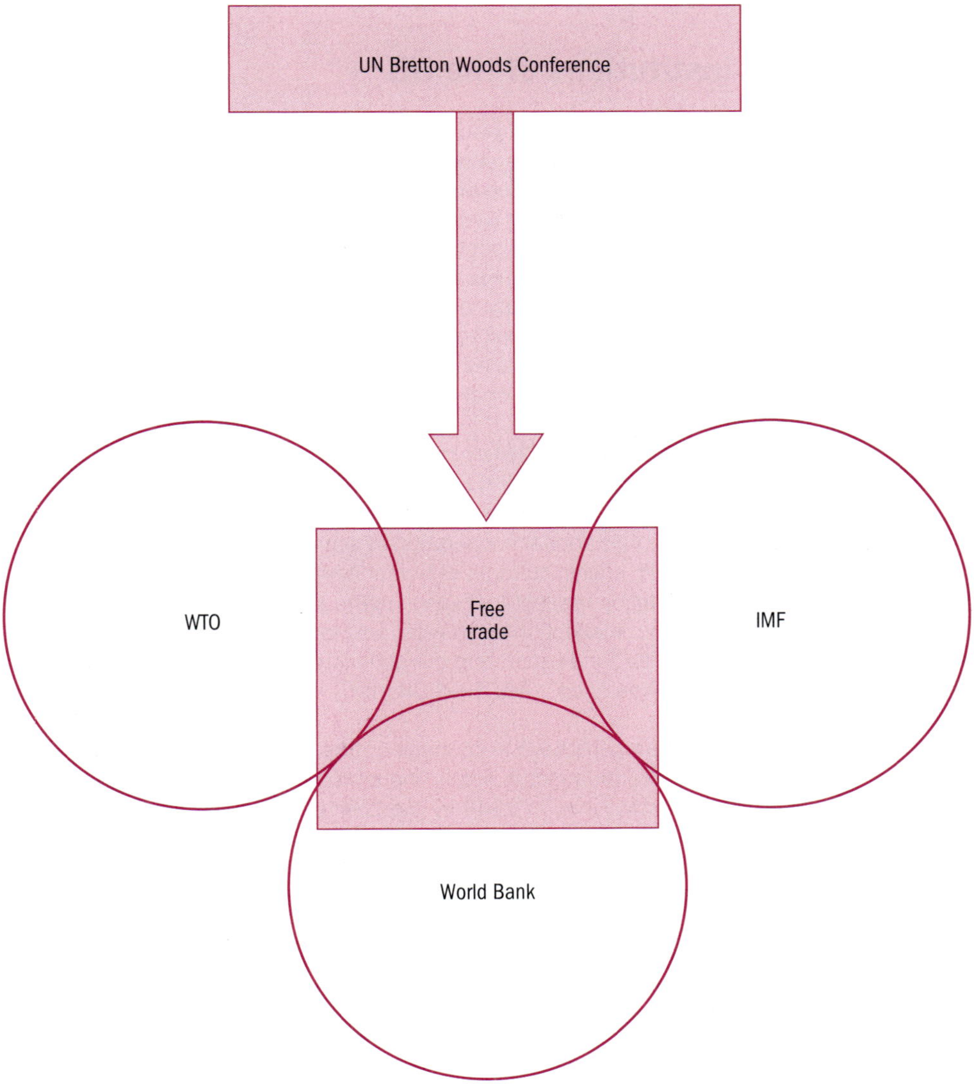

At the end of the Bretton Woods-conference, the American delegate Henry Morgenthau emphasized the relation between peace and free trade:
'To seek the achievement of our aims separately through the planless, senseless rivalry that divided us in the past, or through the outright economic aggression which turned neighbors into enemies would be to invite ruin again upon us all. Worse, it would be once more to start our steps irretraceably down the steep, disastrous road to war. That sort of extreme nationalism belongs to an era that is dead.
Today the only enlightened form of national self-interest lies in international accord. At Bretton Woods we have taken practical steps toward putting this lesson into practice in monetary and economic fields.
I take it as an axiom that this war is ended; no people-therefore no government of the people-will again tolerate prolonged or wide-spread unemployment. A revival of international trade is indispensable if full employment is to be achieved in a peaceful world and with standards of living which will permit the realization of man's reasonable hopes.'
(Morgenthau, 1944)

4.2 The institutions of the UN

The United Nations is a complex organization with numerous bodies that operate in all kinds of areas. After all, the ambitious job description of the United Nations could not have been more broad.
'The Purposes of the United Nations are:

1. To maintain international peace and security, and to that end: to take effective collective measures for the prevention and removal of threats to the peace, and for the suppression of acts of aggression or other breaches of the peace, and to bring about by peaceful means, and in conformity with the principles of justice and international law, adjustment or settlement of international disputes or situations which might lead to a breach of the peace;
2. To develop friendly relations among nations based on respect for the principle of equal rights and self-determination of peoples, and to take other appropriate measures to strengthen universal peace;
3. To achieve international cooperation in solving international problems of an economic, social, cultural, or humanitarian character, and in promoting and encouraging respect for human rights and for fundamental freedoms for all without distinction as to race, sex, language, or religion; and
4. To be a center for harmonizing the actions of nations in the attainment of these common ends.' (Art. 1 UN Charter)

What all these organs have in common is that they are entrusted to organize matters on a global scale. The primary bodies of the United Nations are established in 1944 by the Charter of the UN (Article 7):

- The General Assembly, in which all Member States are represented.
- Three councils, with more specified competencies in which not all Member States are represented permanently: the Security Council, the Economic and Social Council, the Trusteeship Council.
- Two bodies composed of neutral individuals, not representing states: the International Court of Justice, and the UN Secretariat (Malenczuk, 1997a).

Furthermore, these primary bodies have installed numerous subsidiary organs to facilitate them in their duties, and joined partnerships with other international organizations that were installed by treaties. As a result, a complex web of UN related institutions forms the engine of global interaction, discussion, political exchange and law making.

Please note that the Trusteeship Council has suspended its activities since 1994, and therefore, this institution will not be discussed any further in this section. The Trusteeship Council was originally installed to oversee the governance of decolonized territories until such territories were self-governing (Chapters XI and XII UN Charter).

4.2.1 The General Assembly

The General Assembly functions as the main political body of the United Nations. It is the only body in which all Member States of the UN are represented. In decision-making processes, each Member (that is, as long as they pay their contributions) has one vote. However, it has become a common practice to adopt decisions by consensus, and therefore without voting. Normally, the General Assembly convenes once a year, from September till December or January. Next to that, special sessions or emergency sessions may be called when needed. There are six committees that prepare the General Assembly sessions and write draft resolutions. In fact, a large part of the political debate and negotiations preceding the adoption of a resolution happens within these committees.

The General Assembly has legally binding powers and legally non-binding powers.

Legally binding powers

The legally binding powers of the General Assembly are:

- to approve the budgets of the UN and the contribution each member state has to pay;
- to appoint members of the other primary UN organs. More specifically they appoint: the non-permanent members of the Security Council (Art.23 UN Charter), the members of the Economic and Social Council (Art. 61 UN Charter), and the Secretary-General (upon the recommendation of the Security Council, Art. 97 UN Charter).

Legally non-binding powers

All other competencies do not involve the adoption of legally binding decisions, but rather involve the consideration and recommendation on the various matters that fall within the scope of the UN Charter. This then results in the voting on resolutions of a non-binding nature on all kinds of topics in the sphere of peace and security, social and economic development and human rights.

On the one hand, the power of the General Assembly should not be overestimated. In fact, this is pretty much a political body rather than a legislative institution. Its competencies to adopt legally binding decisions are therefore quite limited. Therefore, the great majority of all work done by the General Assembly results in recommendations. However, since such recommendations are not legally binding, there are no real consequences when a member state chooses to disregard them. Especially when the Assembly – or one of its subsidiary institutions – recommends member states to adopt measures to live up to their obligations under international law, such recommendations are more than once ignored.

For instance, until 2015, the U.S.A. has uphold economic sanctions against Cuba for decades – a remnant of the cold war. These sanctions were upheld despite the frequent request of the General Assembly to end such sanctions, as you can see in the newspaper item. Only when the Obama administration decided that it was time to restore the connections with Cuba in early 2015, these sanctions were lightened (Tannebaum & Stokes, 2014).

4

REUTERS, 28 OCTOBER 2014

For 23rd time, U.N. nations urge end to U.S. embargo on Cuba.

BY: MIRJAM DONATH & LOUIS CHARBONNEAU

The U.N. General Assembly on Tuesday voted overwhelmingly for the 23rd time to condemn the decades-long U.S. economic embargo against Cuba, with many nations praising the island state for its response in fighting the deadly Ebola virus that is ravaging West Africa.

In the 193-nation assembly, 188 countries voted for the nonbinding resolution, titled "Necessity of Ending the Economic, Commercial and Financial Embargo imposed by the United States of America against Cuba."

As in previous years, the only countries that voted against the declaration were the United States and an ally, Israel. The Pacific island nations Palau, Marshall Islands and Micronesia abstained. The voting result was identical to last year's. (...)

On the other hand, the competencies of the General Assembly should also not be underestimated. It is the only political organ in the world in which almost all states of the world are represented based on equal representation (one vote per country). A resolution adopted by the General Assembly surely has some political weight, but may also have a legal effect. Although there is some scientific debate about the matter, a General Assembly Resolution that is widely recognized amongst the Member States (for instance due to the fact that it was adopted by unanimous voting) may be evidence of customary law (Öberg, 2005; Kerwin, 1983). For instance, the International Court of Justice ruled in their Nuclear Weapon opinion that previous General Assembly Resolutions, in which Member States explicitly agreed that the threat and use of nuclear weapons would be in violation of international law, could be evidence of customary law:

> 'The Court notes that General Assembly resolutions, even if they are not binding, may sometimes have normative value. They can, in certain circumstances, provide evidence important for establishing the existence of a rule or the emergence of an opinio juris.' (ICJ, 1996)

Furthermore, while a resolution of the General Assembly may not be legally binding, it is often the starting point of legal development. For instance, most international human rights treaties are first adopted as a resolution by the General Assembly, and later signed and ratified by states. In 1948, the Universal Declaration on Human Rights was adopted by the Assembly (GA

Resolution 217 A(III), 1948), and was merely a solemn declaration. Currently, the international human right arsenal is expanded to many multilateral treaties, that all started as resolutions adopted by the General Assembly (Wernaart, 2013).
Lastly, it needs to be noted here that landmark international agreements such as the Millennium goals (GA Resolution 55/2, 2000) and the decisions taken as a result of the 2005 Wold Summit (GA Resolution 60/1, 2005) are concluded in the context of the General Assembly. Such documents, although not as hard as a legally binding treaty, cause quite a stir in the international political arena, and most certainly contribute to the realization of the included goals. In other words: while not legally binding, it sets development in motion.

4.2.2 The Economic and Social Council

Under the supervision of the General Assembly (Art. 60 UN Charter), the Economic and Social Council is 'the principal body for coordination, policy review, policy dialogue and recommendations on economic, social and environmental issues, as well as for implementation of the internationally agreed development goals' (UN, 2015). This means that the Economic and Social Council initiates studies, makes recommendations, prepares draft resolutions and conventions for submission to the General Assembly, and call international conferences (Art. 60 UN Charter).
The Council plays an important role in the coordination of the various special agencies that are installed by or work in cooperation with the United Nations (64 UN Charter). Furthermore, in the context of the Council, non-UN entities may participate in the various sessions, such as business representatives, NGO's, and academics. There is even a youth forum in which the viewpoints of young people can be expressed.

Composition of the Council

The Council is composed of representatives of 54 Member States, elected by the General Assembly. The states that participate in the council are elected for three years, and are allotted based on a geographical subdivision. This means that African states have fourteen, Asian states eleven, Eastern European states six, Latin American and Caribbean states ten, and Western European and other Western countries are allocated thirteen seats. Just like the General Assembly, the Economic and Social Council installed several subsidiary commissions and committees that prepare the sessions of the Council.

4.2.3 The Security Council

Legally binding powers

Perhaps the most famous UN body is the Security Council. This Council is authorized to adopt legally binding resolutions in the field of peace and security (Art. 25 UN Charter). In chapters VI and VII of the UN Charter the most important competencies of the Security Council are enshrined. In Chapter VI, the peaceful settlement of international disputes is organized, where in Chapter VII, the Council is authorized to take action in case of a threat to peace, a breach of peace, or acts of aggression. Such actions are always non-violent first, such as economic sanctions (Art. 41 UN Charter). When non-violent action proves to be inadequate, the Council may decide take more further-reaching measures, and bring in the troops:

> 'Should the Security Council consider that measures provided for in Article 41 would be inadequate or have proved to be inadequate, it may take such action by air, sea, or land forces as may be necessary to maintain or restore international

peace and security. Such action may include demonstrations, blockade, and other operations by air, sea, or land forces of members of the United Nations.' (Art 42 UN Charter)

UN operations

When it is decided to take action under Article 42 of the UN Charter, the Council usually requests the aid of several Member States to contribute to a military operation (Art. 43 UN Charter). In the past, UN armies have in some shape of form intervened in various conflicting areas. Most of the times, such mandates were in the sphere of contributing to peacekeeping. Occasionally however, UN authorized forces intervened more profoundly, to the extent of using arms to enforce peace or even defeat another army. Findlay (2002) distinguishes the following types of UN operations whose mandated is based on Article 42 UN Charter:

- Traditional peacekeeping involves armed forces that mainly observe and verify whether conflicting parties comply with military agreements. Such mandates usually have a limited role, but may last for a while until the point of a permanent peace force. Examples are the UNMOGIP (since 1949), to observe the peace agreements between India and Pakistan, and UNTSO (since 1948) in the Middle East, to monitor the compliance with various peace agreements.
- Expanded peacekeeping reach beyond the observatory role, and include the supervision of an entire peace process or the transition of a governmental system. Examples are the UN mission to Cambodia (UNTAC , 1992-1993), Mozambique (ONUMOZ, 1992-1994) and Mali (MINUSMA, since 2013).
- Peace enforcement involve a more active role, in the sense that they use their armed forces to enforce peace. The main goal is enforcing peace, not defeating parties that are involved in the conflict. An example is the mission in Sierra Leone (UNAMSIL, 1998-1999).
- Enforcement is the most radical type of operations, that aim to defeat a party that is involved in a conflict and acts against the will of the international community. An example is the UN authorized forces hat liberated Kuwait in 1991 from the Iraqi occupation.

An overview of the current UN operations is available at www.un.org.

Composition of the Council

The Security Council consists of fifteen Member States, including five permanent members (Art. 23, amended in 1966, UN Charter). The latter are the main victories of the Second World War: China, France, Russia, the UK, and the U.S.A. The non-permanent members are elected for a period of two years by the General Assembly, and are allotted based on a geographical subdivision. This means that amongst the non-permanent members, three seats are allocated to African, two seats to countries from Asia and the Pacific, one seat to Easter European countries, two seats to Latin American and Caribbean countries, and two seats to Western European and other Western countries. States who are not represented in the Council may participate in the sessions of the Council when its interest is affected by the topic involved. However, such participation is always without a vote. For instance – as you can see in the news item – the Dutch minister of foreign affairs addressed the security council in a session in which a resolution was adopted concerning the plane crash of MH17 (S.Res. 2166, 2014), since the lives of many Dutch citizens were lost as a result of the downing of the plane. At that time, the Netherlands was not a member of the Security Council.

ELITE DAILY, JUL 22, 2014

Dutch Foreign Minister Gives Emotional And Powerful UN Address About The MH17 Crash

BY: ALEXIA LAFATA

On Monday, Dutch Foreign Minister Frans Timmermans gave an emotional address to the UN Security Council about a UN resolution that would give his country access to the crash site of the MH17 - something that Russia has been hesitant to allow.

Timmermans' speech opened up with a disheartening thought:

'I've been thinking how horrible it must have been - the final moments of their lives when they knew the plane was going down. Did they lock lands with their loved ones? Did they hold their children close to their hearts? Did they look each other in the eyes, one final time, in a wordless goodbye? We will never know.

The loss of almost 200 Dutch citizens "has left a hole in the hearts of the Dutch nation," causing much anger, grief and despair.

(...)

To my dying day, I will not understand that it took so much time for the rescue workers to be allowed to do their difficult jobs and that human remains should be used in a political game. It is despicable.

Thankfully, the UN resolution to grant the Netherlands access to the site was passed.'

Voting mechanism

The voting mechanism of the Security Council is infamous: each Member has one vote, though the permanent members have a veto on non procedural matters. This practically means that any legally binding decision in the field of peace and security cannot be adopted without the consent of the fiver permanent members.

4.2.4 The Secretariat

The UN Secretariat is the main administrative organ of the UN, and is headed by the Secretary-General. The Secretariat employs about 8700 employees located in UN quarters around the world. They are responsible for the day-to-day functioning of the UN, supporting and administering the programmes and policies that are laid down by the other UN bodies. The Secretary General is the main representative of the United Nations, and in this capacity plays an important ceremonial, but also political role.

In principle, the Secretariat is politically neutral, and is bound to the political agenda set by especially the General Assembly and the Security Council. For sure, employees of the Secretariat are not allowed to act according to the instructions of any government or other authority (Art. 100 UN Charter). However, Article 99 UN Charter leaves some margin of discretion for the Secretary General, for he is authorized to 'may bring to the attention of the Security Council any matter which in his opinion may threaten the maintenance of international peace and security'. This Article suggests that he does not have a mere executive function, but is supposed to also take his own political initiative when appropriate (Kennedy, 2007; Franck, 1996). In practice, this is noticeable when a Secretary-General uses his function to condemn violence, call conflicting parties to stand down, or offers his services as a mediator in a conflict. An example of the latter is the offered mediation between India and Pakistan in their territorial conflict on the Kashmir region, as you may see in the newspaper item.

THE HINDUSTAN TIMES, 8 FEBRUARY 2014

UN ready to mediate on Kashmir issue: Ban Ki-moon

The UN is available to mediate between India and Pakistan if the two neighbours request such assistance in resolving the Kashmir issue, a spokesperson for UN Secretary General Ban Ki-moon has said. 'On Kashmir, (as with other conflicts around the world), our good offices are available if both sides (India and Pakistan) were to request that. And that remains the case today,' Acting Deputy Spokesperson for the Secretary-General Farhan Haq said. Haq was responding to a question on whether the UN chief would propose to India to sit down and talk with Pakistan to resolve the longstanding Kashmir issue. Among the most vital roles played by the Secretary General is the use of his 'good offices,' which are steps taken publicly and in private, drawing upon his independence, impartiality and integrity, to prevent international disputes from arising, escalating or spreading.
'Good offices' are employed to help bring warring parties toward peace or to prevent political and armed conflicts from escalating.

Voting mechanism

The secretary-General is appointed by the General Assembly upon recommendation of the Security General (Art. 97 UN Charter). This means that both organs should agree. The veto-procedure within the Security Council also applies to recommending on the Secretary-General.

4.2.5 The International Court of Justice

Jurisdiction of the Court

The International Court of Justice (ICJ) is seated in the Hague in the Netherlands. The Court, also referred to as the World Court, has jurisdiction to:
- settle disputes based on international law submitted by states (Chapter II, Statute of the ICJ), and
- give advisory opinions on international law on the request of UN organs or related agencies Chapter IV, Statute of the ICJ.

However, it appears that in practice the jurisdiction to rule in legal disputes is rather restricted. In the first place because only states can be a party in such a legal dispute (Art. 34 Statue of the ICJ). This excludes amongst others individuals, businesses, ethnic groups and NGOs. This is perhaps a somewhat outdated approach, since increasingly, non-state entities are also involved with international law (Malenczuk, 1997b).
In the second place, the jurisdiction of the Court to settle disputes is based on the consent of states. This means that the Court can only rule in a dispute if the conflicting states all agree on the jurisdiction of the Court (Alexandrov, 2006). This consent can be expressed in various ways:

- States may give their consent per case separately, and thus decide per situation whether or not they accept the jurisdiction of the Court.
- States may give their unconditional consent on the jurisdiction of the Court on a permanent basis by submitting a declaration to the Secretary General of the UN.
- States may give their consent on the jurisdiction of the Court on a permanent basis, with the condition of reciprocity: any future conflicting parties should also accept the jurisdiction of the Court.
- States may be indirectly bound by the jurisdiction of the Court because they are a state party of a treaty that recognizes the ICJ as the competent court to rule in matters of dispute related to that treaty. Examples of such treaties are the Convention on the Prevention and Punishment of the Crime of Genocide (1948), the international Convention on the Elimination of All Forms of racial Discrimination (1966), and the Convention on the Law of Treaties (1969).

A majority of the UN Member States seem to be hesitant in submitting a declaration of recognizing the jurisdiction of the court on a permanent basis. In 2015, only 72 states had filed such a declaration, while some of the most powerful countries in the world, such as the U.S.A., China, Russia and France did not. For instance, as you can see in example 4.2, the U.S.A. was able to successfully obstruct course proceedings in a case against them.

EXAMPLE 4.2

Nicaragua v. United States

In 1986, Nicaragua filed a case against the United States of America before the International Court of Justice. According to Nicaragua, the U.S.A. had acted in violation of international law by supporting a rebel-group against the left-winged Sandinista National Liberation Front. This support consisted of financial support and military training. This eventually led to the eruption of a civil war in Nicaragua that lasted until 1989.
While the International Court of Justice ruled in favour of Nicaragua (ICJ, 1986), the U.S.A. refused to participate in the proceedings. Also, the compensation that was awarded to Nicaragua was never executed, because the U.S.A. used its veto power in the Security Council against measures to effectuate the verdict.

Composition of the Court

The International Court of Justice consists of fifteen permanent judges who are elected by the General Assembly and the Security Council. The judges must all have different nationalities, and must represent the main forms of civilization and legal systems around the world. In practice, this means that usually five judges are from Western countries, three from African countries, two from Eastern European countries, three from Asian countries, and two from Latin American/Caribbean countries.
In addition, when the nationality of a disputing parties is not apparent amongst the permanent judges, a judge from this nationality has the right to sit in that case and will be added as an *ad hoc* judge. The idea is that judges from the nationality of conflicting parties may have insight in the

legal particularities and systems that are involved that may otherwise be overlooked (Malenczuk, 1997b).

The International Court of Justice should not be confused with the various international tribunals that are installed by the Security Council to rule in matters of war crimes in particular regions, such as the tribunals for Rwanda, the former Yugoslavia, Lebanon and Sierra-Leone.
Nor should the International Court of Justice be confused with the International Criminal Court, that is also seated in The Hague, the Netherlands. In this court, war criminals in general can be tried under the Rome Statue: a treaty that is not directly related to the United Nations (Rome Statute, 1988).

4.2.6. Subsidiary bodies and partnerships

The General Assembly, the Economic and Social Council and the Security Council may install subsidiary organs (Art. 22, 29 and 68 UN Charter) to support them in their duties. Such institutions are supervised by the founding UN body. Furthermore, the UN may enter into partnerships with specialized agencies installed by a treaty (Art. 57 Charter). Such institutions do not necessarily respond to the UN primary institutions, and have their own mandate which is mostly enshrined in international treaties.

Subsidiary bodies

> Subsidiary bodies are institutions installed and supervised by the General Assembly, the Economic and Social Council or the Security Council in support of their mandates under Articles 22, 29 or 68 UN Charter.

- An examples of subsidiary bodies installed by the General Assembly is for instance the Human Rights Council.
- Examples of subsidiary bodies that are jointly supervised by the Assembly and the Economic and Social Council are the United Nations Development Programme (UNDP), the United Nations Conference on Trade and Development UNCTAD, and the United Nations Children's Fund (UNICEF).
- Examples of subsidiary bodies that are installed by the Security Council are the International Tribunals that settle disputes related to troubled regions, such as the International Criminal Tribunal for Rwanda and the former Yugoslavia (ICTR and ICTY), the Special Tribunal for Lebanon (STL), and the Special Court for Sierra Leone (SCSL). Naturally, also the UN missions are installed by the Security Council.

Specialized agencies

> Specialized agencies are autonomous institutions in partnership with the UN under Article 57 UN Charter.

Examples of such agencies are the World bank Group, the International Monetary Fund (IMF), the Food and Agriculture Organization (FAO), the World Intellectual Property Organization (WIPO) and the International Labour Organization (ILO). It needs to be noted here that the World Trade Organization is technically not a specialized UN agency, but has very strong ties with the organization via a special agreement (WT/GC/W/10, 1995).

The establishment of subsidiary bodies and specialized agencies has resulted in a rather large, and to be honest cumbersome web of actors that are involved in gathering data, doing research and advise on all kinds of worldwide matters (Wernaart, 2010). This occasionally results in situations in which UN or UN related institutions may have opposing interests and views. For instance, when the recognition of human rights is involved, it is no secret that the subsidiary bodies that operate in the human rights sphere are composed of individuals that strongly support far-reaching obligations for states. This is in contrast to the view of other actors within the UN context that operate in the field of economics: the policies of the IMF and the World Bank are criticized by some as counterproductive to the realization of equality and other human rights. A former rapporteur on the Right to Food (a post installed by the Human Rights Council) called this phenomenon the 'schizophrenia of the UN' (Ziegler et al. 2010). It is therefore hardly possible to speak of the UN as if it is one coherent organization with one clear objective, as you might see in example 4.3.

EXAMPLE 4.3

Black Pete could be racist, according to the UN. But who is the UN?

Each year on December 5th, the Dutch celebrate an old tradition known as Sinterklaas. There are some similarities with the worldwide known Santa Claus: a man who is hundreds of years old gives presents to children. There are also differences: where Santa Claus arrives on a sleigh with reindeers, and is aided by numerous elves, Sinterklaas arrives on a big steamboat and is aided by numerous clumsy 'Black Petes'. Some consider Black Pete as an innocent character in a tradition for children, where others consider it as a stereotyped and painful reminder of black slaves. The first group points out that 'Black Pete' is part of the Dutch tradition, and should not be tempered with. The latter considers the character as sheer discrimination. The two camps have engaged in fierce debates, demonstrations and even occasional fighting in the Netherlands for some years now.
Also abroad, the phenomenon of 'Black Pete' did not go unnoticed. In a joint declaration, several UN Rapporteurs in the field of minorities and racial discrimination concluded that: 'the character and image of black Pete perpetuate a stereotyped image of African people and people of African descent as second-class citizens, fostering and underlying sense of inferiority within the Dutch society and stirring racial differences as well as racism' Stephard et al. 2013. A viewpoint that was later reaffirmed by the UN Committee on the Elimination of Racial Discrimination: 'Considering that even a deeply-rooted cultural tradition does not justify discriminatory practices and stereotypes, the Committee recommends that the state party actively promote the elimination of those features of the character of Black Pete which reflect negative stereotypes and are experienced by many people of African descent as a vestige of slavery'. (CERD, 2015)

Media around the world reported on the fact that the 'UN' considered Black Pete a racist tradition. However, the question could be addressed who the UN is in this context. It seems that the average newspaper has no idea about the internal structure of the United Nations. In fact, there have been Special Rapporteurs, who advise the Human Rights Council on an individual basis, and a specialized agency that was installed by a treaty (the CERD) who condemn the tradition of 'Black Pete'. None of these organs have any legally binding powers, and do most certainly not represent a unanimous view of all countries in the world. It seems to be a bit dramatic therefore to identify these rapporteurs and the CERD with the entire UN. On the other hand, the political significance should not be underestimated, for it seems that the criticism on 'Black Pete' in general leads to a slow development within the Netherlands in which the stereotyping gradually disappears (Sas, 2015).

4

Figure 4.2 shows a schematic overview of the institutions of the United Nations.

FIGURE 4.2 The institutions of the United Nations

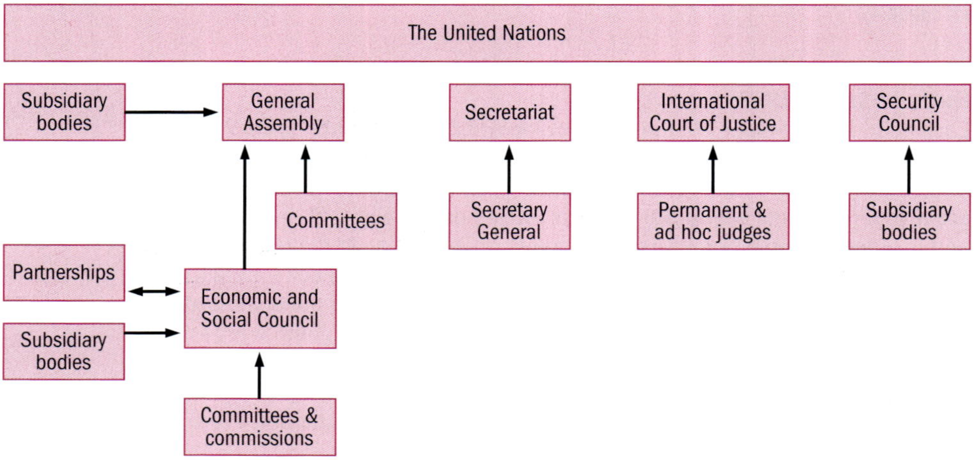

Summary

- The United Nations is the primary organization for global cooperation.
  - The UN is the successor of the League of Nations.
  - The UN was founded in 1945.
  - The core document of the UN is the UN Charter, adopted in 1945.
  - Within the framework of the UN, the Bretton Woods Conference was held in 1944.

- As a result of the Bretton Woods Conference, three main international institutions for economic cooperation were founded:
  - the International Monetary Fund (IMF);
  - the World Bank (WB);
  - the WTO (World Trade Organization), previously the GATT (General Agreement on Tariffs and Trade).

- The main philosophy of the Bretton Woods Conference was that lowering trade barriers was a key to lasting peace.

- The United Nations has a broad mandate, which includes:
  - maintaining international peace and security;
  - developing friendly relations amongst nations;
  - achieving international cooperation in solving international problems of an economic, social, cultural or humanitarian nature, and in promoting human rights;
  - being a centre for harmonizing the actions of nations in the attainment of these common ends.

- The primary bodies of the UN are:
  - the General Assembly;
  - the Security Council;
  - the Economic and Social Council;
  - (the Trusteeship Council, which is currently inactive);
  - the International Court of Justice;
  - the Secretariat.

- The General Assembly is the main political body of the UN in which all Member States are represented.
  - The General Assembly has the legally binding powers to:
    - approve the budgets of the UN and the contribution each member state has to pay;
    - appoint members of the other primary UN organs.
  - The General Assembly has the legally non-binding powers to consider and recommend on the various matters that fall within the scope of the UN Charter.

- ► The Economic and Social Council is the principal body for coordination, policy review, policy dialogue and recommendations on economic, social and environmental issues, as well as for implementation of the internationally agreed development goals.
  - The Council consists of representatives of 56 member states, elected by the General Assembly.

- ► The Security Council adopts legally binding decisions in the field of peace and security.

- ► The Security Council consists of fifteen Member States, including the five permanent members, who have a veto on non-procedural matters. The non-permanent members are elected by the General Assembly.
  - In case of a threat to international peace and security, the Council adopts non-violent measures first, such as economic sanctions.
  - The Council may adopt the decision to start a UN operation, that involves military action in different shapes of form:
    - traditional peacekeeping: observatory and verification missions;
    - expanded peacekeeping: supervision of a peace process or transition of government structure;
    - peace enforcement: enforcement of peace by military intervention;
    - enforcement: enforcement by defeating a party that is involved in a conflict and acts against the will of the international community.

- ► The Secretariat is the main administrative organ of the UN.

- ► The Secretariat is led by the Secretary-General, the main representative of the United Nations.

- ► The International Court of Justice has the jurisdiction to:
  - settle disputes based on international law submitted by states;
  - give advisory opinions on international law on the request of UN organs or related agencies.

- ► This jurisdiction is restricted in two ways:
  - only state parties may be a party in a legal conflict settled by this court;
  - the Court may only rule in a conflict between state parties who accepted the jurisdiction of the court by expressing their consent.

- ► The General Assembly, the Economic and Social Council and the Security Council may install subsidiary organs to support them in their duties.

- ► The UN may set up a partnership with a specialized autonomous agency in support of its duties.

Practice questions

Open questions

Please, read the following part of a UN resolution:

16. Decides that the mandate of MINUSMA shall be the following:

(a) Stabilization of key population centres and support for the reestablishment of state authority throughout the country

(i) In support of the transitional authorities of Mali, to stabilize the key population centres, especially in the north of Mali and, in this context, to deter threats and take active steps to prevent the return of armed elements to those areas;

(ii) To support the transitional authorities of Mali to extend and re-establish state administration throughout the country;

(iii) To support national and international efforts towards rebuilding the Malian security sector, especially the police and gendarmerie through technical assistance, capacity-building, co-location and mentoring programmes, as well as the rule of law and justice sectors, within its capacities and in close coordination with other bilateral partners, donors and international organizations engaged in these fields, including the EU;

(iv) To assist the transitional authorities of Mali, through training and other support, in mine action and weapons and ammunition management;

(v) To assist the transitional authorities of Mali in developing and implementing programmes for the disarmament, demobilization and reintegration (DDR) of former combatants and the dismantling of militias and self-defence groups, consistent with the objectives of reconciliation and taking into account the specific needs of demobilized children;

4.1 Considering the nature and content of this resolution: which UN organ adopted this resolution, and is it legally binding?

4.2 Could you refer to the relevant Article of the UN Charter that supports this view (see www.un.org for the entire charter)?

4.3 In 2016, the people in Great Britain voted to leave the European Union in a so-called 'Brexit'. Besides what one politically believes about this, which lesson in history regarding the League of Nations did the 'Brexitters' not consider?

4.4 Please explain the primary role of the UN Secretary General.

Essay question

The jurisdiction of the International Court of Justice is only recognized by 72 countries. Do you think this court has any chance of success in the future, and would you recommend that? Please write an essay in which you discuss your opinion on the matter.

Multiple choice questions

4.1 See the resolution that is quoted in open question 1. What kind of a mission is described here?

a traditional peacekeeping
b expanded peacekeeping
c peace enforcement

4.2 The UN General Assembly has:

a legally binding powers to approve the UN budget
b legally binding powers in resolutions about economic cooperation
c no legally binding powers at all

4.3 The ECOSOC Council is composed of:

a 15 UN member states
b 54 UN member states
c All UN member states

4.4 Which country has not Veto power in the UN Security Council?

a U.S.A.
b France
c Germany

IMF
IT'S ALL DRIED OUT!!
Sandor

5 International Cooperation: The Bretton Woods Institutions

In this chapter, we will further explore the economic institutions that were founded as a result of the Bretton Woods conference: the International Monetary Fund, the World Bank Group, and the World Trade Organization. Since these institutions are not unchallenged, we will also discuss an alternative global attempt to encourage international economic cooperation; the Asian Infrastructure Investment Bank.

5.1 The International Monetary Fund

The IMF was founded in 1944 at the Bretton Woods Conference. Although it is a specialized agency of the United Nations, the organization acts autonomously.

International Monetary Fund

> The International Monetary Fund is a UN specialized agency that promotes financial stability and monetary cooperation on the global level.

During the Bretton Woods Conference, the need was felt to install a global organization that would oversee the international currency system. This was mainly due to avoiding drastic global currency crises, such as during the Great Depression in the 30ies. During this depression, a true currency war erupted, in which states competed with the value of their currencies, a phenomenon that is called competitive devaluation.

Competitive devaluation

> Competitive devaluation is the competition between states in exchange rates in order to stimulate export and discourage import.

As you can see in example 5.1, state policies that tried to establish competitive devaluation were considered a cause for worsening the results of the economic crisis in the 30ies, leading to the Great Depression. Also recently, during the crises since 2008, currency wars seem to damage the global economy, as you may see in the news item 'World gripped by 'international currency war'.

EXAMPLE 5.1

Currency wars and economic crises
When a global economic crises broke out in the 30ies, the monetary policies of states were believed to profoundly worsen the economic problems. During this period, states gradually let go of the gold standard. This means that currencies were not expressed in gold value anymore and a system of floating currencies was created. To stimulate their domestic economies, countries tried to lower the exchange rates of their currencies. The intended result was that import would become more expensive, while export would be cheaper. This then should result in a growing demand for domestic products from both national and foreign markets. However, given the fact that many countries tried to implement such policies, and competed against one another with ever-lowering exchange rates, a race to the bottom followed. The result was that the global monetary system collapsed, with dramatic consequences for the world economy (Eichengreen & Sachs, 1986).

THE GUARDIAN, 28 SEPTEMBER 2010

World gripped by 'international currency war'

BY: TIM WEBB
The world is in the midst of an 'international currency war' according to Brazil's finance minister as governments force down the value of their currencies to boost their struggling economies.
The comments are the first public admission made by a senior policymaker about a practice which has become increasingly widespread since the global economic downturn.
Many countries, notably China, have been deliberately weakening their currencies by selling them on foreign exchanges or keeping interest rates artificially low to make their exports cheaper.
Economists fear that such moves are resulting in increasing currency volatility and instability. Increasing competition among individual countries to devalue also makes it harder to mount a co-ordinated policy response to the economic downturn, particularly amid fears of a renewed slowdown.
The issue is likely to be high on the agenda at the upcoming G20 meeting in November in South Korea. China has resisted pressure from the U.S. to allow the value of its currency, the yuan, to rise.
Many countries in Asia, including the host, are reluctant to raise the issue for fear of antagonising China, a major trading partner.

5.1.1 The mandate of the IMF

In order to stabilize the global monetary system, the IMF is mandated to oversee the global monetary system. Therefore, the IMF employs the following activities: surveillance and technical assistance, lending money, and supervising the system of Special Drawing Rights (SDRs).

Surveillance

In Article IV of the IMF Articles of Agreement, the Fund is mandated to oversee the international monetary system, and monitor whether the member states act in compliance with the obligations for member states. To this end, economists of the IMF annually undertake country visits: the so-called 'bilateral surveillance'. During such a visit, the country's financial status and policies are discussed with the most important domestic actors, such as the head of state, the head of the central bank, parliamentarians, and the main actors in the business sector. On his return, the IMF representative will present a report to the Executive Board, and communicate his findings and through a press release. You may find an example of bilateral surveillance in example 5.2.

Bilateral surveillance

5

EXAMPLE 5.2

Visiting Kazakhstan: from economic slowdown to fundamental reforms

As part of the IMF surveillance program the director of the IMF's Middle East and Central Asia Department – Masood Ahmed – undertook a journey to Kazakhstan on 2-4 September 2015. During his stay, he had several debates about the financial status quo of Kazakhstan, and their financial policies that were employed to stabilize and further improve the Kazakhstan economy. Amongst others, he met the Kazakhstan Prime Minister, and the National Bank Governor.
At that time, the domestic economy of Kazakhstan was greatly affected by external factors, such as a low oil price, a slowdown in the economies of their direct neighbours – Russia and China – and long term effects of global financial crises. However, mr. Ahmed welcomed the way that Kazakhstan authorities responded to such matters. For instance, one of the measures adopted by the Kazakhstan Central Bank was to float the domestic currency: the tenge. An expected consequence of such a policy is that exchange rates are more flexible, and therefore the pressure on the national reserves is – to a certain extent – reduced.
To support such policies, mr. Ahmed advised to speed up efforts to build confidence in the Kazakhstan economy. Amongst others, he recommended to strengthen the supervision on banks, improve the communication regarding domestic financial policies to manage expectations in the financial sector, and reform the governmental financial institutions to a more open marked oriented economy (IMF, 2015).

Furthermore, the IMF undertakes studies to monitor the regional and global economies: the so called 'multilateral surveillance'. This does not only include annual publications such as the World Economic Outlook, the Global Financial Stability Report and the Fiscal Monitor: multilateral surveillance

Multilateral surveillance

may also include the contribution of the IMF in a so-called 'mutual assessment process', in which Member States are engaged in a debate on joint policy action to tackle global financial problems. Moreover, this process was created by the G20 countries: the twenty largest economies in the world.

In conclusion, as part of their surveillance mandate, the IMF supports the sharing of accurate data on economic and financial issues. This is done by standardizing the form in which economic and financial data is communicated to make it easily accessible and understandable for countries and other actors. For this reason, the IMF created the General Data Dissemination System (GDDS) and the Special Data Dissemination System (SDDS). The first sets standards for countries to develop statistical systems in the first place, ensuring that all data is comprehensive and reliable. The latter sets standards for communicating data in the financial sector, as you can see in example 5.3.

EXAMPLE 5.3

The Special Data Dissemination System into more detail

The system is based on formal and substantive dimensions. The formal dimensions are about the way data is obtained and communicated, while the substantive dimensions are about the content of this data (IMF, 2013).

Formal dimensions

There are four formal dimensions:

- Data should be complete, frequent and accurate (in time). In practice, some data must be updated in standard frequencies, which may be annually, monthly or even weekly, depending on how fast such data changes.
- Data should be accessible by the public, so that all actors in the financial sector may benefit from the gathered information.
- The data should be trustworthy, and therefore collected with integrity.
- The data should be of a high quality, based on sound methods and reliable sources.

Substantive dimensions

The content of the data that is collected and communicated can also be categorized in four groups.

- Data regarding the real sector, which includes statistics about the Gross Domestic Product, the labour market and price indexes – that is, the extent to which consumer or wholesale prices change over time.
- Data regarding the fiscal sector, which includes statistics about basically government spending and dept.
- Data regarding the financial sector, which includes data bout depository institutions (that is the Central bank, commercial banks, credit unions and savings institutions), interest rates, and stock exchange rates.
- Data regarding the external sector, which includes data regarding the balance of payments (transactions with other countries) and international reserves (funds that can be passed between central banks, such as Special Drawing Rights or foreign currencies).

Technical assistance

The IMF provides for technical assistance in the field of its expertise: macro/economic financial issues. This is mostly done through the IMF Institute for Development Training Program. Around the globe, the IMF installed several training centres through, in which training and education on financial affairs is generated. Through these centres, but also directly, IMF staff advises governments and Central Banks on their economic and financial policies (IMF 2015c).

Lending money

In its essence, the IMF is a fund. This means that IMF member states pay a quota to the IMF as contribution for their membership. The quotas are based on the relative seize of the economy of the countries through a formula. For instance, in 2015, the U.S.A. had the largest quota of $58 billion, where Tuvalu had the smallest quota of $2,47 million (IMF, 2015a). This fund may be used to finance loans when a country requests one. This is mainly the case when a member state faces difficulties in financing their foreign debts. In exchange for the loan, the borrowing state has to agree to a 'letter of intent', in which the country clarifies the economic and financial policies it will undertake to resolve the payment problems. In practice, this means that in exchange for a loan, the IMF has a certain influence on the domestic policies. If the government of a state is not willing to reform or change policies when necessary, the loan will simply not be granted. After all, the Executive Board of the IMF will have to agree on the loan. This approach is called 'IMF conditionality'(Jensen, 2004), and has a legal basis in Art. I, section V of the IMF Articles of Agreement.

> IMF conditionality is the principle that IMF financial support is granted under the condition that the involved member state adopts certain economic and financial policies.

IMF conditionality

The principle of conditionality is not uncontested. Where the IMF claims that a loan will be ineffective without structural reforms, the effects of such 'enforced' policies are hard to measure (Dreher, 2009). Next to that, the sentiment in the borrowing countries is that an external entity interferes with their sovereignty. For instance, the economic and financial reforms that were a condition for further loans to Greece in 2015 were heavily debated amongst the Greek and in Greek politics. As you can see in the news item, Greece was hesitant in accepting the conditions for more loans set by both the IMF and the European monetary union.

CNN/MONEY, 30 JUNE 2015

Greek defaults on $1,7 billion IMF payment

BY: MARK THOMPSON AND ELINDA LABROPOULOU

In a dramatic but widely expected step, Greece formally defaulted on a $1,7 billion payment to the International Monetary Fund early Wednesday in Athens.

Greece became the first developed country to default to the IMF, an organization of 188 nations that tries to keep the world economy stable.

Greece will now be cut off from access to IMF resources until the payment is made.

The move came hours after the country made a desperate attempt Tuesday to halt its plunge into economic chaos by requesting a new European bailout.
Greece asked for a two-year bailout from Europe, its third in six years. The bankrupt country is reported to be asking for 29 billion euros ($32 billion).
(...)
Greece is fast running out of money. It rejected the conditions Europe and the IMF set for releasing the remaining billions from its existing bailout at the weekend. That bailout expired Tuesday.
'The last chance to get a solid extension of the old program has gone by,' Dijsselbloem said. 'We are now in a difficult situation.'
Greece is now on its own financially, and can't pay all its bills.

There are various types of loans a country may opt for. Traditionally, an IMF loan is non-concessional, meaning that such a loan is subject to interest. Such interest is mostly based on the interest rates of the Special Drawing Rights. However, since 2010, also concessional loans are granted, with a very low interest rate to the extent of 0 per cent. Such loans are granted to countries with high poverty rates (IMF, 2015b).

Special Drawing Rights (SDRs)
To understand what Special Drawing Rights are, one needs to know a little more about IMF's recent developments. After all, the role of the IMF has changed significantly when the global financial system was changed, especially in the 70ies.

In essence, Special Drawing Rights is a unit that reflects the value of a large money basket in which the four most accepted international currencies are 'injected' the U.S. dollar, the pound sterling, the euro and the yen. These currencies are perceived to be the 'hardest' and most stable currencies in the world. Special Drawing Rights are allocated to IMF Member States, in quantities that reflect the relative size of their economies. The purpose of SDRs are to establish a 'neutral' global unit that can be used amongst central banks to complement their national reserves in a globally accepted unit.

The history of SDRs
In the sixties, the global financial system was heavily depending on the U.S. dollar, and to a lesser extent the UK pound. The main reason for that was that especially the dollar was directly linked to gold. This means that one could hypothetically exchange a dollar for gold. This is also called the 'gold standard'. As a result, the dollar was perceived as a strong and reliable currency, due to the fact that it would ensure possible transformation to gold. Consequentially, the dollar was widely accepted as a currency for foreign payments. Since other domestic currencies in the world were not linked to gold, they were not preferred currencies in international trade. National banks then would convert part of their local currencies to dollars to facilitate foreign payments in international trade. The 'monopoly position' for using the dollar for foreign payments had the side effect that the global economy was largely depending on the domestic policies of the U.S. government. After all, they took the decisions that would affect the dollar for it is their national currency. Another effect was that this global usage of the dollar amongst Central Banks caused too much pressure on the dollar.

Gold standard

To tackle this problem, the IMF introduced the Special Drawing Rights. In fact, these rights are nothing more than entries in book keepings that resemble hypothetical claims to a money basket that consists of a mixture of four stable currencies: the U.S. dollar, the pound sterling, the euro and the yen. All members of the IMF were allocated a certain amount of SDRs, depending on their relative size of their economies. These book entries – Special Drawing Rights – could now be used as a payment method between Central Banks to pay foreign debts, or receive payment from other countries. The idea is the same however: where the dollar was hypothetically exchangeable for gold, and therefore a strong currency, a Special Drawing Rights is hypothetically exchangeable for a share of the money basket, consisting of a mixture of four strong currencies. The big difference is that the Special Drawing Rights were now supervised by the IMF and involved four currencies, instead of a U.S. governed single currency. Figure 5.1 shows a visualization of the dollar when using the gold standard, and the Special Drawing Rights.

FIGURE 5.1 The dollar and Special Drawing Rights

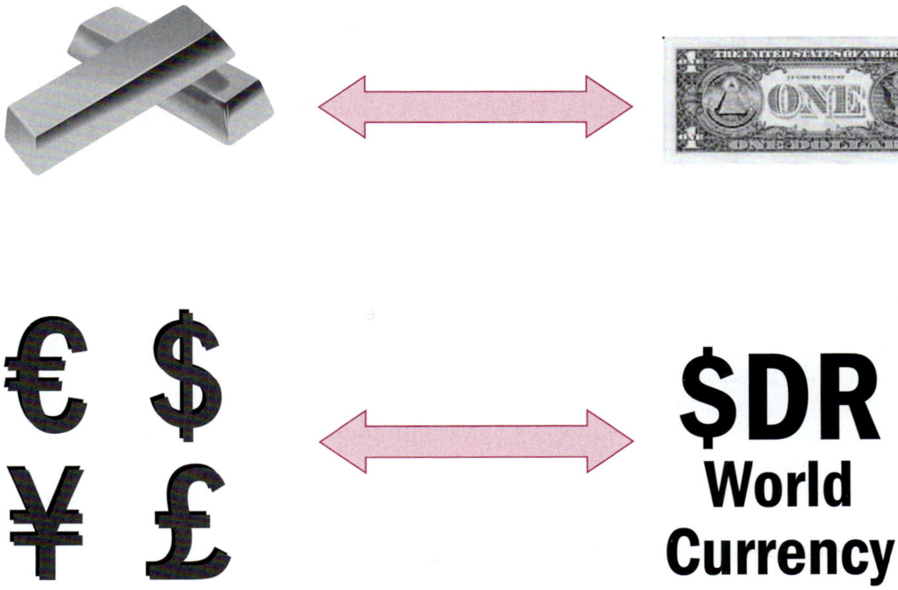

The modern use of SDRs

However, shortly after the introduction of the system of SDRs, the global monetary system changed. The U.S. government decided to let go of the gold standard, and transferred to a floating system. This means that the dollar was no longer linked to gold, and therefore no longer represented as a fixed value. Instead, the value of the dollar, as all other currencies in the world, was now floating. This means that the value of all currencies were now determined by a system of supply and demand. The effect of this floating system was that the SDRs would now be less relevant. After all, the principle of supply and demand would now automatically take away the pressure on currencies. When, say, there was a high demand for dollars, the

Floating system

price of that dollar would simply increase to the point that the demand would be less (Mudd, 1978).
For a long time, it was more convenient for countries to use this floating system in their advantage and build their own foreign reserves. Such foreign reserves would then consist of strong foreign currencies that could be used to pay foreign debts and therefore settle so-called balance of payment deficits. The usage of Special Drawing Rights was out of fashion, so to say. However, the global financial crises that erupted since 2008 have caused a renewed attention for the SDRs. The IMF allocated new SDRs worth 182,6 billion U.S. dollars to its member states, in order to supplement the countries reserves that could be used for immediate payments (Bird, 2010). Amongst others, Greece used these SDRs to settle international debts when they were dramatically running out of liquid assets for the short term in the summer of 2015. More details about the Greek SDR drawings can be found in the Financial Times article.
Since then, the future and potential of SDRs are debated in the international financial arena. After all, SDRs were for a long time seen as a relic from a financial system that was replaced, but its more recent use certainly seems to open new possibilities (Obstfeld, 2011; IMF, 2011).

THE FINANCIAL TIMES, 12 MAY 2015

Greece taps IMF reserves to pay €750m debt

BY: KERIN HOPE AND SHAWN DONNAN

Greece took the unusual step of raiding its holdings of the International Monetary Fund's de facto currency to make a €750m payment to the fund on Tuesday, in another sign of the country's increasingly desperate cash crunch.
The €750m payment to the IMF on Tuesday was the biggest Athens has made to the fund so far this year. But it is just the first in a series of major payments to the IMF and the European Central Bank due in the coming months that have raised the spectre of a Greek default and exit from the eurozone.
Athens drew €650m from its holdings of the IMF's Special Drawing Rights to make the loan payment and also give it room to disburse nearly €1bn on Wednesday to pay public sector salaries.

5.1.2 The organization of the IMF

In principle, the IMF is governed by the Board of Governors. However, this board has delegated most of its executive powers to the Executive Board. Next to that, the Fund is managed under the supervision of a Managing Director. The voting systems within the Board of Governors and the Executive Board are led by the financial contribution of member states to the IMF. This contribution depends on the relative sizes of the economies of the member states. This voting system is called 'weighted voting' (Gianaris, 1990).

Weighted voting is a voting system in which a vote of a member state has unequal weight, and instead is weighted in accordance with their financial contribution to the international institution.

Weighted voting

This results in the fact that the IMF is for the major part led by the richest – mostly Western – countries in the world. There is an ongoing debate about the fairness of this system, and the role developing countries may play (IMF, 2010; Mahbubani, 2008).

The IMF Board of Governors

The Board of Governors is the highest political body in the IMF (Art. XII, section 2 IMF Articles of Agreement). This Board is a non-permanent body, and is normally convened once a year. Each Member State is represented by a Governor in this Board, which is usually the minister of finance, or the head of the central national bank. The voting power of each governor however is not equal, but instead depending on the relative seize of the economy of the state he represents. This means practically, that the world's largest economies have most power within the IMF. For instance, since the 2008 Amendment on Voice and Participation, the U.S.A. has a voting power of 16,74 per cent, while Bhutan has a voting power of 0,03 per cent in the Board. An overview of the voting power per Member State can be found at www.imf.org.

As stated above, the Board has delegated most of its executive powers to the Executive Board, but retains the exclusive mandate to approve of quota increases, allocate Special Drawing Rights, admit or withdraw member states, and amend the IMF Articles of Agreement (IMF 2015d).
The Board of Governors installed two advisory committees: the International and Financial Monetary Committee, and the Development Committee. The latter is a joint body of the IMF and the World Bank. In the context of both committees, a great deal of political debate and consensus building takes place.

The IMF Executive Board

The Executive Board is a permanent body that has the daily executive power if the IMF (Art. XII, section 3 IMF Articles of Agreement). While the board only consists of 24 Governors, all IMF Member States are represented through a complex system of constituencies. Also here, power depends on the relative seize of the economy. This means that the largest economies of the world, such as Chine, France, Germany, Japan, the Russian Federation, Saudi Arabia, the UK and the U.S.A. have a seat of their own. Other states are represented jointly by one seat. It must be noted here that also the voting power may differ per seat. For instance, Azerbaijan, Kazakhstan Kyrgyz Republic, Poland, Serbia, Switzerland, Tajikistan and Turkmenistan are represented by one Board Member, having a voting power of 70,447 votes out of a total of 2,520,571 votes. An overview of the voting power per constituency can be found at www.imf.org.

The IMF Managing Director

The IMF personnel and staff are managed by a managing director. Next to that, this managing director is also the 'face' of the IMF, representing the organization as such. The director is appointed by the Executive Board. The former head of the IMF, Dominique Strauss-Kahn, attracted a great deal of media attention in 2011 just before he resigned, as you can read in the newspaper item. He was replaced by Christine Legarde.

THE NEW YORK TIMES, 14 MAY 2011

I.M.F. Chief, Apprehended at Airport, Is Accused of Sexual Attack

BY AL BAKER AND STEVEN ERLANGER

The managing director of the International Monetary Fund, Dominique Strauss-Kahn, was taken off an Air France plane at Kennedy International Airport minutes before it was to depart for Paris on Saturday, in connection with the sexual attack of a maid at a Midtown Manhattan hotel, the authorities said.

Mr. Strauss-Kahn, 62, who was widely expected to become the Socialist candidate for the French presidency, was apprehended by detectives of the Port Authority of New York and New Jersey in the first-class section of the jetliner, and immediately turned over to detectives from the Midtown South Precinct, officials said.

The New York Police Department arrested Mr. Strauss-Kahn at 2:15 a.m. Sunday 'on charges of criminal sexual act, attempted rape, and an unlawful imprisonment in connection with a sexual assault on a 32-year-old chambermaid in the luxury suite of a Midtown Manhattan hotel yesterday' about 1 p.m., Deputy Commissioner Paul J. Browne, the department's chief spokesman, said.

Reached by telephone, Benjamin Brafman, a lawyer, said he would be representing Mr. Strauss-Kahn with William Taylor, a lawyer in Washington.

5.2 The World Bank

World Bank Group

The World Bank is not one institution, but two: the International Bank for Reconstruction and Development (IBRD) and the International Development Association (IDA). The term 'World Bank' should not be confused with the 'World Bank Group', of which the World Bank is a part. The World Bank Group consists of the already mentioned IBRD and IDA, and furthermore of the International Finance Cooperation (IFC), the International Centre for Settlement of Investment Disputes (ICSID), and the Multilateral Investment Guarantee Agency (MIGA). Figure 5.2 shows a schematic overview of the World Bank Group.

5.2.1 The mandate of the World Bank and the World Bank Group

Poverty reduction

In discussing its mandate, it is impossible to separate the World Bank from the other institutions in the World Bank Group. After all, their tasks complement one another in the pursuit of the same goals, which is twofold. First, the group aims to provide low interest loans (or zero interest loans) to developing countries. Second, the group provides support to these developing countries through policy advice, research and analysis, and technical assistance (www.worldbank.org, 2015). This is all done to achieve worldwide poverty reduction.

FIGURE 5.2 The World Bank and the World Bank Group

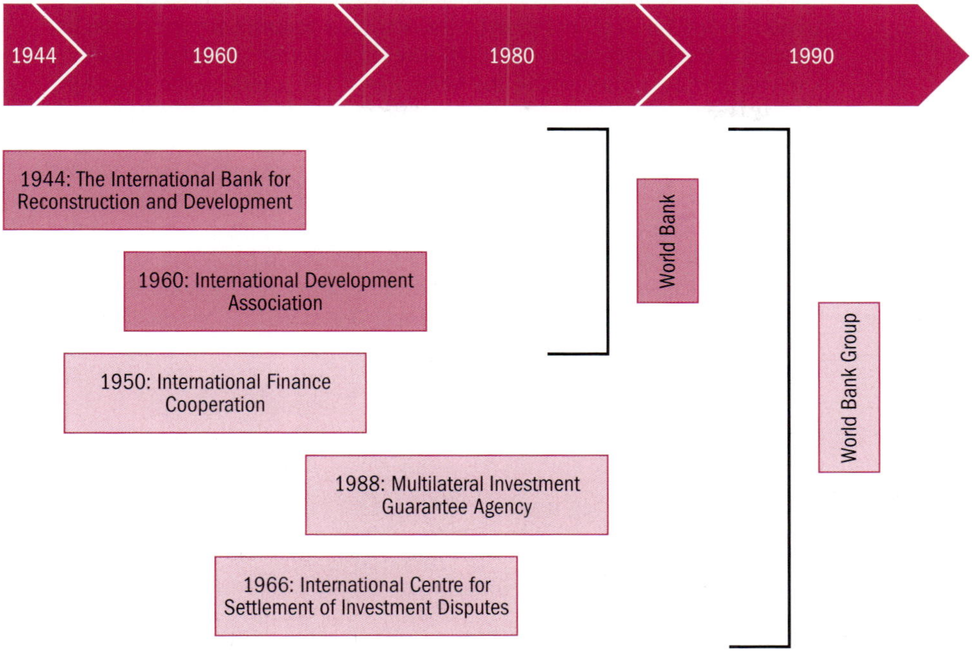

World Bank Group

The World Bank Group is a combination of five international institutions that are specialized UN agencies, with the aim to reduce poverty by lending money and providing for technical support to developing countries.

The mandates of the five institutions of the World Bank Group are defined as follows (The World Bank, 2011):
'**The International Bank for Reconstruction and Development (IBRD)** lends to governments of middle-income and creditworthy low-income countries.
The International Development Association (IDA) provides interest-free loans – called credits – and grants to governments of the poorest countries.
The International Finance Corporation (IFC) provides loans, equity, and technical assistance to stimulate private sector investment in developing countries.
The Multilateral Investment Guarantee Agency (MIGA) provides guarantees against losses caused by non-commercial risks to investors in developing countries.
The International Centre for Settlement of Investment Disputes (ICSID) provides international facilities for conciliation and arbitration of investment disputes.'

So, in essence, the IBRD lends money to governments who are credit worthy and could be classified as middle income countries. Its original purpose was to help restore the economies of European countries after the Second World War, and gradually expand to other places in the world. Its main goal is to support economic stability for the longer term.

The IDA lends money to low-income countries that are not necessarily credit worthy on favourable terms. Its main focus is to reduce poverty.
The IFC and MIGA do not direct their activities towards governments, but towards the private sector. The IFC invests in private undertakings in developing countries, where the MIGA tries to help reduce the risks for foreign investors in developing countries. In addition, the ICSID was installed to create a mediation board that can help when foreign investors are in conflict with a government of a developing country. Such a mediation board may help to facilitate smooth investments in developing countries.
Figure 5.3 shows a schematic overview of the different mandates of the World Bank Group institutions. Of course, the World Bank Group Institutions cooperate closely in their combined efforts to reach their shared goals. An example of a project in which World Bank Group institutions participate can be found in example 5.4.

FIGURE 5.3 The mandates of the World Bank Group

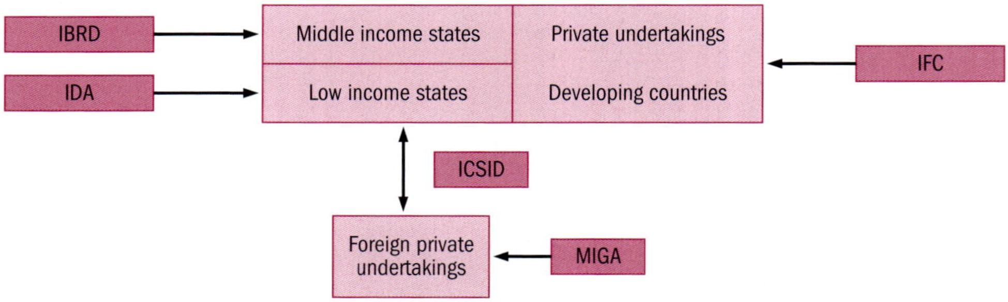

EXAMPLE 5.4

Improving urban services in Bogota

Bogota is the capital of the Latin American State Columbia. In the 60ies and 70ies, the city experienced a huge urbanization, resulting in the fact that its population grew rapidly with an annual population growth over 10 per cent. This has led to almost an uncontrolled expansion of the city, without proper city planning and transportation means. The practical result of this was that especially people who lived in dangerous self-built slums had a difficult access to the main parts of the city where they could find employment. This is one of the contributing factors to high employment rates (UN-Habitat 2003).

In the form of several loans and technical assistance of the IBRD to the city of Bogota and the Columbian government, the Bogota Urban Service Project was set up. This project originated from 2003, and was closed in 2014. The entire project cost 272,67 million U.S. dollar, of which approximately 100 million was borrowed from the IBRD. Amongst others, transport systems were financed that benefit 160 thousand women and 155 thousand men each day, since their travel time to their work is now reduced with 25 per cent. Next to that, the Project supports urban upgrading in the form of improvements in the usage of urban space. For instance, the project funded the building of parks, better infrastructure for pedestrians. As a result,

1,2 million inhabitants have benefitted from these improvements, including 1.995 households of which the living conditions were significantly improved by relocating their living safer areas with lower risks (World Bank Group, 2015).

Furthermore, an ambitious water and sanitation project was launched to create better, safer and more hygienic water supply and access to sewage connections (Browder, 2010).
Also in terms of governance, the project provided for technical assistance in reorganizing fiscal management and governance of the city. Amongst others, the illegally built slums were partly legalised, and its citizens were now not longer excluded from democratic decision-making processes in the city.
The IBRD does not operate alone, but rather engages in partnerships. For instance, the Bank has set up partnerships with local governmental institutions, such as the Bogota's Financial Secretariat, the local Urban Development Institute, the Popular Housing Unit and the Bogota Water and Sewage Company. In the broader context, the Bank cooperates with other governments through the Water Partnership Program through which the Netherlands, the UK, Denmark and Australia cooperate in funding projects and sharing their expertise in water management.

Parallel to the IBRD work, the International Finance Corporation (IFC) focuses on private investments in Bogota, with a focus on the transport sector (www.IFC.org, 2015). As of October 2013, the IFC has invested 2,9 billion U.S. dollar in the private sector of Colombia.

5

5.2.2 The organization of the World Bank and the World bank Group

The organization of the institutions of the World Bank Group shows many similarities. While technically, these institutions are UN specialized agencies, they act autonomously and have their own organizational structure.
In essence, the institutions are owned by the Member States, who are the shareholders. As a result, the voting power of the countries resembles the seize of their shares, and as a result may differ significantly. Also here, the phenomenon occurs that richer countries, who have larger shares in the Bank, have a strong power position. Historically, the U.S.A. has large shares in the World Bank, which results in the remarkable situation that the U.S.A. can block important decisions on their own. As a matter of fact, this results in a *de facto* veto power for the U.S.A. when a qualified majority is needed (World Bank, 2013).

Weighted voting

The governance system of the World Bank Group institutions is rather identical, and inspired by the original method of governing the IBRD. In essence, the IBRD Board of Governors and Board of Directors consist of the same individuals as the equivalent bodies of the IDA, IFC, MIGA and ICSID. The only difference is that the MIGA has a council of governors instead of a board (it's in the name), and the ICSID does not have an executive body. Perhaps the figure 5.4 will clarify these minor differences a bit more. Although in this section we will focus on the IBRD institutions, please note that they are for the major part identical to the other equivalents in the World Bank Group.

FIGURE 5.4 The organizational structure of the World Bank Group

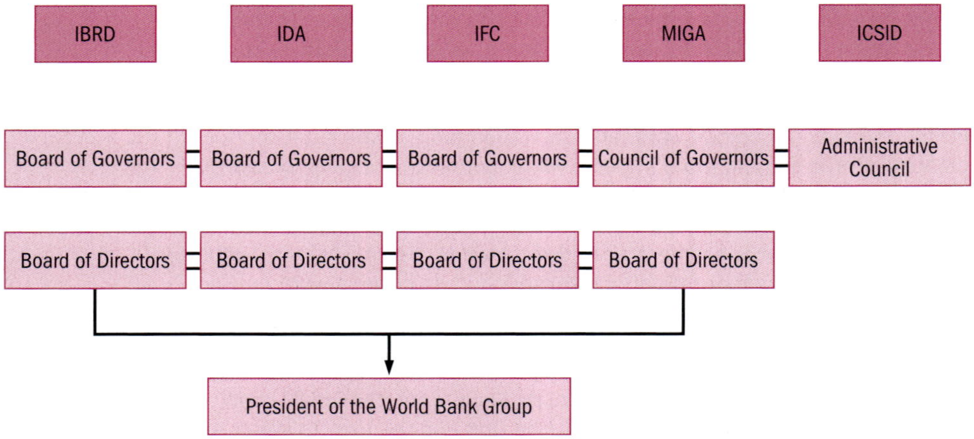

The Board of Governors

Board of Governors

As a shareholder of the IBRD, each Member State appoints a Governor. In practice, this is usually the minister of financial affairs or the head of the central national bank. This Governor represents the country in the board of governors, and has a weighted vote that resembles the share of the state he represents (Article V, Section 2, IBRD Articles of Agreement). The Board of Governors meet annually, that is twice a year. They gather in a combined session with the IMF Board of Governors. These are the so called annual and spring meetings. Since the board only meets twice a year, they have delegated most of its powers to the executive board. As a result, the Board of Governors is mostly occupied with:

- Admitting and suspending members;
- Increasing or decreasing the capital stock;
- Determining the distribution of the net income of the Bank;
- Deciding on appeals from interpretations of the Articles of Agreement by the Executive Directors;
- Making arrangements to cooperate with other international organizations;
- When needed, suspending permanently the operations of the Bank;
- Increasing the number of elected Executive Directors; and
- Approving on amendments to the Articles of Agreement (www.worldbank.org, 2015).

The Board of Directors

Board of Directors

All other executive duties are delegated to the Board of Directors. This board consists of 25 Executive Directors,. Just like the IMF Executive Board, all member states are represented, although mostly in constituencies consisting of more countries. Only the biggest shareholders of the IBRD have an executive director of their own, including China, France, the Japan, Saudi-Arabia, the UK and the U.S.A. Also the voting power within the board is weighted, and depends on the share of the Member State.

The World bank Group President

The managerial organization of the World Bank Group is attributed to a president, who is appointed by the Boards of Executive Directors.

Traditionally, the president is always a U.S.A. citizen. The president is appointed for a term of five years, and may be reappointed. The president is president of all five World Bank Group institutions.

5.3 The World Trade Organization

While there were plans to install a global organization for international trade during the Bretton Woods Conference in 1994, The World Trade Organization was founded only in 1994. Before that time, there was but a treaty with the purpose to regulate and reduce tariffs and other boundaries to trade in international business: the General Agreement on Tariffs and Trade (GATT). This was due to the fact that intended creation of an International Trade Organization (ITO) failed, mainly as a result of the fact that the U.S.A. did not adopt its charter in 1950. However, the GATT was already in force, and consequentially this treaty formed the basis of international trade rules, albeit without a formal institution to support its implementation. In the end, the GATT was for practical reasons considered as some sort of unofficial international organization, with staff and annual meetings, to still be able to support trade liberalization. In negotiation rounds, the GATT Member States gradually adopted other international trade agreements on various issues in order to further liberalize trade. It would take until 1994 before an official institution came into being to support all these agreements: the World Trade Organization (Matsushita et al, 2006a).

5.3.1 The mandate of the World Trade Organization

The World Trade Organization was founded by the Agreement Establishing the World Trade Organization, on 15 April 1994 in Marrakesh (WTO Agreement). Its functioning is greatly inspired by the works of the liberal economist David Riccardo, as you may see in example 5.5.

World Trade Organization

> The World Trade Organization is a global institution with as its main goal to liberalize trade.

FIGURE 5.5 The World Trade Organization

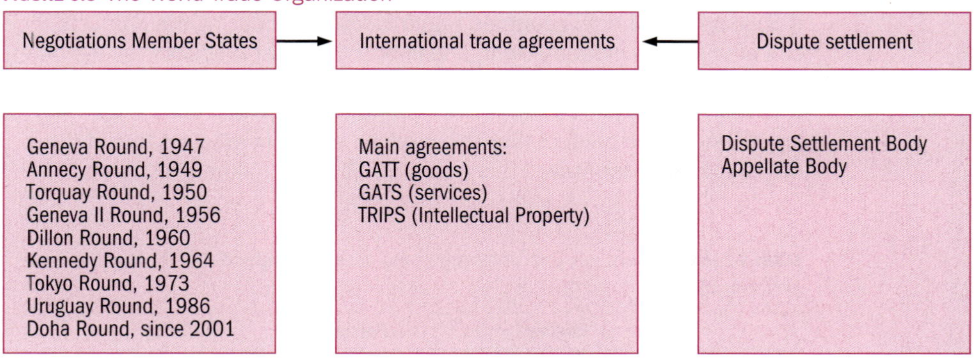

The WTO has three main roles in relation to international trade liberalization (WTO, 2011). First, it is a negotiation forum for its member states in which trade matters are discussed, and new agreements are closed. Second, based on these agreements, the WTO is a law-making body that sets standards for global trade liberalization. Third, the WTO serves as a dispute settlement body, in case Member States have a conflict in the interpretation of these WTO agreements. Figure 5.5 shows a schematic overview of the three main roles of the WTO.

5

EXAMPLE 5.5

David Ricardo and the case for free trade

In the works of David Ricardo, he makes a plea for free trade on a global level. According to him, all will be better of without domestic protection of trade and other trade barriers. He frequently uses a variation of the following example.

Imagine there are two countries that do business with each another when there is free trade between them. Let's say those countries are England and Portugal. Their main business concerns garment and wine. However, in England, people are able to produce garment a bit more efficiently compared to the production of wine. In Portugal, it happens to be the other way around: Portuguese businesses are more efficient in wine making, compared to the production of garment. All this can be deduced from table 1, in which you can find the labour hours both countries need to produce a unit of wine and a unit of garment. In the terminology of Ricardo, England has an absolute advantage over Portugal in producing garment, while Portugal has an absolute advantage over England in producing wine.

TABEL 1 Labour hours per unit of garment and wine for England and Portugal

	England	Portugal	Total
Unit of garment	90 hours	100 hours	190 hours
Unit of wine	100 hours	70 hours	170 hours
Total	190 hours	170 hours	350 hours

It appears that if both countries would focus on producing the products they can produce the most efficient, and import the other product from the other country, all will benefit. However, this would only be possible in a situation where there truly is free trade. Both countries could then double the production of the product they can produce the most efficient to suit the demand in both countries. This would result in the following numbers:

TABEL 2 Labour hours per unit of garment and wine for England and Portugal in case of free trade

	England	Portugal	Total
Unit of garment	180 hours	0 hours	180 hours
Unit of wine	0 hours	140 hours	140 hours
Total	180 hours	140 hours	320 hours

The result is that not only the labour hours per product, but also the labour hours for each country are reduced. In other words: everyone is better off this way.
However, the question arises what would happen if one of the two countries is better in producing both articles. Does this approach then still lead to a better situation for the country that spends most labour hours for all products? Assume such a situation would look like this:

TABEL 3 Labour hours per unit of garment and wine for England and Portugal, in which England is better in the production of both products

	England	**Portugal**	**Total**
Unit of garment	90 hours	110 hours	200 hours
Unit of wine	100 hours	105 hours	205 hours
Total	190 hours	215 hours	405 hours

Ricardo proposes to apply his theory also in this particular situation. When applied, you may deduce from table 4 that it still leads to a save in the costs for England when they import the wine from Portugal, even when England would be able to produce wine more efficiently. This can be explained by the fact that from the two products, England is able to produce garment the most efficient. In the terminology of Ricardo, this is the principle of comparative advantage. England is much better in making garment, compared to Portugal, and slightly better in making wine. It would therefore be wise to spend all their available labour hours on the production of garment, and still import the wine from Portugal. Even when in absolute terms, England is also better in producing wine.

TABEL 4 Labour hours per unit of garment and wine for England and Portugal in case of free trade

	England	**Portugal**	**Total**
Unit of garment	180 hours	0 hours	180 hours
Unit of wine	0 hours	210 hours	210 hours
Totaal	180 hours	210 hours	390 hours

The conclusion is that each country should specialize itself in producing that which they can produce the most efficient. On the longer term this will yield to better economical results for all, as long as there is free trade. The World Trade Organization embraces this theory, and tries to act accordingly.

Negotiation forum

During so called 'trade rounds', the Member States of the WTO negotiate over trade issues and agree on lowering trade barriers. In total, 9 rounds were convened, with mixed success. The first round was a GATT round, in Geneva, and the most recent one was the Doha round, which is not formally concluded yet and seems to go on forever. During these rounds, amongst others, the World Trade Organization was founded (Uruguay Round), and the most important trade agreements were adopted. As it seems, trade negotiations became more complex and difficult during the Doha Round. The Round, named after the place where it was launched, carries on for years now, without yielding any results. Several factors play an important role in the collapse of various attempts to close the round. The developing countries that have organized and coordinated their arguments well, are a new force to consider in the trade negotiations. They are at odds with the wealthier countries over market protection, especially in the agricultural sector. Whilst the WTO is an institution that aims at trade liberalization, it is difficult to reach an understanding on the lowering of trade barriers to agriculture, especially since developed countries seem to have a commercial in subsidizing their own agricultural sector. Developing countries find it hard to compete with subsidized products, and therefore want to protect their own markets from especially the EU and U.S.A. agricultural markets (Beierle, 2002). Since decision making in the WTO is not based on weighted voting – like it is in the World Bank Group and the IMF, developing countries are able to establish a serious power block in this context.

The repeating collapse of the trade negotiations of the Doha Round has led to a broad worldwide discussion on the functioning of the WTO. With good arguments, some defend its goal to liberalize trade (Panagariya, 2005), where some question this goal and propose alternatives (Serfati, 2015). One of those alternatives is to allow developing countries to adopt protective measures to safeguard domestic agricultural production in order to remain self-sufficient in food production, and secure food security amongst their citizens (Laroche-Dupraz & Postolle, 2011). On the other hand, some defend that when developed countries – especially the EU and the U.S.A. – would truly lower their own barriers to trade, it would allow developing countries to enter those markets, and expand their export in agricultural products. In line with the theory of David Ricardo, this would potentially lead to a better trade position of developing countries, more jobs, and a higher GDP (McCalla & Nash, 2007).

Law-making body

In the various negotiation rounds that took place over the years, the WTO Member States agreed on many treaties, including the core treaties of the WTO: the General Agreement on Tariffs and Trade (GATT) which aims to lower trade barriers on goods, the General Agreement on Trade in Services (GATS) which aims to lower trade barriers on services, and the Trade Related aspects of Intellectual Property Rights (TRIPS), which aims to lower trade barriers on intellectual property. These treaties form the basis of a large variety of specialized treaties that further specify trade rules in particular markets.

Although the core treaties cover different aspects of trade, they have certain principles in common, that form the foundation of trade liberalization within the WTO (WTO, 2011). These principles are:

- No discrimination to trade;
- Lowering trade barriers;
- Fair competition;
- Encouraging developing countries.

Non-discrimination

Countries are not allowed to discriminate in trade. This non-discrimination principle has two fundaments: the most-favoured nation principle, and the national treatment principle.

Most-favoured nation principle

> The most-favoured nation principle (MFN) means that foreign businesses should be treated equally.

In short, this means that countries in their rules and regulations on import and export have to apply the most favourite rules they offer to one country, to any country. The idea behind this principle is that equal treatment will lead to a situation in which countries will import from the country that is able to offer a product or service the most efficient, in line with the theory of David Ricardo. If countries would apply different trade rules to their trading partners, these differences would distort this process, as you can see in example 5.6: one of the longest disputes on international trade since the WTO came into being.

To this principle, some exceptions are allowed. For instance, countries may apply different standards when they are a member state of a free trade zone. In that case, the countries within the zone naturally do business with each other under more favourable conditions compared to other countries outside this zoned. Another exemption is that countries may support developing countries by offering them favourable trade terms. A last exception is that countries apply less favourable conditions or even raise barriers to trade against products or services that are traded unfairly (WTO, 2011).

EXAMPLE 5.6

The war on bananas

Since the early nineties, the European Union was in conflict with the United States of America and a group of Latin American countries over banana trade. The European Union upheld very favourable conditions to the import of bananas from the former French and British colonies. In essence, the European Union imposed a licencing system on the import of bananas which established quotas. However, these quotas were more favourable for the former European colonies, and blocked Latin American countries such as Equador, Guatamala, Mexico and Honduras, as well as some big multinational companies from the United States, such as Chiquita, which operate in these countries. The U.S.A. and the Latin American countries filed a complained at the Dispute Settlement Body in 1996. As a result, the European Union adjusted its regulation on the import of bananas in January 1999 (DSB, 1997). However, the Dispute Settlement Body still considered these new trading rules to be incompatible with the GATT and other WTO agreements. Amongst others, the DSB authorized the U.S. and Honduras to impose economic sanctions against the EU in retaliation to their banana regulations.

In 2001, the EU, the U.S.A. and Ecuador reached an agreement in which on the one hand, the economic sanctions were dropped in exchange for yet another European regime in banana import (DSB, 2001). The European quota rules were now replaced by tariff-based import regulations. As it appeared however, these tariffs were not applied to the former colonies of the European countries, and therefore put the Latin American countries yet again at a disadvantage. In the end, the European Union reached an agreement that settled one of the longest trade disputes since the WTO came into existence. In the agreement, the European Union will gradually end the preferential treatment of its former colonies on the import of bananas. In exchange, the Latin-American countries as well as the U.S.A. will stop any legal proceedings at the WTO level nor will they try to negotiate further terms in the Doha trade talks (European Parliament, 2011).

5

National treatment principle

The national treatment principle means that foreign and domestic businesses should be treated equally.

This means that WTO Member States may not discriminate against foreign products in favour of domestic products once foreign products have entered the market. So, this principle does not focus on export or import, but on the situation after a foreign product entered a domestic market. In assessing whether a member state violates this principle, the WTO Dispute Settlement Body (DSB) will determine whether a domestic policy or rule *de facto* leads to the distortion of competition in this domestic market (Matsushita et al. 2006b). See for instance the Korean Beef case in example 5.7.

EXAMPLE 5.7

Korean Beef

A 1990 guideline in South Korean Law established a system of two distinct retail systems for the sales of beef: one for domestic beef, and a separated one for imported beef. This resulted in the fact that small retailers could either sell domestic or foreign beef, but not both. In case of supermarkets – large retailers – selling both domestic and foreign beef was allowed, as long as they were offered in separate sales areas, and the domestic beef was displayed with the sign 'specialized imported beef store' (Guidelines Concerning Registration and Operation of Specialized Imported Beef Stores, 1990; Regulations Concerning Sales of Imported Beef, 1998; Management Guideline for Imported Beef, 1999).
This policy was contested by Australia and the U.S.A. for both countries argued that due to this policy, they lost market share of beef in Korea. According to them, Korea violated the national treatment principle. The Appelate Body ruled that the policy in itself did not necessarily violate this principle; countries may adopt rules on the sales of foreign products, as long as it does not distort the domestic competition. However, the Appelate Body did conclude that since the introduction of this policy, the market share of foreign beef dropped considerably. In other words: while the policy in itself was not necessarily discriminating, the noticeable consequences of this policy were (DSB, 2000).

In line with the macro-economic theories on which the WTO is founded, especially those of David Ricardo, the idea is to lower trade barriers. This goal is partly pursued by the non-discrimination measures that can be found in the core WTO agreements. Furthermore, the trade rounds in itself are mostly used as a negotiation forum to reach further agreement on the lowering of tariff rates and other barriers to trade. For instance, technical regulations for products could be a trade barrier. Especially when such regulations are unrealistic, the number of regulations is out of control or the procedures to verify compliance with regulations are costly and time consuming (Matsushita et al. 2006c). Therefore, the WTO Member States adopted the Agreement on Technical Barriers to Trade (TBT Agreement). In this agreement, the states commit themselves to apply the non-discrimination principle to technical regulations in international trade. Next to that, the member states agreed to apply international technical standards where possible. As a result, it should be easier for companies to sell their products in multiple countries without being restricted too much by all kinds of different technical regulations for the same product.

Fair competition

Another WTO principle is fair competition. In a free market economy, companies should compete on fair terms. Fair competition could be distorted by various elements, such as discrimination to trade and trade barriers, as we have seen above. Furthermore, countries may subsidize their domestic markets and as a result create a situation of unfair competition. After all, the domestic producers have an advantage over foreign producers that is not caused by the 'natural' market forces, but artificially upheld by governmental interference. Another example of unfairness in competition could be the phenomenon of dumping.

Dumping

> Dumping is the sales of products or services for a lower price in an export market than in the domestic market, in order to gain market share (UNCTAD, 2004).

Although there is debate about the question whether dumping is unfair under all circumstances (Lindsey & Ikenson, 2002; Klitgaard & Schiele, 1998), the WTO members have adopted the Anti Dumping Agreement. This agreement aims to reduce dumping practices and stimulate fair trade.

Encouraging developing countries

The last principle of the WTO is to encourage developing countries. The ultimate goal of the WTO is to realize a global economy that is founded on free trade. However, developing countries might need more time to adjust their domestic policies and economic affairs in line with the WTO agreements compared to developed countries. Next to that, developing countries usually do not have equal access to global markets compared to developed countries. Therefore, it is common to adopt special provisions for developing countries to stimulate and facilitate their access to these global markets. For instance, part IV of the GATT deals with the issue of trade and development in particular. Article 8 of this part stipulates that:

> 'The developed contracting parties do not expect reciprocity for commitments made by them in trade negotiations to reduce or remove tariffs and other barriers to the trade of less-developed contracting parties.'

In short, this means that in case a developed country applies favourable terms to trade on a developing county, the developed country does not necessarily expect similar favours in return.

Since about two third of the WTO members are developing countries, and voting in the WTO is based on equal votes, the developing countries are a serious power block (Michalopoulos, 2013). This was clearly visible in the failed negotiations that were part of the Doha round.

Dispute Settlement

Next to a negotiation forum and a law making body, the WTO is also a forum to settle international trade disputes. The procedures of dispute settlement are laid down in the second annex of the WTO Agreement: the Understanding on rules and procedures governing the settlement of disputes (DSU).

The general approach is that international disputes on trade should be settled fast, effective, equitable and on the basis of mutual consent (WTO, 2011). Especially the last is important, and in this the dispute settlement procedures are different from court rulings in which the winning party wins all and the losing party suffers the consequences. At any stage of a dispute settlement procedure, negotiation and diplomacy are most important, if need be with the help of other WTO members.

Good office, conciliation and mediation

Regardless the stage of the dispute settlement procedure, disputing states are at any time encouraged to make use of alternative dispute settlement techniques to solve their problem. These alternatives are good office, conciliation and mediation (Art. 5. DSU). In these alternate proceedings, a third party is involved that at some point facilitates the disputing parties in reaching an agreement on settling the dispute. This could be the Secretary General of the WTO, or one of his staff members.

Good office

> Good office is the provision of logistical support by a third party to help the conflicting parties to settle their trade dispute.

In fact, the third party offers its facilities to negotiate on neutral ground, but is not actively involved in settling the dispute. This is different in the case of conciliation and mediation. While in some parts of the world, these words have different meanings (Squbini et al, 2004), in the WTO context they are understood as follows:

Conciliation

> Conciliation is the direct involvement of a third party in a trade dispute, facilitating the discussions and negotiations between the conflicting parties.

Mediation

> Mediation is the direct involvement of a third party in a trade dispute, facilitating the discussions and negotiations between the conflicting parties and proposing solutions to end the dispute.

So, in the case of conciliation, the involved third party supports the disputing parties in its involvement in the discussions, where in the case of mediation, the third party also proposes solutions to the conflicting parties. As promising as such alternative dispute settlement procedures may sound, WTO members seem to be very hesitant in using such a formal alternative to a dispute settlement procedure. In 2015, only in one case a mediation procedure was started in a trade dispute between Thailand and the Philippines on the one hand, and the European Community on the other (WTO, 2002).

Consultations

Normally, when countries are in a trade dispute, the dispute settlement procedure is started when one of the disputing countries formally requests for consultations (Art. 4 DSU). This means that at least one WTO Member State files a complaint at the Dispute Settlement Body against at least one other Member State. In practice, other countries may join the dispute on any of the conflicting sides when they feel that the case also concerns them. Therefore, it is quite common that more than two countries are involved in a trade dispute. When the official request for consultation is filed, the conflicting parties have a 'cooling down-period' of 60 days before they are allowed to present their case to the Dispute Settlement Body. This cooling down period can be reduced to 20 days in cases of emergency. During this period, they are obliged to seek for a solution through negotiation and diplomacy through 'consulting' one another on possible solutions to the problem. In other words: before a real procedure is started, the conflicting parties have to try to sort things out amongst themselves. Theoretically, good office, conciliation and mediation might play a role in especially this stage of the dispute settlement process.

Dispute settlement body

If there is no other way, and all other forms of diplomacy have failed, disputing parties may request the formation of a panel (Art. 6 DSU). This panel consists of 'well-qualified governmental and/or non-governmental individuals' that are chosen from a list of the Secretariat. These individuals may not be citizens of the disputing parties. Normally, such a panel consists of three or five members (Matstsuhita et al, 2006d). Forming this panel will normally take up to 45 days. This panel will, after hearing the case as presented by the disputing parties, prepare a final report with their findings, within 6 months. The panel then will submit this report to the Dispute Settlement Body (DSB). The DSB is actually the General Council of the WTO, but now with a different name. Within 60 days after the final report is submitted, the DSB has to decide on the case (Art. 16 DSU). Normally, the DSB will decide in line with the panel report. This is due to the fact that the DSB may only reject the panel's findings with consensus. This means that all the members of the DSB have to vote against the adoption. This will hardly be the case, since the party who 'wins' the case according to the panel also votes on the adoption of the report in the DSB. This winning party would then also have to vote against their own case to block adoption of the report, which of course will rarely occur.

Appellate Body

It is possible to appeal from the panel's views. When a party involved in a trade conflict wishes to appeal from a panel decision, an Appellate Body will be installed. This body consists of seven members, and has the authority to 'uphold, modify or reverse the legal findings and conclusions of the panel (Art. 17 (13) DSU).' The Appellate Body will adopt a final report with its findings within 60 to 90 days. The DSB will adopt the report within 30 days, using the same procedure as with a panel report (Art. 17 (14) DSU). This means that mostly, a procedure before the appellate body takes about three months.

Compliance

When the dispute is settled by the DSB, the 'losing' party is bound to comply with the adopted report. This could be for instance to lower certain trade barriers by changing tariffs or altering rules and regulations that relate to the trade dispute. In the next DSB meeting, which shall be held within 30 days after the adoption of the report, the losing party has to inform the DSB about their intentions on how to comply with the report (Art. 21 (3) DSU).

The losing side has to comply immediately, and if that is not possible, within a reasonable time. Normally, the verdict will define what such a reasonable time will be.

Compensation

However, if the losing party does not seem to comply, the conflicting parties have to negotiate a mutually acceptable compensation. In other words, the losing party has to compensate the winning party for continuing to uphold the disputed barrier to trade. For instance, such compensation could be in the form of a temporary tariff reduction in the product category of the trade dispute. If the parties do not reach an agreement on such compensation within 20 days, the winning party may request permission to the DSB to adopt retaliation measures (Art 22 DSU). Such measures are in the form of suspending concessions. In other words: the winning party may in return uphold barriers to trade against the losing party in retaliation for not complying with the DSB decision.

Retaliation

There are three types of retaliation measures (Art. 23 (3) DSU):
- Parallel retaliation: the suspension of concessions is done within the same sector as that in which the panel or Appellate Body has found a violation or other nullification or impairment.
- Cross-sector retaliation: the suspension of concessions is done within the same trade agreement as that in which the panel or Appellate Body has found a violation or other nullification or impairment.
- Cross-agreement retaliation is done within another trade agreement as that in which the panel or Appellate Body has found a violation or other nullification or impairment.

Cross sector retaliation will only be allowed when parallel retaliations seems impossible, for instance due to the fact that the country that wants to retaliate does not export products in the same sector. Furthermore, cross-agreement retaliation will only be allowed when cross-agreement retaliation seems impossible, due to the fact that the country that wants to retaliate is unable to do so within the margin of the same trade agreement. In practice, retaliation is a complex issue. It is not easy to determine what the extent should be of fitting retaliation actions (Read, 2007). Furthermore, retaliation measures are traditionally adopted in trade disputes that relate to goods. Applying retaliation measures in other areas, such as the service markets (Appleton, 2009), or intellectual property, is a rather unexplored area. A remarkable example in which both services and intellectual property are involved is the case between the U.S.A. and Antigua and Barbuda: example 5.8.

EXAMPLE 5.8

Gambling in the U.S.A.

One of the smallest economies in the world, Antigua and Barbuda, challenged the biggest economy in the world before the DSB. The trade dispute dates back from 2003, and concerned a U.S. internet block on online gambling from foreign countries, such as Antigua and Barbuda. According to the small state, online gambling forms approximately 5 per cent of the countries employment. The internet block was considered to be violating the principle of the National Treatment Principle, since the U.S.A.

did allow online betting on horseraces when it would be offered by domestic websites.
In a series of decisions, the DSB ruled that indeed the U.S.A. violated the WTO rules by maintaining this internet blockage.

However, since the decision in 2005 of the Appellate body, the U.S.A. and Antigua and Barbuda disagreed on whether the U.S.A. acted in compliance with the report. Where the U.S. had altered some of its regulations regarding to online gambling, and negotiated terms on the matter with other countries, Antigua and Barbuda could still not access the U.S. market properly. In the end, Antigua and Barbuda requested authorisation from the DSB to adopt retaliation measures. However, it would be very unlikely that at any point parallel or cross-sector retaliation would have any effect, since people from Antigua and Barbuda would hardly use U.S. websites for online gambling. To this end, the DSB allowed Antigua and Barbuda to adopt cross-agreement retaliation measures (DSB, 2007). To be precise, Antigua and Barbuda were now allowed to adopt retaliation measures in the field of intellectual property rights. For instance, they could allow its citizens to download movies or music from the U.S. industry for a very low price, up to a certain threshold. The result would be that consumers from Antigua and Barbuda would hardly pay any royalties to the U.S. companies in retaliation for the U.S. internet block on online gambling.

FIGURE 5.6 The WTO dispute settlement procedure.

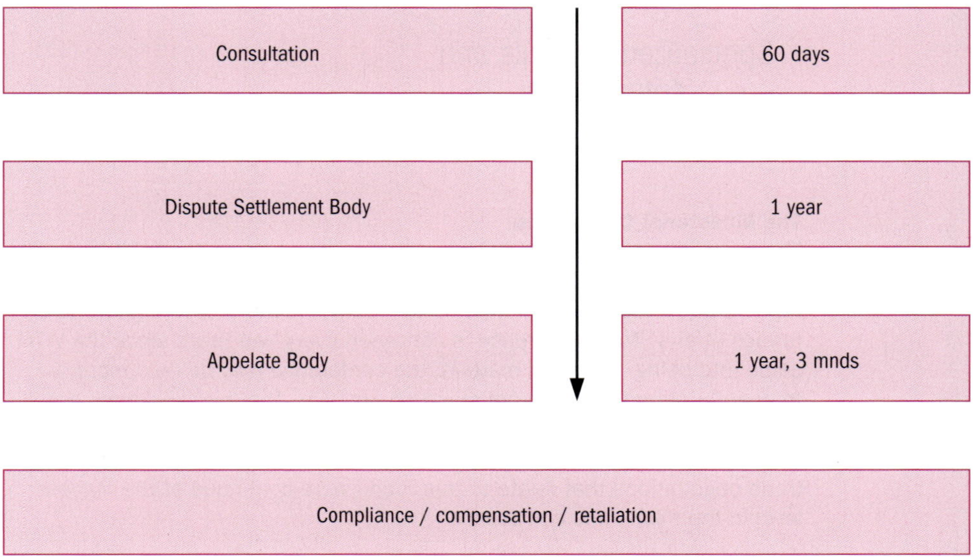

5.3.2 The organization of the WTO

The idea is that all WTO members may participate in each council or committee governing the WTO, except – for practical reasons – the dispute settlement panels and the appellate body. The WTO is governed on three levels: the highest level is the Ministerial Conference. The General Council operates on the second level, and specialized councils and committees operate on the third level. The WTO administration is led by the Director-General, who has no deciding powers. In Figure 5.7 you may find a visualization of these main bodies of the WTO.

FIGURE 5.7 The main bodies of the WTO

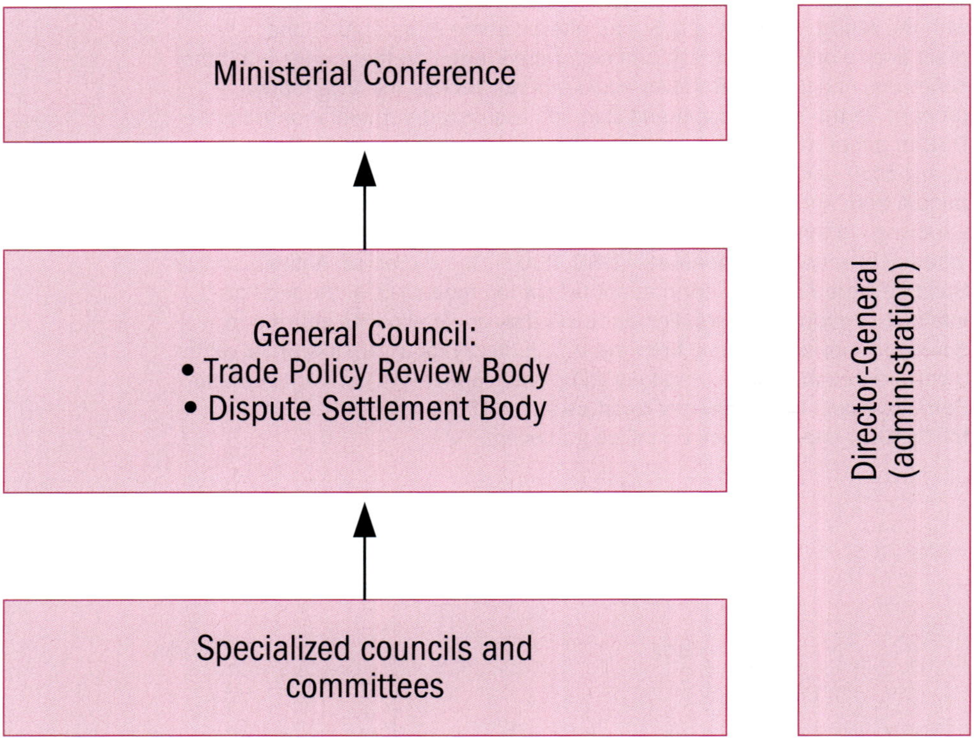

The Ministerial Conference

Ministerial Conference

The highest and most important decision-making body in the WTO is the Ministerial Conference. This conference consists of high-level representatives of the WTO members, mostly ministers of foreign trade or foreign affairs. This conference is convened every two years since the WTO came into being. In urgent matters, the conference may be held more frequently, although this is not common practice. The 'big' decisions are taken by the ministerial conference. For instance, the Doha trade round was launched during the fourth ministerial conference in 2001. Since then, the trade negotiations that relate to this round were continued at the highest level in the ministerial conference.

The General Council

General Council

Where the ministerial conference is not a body that functions day to day, theGeneral Council is. This Council reports directly to and acts on behalf of the Ministerial Conference. Also in the council, all WTO members are represented, but now on a permanent basis. The council usually meets in different capacities however.

Its first capacity is that of a Trade Policy Review Body (TPRB), in which the body discusses and evaluates the trade policies of its member states. Member states are reviewed in a frequency that relates to their relative seize of the world economy. In practice, this means that the four largest economies in the world (the European Communities, the United States of America, China and Japan) are reviewed every two years, where other economies are reviewed every four or even six years. The idea is that such reviews encourage the functioning of the WTO system, and most of all lead to transparency of domestic trade policies around the world.

Its second capacity is that of a Dispute Settlement Body (DSB). The functioning and procedures of this body are already discussed above.

Specialized Councils and Committees

In support of the General Council, there are several councils and committees that report to the General Council. Mainly, these are the Council for Trade in Goods, the Council for Trade in Services and the Council for Trade-Related aspects of Intellectual Property. These councils relate to the core WTO agreements (the GATT, GATS and TRIPS). Their core purpose is to facilitate the smooth functioning of those agreements. The councils usually have subsidiary bodies to support their functioning.
Next to these councils, there are various smaller committees on particular trade related aspects that report to the General Council, such as the Committee on Trade and Development, the Committee on Regional Trade Agreements, the Committee on Balance of Payments Restrictions and the Committee on Budget, Finance and Administration.

Decision-making procedures

In line with the GATT practice that was followed since 1947, the WTO bodies continue to take decisions by consensus(Art. IX WTO Agreement). Please note that this does not mean that all members should agree on something, but rather that no WTO member objects to a decision. Consequentially, a majority in a decision-making process is bound to negotiate with a minority to make sure they will not actively oppose a trade decision. The idea is that in a complex world with different ideologies, adopting decisions with consensus is seen as the most fruitful way. After all, to some extent, everyone is bound to take into account everyone's interest. This prevents that majorities rule over minorities, causing tense relations (Footer, 1997). However, it can be questioned whether this 'fairness' in the system truly works. After all, not every country can afford itself to veto decisions in the WTO, considering its position in the global market (Ehlermann & Ehring, 2005). Next to that, especially in case of a stale mate in negotiations, this system also results in rather slow decision making, as we have seen in the context of the Doha trade round. Consensus
Hypothetically, only in case when a decision cannot be made by consensus, a decision may be adopted by voting. In that case, each state has an equal vote. However, it is a rarity that in a WTO body, surely in the highest bodies, decisions are adopted after voting. Voting

Director-General

The WTO personnel and administration is led by the Director-General. He has no true policy powers, since the WTO members take all such decisions in the therefore installed WTO bodies. The Director-General may however Director-General

play a role in dispute settlement through advice and counselling, and officially represents the WTO in the international arena.
The Director-General is appointed by the Ministerial Conference (Article VI, WTO Agreement), for a four-year term. Occasionally, a Director-General is reappointed for another four-year term. For instance, the Pascal Lamy (France) served as Director-General from 2005-2013. He was succeeded by Roberto Azevedo (Brasil).

5.4 Alternatives

Asian Infrastructure Investment Bank

Especially due to the system of weighted voting in the IMF and the World Bank Group, the power of the world's largest economies is often criticized. A notable alternative to the World Bank was a Chinese initiative in 2014, to set up the Asian Infrastructure Investment Bank (AIIB). This bank is destined to function as a regional investment Bank to support developing regions in Asia (Chapter I, Articles of Agreement AIIB). The function of this bank is therefore pretty much alike the already existing World Bank, or its regional twin, the Asian Development Bank. Both are however greatly dominated by the U.S.A. and Japan, who are not prospective founding member of the AIIB. It is no secret that especially the U.S.A. considers the AIIB as a rival to the World Bank, and publicly regrets the fact that most of their allies do join the Chinese initiative, as you can see in the newspaper article.
At the time of writing, the Asian Infrastructure Investment Bank did not yet start operations effectively, for its 57 prospect founding members have to sign and ratify the AIIB Articles of Agreement. Only when ten potential Member States representing 50 per cent of the intended capital signed and ratified these articles, the Bank will start to function (Art. 59, Articles of Agreement AIIB). These requirements were fulfilled in January 2016, and since then the bank is up and running.

THE GUARDIAN, 13 MARCH 2015

US anger at Britain joining Chinese-led investment bank AIIB

BY: NICHOLAS WATT, PAUL LEWIS AND TANIA BRANIGAN

US statement says of UK membership that it is 'worried about a trend of constant accommodation' of China, in a rare public breach in the special relationship

The White House has issued a pointed statement declaring it hopes and expects the UK will use its influence to ensure that high standards of governance are upheld in a new Chinese-led investment bank that Britain is to join.
In a rare public breach in the special relationship, the White House signalled its unease at Britain's decision to become a founder member of the Asian Infrastructure Investment Bank (AIIB) by raising concerns about whether the new body would meet the standards of the World Bank.
The \$50bn (£33,5bn) bank, which is designed to provide infrastructure funds to the Asia-Pacific region, is viewed with great suspicion by Washington officials, who see this as a rival to the World Bank. They believe Beijing will use the bank to expand its soft power in the region.

Summary

The IMF

- The International Monetary Fund International Monetary Fund, IMF is a UN specialized agency that promotes financial stability and monetary cooperation on a global level.
  - One of the direct causes to the instalment of the IMF was the phenomenon of competitive devaluation: the competition between states in exchange rates in order to stimulate export and discourage import.

- The IMF employs the following activities:
  - Surveillance: through bilateral and multilateral surveillance, the IMF monitors whether the member states act in compliance with the obligations for member states, and supports sharing accurate data on economic and financial issues.
  - Technical assistance: The IMF provides for technical assistance in the field of its expertise: macro/economic financial issues. This is mostly done through the IMF Institute for Development Training Program.
  - Lending money: the IMF may be used to grant loans to countries that request this. A loan is granted when the lending party complies with the principle of conditionality. This means that IMF financial support is granted under the condition that the involved Member State adopts certain economical and financial policies.
  - Supervise the system of Special Drawing Rights. Special Drawing Rights is a unit that reflects the value of a large money basket in which the four most accepted international currencies are 'injecting' the U.S. dollar, the pound sterling, the euro and the yen. Countries are allocated drawing rights, depending on the relative size of their economies. A SDR is exchangeable for a bite of the money basket, consisting of a mixture of four strong currencies.

- Decision-making in the IMF is based on weighted voting: a vote is weighted in accordance with the financial contribution of a Member State to the IMF.

The IMF is governed by three main bodies: the Board of Governors, the Executive Board, and the Managing Director:

- The Board of Governors is the highest political body in the IMF, and is convened once a year. Each member state is represented in this body. The Board has delegated most of its executive powers to the Executive Board.
- The Executive Board is a permanent body that has daily executive power in the IMF. While the board only consists of 24 Governors, all IMF Member States are represented through a system of constituencies.

► The IMF personnel and staff are managed by a managing director, who also represents the IMF in the international arena.

The World Bank

The World Bank Group is a combination of five international institutions that are specialized UN agencies, with the aim to reduce poverty by lending money and providing for technical support to developing countries.

- The International Bank for Reconstruction and Development (IBRD) lends to governments of middle-income and creditworthy low-income countries.
- The International Development Association (IDA) provides interest-free loans – called credits – and grants to governments of the poorest countries.
- The International Finance Corporation (IFC) provides loans, equity, and technical assistance to stimulate private sector investment in developing countries.
- The Multilateral Investment Guarantee Agency (MIGA) provides guarantees against losses caused by non-commercial risks to investors in developing countries.
- The International Centre for Settlement of Investment Disputes (ICSID) provides international facilities for conciliation and arbitration of investment disputes.

► Decision-making in the World Bank Group is based on weighted voting.

► The World Bank Group is practically organized by the same institutions, under a different name.
  - The Board of Governors is the highest political body in the WBG, and delegated most of its executive competencies to the Board of Directors. The board convenes twice a year.
  - The Board of Directors consists of 25 executive directors, representing all member states through a system of constituencies. The board operates on a day to basis.
  - The World Bank President is appointed by the Board of Directors, and supervises the managerial operations of the World Bank. The President represents the World Bank Group in the international arena.

The WTO

► The World Trade Organization is a global institution whose main goal is to liberalize trade
  - The World Trade Organization was founded in 1994, and is the successor of the GATT.
  - The philosophy of the WTO, to liberalize trade, is founded on the macro-economical theories of David Ricardo.

► The WTO is a negotiation forum: in trade rounds, the WTO members try to negotiate new trade rules to further liberalize trade.

► The WTO is a law-making body: important core treaties are adopted by the WTO members, such as the GATT, the GATS and the TRIPS. These treaties have the following principles in common:
  - The most-favoured nation principle: this means that foreign businesses should be treated equally;

- The national treatment principle: this means that foreign and domestic businesses should be treated equally;
- The lowering of trade barriers;
- Fair competition;
- Encouraging developing countries.

► The WTO facilitates Dispute Settlement.
- At any stage of a dispute settlement procedure, negotiation and diplomacy are most important, if need be with the help of other WTO members. This could be through:
  - Good office: the provision of logistical support by a third party to help the conflicting parties to settle their trade dispute;
  - Conciliation: the direct involvement of a third party in a trade dispute, facilitating the discussions and negotiations between the conflicting parties;
  - Mediation: the direct involvement of a third party in a trade dispute, facilitating the discussions and negotiations between the conflicting parties and proposing solutions to end the dispute.
- A dispute settlement procedure potentially consists of three parts:
  - Consultation: the conflicting parties have a 'cooling down-period' of 60 days before they are allowed to present their case to the Dispute Settlement Body.
  - Panel report: a panel composed of well-qualified governmental and/or non-governmental individuals writes a report with their findings about the case. The report may be adopted by the Dispute Settlement Body. Together with the consultation period, this procedure takes up to one year.
  - Appeal procedure: an appellate body is installed, which has the authority to uphold, modify or reverse the legal findings and conclusions of the panel. Together with the previous proceedings, this process takes up to 1 year and three months.

► The WTO is governed by the Ministerial Conference, the general Council, specialized commissions and committees and the Director-General.
- The Ministerial Conference is the highest political body, and is convened every two years. All WTO members are represented.
- The General Council functions on a daily basis, and mainly serves as a Trade Policy Review Body and Dispute Settlement Body.
- In support of the General Council, various specialized Councils and Committees are installed.
- The Director-General supervises the personnel and administration of the WTO. He furthermore represents the WTO in the international arena.

► Usually, WTO bodies take decisions by consensus. This means that a decision is adopted if no member state opposes its adoption.

The AIIB

► Due to the system of weighted voting in the IMF and the World Bank Group, the power of the world's largest economies is often criticized. Therefore, as an alternative to the World Bank, the Chinese set up the Asian Infrastructure Investment Bank in 2014.

Practice questions

Open questions

5.1 The WTO DSB concludes in its final report that the EU is violating the GATT. The EU maintains a practice in which banana import from African countries is duty free. Companies that import bananas with an origin in the U.S.A. however, must pay 7 per cent import tax when entering the EU market. Since the verdict, the EU seems to continue its practice, regardless the conclusion of the DSB. In addition, the EU is unwilling to pay for compensation to the U.S.A. The U.S.A. imports no bananas from the EU, but does import apples on a large scale (the fruit species, not the computers). Banana import and apple import were never included in the same trade agreements between the EU and the U.S.A. Consider that there is no trade agreement between the EU and the U.S.A. about fruit.

Please, explain what retaliation-actions you would advise the U.S.A. to undertake.

5.2 'The unit of currency is the Tunisian dinar (TD), which is divided into 1000 millimes (mills). It's illegal to import or export dinars and they are not accepted in the duty-free shops at Tunis Airport.
You can re-exchange up to 30 per cent of the amount you changed into dinar, up to a limit of TD100. You need bank receipts to prove you changed the money in the first place.
Major credit cards such as Visa, American Express and MasterCard are widely accepted at big shops, tourist hotels, car-rental agencies and banks. ATMs are found in major towns and resort areas. Cash advances are given in local currency only.' Source: www.lonelyplanet.com

Please explain how this policy relates to the 'floating system' of currencies, and why this could be beneficial to the Tunisian economy.

5.3 Japan imposes a higher national Value Added tax (VAT) on grape wines (40 per cent). 80 per cent of all the grape wines are imported products from predominantly European Countries. The reason for this is the expected health damage as a result of overconsumption. It is however curious that such a VAT is not imposed on Japanese Rake (Rice Wine), and the lower percentage (21 per cent) is applied.

How would you judge this tax policy in the context of WTO trade rules?

5.4 Japan restricts the import of grape wines from Europe by establishing a quorum. However, beer from china is allowed on the domestic Japanese market without any restrictions.

How would you judge this tax policy in the context of WTO trade rules?

Essay question

The IMF voting mechanism is often criticized, as we can see in this chapter. How would you judge the IMF voting mechanism in relation to the principle of IMF conditionality? Write an essay in which you explore the relation between the IMF voting mechanism and this principle, and conclude with your own opinion on the matter. In writing, select one of the following titles;

- The principle of conditionality is a justified mechanism to guarantee the security of IMF investments.
- The principle of conditionality is a corrupt mechanism that even further enriches the rich countries in the world.
- The principle of conditionality might work but should be reviewed.

Multiple choice questions

5.1 The latest IMF report on the functioning of the economies in Latin America is an example of:

a bilateral surveillance
b regional surveillance
c multilateral surveillance

5.2 The Central African Republic is one of the poorest countries in the world. Nestlé considers investing in the country, but is unsure about this considering the risk of political instability and occasional eruptions of violence.

Which World Bank Group institution might be of help here?

a the Multilateral Investment Guarantee Agency
b the International Finance Corporation
c the International Development Association

5.3 The daily affairs of the World Bank and related institutions are run by:
a the Board of Governors
b the Board of Directors
c the World Bank Group President

5.4 The U.S.A. is not a member of the:
a Asian Development Bank
b Asian Infrastructure Investment Bank
c International Bank for Reconstruction and Development

FREE TRADE LAW
USED TYRES-comp.
URUGUAY
BRAZIL
TYRE
BURNING
LOCATION
Sandor

6 Regional economic integration

In this chapter we will explore the various forms of regional economic integration. In all parts of the world, countries choose to intensify economic cooperation with their trading partners. This is done by closing agreements that lead to the reduction of barriers to trade. Such agreements come in various grades of economic integration. First, we will explore the forms of economic integration: the free trade zone, the customs union, the common market, the economic union and the monetary union. Second, we will discuss various examples of such forms into more detail: the NAFTA (free trade zone), the SACU (customs union) and the MERCOSUR (common market). Please note that in chapter 7, we will discuss the European Union into more detail (economic and monetary union).

6.1 Regional economic integration

Parallel to the attempts on a global level to liberalize trade and reduce barriers to trade, there are uncountable regional initiatives to realize such goals. Usually, it is easier to reduce barriers to trade between befriended, nearby countries with a long trading history compared to the worldwide attempts. Agreements to reduce trade barriers regionally is therefore usually more intense and successful compared to the WTO agreements. It needs to be noted here that for this reason, the WTO most favoured nation principle does not apply to regional attempts that lead to closer economic cooperation. In other words: when a group of countries decide to lower trade certain barriers between them, they are not necessarily bound to apply these agreements – for they are more favourable – to other countries (WTO 2011).

Relation with WTO agreements

6.1.1 Forms of regional economic integration

Usually, regional economic integration progresses in several steps. When there is nothing agreed between countries, countries usually seek to artificially protect their domestic markets by upholding barriers to trade. Such barriers are usually either tariffs or import quotas. To this end, the domestic production is favoured over foreign producers, since foreign producers face more difficulties to enter the domestic market. However, it may be beneficial to ban such trade barriers amongst a group of countries. After all, we have seen in the previous chapter that several macro-economic theories point out that reducing trade barriers benefits all when applied properly. To do so, a first step in economic cooperation is the creation of a free trade zone.

Free trade zone

> A free trade zone is a zone in which the involved countries agreed to abolish tariffs and quotas to trade.

This means that on the one hand, the most important obstacles to trade are banned amongst the member countries. Simultaneously, on the other hand, the involved countries have their own policies in upholding trade barriers to third countries that are not a part of this zone. This can be done in two ways: with closed and open borders. In the case of closed borders, the members of a free trade zone may adopt rules of origin, meaning that only products that originate from within the zone may enjoy the preferred treatment. An example is the NAFTA, as we will see below. This does mean that the borders remain 'closed', and products are checked at each border. When an originating product crosses the border, it may do so under the more favourable rules of the free trade zone. When a product is non-originating, it will be treated just like before the free trade zone was installed, and each country will then determine at their borders what to do with these products. The pro of this approach is that the members of a free trade zone keep control on how products are allowed in their country. The con is that it always leads to border controls, which delays trade, including trade in originating products.

Another option therefore is to establish a free trade zone with open borders. The result is that once a product enters the zone, it can be sold anywhere without being restricted by tariffs or quotas. The advantage is that between the free trade zone members, no more border controls are necessary. The disadvantage is that producers from third countries will then probably try to enter the zone through the country that upholds the lowest barriers to trade non/originating products. The consequence is that then, potentially, all trade will enter the zone through one country, or that the involved countries compete with their rules on trade barriers to third countries. After all, especially the logistic sector in the country through which trade enters the zone will prosper. This phenomenon is called trade deflection. This problem can easily be solved by installing a customs union.

Customs union

> A customs union is a free trade zone in which the countries harmonized their external tariffs and quotas to trade.

In fact, this is a free trade zone with a common external tariff, and common quotas to trade. In harmonizing those, it makes no difference for third countries as to where they enter the zone. Consequentially, all members of

the customs union enjoy the benefits of the customs union equally, and within the zone, the borders can remain 'open'.
A customs union focuses on the trade in goods. However, one could also apply the principles of a customs union to more than that. A logical next step to regional economic integration is to form a common market, in which the banning of tariffs and quotas, as well as a common external approach towards barriers to trade, is extended to services, personnel, and capital.

Common market

> A common market is a customs union that extends to services, personnel and capital.

It needs to be noted here that in this stage of economic cooperation, the terminology is somewhat confusing. Next to the term 'common market', we also find terms such as 'single market' and 'internal market'. While the exact distinction between those concepts is not very clear, it is generally accepted that the words 'single market' and 'internal market' reflect a closer integration compared to a 'common market', in which also political aspects are harmonized. They are, as a manner of speaking, somewhere in between a common market and the next step of economic integration: the economic union.
After all, a close economic integration such as a common market mostly requires a bit more than solely banning barriers to trade. If the 'rules of the game' are different in each country, there will be regulatory competition. This means that the country with the lowest product standards, or most flexible labour law will attract the most business. To rule out such forms of competition, and equalize trade opportunities even further, it is necessary to also harmonize economic laws and policies. This next step is called an economic union.

Economic union

> An economic unionis a customs union in which economic laws and policies are harmonized.

The result of such a union is that the 'rules of the game' are the same, and business opportunities are not influenced by differences in legislation. At this stage, most barriers to trade and other influences that cause differences in business opportunities are ruled out. However, there is one issue that remains, which is the fluctuating of currencies. Countries may have equalized business opportunities as much as possible, but if the involved countries use different currencies, the fluctuation of the value of these currencies against one another may still interfere the idea of fair trade. To deal with this, a monetary union may be installed. This is the ultimate form of economic integration.

Monetary union

> A monetary union is an economic union with a shared monetary unit.

When countries pay with the same currency, the differences in value of currencies play no further role in business, creating an atmosphere of fair trade based on equal opportunities.
Please note that in some cases, countries happen to pay with the same currency unit, but do not necessarily cooperate as close as an economic union. For instance, the fact that in Cambodia it is quite normal to pay with American dollars does not make Cambodia and the U.S.A. an economic union.

6.1.2 Political Struggle

Typically, the integration of economics goes hand in hand with fierce political debate and struggle. This mostly relates to the fear of losing jobs and losing competitiveness when boarders are opened for foreign trade. Another issue is the so-called 'race to the bottom' regarding rules and regulations on product standards: when borders are opened, foreign products may enter your markets that do not meet your own standards.

An example of such debate is the existence of the North American Free Trade Agreement (NAFTA). We will explain this agreement into more detail in the next section. Politically, the NAFTA has always been a loathed issue. In all three member states politicians have pointed out the pros and cons of such a zone for the domestic markets. Also in the media, wild speculations about the effects of the NAFTA have circulated ever since the zone came into being. A striking example is formed by the two news articles below, published on exactly the same date, while drawing opposite conclusions with very contradicting statistics. In all honesty, the political debate has mostly been very far away from economic reality, and not necessarily academically substantiated (Fatemi, 1994). Moreover, similar discussions can be observed in the case of the SACU, the MERCOSUR and the European Union.
Whatever political debate there is, the NAFTA as an institute is – not surprisingly – very positive about its own existence. In 2015, it reported that since its existence, trade amongst the three countries had tripled, the North American economy had more than doubled in size, and employment levels had climbed nearly 23 per cent (www.NAFTANOW.org, 2015).

THE ECONOMIST, 4 JANUARY 2014

Deeper, better, NAFTA

North America's trade deal has delivered real benefits. But the job is not done

The arguments for and against the North American Free-Trade Agreement (NAFTA) before its launch on January 1st 1994 were hyperbolic. Twenty years on, NAFTA's backers have won the argument.
The American and Canadian economies were already pretty well integrated before the creation of NAFTA, so there was no great leap in trade between the two. But America's trade with Mexico increased by 506 per cent between 1993 and 2012, compared with 279 per cent with non-NAFTA countries. (...) The 'giant sucking sound' that Ross Perot, a presidential candidate, predicted would be heard as Mexico hoovered up American jobs never materialised; if jobs have moved anywhere in the past two decades, they have gone to China, not Mexico. Industries from aerospace to cars have woven supply chains back and forth across North America's borders. Some 40 per cent of the content of imports from Mexico into the United States, and 25 per cent of the content of imports from Canada, originated in the United States itself.
Helped by rising energy production in all three countries, Factory North America is being created.

THE GUARDIAN, 4 JANUARY 2014

NAFTA: 20 years of regret for Mexico

BY: MARK WEISBROT

It was 20 years ago that the North American Free Trade Agreement between the U.S., Canada, and Mexico was implemented. (...) it is easy to see that NAFTA was a bad deal for most Americans. (...)

But what about Mexico? Didn't Mexico at least benefit from the agreement? Well, if we look at the past 20 years, it's not a pretty picture. (...) From 1960-80 Mexico's GDP per capita nearly doubled. This amounted to huge increases in living standards for the vast majority of Mexicans. (...) But Mexico, like the rest of the region, began a long period of neoliberal policy changes that, beginning with its handling of the early 1980s debt crisis, got rid of industrial and development policies, gave a bigger role to de-regulated international trade and investment, and prioritized tighter fiscal and monetary policies (sometimes even in recessions).

For Mexico, NAFTA helped to consolidate the neo-liberal, anti-development economic policies that had already been implemented in the prior decade, enshrining them in an international treaty. It also tied Mexico even further to the U.S. economy, which was especially unlucky in the two decades that followed...

6

6.2 The free trade zone: NAFTA

A famous example of a free trade zone is the North American Free Trade Agreement(NAFTA) between Canada, Mexico and the United States of America. The agreement went into effect on the 1th of January 1994, after – not surprisingly – a long period of political struggle. Historically the NAFTA is a special free trade zone, since the zone includes two developed and one developing country (Mexico). Before, Canada and the U.S.A. had already established a free trade zone in 1989 (CUSFTA). The NAFTA in fact enlarged this zone to Mexico, albeit with different terms and conditions. Please note that in essence, the NAFTA is a free trade zone with closed borders.

6.2.1 Free trade under the NAFTA

The NAFTA in itself is a lengthy document (over 2.000 pages!) specifying the free trade agreement of North America. Most important are the reduction of tariffs and quotas, the rules of origin, and the application of the most favoured nation principle in other economic areas.

Tariffs and quotas

Import/export tariffs

At the core of the NAFTA agreement is the ban of import/export tariffs between its Member States concerning a significant amount of goods, and the reduction of tariffs of many more goods (Art. 301 NAFTA). Under the latter category fall the more delicate markets such as the agriculture, automobile and textile markets. As in many free trade zones, it is always difficult to reach an agreement on fully dropping import/export duties on these markets. Main characteristics of the NAFTA is that while the Member States banned most of the barriers to trade internally, they have their own distinct laws and policies towards trade with third countries: this is not harmonized.

Next to the elimination or reduction of tariffs, no prohibition or restriction to trade may be adopted nor maintained (309 NAFTA). This means that quotas to trade are to be eliminated. A quota to trade is also referred to as a quantitative restriction.

Quantitative restrictions

Quantitative restrictions are limitations to import or export to the volume or value of goods.

Such quotas can only be justified when they are in compliance with Article XI of the GATT. The NAFTA refers to the older GATT rules for practical reasons: its members already agreed on this treaty. Such a justification of a quantitative restriction will hardly occur, for such exceptions to the rule can only be invoked in rather dramatic times. For instance, when a country faces a shortage in food, a quota on the export of foodstuff may be imposed to prevent a famine.

Rules of Origin

A free trade zone with closed borders, trade deflection, also proves to be a challenge. Companies might try to abuse the favourable free trade zone rules. For instance, they might set up an establishment in the zone and only perform the last stage of processing to an end product just to make it look like a product that originates from the zone. To avoid this kind of trade deflection, a complex web of regulations that determine the origin of a product was established. The purpose of these rules is to establish whether or not a certain product may benefit from the preferred treatment that applies within the zone. When a product does not fall under this category, each NAFTA Member States will apply its own rules and regulations on international trade. This is, by the way, a quite common approach in case of regional economic cooperation in relation to third countries (Brenton, 2003). It is important to be well aware of these rules when a company is involved in international trade in the NAFTA zone to be able to predict the exact tariffs and other rules that apply to their products.

Rules of origin

Article 401 NAFTA defines when a product originates from the NAFTA zone. Obviously, there is no real problem when goods are wholly obtained or produced in the NAFTA region. Such products contain no foreign materials or parts from outside the NAFTA countries. Article 415 NAFTA further defines these goods. Examples are: mineral goods extracted in a NAFTA country, vegetables, harvested in a NAFTA country, live animals born and raised in a NAFTA country, and sea products taken from the sea in a NAFTA country. However, the situation is more complex when end products are created within the region while some of its substances are imported from outside the NAFTA zone. To this end, the NAFTA provides for additional rules defining what type of products may be classified as 'originating' from the NAFTA zone.

First, there are goods meeting the Annex 401 origin rule. These are goods that are partly composed of materials coming from non-NAFTA countries, but may still be considered as originating from the NAFTA zone, as long as they are in compliance with the rather lengthy Annex 401. This means practically, that the end product, even if it is partly composed of materials that do not originate from the NAFTA zone, is considered to originate from the NAFTA zone, as we can see in example 6.1.

EXAMPLE 6.1

Goods meeting the Annex 401 origin rule: pork sausage

A company situated in the United States imports pork meat from Hungary. The company adds spices to the meat that originates from the Caribbean, and cereal that originates from the United States. The end product is pork sausage. In Annex 401, the end product 'pork sausage' is classified in a certain category that allows the composition of the Hungarian meat and Caribbean spices without losing its classification as 'originating' from the NAFTA zone (U.S. Custom and Border Protection, 2015).

Second, there are goods produced in the NAFTA region wholly from originating materials as we can see in example 6.2. In other words: a product may be composed of several other products. As long as these products fall under the first two categories, the new end product is considered to be originating from the NAFTA zone. This means that hypothetically, a product may be composed of several end products from the Annex 401 list, and therefore may be partially composed of non-NAFTA materials.

EXAMPLE 6.2

Goods produced in the NAFTA region wholly from originating materials: leather eyeglass cases

A company situated in Mexico imports raw cowhide from Argentina. The company processes the skin into an end product: leather. According to Annex 401, this end product is a product originating from the NAFTA zone. This leather is purchased by a company in the United States and used to produce leather eyeglass cases. These cases are made of products that originate from the NAFTA zone, while in essence, Argentinian leather is used (U.S. Custom and Border Protection, 2015).

Third, there are unassembled goods and goods classified with their parts which do not met the Annex 401 rule of origin but contain 60 per cent regional value content using the transaction method (50 per cent using the net cost method). These are goods that do not match any of the above criteria. However, due to the fact that a company in the NAFTA zone adds a certain value to the product, the free trade zone rules may be fully, or partially, applied. See for instance example 6.3.

EXAMPLE 6.3

Unassembled goods and goods classified with their parts which do not met the Annex 401 rule of origin: bicycles

A Canadian company imports basic materials for bicycles in Germany, Belgium, China and Japan. On their own, these basic materials represent a low value. However, when these materials are assembled into a bike, using the companies applied skills and knowledge, the value is significantly increased. When the increase of the value exceeds a certain threshold, the bikes may be qualified as originating from the NAFTA zone (U.S. Custom and Border Protection, 2015).

Other economic cooperation

One important aspect of the NAFTA is that the member states maintain a great deal of sovereignty in trade laws. There is no explicit desire to create some sort of pan-North-American legislative system in which all rules on trade aspects are harmonized. However, the NAFTA is not only about the elimination or reduction of tariffs and quota to trade.

On most trade aspects in the NAFTA, it is stipulated that while the members of the NAFTA may enjoy this sovereignty in their trade laws, they should not misuse them as a barrier to trade. This is for instance explicitly stipulated in the context of intellectual property, standard related measures, and sanitary and phytosanitary measures. In the case of Intellectual Property, the Member States agreed to adequately protect such things as copyrights, patents and trademarks while simultaneously guaranteeing that such rules do not result in a barrier to trade. In case of standards (for instance for products) or sanitary and phytosanitary measures (for instance on food quality), countries may uphold their own laws and regulations, as long as such standards are proportionate to its legitimate goal and do not result in discrimination against other members of the NAFTA.

Most favoured nation principle

National treatment principle

To this end, on most trade related aspects, the most favoured nation principle and the national treatment principle applies to many aspects of trade. Therefore, the most favoured trade laws should apply to all members of the NAFTA, and domestic trade laws should not create a distinction between foreign trade and domestic trade. For instance, these two principles apply to services, financial services, and foreign investments.

6.2.2 The organizational structure of the NAFTA

The NAFTA is not centrally led by supranational bodies, such as the European Union. Rather, it has a sober institutional structure mainly consisting of the Free Trade Commission and the Secretariat. The Commission was installed to oversee the implementation of the Agreement and dispute settlement procedures under chapter 14, 19 and 20 (Art. 2001 NAFTA). The Secretariat supervises the administration of the NAFTA (Art. 2002 NAFTA). It needs to be noted however, that both NAFTA bodies have no legislative powers over their Member States, and therefore cannot take binding decisions.

6.2.3 Dispute settlement under the NAFTA

In the NAFTA, there are four different types of dispute settlement procedures. They are usually named after the NAFTA chapter in which they are stipulated. These are the Chapter 20, 11, 14 19 procedures. A remarkable aspect of NAFTA dispute settlement is the possibility for private parties in particular disputes to sue a government (Chapter 11 and 19 procedures). All procedures move beyond mediation, and have a firm legally binding effect.

Chapter 20 procedure

The Chapter 20 procedure is the most general procedure. When member states are in a dispute about the interpretation of the NAFTA, they may seek legal remedies through this procedure. It needs to be noted here that a Chapter 20 procedure cannot be used for matters covered under any of the other three procedures.
First, the disputing parties have to attempt to resolve the dispute in a formal consultation process in which they try to settle the dispute friendly on a governmental level. When this fails, the ministers of trade have to try to settle the dispute within the context of the Free Trade Commission. When this does not lead to an agreement, a process may be started in which an arbitration panel is installed. This panel makes a legally binding ruling on the matter. When the losing party does not act in compliance with the panel's final report, the winning party may adopt retaliation measures.
In essence, this procedure is pretty much like the WTO dispute settlement system.

Chapter 11 procedure

Under the Chapter 11 procedure investors from NAFTA countries may sue another NAFTA government for not complaining with the obligations stipulated in Chapter 11. The most important obligations in this chapter are the national treatment principle, the most-favoured nation principle, and the principle of fair and equal treatment (Articles 1102, 1103 and 1105). Chapter 11 does not regulate the forming of a panel that rules in the matter. Instead, the complaining party may choose between three already existing arbitral systems from the World Bank Group or the United Nations Commission for International Trade Law. In example 6.4, the complaining party made use of the latter.

EXAMPLE 6.4

Toxicity!

S.D. Meyers Inc. v. the Government of Canada

PCB waste consists of toxic chemicals, mostly used as coolers in for instance fridges, or insulating fluids in transistors and capacitors. Currently, the application of PCBs is for the greater part forbidden.
An Ohio-based company, S.D. Meyers Inc., is specialized in the procession, transportation and disposure of such PCB waste. A rather specialized market, with not too many competitors. S.D. Meyers Inc. was active on the Canadian market, and had several contracts with Canadian parties worth over 50 million U.S. dollars. However, in the period November-December 1995, the Canadian government adopted several export orders that forbade the exportation of PCB waste. Amongst other arguments, the Canadian government held that the import or export of hazardous toxics is not a very good idea and that the waste should be disposed domestically. Especially since the U.S.A. seemed to have more flexible rules on the disposal of such waste, and therefore it could not be guaranteed that S.D. Meyers Inc. would act in line with the high standards of environmental laws that were applicable in Canada (Government of Canada, 1999). However, on the other hand, the Canadian ban resulted in the fact that one Canadian company now got all the contracts, for a much higher price and very far away from most PCB waste locations. In the view of S.D. Meyers, this was a barrier to trade, leading to disfavouring a U.S. company over a Canadian.

In 1999, a tribunal was appointed under the UNCITRAL arbitration rules, to settle the dispute.
The company's activities in Canada were considered a foreign investment, and the Canadian Orders were – amongst others – considered a violation of the national treatment principle (Art. 1102 NAFTA), and the principle of equal treatment (Art. 1105 NAFTA). After all, the U.S. company was indeed discriminated compared to the Canadian company (NAFTA arbitration tribunal, 2000). In the end, the tribunal ruled that Canada had to pay compensation damage of 8.231 million U.S. dollars to S.D. Meyers Inc. Since Canada had already changed their import and export rules on PCB Waste, no alteration of such laws was needed.

Chapter 14 procedure

The Chapter 14 procedure is a procedure designed for the settlement of disputes on financial services. However, since it appears that the other procedures offer adequate legal remedies in this field, the Chapter 14 procedure has never been used as of yet.

Chapter 19 procedure

The Chapter 19 procedure is a rarity in international law. In essence, the procedure is an alternate appeal procedure against decisions of authorities from a NAFTA Member State in the field of antidumping or countervailing duty laws.
In short, an antidumping duty is imposed on an imported product when it is sold below the home-market price or cost price. A countervailing duty is a duty imposed on imported products that are subsidized in a home country, see example 6.5. In both cases, the extra duty is imposed to create a fair competition. After all, when producers try to dump their products on another market, or received some subsidy from their own government in producing the product, they surely have an advantage over competing producers in the other market (Macrory, 2002).

EXAMPLE 6.5

U.S. countervailing duties on Canadian softwood lumber

When a producer in Canada receives a subsidy to producer softwood lumber, the production costs are lower compared to its competitor in the U.S.A. After all, the U.S. producer did not receive such a subsidy from its own government. When crossing the border, the U.S. custom authorities impose an additional duty on the Canadian softwood lumber to eliminate this difference so that both producers may compete fairly on the U.S. market. This additional duty is called a countervailing duty, to literally countervail the Canadian subsidy.

While all NAFTA members are allowed to adopt their own laws and policies on antidumping and countervailing duties, the competent authorities should of course act in compliance with their own laws. The Chapter 19 procedure offers an alternative legal remedy for companies from a NAFTA country that feels that authorities do not act in compliance with their own antidumping or

counterbalance laws. Such a company might seek legal remedies at the competent national courts, but may also choose to start a procedure under chapter 19 NAFTA.
In this procedure, a panel is formed composed of representatives from the two countries that are involved (the importing and exporting country). This panel simply reviews the disputed action of the authority that imposes the duty against its own legislation. However, the decision of such a panel is legally binding, and the involved authority has to respect this decision. What we see here is a unique hybrid legal system in which a supra-national ad hoc panel is formed that reviews and applies national law (Powell, 2010).

6.2.4 The side agreements to the NAFTA

As noticed above, it is not the intention of the drafters of the NAFTA to create harmonized rules on trade. However, as we may have seen in the case 'S.D. Meyers Inc. v. the Government of Canada' above, this may result in the fear that companies will cross the border just to make use of more flexible regulations. In itself, this is just a side effect of opening the borders to trade. Simultaneously, it may have rather dramatic consequences for controversial issues such as the environment and the wellbeing of employees. After all, companies will most likely prefer to produces in the country with the least strict rules in environmental or employee protection, for the simple reason that they can produce for a lower cost price. To respond to this fear of unwanted negative effects of the NAFTA in terms of environmental issues and employee protection, two side agreements were adopted to the NAFTA: the North American Agreement on Environmental Cooperation, and the North American Agreement on Labour Cooperation.

North American Agreement on Environmental Cooperation (NAAEC)

The goal of the North American Agreement on Environmental Cooperation (NAAEC) is to make sure that economic integration does not 'displace ongoing cooperation and continuous improvement in the environmental performance of each country' (CEC, 2010). To this end, the treaty installs the Commission for Environmental Cooperation, which is responsible for assessing the effects of free trade on the environment, and where possible encourage a combined approach towards environmental policies and law-making. It is hailed for adequately realising this first goal, though there are doubts whether the commission is politically powerful enough to truly contribute to a combined environmental approach amongst the three NAFTA members (Duncan & Mumme, 1997).
Next to that, the Commission monitors whether the Member States implement their environmental laws properly. To this end, two complaint procedures are adopted. One for states towards the other, and one for private parties. Through this latter procedure, NGOs and involved private parties may file a complaint against a member state that allegedly violates its own environmental laws (Art 14 and 15, NAAEC). However, there are some doubts about the effectiveness of this procedure, since the involved CEC institute seems hesitant in reviewing the more general environmental policies, and only limits its competency to narrow topics (Wold et al, 2004).

North American Agreement on Labour Cooperation (NAALC)

A similar approach was mustered in the sphere of labour standards. Typically in the field of labour, the fear for the 'race to the bottom' has always been a source for wide political debate. To this end, the North American Agreement on Labour Cooperation (NAALC) was adopted. The purpose of this treaty is to encourage its member states to 'ensure that its labour laws and regulations provide for high labour standards, consistent with high quality and productivity workplaces, and shall continue to strive to improve those standards in that light' (Art. 2 NAALC). One of the most important aspects here is that individuals are guaranteed the right to effectively invoke these labour standards in a court (Art. 4 NAALC). The Commission for Labour Cooperation was installed to oversee the implementation of the NAALC, as well as complaint procedures.

While it is explicitly not the intention to unify law or create supranational labour law, some common core labour principles are recognized in the first annex to the NAALC, such as the freedom of association, the right to collective bargaining, the right to strike, minimum employment standards, the elimination of discrimination and the protection of migrant workers. In case of an alleged violation of one of those principles, individuals, NGOs, trade unions and human rights advocates may file a so-called 'public communication' against a state. The procedure that follows focuses on the exchange of views, open dialogue and mediation, rather than legal enforcement. The only case in which a government may be fined is in case of persistent pattern of failure to effectively enforce its domestic occupational safety and health, child labour, or minimum wage technical labour standards. Obviously, the advantage of such a procedure is that it leads to an increase in the dialogue between the member states on labour standards, and more awareness of the importance of the wellbeing of employees (Compa, 1999; Kay, 2011). Simultaneously, the disadvantage of such a mechanism is that in practice it hardly leads to enforcement of the labour principles, nor on actually fining states that violate these principles consistently (Brower, 2008). However, considering the fact that this procedure was installed on top of the existing national legal remedies to enforce labour laws, this 'disadvantage' should be weighted in the right proportion.

6.3 The customs union: the SACU

Dating back to 1889, the Southern African Customs Union (SACU) is the oldest customs union in the world. The current member states of this union are Botswana, Lesotho, Namibia, South Africa and Swaziland. Historically, the colonial past of the region played a profound role in the way the union was formed, and reformed. Where in 1889, the customs union had a strong colonial focus, with a dominant position for Great Britain, the reforms in 1910 and 1969 put the now sovereign South African Union in a dominant position both in terms of the distribution of duty incomes and decision-making processes. This was perfectly in line with the apartheid regime that was put into place in South Africa in the period 1948-1994. Since 2002 however, Botswana, Lesotho, Namibia and Swaziland (the so called BLNS countries) were recognized as 'equals' in the SACU system. This is mostly reflected in the fact that the decision-making processes in the Union are now more democratic, instead of South Africa being the sole authority within the Union, and the fact that the BLNS countries receive more income resulting the duties earned in the customs union (Gibb, 2006).

The SACU is characterized by big differences in the economies of its member states (Kirk & Stern, 2003). On the one hand there is South

Africa, one of the biggest and most powerful economies of Africa. On the other hand, there are the BLNS countries, greatly depending on their trade with South Africa. However, also within the BLNS countries there are also big differences. The most notable extremes are Botswana, with an ever-increasing economy and GDP, and Lesotho, one of the poorest countries in the world. Another interesting detail is the dominance of the South African currency, the Rand. Except for Botswana, all the SACU countries are a member of or otherwise linked to the Common Monetary Area in Southern Africa. This means in practice, that the South African rand circulates freely and is an accepted currency in all SACU countries except Botswana. While next to that Lesotho, Namibia, and Swaziland do have their own currencies, their exchange rate is not flexible, but linked to the value of the rand.

Common Monetary Area in Southern Africa

6.3.1 Free trade under the SACU

In the Southern African Customs Union, a free trade zone is established. In practice, this means that there is, with a few exceptions, free trade without tariffs to trade or quantitative restrictions (Art. 18, 2002 SACU Agreement). The main benefit in the SACU lies in the fact that while the member states can do business with one another without tariffs or quantitative restrictions, they uphold a relatively high common barrier to trade to the outside world (Kirk & Stern, 2003).

Common external tariff

It is the common external tariff that characterizes this economic cooperation, for it makes the SACU a customs union. Next to that, the member states harmonized the excise duties on certain products, such as alcohol, fuel, tobacco and luxury products (see for an overview the website of the South African Revenue Service: www.sars.gov.za).

Excise duties

> Excise duties are fixed taxes imposed on certain products.

The obvious difference between excise duties and 'normal' Value Added Tax (VAT) is that an excise duty is a fixed sum, and not depending on the sales price. This results in the fact that the governments imposing this tax are guaranteed a certain income. Practically, this form of taxation is usually applied to discourage the consumption of certain harmful products. These excise duties are, as stated above, harmonized in the SACU zone.

The revenue of both the external tariffs and the excise duties are collected jointly in a Common Revenue Pool. The pool is then distributed between the member states of the SACU, through a rather complex distribution formula (if you really want to know how that works, check: Ngalawa, 2013). This formula is referred to as the Revenue Sharing Formula. Traditionally, the formula is rather favourable to the emerging economies (the BLNS countries). They receive a so-called 'development component', resulting in a slightly higher share of the pool. The background of this practice was to compensate South Africa's dominance in the decision-making processes until 2002. However, since the SACU is now more democratic, the BLNS countries are still allocated their favourable shares, while South Africa will receive the remainder of the Pool. Next to that, South Africa is the 'custody' of the pool, meaning that their Central Bank will financially guarantee the payments to other countries, and even pay their expected shares in advance, to boost the economy.

There are pros and cons to this. The pro is that the BLNS countries enjoy guaranteed payments from the Common Revenue Pool, inserting a stabilizing factor in their economies. Just to put things in perspective, the revenue payments to the BLNS form a significant part of the government income. Occasionally, this has been for countries as Lesotho and Swaziland even over 50 per cent of the total annual governmental budget (Kirk & Stern, 2003). This is simultaneously the big dilemma for the BLNS countries: they might consider themselves too dependent on the SACU trade, or – more directly – on South Africa. After all, when the SACU in general faces economic difficulties, this has its effect on the government budgets of the member states, as we can see in the newspaper item on Namibia. There is another issue in South Africa: while on the one hand the country benefits from economically stable neighbours, the question is raised to what cost this is acceptable. In practice, South Africa pays a large sum of money to their fellow SACU members under the SACU Common Revenue Pool rules. As we can see in the newspaper item below, this is politically a sensitive topic.

Namibia not overly dependent on SACU revenue

BY MATHIAS HAUFIKU

WINDHOEK - The Minister of Finance Saara Kuugongelwa-Amadhila says the country is not overly dependent on revenue from the Southern African Customs Union (SACU).

She says the problems which SACU experienced, especially during the time of the global economic crisis, did present destabilizing threats to the national budget. She made the remarks in the National Assembly on Monday during the finance ministry's budget allocation debate.

'SACU's importance in terms of the ratio of the income coming from SACU has been on a declining trend and that is good for us as a country, because it shows that we are not overly dependent on revenue from SACU,' explained the finance minister. Two parliamentarians, Nahas Angula and Ignatius Shixwameni, wanted to know how the country would generate its own revenue in light of the declining SACU revenue. "Looking on the revenue side, about 30 per cent of our revenue comes from SACU and about 20 per cent from personal income tax. This means that the production sector is not really making much of a contribution," said a worried Angula, who is also the Minister of Defence.

INVESTORS MONTHLY

SA sticks to its guns over SACU revenue deal

BY: LINDA ENSOR

SA was pushing hard for the 'unfair' revenue-sharing agreement between the Southern African Customs Union (SACU) members to be reworked, both in terms of the formula itself and the way in which the money was used once it had been distributed, Finance Minister Nhlanhla Nene said on Tuesday.

SA was the 'the cash cow' in the arrangement and had encountered resistance when it raised issues, the minister said.

He said a proposal would be presented to this year's as yet unscheduled annual meeting of the heads of state of SA, Botswana, Lesotho, Namibia and Swaziland for them to resolve the matter 'once and for all'.

(...)

The five SACU countries share a common external tariff and share the proceeds of customs and excise duties in accordance with a separate revenue-sharing formula for each element.

In addition, a developmental subsidy is built into the excise duty formula so that SA can aid its poorer neighbours.

This results in significant revenue flows to the other four countries in the union.

6.3.2 The organizational structure of the SACU

In general, it needs to be noted here that all amendments to existing SACU treaties need to be signed and ratified by the heads of states and governments of the member states. In case this is required, a summit is organized in which all governments are represented by their heads of state.

Council of Ministers

However, on a more permanent basis, the highest organ within the SACU is the Council of Ministers (Art. 8, 2002 SACU Agreement). This council is composed of all ministers of finance and trade of each member state. The council oversees the implementation of the SACU agreements. To this end, the council – amongst others – approves the external tariffs, excise duties, and matters that relate to the Common Reserve Pool. The council – as do all SACU bodies – adopts decision by consensus: a huge difference with the past, in which South Africa had the sole right to decision-making in the SACU (Art. 17). Furthermore, the Council appoints most other SACU bodies.

Customs Union Commission

On an executional level, there is the Customs Union Commission (Art. 9 2002 SACU Agreement). This commission, appointed by the council, executes the council's decisions. In this light, its most important task is to oversee and manage the Common Revenue Pool. Substantially, the commission is supported by five so called Technical Liaison Committees. These committees assist and advise the commission in the field of agriculture, customs, trade and industry, transport and finance.

Secretariat

There is a secretariat, chaired by an executive secretary (Art. 10 SACU Agreement). This institution is responsible for the day to day administration of the SACU. It is located in Windhoek, Namibia. In practice, the executive secretariat plays a strong facilitating role, in which it contributes to implementing the SACU agreements by hosting meetings of SACU bodies and coordinating trade negotiations.

6.3.3 Dispute settlement under the SACU

Currently, the SACU countries are preparing to set up an ad-hoc tribunal, that may adopt legally binding decisions in case of a dispute regarding the SACU agreements (Art. 13, 2002 SACU agreement).

6.4 The common market: MERCOSUR

The Mercado Común del Sur (MERCOSUR), which is Spanish for Southern Common Market, is an example of a common market. On the one hand, this trading bloc seeks to realize free trade for goods and the recourses necessary to produce them: personnel, services and capital. On the other hand, political and legislative cooperation is limited and hardly harmonized. The MERCOSUR was initially established by the treaty of Asuncion, in 1991. Its original members were Argentina, Brazil, Paraguay and Uruguay. Since 2012, Venezuela is a full member. In 2015, Bolivia was accepted as a full member of MERCOSUR on a Presidential Summit, however, at the time of writing, the accession still needed to be approved by the parliaments of some member states. Furthermore, several countries joined as associate countries, and observer countries. The associate countries are Chile, Peru, Colombia and Ecuador. These countries on the one hand enjoy the more favourable treatment that is mustered within the MERCOSUR zone, but do not participate fully in decision-making processes nor do they apply the common external tariffs to trade. The observer countries are New Zeeland, Mexico and Japan. While these countries participate in the summits and gatherings of the MERCOSUR, they have no voting rights nor do they make use of any trade rules that apply in the MERCOSUR zone.

6.4.2 Free trade under the MERCOSUR

The urge to establish the MERCOSUR was twofold. First, the trade bloc was create to counterbalance other trade blocs such as the European Union and the NAFTA. Second, the customs union was installed to create more stability in the region. Especially Brazil and Argentina have a long history of conflicts. The MERCOSUR was considered as a means to facilitate a more friendly relation between the two countries, based on mutual trade benefits.

Therefore, the MERCOSUR goals laid down in Article 1 of the treaty of Asuncion are ambitious.
'This common market shall involve:

- The free movement of goods, services and factors of production between countries through, inter alia, the elimination of customs duties and non-tariff restrictions on the movement of goods, and any other equivalent measures;
- The establishment of a common external tariff and the adoption of a common trade policy in relation to third states or groups of states, and the co-ordination of positions in regional and international economic and commercial forums;
- The co-ordination of macroeconomic and sectoral policies between the States Parties in the areas of foreign trade, agriculture, industry, fiscal and monetary matters, foreign exchange and capital, services, customs,

transport and communications and any other areas that may be agreed upon, in order to ensure proper competition between the States Parties;
- The commitment by States Parties to harmonize their legislation in the relevant areas in order to strengthen the integration process.'

However, the coordination of politics and law did not quite evolve, due to differences in political insights between the member states. Especially in the late nineties and the greater part of the zeroes, the progress in economic integration was halted by tensions and disputes between its members (Gómez-Mera, 2009). A change in political leadership in especially Argentina and Brazil led to more a protectionist approach towards trade, resulting in various trade disputes. Another issue was the accession of Venezuela in 2012, as you can see in example 6.6.

EXAMPLE 6.6

Killing farmers and democracy
Paraguay was against the admission of Venezuela, due to the fact that it was concerned about the lack of democracy in Venezuela. It is ironic therefore, that in 2012 Paraguay was suspended as a member of the MERCOSUR, due to the fact that its president – Fernando Lugo – was removed from his office following the death of farmers in a confrontation with the Paraguayan police. The other MERCOSUR countries held that such incidents were not in compliance with the democratic goals of the common market. Simultaneously, Venezuela was promptly admitted as a MERCOSUR member, circumventing the veto of Paraguay by its suspension.

The future will tell whether the MERCOSUR will predominantly remain a common market facilitating free trade, or move towards the direction of a more integrated political unity, such as an economic union (Arieti, 2006).

6.4.2 The organizational structure of the MERCOSUR

In essence, the MERCOSUR is an intergovernmental organization. This means that decision-making is done by consensus.

Common Market Council

The Common Market Council is the highest authoritative body in the MERCOSUR. It is composed of all ministers of foreign affairs and economic affairs of all Member States (Art. 11. treaty of Asuncion). This is a non-permanent body, for it meets twice a year, and furthermore whenever it is convened when necessary. At least once a year, the heads of states of the Member States participate in its meetings. The mandate of the Council is to oversee the implementation of the treaty of Asuncion and other MERCOSUR agreements. Next to that, it is the forum through which trade policy is discussed and when possible harmonized. As stated above, this has been proved to be difficult in the past (Art. 10 treaty of Asuncion).

Common Market Group

The Common Market Group is the highest executive organ of the MERCOSUR. It is composed of four permanent and four alternate members of each country. The members should represent the ministries of foreign affairs and economic affairs, and the central banks of each country. The mandate of the Common Market Group is to monitor the compliance of the member state with the MERCOSUR agreements. Next to that, the Group may propose draft decisions to the Council, when they see the urge to adjust certain trade rules. Furthermore, the Group may adopt its own decisions and policies in order to implement the MERCOSUR agreements (Art. 14, Protocol of Ouro Preto). The Group is supported by several working subgroups and specialized assemblies in which part of the negotiations are conducted and through which advice and knowledge is gained.

Trade Commission

On a more permanent basis, the Trade Commission deals with executive trade matters. The commission supports the Common Market Group. It is mandated to oversee the daily trade affairs that relate to implementing the MERCOSUR agreements (Art. 16 Protocol of Ouro Preto). This commission is composed of four permanent members and four alternate (flexible) members per member state.

MERCOSUR parliament

One of the challenges of the MERCOSUR has always been to uphold the domestic ambition to integrate economically. Due to changes in the political landscape of the MERCOSUR countries, its progress has been not as smooth as was originally foreseen. To solve this (Art. 25 Protocol of Ouro Preto), and to include a direct democratic element in the institutional structure of the MERCOSUR, an intergovernmental parliament was installed in 2007. This parliament was originally named the Joint Parliamentary Commission, although currently, one speaks of the MERCOSUR parliament. It is composed of 188 parliamentarians: 76 from Brazil, 43 from Argentina, 33 from Venezuela, 18 from Uruguay and 18 from Paraguay. The Parliament has limited powers, and may at most adopt recommendations to the Common Market Council or the Common Market Group (Art. 26 Protocol of Ouro Preto).

Structural Convergence Fund of MERCOSUR

Since 2010, there is the Structural Convergence Fund of MERCOSUR. This fund is used to invest in regional infrastructure to stimulate and facilitate trade. In practice, the fund is allocated to make lesser developed regions more competitive. This means that Brazil provides for about 70 per cent of the fund, while most of the money is invested in Paraguay and Uruguay (www.mercosur.int/focem, 2015).

Administrative Secretariat

Finally, there is an Administrative Secretariat, to provide for operational support, seated in Montevideo and headed by a Director. This body is truly an administrative institution, mostly archiving documents, circulating information and providing for logistic support when needed, such as the organization of a summit (Art. 32, Protocol of Ouru Preto).

6.4.3 Dispute settlement

The MERCOSUR member states have adopted a dispute settlement procedure. This system has gradually evolved in several steps (Vinuesa, 2005). Under its most recent revision by the Protocol of Olivos, the procedure mostly involves negotiation and arbitration rather than supranational litigation. The proceedings are inter-governmental, which means that private parties have no direct legal remedies based on MERCOSUR agreements.
In case of a dispute over MERCOSUR agreements, the first step is always to negotiate a solution between the involved State Parties. If this does not

work out, national governments may start a procedure before an ad hoc arbitrational tribunal. However, it needs to be noted here that a government may choose to do so on behalf of a private party. This means that private parties are relying on the willingness of a government to invoke the MERCOSUR agreements. These ad-hoc arbitrational tribunals have proven to be controversial since the outcome of its judgements were not quite consistent. To tackle this, and guarantee a more consistent interpretation of the MERCOSUR agreements, the Protocol of Olivos provides for a Permanent Court of Review. This Court reviews decisions of ad hoc tribunals on the request of the involved parties, and has a final say in the matter. An example of a case before an ad hoc arbitrational tribunal can be found in example 6.7.

EXAMPLE 6.7

Burning used tyres in Brazil: a trade dispute

In 2002, Uruguay started proceedings before a MERCOSUR ad hoc arbitrational tribunal against Brazil. The dispute concerned Brazilian trade laws that restricted the import of remodelled/used tyres from Uruguay. In fact, the usage or burning of used tyres is a serious environmental problem, in particular in Brazil. To tackle this, Brazil banned the import on used tyres, and fined importers who would still import used tyres from abroad. However, this affected existing commercial routes between Uruguay and Brazil, and created a sudden – not anticipated – impact on the Uruguay markets. The trade in used tyres had existed for years, and has always been a legal business. The ad-hoc tribunal decided that the Brazilian law was against the MERCOSUR principles of free trade, and ruled that Brazil had to adjust its laws. After all, one of the MECOSUR principles of free trade is that countries may not impose any new restrictions to trade, as is stipulated in Article 1 of the treaty of Asuncion (Ad hoc Arbitrational Tribunal, 2002). Brazil did comply, mainly by not enforcing the fines on existing trade relations.
An interesting side note here is that Brazil faced a similar case before the WTO Dispute Settlement Body. The European Union started proceedings against Brazil regarding its trade laws on used tyres. However, this time, Brazil was more successful, for it could invoke article XX(b) of the GATT, which provides for exemptions to the ban on trade barriers when it is necessary to protect human life or health (DSB, 2009). An equivalent provision cannot be found in the MERCOSUR Agreements.

Summary

6

- There are various forms in which regional economic cooperation can take place. These are usually the following:
  - A free trade zone, which is a zone in which the involved countries agreed to abolish tariffs and quotas to trade;
  - A customs union, which is a free trade zone in which the countries harmonized their external tariffs and quotas to trade;
  - A common market, which is a customs union that extends to services, personnel and capital;
  - An economic union, which is a customs union in which economic laws and policies are harmonized;
  - A monetary union, which is an economic union with a shared monetary unit.

- Typically, the integration of economics goes hand in hand with fierce political debate and struggle.

- An example of a free trade zone is the North Atlantic Free Trade Zone (NAFTA)
  - In the NAFTA, import and export tariffs are increasingly banned, as well as quotas.
  - The more favourable rules within the zone only apply to goods that originate from the NAFTA Member States. To determine whether a product originates from a NAFTA country, rules of origin apply.
    - Products that are wholly obtained or produced in the NAFTA region;
    - Products that are partly composed of materials coming from non-NAFTA countries but still considered as originating from the NAFTA zone.
  - Regarding most trade laws, the most favoured nation principle applies amongst the NAFTA countries.
  - The NAFTA is governed by the Free Trade Commission, and has a Secretariat.
  - The NAFTA has a profound dispute settlement system, in which four types of procedures can be used in case of an alleged violation of the NAFTA Articles. These are the so-called Chapter 20, 11, 14 and 19 procedures.
  - Two side agreements were closed to protect the environment and the wellbeing of employees against a race to the bottom in flexible rules between the NAFTA Member States: the North American Agreement on Environmental Cooperation, and the North American Agreement on Labour Cooperation.

- An example of a customs union is the South African Customs Union (SACU).
  - In the SACU, a free trade zone is established;
  - A common external tariff is imposed on all non-SACU products;
  - Excise duties within the SACU zone are harmonized;
  - The incomes of the common external tariff and excise duties are collected jointly in a common revenue pool, and distributed amongst the member states through a distribution formula, guaranteeing the governments a certain income.
  - The SACU is governed by several institutions:
    - The Council of Ministers, which oversees the implementation of the SACU agreements;
    - The Customs Union Commission, which is the executive body;
    - The secretariat, responsible for the administration of the SACU and coordination of trade negotiations.
  - An ad hoc-tribunal to settle disputes is expected.

- An example of a common market is the Mercado Común del Sur (MERCOSUR).
  - The Mercosur was intended to be a common market in which economic laws were harmonized. This has not yet been fulfilled as planned. However, there is a free trade zone, and a common external tariff.
  - Decisions within the MERCOSUR is done by consensus.
  - The MERCOSUR is governed by various institutions:
    - The Common Market Council, which is the highest authoritative body, overseeing the implementation of the MERCOSUR agreements;
    - The Common Market Group, which is the highest executive organ, supported by the Trade Commission;
    - The MERCOSUR parliament adopts recommendations for the Common Market Council or Common Market Group, and strengthens the domestic implementation of the MERCOSUR agreements;
    - The Structural Convergence Fund of MERCOSUR invests in regional infrastructure to facilitate trade;
    - The Administrative Secretariat provides for operational support.
  - Dispute settlement regarding MECRCOSUR agreements is firstly done through mediation. When this fails, an ad-hoc tribunal may be installed. Decisions of ad-hoc tribunals may be reviewed by the Permanent Court of Review. Private parties may request their government to start procedures on their behalf.

Practice questions

Open questions

6.1 What are the main pros and cons of the SACU Common Revenue Pool?

6.2 Please read the case 'Burning used tyres in Brazil: a trade dispute' in this chapter again. How would this dispute be resolved if the conflicting parties were both NAFTA countries?

6.3 Please read the case 'Burning used tyres in Brazil: a trade dispute' in this chapter again. How would this dispute be resolved if the conflicting parties were both SACU countries?

6.4 Which part of the common market has not quite evolved within the MERCOSUR, and why?

Essay question

The international economic cooperation amongst the NAFTA, SACU and MERCOSUR is fundamentally different. Write an essay in which you point out the main features of these differences.

Multiple choice questions

6.1 In the NAFTA, a product constructed of foreign (non-NAFTA countries) basic materials but where the value to the product is predominantly added within the NAFTA is:
a considered an originating product
b partly considered an originating product
c not considered an originating product

6.2 The NAFTA rules of origin are predominantly adopted to avoid:
a regulatory competition
b abuse of dominant market positions
c trade deflection

6.3 The side agreements to the NAFTA were adopted to avoid:
a regulatory competition
b abuse of dominant market positions
c trade deflection

6.4 The highest political organ of the SACU is the:
a Customs Union Commission
b Council of Ministers
c Executive Secretary

HIPS!
THAT'S NOT LIQUOR!... THAT STUFF DOESN'T GET YOU DRUNK!
DIJON
CASSIS
Sandor

7 The European Union

In this chapter, we will explore an economic and monetary union: the European Union. First, we will discuss the historic background of economic integration in Europe, and the supranational character of European Union law. Then, we will explore free trade in Europe, in which the four freedoms to trade, harmonization in trade law and competition rules play a profound role. Furthermore, we will briefly explain the organizational structure of the EU, and last, hoe disputes are settled by the European Court of Justice.

7.1 Economic integration in Europe

The forming of the European Union (EU), and its predecessors, must be viewed in the light of war and peace. The lesson learned from the Second World War was that economic integration would be a key to lasting peace. Therefore, in 1952, Belgium, France, (West)-Germany, Italy, Luxembourg and the Netherlands installed the European Coal and Steel Community. Since coal and steel were the most important materials for weapon production, it was believed that mutual dependence on trade in these basic materials would guarantee peaceful relations between the former combatting countries. Based on similar ideas, the European Atomic Energy Community was established in 1985. However, the economic cooperation did not stop here. Gradually, throughout the years, the nature of the economic cooperation became more intense. From the creation of a common market in 1958, economic cooperation progressed through a single market in 1987, an economic union in 1993, and a monetary union in 1999 (Fairhurst, 2012). Also, the number of participating member states increased from 6 in 1958 to 28 in 2015.

It needs to be noted here that not all EU member states are simultaneously a member of the monetary union. For instance, the United Kingdom is a EU member, but chose not to participate in the monetary union. In 2016, the UK held a referendum regarding their EU membership, and decided to leave the EU. It remains to be seen how this so-called 'Brexit' will take shape.

Brexit

The European Union is characterized by its supranational law and organization. The EU legislative bodies and the European Court of Justice have played a profound role in the forming of European Law: a field of law in its own right that is applicable in the domestic legal orders of its member states.

7.1.1 Supranational law

Already in the early days of European economic integration, the European Court of Justice (ECJ) ruled in two ground-breaking verdicts that European law is supranational, as you may see into more detail in example 7.1.

Directly applicable

Superior

This means two things. First, European law is directly applicable in its member states. This means that each citizen may invoke European law effectively. This is a rarity in international law, since international standards are mostly rules between states. In Europe, the individual can use European law to stand his ground. Second, European law is superior to domestic law. This means that all domestic legislation that is not in compliance with European law may not be applied. Instead, the European standard should be used.

EXAMPLE 7.1

The Van Gend en Loos and COSTA v. ENEL cases

In two ground-breaking rulings, the European Court of Justice recognized that European Union law is supranational. In the Van Gend en Loos ruling (ECJ, Case 26/62, 1963), the Court held that EU law was directly applicable. In the COSTA/ENEL ruling (ECJ, Case 6/64, 1964), the Court recognized the supremacy of EU law over domestic law.

Van Gend en Loos

The Dutch transport company Van Gend en Loos imported basic materials for the production of plastic from Germany. However, the Dutch customs authority charged an import tariff on each transport. According to Van Gend en Loos, this was in clear violation of an Article that is now equivalent to Article 30 of the Treaty on the Functioning of the European Union (TFEU). This Article prohibits all custom duties on imports and exports between Member States. As it seems, the Dutch government did not yet implement this European standard in the domestic legal order. The Dutch customs agency held that an individual or company could not invoke European standards, and therefore, the Van Gend en Loos claim was invalid. However, the European Court of Justice thought otherwise, and ruled that European Law had direct effect: Article 30 TFEU could be invoked by individuals such as Van Gend en Loos. The fact that a government was neglectful in implementing European rules did not mean that individuals should suffer the consequences. Ultimately, the customs authority had to pay back the money Van Gend en Loos had paid under the disputed tariff.

COSTA v. ENEL
In the early sixties, the Italian government nationalized the electricity sector. Mister Flaminio Costa disagreed with this course of affairs, because he owned shares in a small private electricity company that was now being merged into a state owned company: ENEL. As reprisal, he refused to pay his electricity bills, with a total sum of almost 2000 Lire. In the Italian court, he argued that the nationalization was against European Law. The Italian government however, held that under no conditions, a domestic court could set aside national law. In the end, the European Court of Justice ruled that in this case the nationalisation of the electricity sector was a matter the European Commission should deal with, since the commission was competent to review such acts against European Law. *In casu* therefore, mister Costa did not win the argument. However, the court was very clear on one thing: the Italian government was wrong in assuming that no domestic court could set aside domestic law. After all, European law was of a higher legal order than Italian law. The national courts therefore should always let European Law prevail over contrary Italian law.

7.2 Free trade under the EU

In the European Union, the concept of free trade is organized in three main areas:
1 The four freedoms;
2 Harmonization of law;
3 Competition rules.

In essence, the four freedoms constitute the common market in which there is free movement of goods, people, services and capital. To avoid regulatory competition, many economic laws have been harmonized. Next to that, the rules of the game for companies are also equal, in which they are bound to 'behave' themselves and not distort the markets. To this end, in the EU, competition rules are adopted.

7.2.1 The four freedoms

In the European Union, free trade is realized by recognizing four fundamental freedoms: the free movement of goods, personnel, services and capital. While all four are indisputably important to promote free trade, the evolvement of the free movement of goods usually attracts most attention. Not in the least because the legal doctrine of the free movement of goods has set the agenda of the development of the other freedoms.

The free movement of goods
The free movement of goods is in fact built around two concepts: first, a ban on all fiscal restrictions, and second, the elimination of all quantitative restrictions to trade in goods.

Fiscal restrictions

To start with the ban on fiscal restrictions, this prohibition is specified in two articles: Article 30 and Article 110 TFEU. The ban on custom duties is stipulated in Article 30, a logical consequence of the fact that the origin of the EU is a customs union (Art. 28 TFEU). To make sure member states do not circumvent this ban by the clever use of national taxes, Article 110

TFEU prohibits the use of national taxation to discriminate against foreign products.

Article 30 stipulates that any charges at some point relate to the fact that a product crosses a border between EU Member States are illegal. This does not only include the obvious customs or charges that relate to import or export. After all, in this phase of economic integration, such duties hardly exist anymore. However, the Court of Justice built a solid chain of case law around this provision, understanding its content broadly. The main things you should know about that are the following rules:

- All import and export duties are forbidden, even if they are not intended to protect a market, but instead should serve a social cause. For instance: an Italian export tax on products of an artistic, historical and archaeological or ethnographic nature to protect their cultural heritage was considered in contradiction with Article 30 TFEU (EJC, case 7/68, 1968).
- All charges having an equivalent effect are equally prohibited. Sometimes a Member State charges a fee when a product enters or leaves their country, but does not name it an import or export duty. However, whatever the name of the fee is, when it relates to import or export, it is in principal forbidden. For instance, an Italian fee to export products that was charged to cover the costs of collecting data on trade trends was considered in violation with Article 30 TFEU (EJC, case 24/68, 1969). While in essence the purpose of the fee was to contribute to better market insights, which would also be beneficial to the exporting companies, such a fee cannot be justified under Article 30 TFEU.
- The only exception to the above is any fee that is used to directly cover the costs of services provided for by a member state to an importing/exporting company, such as the storage of goods, or the carrying out of inspections. However, such a fee must be proportional to the actual costs of the service provided for. Furthermore, when it concerns inspections, they should be required by the European legislature. For instance, member states may perform inspections on living animals when they cross a border within the EU under Council Regulation 1/2005. The obvious purpose of this regulation is to promote the wellbeing of animals and safeguard public health.

In completion to the ban on import/export duties in Article 30 TFEU, Article 31 stipulates that the European Council (on the proposal of the Commission) is authorized to fix common external duties.

Article 110 reads that internal – national – taxation may not be abused to discriminate against foreign products. After all, Member States could easily circumvent Article 30 TFEU by imposing higher national taxes on products that are predominantly produced in other member states, thereby favouring the domestically produced goods. So, while technically these taxes are not an import or export tax, and applied to all products, they still might constitute a barrier to trade. Therefore, Article 110 forbids discrimination of foreign products through national taxation, such as Value Added Tax or excise duties. In this context, the complexity lies in the question whether a national tax discriminates a foreign product. According to the Article, such taxes may not – directly or indirectly – discriminate similar or competing products, see example 7.2.

EXAMPLE 7.2

Beer, wine: what's the difference, we all get drunk…

In Europe, alcoholic products have been used for ages. However, each country has its expertise. Some countries excel in producing wine, while others are more successful in producing beer or strong liquor, such as whisky. Free trade allows each country to export their product to another country. However, governments, proud of their domestic products, seem to have been protective of their domestic production in this field. Occasionally, the European Court of Justice was confronted with complaints against Member States that imposed excise duties on alcoholic drinks, except the particular drink that was produced domestically. Here are two examples.

In the BENELUX, a common agreement on excise duties resulted in the fact that a special excise duty was charged on Portuguese Madeira, French red wine, French champagne, Italian vermouth and Spanish sherry. However, fruit wines – mostly produced in the BENELUX – were exempted from these charges. The European Court of Justice ruled that since all these products were made of the same kind of agricultural products and by the same process of natural fermentation, the products were likewise products. Therefore, the BENELUX excise duties were in violation with Article 110 TFEU (ECJ Case C-367/93 to C-377/93).

In Great Britain, additional excise duties were charged on wines. It is however no secret that the British do not necessarily excel in the production of wine, but instead produce an enormous amount of beers. Although, such an excise duty was never charged on beers. Of course whine is a different type of product than beer. However, the Court of Justice considered that when taking into account the relevant market, wine and beer were competing products. The result of the excise duties on wine therefore was that the domestic market of British beers was protected against the competition of the imported wines from – amongst others – France. Not surprisingly, the Court ruled that the British duties were in violation of Article 110 TFEU (EJC case 170/78, 1983).

Quantitative restrictions

Not only fiscal restrictions are prohibited. Article 34 and 35 TFEU also prohibits quantitative restrictions on imports and exports. In fact, quantitative restrictions such as quotas are barely an issue within the European Union anymore. Member States know very well that such measures are inconsistent with the TFEU. In the rare occasion in which a quota, directly discriminating foreign goods, is upheld, this will probably fall under the regime of Article 36 TFEU. In this Article, quantitative restrictions to trade may be justified under strict conditions, as will be explained below. Of more importance in this context is the more subtle discrimination caused by domestic legislation of EU member states that create barriers to trade, while they are not a quantitative restriction in itself. In a rich collection of case law, the Court of Justice has further specified to what extent the so-called 'Measures Having Equivalent Effect' (MEE) to quantitative restrictions are in violation with the Articles 34 and 35 TFEU.

Measure Having Equivalent Effect

A Measure Having Equivalent Effect (MEE) is a domestic rule that has the same effect as a quantitative restriction and therefore has a discriminatory effect.

So, in essence, the domestic law does not constitute quotas to trade, but may have the same effect. A Measure Having Equivalent Effect may be distinctively applicable, meaning that they only apply to imported or exported products. Examples are obliged import or export licenses, additional inspections or registration requirements, or more complex commercial rules that do not apply to domestic products. Such measures in itself do not constitute a quota, but most certainly may hinder trade, putting the import or export product in a disadvantage. Therefore, it has the same *effect* as a quantitative restriction.
A Measure Having Equivalent Effect may also be indistinctively applicable. This means that while the measure does not aim to discriminate against import or export goods, it still has a discriminatory effect. In one of the first rulings on the matter, the Court of Justice gives us a clear example of such an indistinctively applicable measure in the Dassonville ruling (example 7.2).

EXAMPLE 7.2

The Dassonville ruling

Indistinctively applicable MEE: whiskey on the rocks

The two Belgian brothers Dassonville own a liquor store in the South of Belgian, near the French border. They sell, amongst others, Scottish whisky. However, in the true spirit of free trade, they do not buy the whisky directly from the Scottish producers, but indirectly, from French wholesale agencies. After all, it is much more efficient to purchase all whiskies at ones through a middle-agency than buying them individually from all producers. Unfortunately, there seems to be a problem: Belgian law demands that for the sales of whisky, a certificate of origin is required. In French law, such a certificate is not required for the sale of whisky. Not surprisingly, the French wholesaler is unable to provide for the certificates, leaving the Belgian brothers with a problem. The Dassonville brothers come up with a provisional solution to the problem by creating fake certificates of origin. When the Brothers were caught by the Belgian authorities and fined for this, they invoked Article 34 TFEU. The brothers held that the Belgian law constituted a barrier to trade.

The purpose of the Belgian rule was to make sure that illegally brewed spirits would not circulate on the Belgian market, not to hinder trade. However, as it seems, this rule practically resulted in a trade barrier when Belgian retailers want to purchase their whiskies in France. After all, it was almost impossible to buy whiskey in France and simultaneously obtain these certificates of origin. The European Court of Justice ruled that while this was not a direct limitation to trade, such as quotas, it had a similar effect. The consequence was that the Belgian brothers won their case, and Belgium had to adjust its laws (ECJ, case 8/74, 1974).

In another ruling, the Cassis de Dijon ruling (example 7.3), the Court further specified its view on indistinctively applicable Measures Having Equivalent Effect. Two rules can be deduced from this ruling:

- The principle of mutual recognition: when a product is lawfully put into circulation in one member state, this product may be sold in other member states under the same conditions;
- The rule of reason doctrine: the principle of mutual recognition does not apply when a member state may invoke a rule of reason, which are for example the effectiveness of fiscal supervision, the protection of public health, the fairness of commercial transactions and the defence of the consumer.

EXAMPLE 7.3

The Cassis de Dijon ruling

Real liquor should contain serious alcohol!?

A German company planned to import the popular French liquor 'Cassis de Dijon'. However, a German law caused difficulties. This law stipulated that something can only be sold as liquor in Germany when it contained at least 25 per cent of alcohol. Cassis de Dijon had an alcohol permillage of 15 to 20 per cent, depending on the product type. According to the German government this rule was perfectly justified for two main reasons. First, the rule was intended to protect human health, for it would discourage the consumption of alcoholic drinks with a modest alcohol percentage, and therefore making the drinking of Cassis de Dijon types of product socially accepted. After all, drinking strong liquor will probably not be socially accepted that easily. Second, the German government claimed that the minimum percentage of alcohol was intended to create fair competition. After all, the alcohol component in the drinks is usually the most expensive. Allowing liquor to be sold under a lower percentage would put the producers like Cassis de Dijon in a competitive advantage, since they have access to the same market, but do not produce with a comparable amount of the relatively expensive alcohol.

The principle of mutual recognition

However, despite those arguments, the European Court of Justice considered the German laws in violation with Article 34 TFEU. The Court considered that in a true free market economy, products that are lawfully produced at one domestic market should have access to the domestic markets of the other Member States without hindering. This is also named the 'principle of mutual recognition'.

The rule of reason

The Court acknowledged on the other hand that in the case of a MEE that is indistinctively applicable, member states may uphold legislation that discriminates when they can invoke a rule of reason. Such a rule is then a justification for the discrimination. The court clarified that such rules of reasons could be the effectiveness of fiscal supervision, the protection of public health, the fairness of commercial transactions and the defence of the consumer. However, in this case, the Court ruled that the German arguments were not convincing. Consequentially, the German government had to adjust its laws (ECJ, Case 120/78, 1979).

7

However, this principle of mutual recognition opened too many possibilities for individuals or companies to try legislation in court, and demand adjustment of domestic laws on a wide variety of themes. After all, many laws and regulation at some point have an effect on international trade, since the differences in law between member states will have some effect on import or export. To this end, the court of justice changed its course in the famous Keck and Mithouard ruling. In short, the court ruled that indistinctively applicable MEE that concern a sales modality were not in conflict with EU law, as long as all market participants were equally affected by this standard.

Sales modality

A sales modality is a trade rule about the circumstances under which a product can be sold.

Examples of sales modalities are rules on opening hours, dumping, or rules on advertisement. Such rules have in common that these rules say little about the product in itself, but rather say something about the circumstances under which the products may be sold. This means that in essence, the regime as developed in the Dassonville and Cassis de Dijon ruling applies to laws that relate to the product itself. For sales modalities, the Keck et Mithouard ruling applies (example 7.4).

EXAMPLE 7.4

The Keck et Mithouard ruling

Supermarket managers & sales modalities

Two supermarket managers in Strasbourg were prosecuted in France for selling Picon beer and Sati coffee below its cost price. In the French law, this was prohibited. However, in some other European Union Member States, such a prohibition did not exist. The supermarket managers claimed that based on the principle of mutual recognition, as was recognized in the Cassis de Dijon ruling, the French law should be adjusted.
However, this was one bridge too far for the European Court of Justice. Ruling in favour of Keck and Mithouard would simply overstretch the competencies and effects of the European Court and European law. Therefore, the Court decided to adjust it course, and ruled that MEE that are indistinctively applicable but relate to a sales modality are not in conflict with Article 34 TFEU, as long as all market participants are affected the same way in the involved domestic market. In other words: a member state may uphold laws that indirectly discriminate as long as this law says something about the circumstances under which a product is sold, and not about the product itself. The law then, must be applied to all market participants and have a similar effect on these participants. In the case of the prohibition to sell below cost price, this certainly was the case. After all: the rule is a sales modality, and all market participants on the French market are equally affected by this rule. Consequentially, Keck and Mithouard lost their case (ECJ, Cases C-267/91 and C-268/91, 1993).

Exceptions

In general, an exemption to the prohibition to quantitative restrictions is stipulated in Article 36 TFEU. While the Article is narrowly understood by the

Court, member states may still discriminate against imported or exported goods...

> '... on grounds of public morality, public policy or public security; the protection of health and life of humans, animals or plants; the protection of national treasures possessing artistic, historic or archaeological value; or the protection of industrial and commercial property.' (Art. 36 TFEU)

An example of a justified ban to a product in the European Union is the 'mad cows' case (example 7.5), in which British meat was banned from the markets of the other EU Member States since the BSE outbreak.

EXAMPLE 7.5

Mad cows & strange ministers
In the early nineties, British cows appeared to be affected by the BSE syndrome (also, more known as the 'mad cow disease'). Therefore, the other EU member states banned British meat from their markets for ten years (1996-2006). The British complained about this course of action, because it was considered a barrier to trade. The British minister of Agriculture of that time, John Gummer, even went this far to eat British meat with his four year old daughter in front of the press to demonstrate that there was nothing to fear about British meat (BBC news, 2000). However, the ban was in the end justified under Article 36 TFEU, for it was a proportionate means to protect human health. After all, the BSE syndrome could cause the Creutzfeldt Jakob disease with humans after consuming the meat, which can lead to someone's death.

A schematic overview of the EU free movement of goods can be found in figure 7.1.

The free movement of persons

One of the main characteristics of the European Union is the free movement of persons. Originally, this right was exclusively reserved for EU nationals who wished to work in another EU country. However, gradually, the principle of free movement of persons has been broadened significantly. Currently, the free movement of workers, establishment and services is quite intertwined, and needs to be understood all together. The general idea is that free movement of persons contributes to the establishment of a free market economy. After all, one needs workers and self-employed people to produce and sell goods. It would not make sense to regulate the free trade of goods in such a profound way as described above on the one hand, and restrict free movement of persons on the other hand. That would still constitute considerable barriers to trade. To this end, the free movement of persons was developed in the European Union.

European Citizenship

In general, all citizens of the EU Member States automatically enjoy the status of being a European citizen. This means, amongst others, that they have 'the right to move and reside freely within the territory of the Member States' (Art. 20 TFEU). Two questions need to be addressed here. First, who can invoke this right, and second, what does this right to move and reside exactly mean? In response to both questions, one needs to take into account the so-called 'free movement of citizens directive', that further specifies Article 20 TFEU (Directive 2004/38/EC, 2004).

FIGURE 7.1 The free movement of goods in the European Union

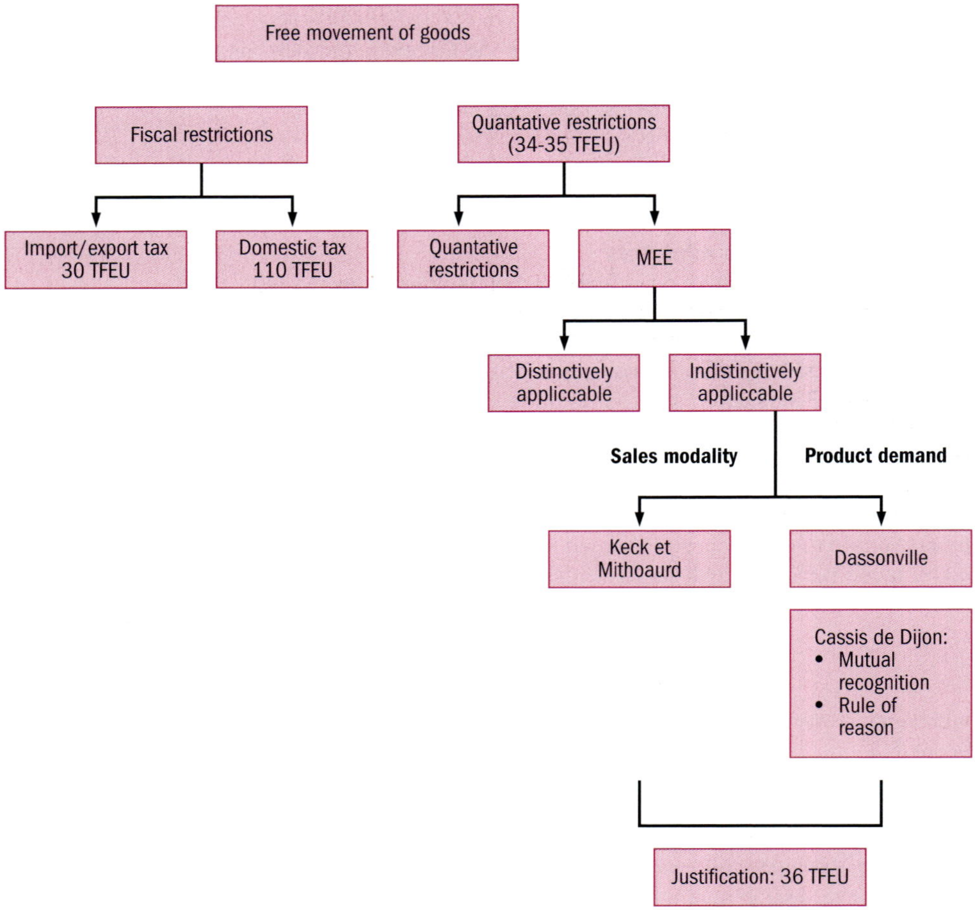

In response to the first question: the right to move and reside is not exclusively reserved for those who are economically active, or are looking for a job. Although this right originally was intended to be a reaffirmation of existing rights to movement, the Court of Justice musters a broad understanding. This resulted in the fact that the right applies to all European citizens, and is not restricted to (potential) workers or self-employed people, as you can see in the case study of Zhu and Chen. Furthermore, the right extends to non-EU citizens who are a family member of a European citizen and accompanies or joints this citizen. This includes for instance spouses, registered partners, direct descendants and relatives in a descending line (such as s father, mother, grandfather, grandmother).

In response to the second question, there are four degrees in which European citizens may enter and reside in another country.

- The first three months of residence: every EU citizen is entitled to enter any other EU country, without any formal requirement (Art. 6, Directive 2004/38/EC, 2004). This means that visa or other formalities that relate to migration are banned. In essence, a host state may not reject this right of residence, as long as the migrant does not 'become an unreasonable burden on the social assistance system of the host Member State'(Art. 14, Directive 2004/38/EC, 2004). See for an application of this principle case study 7.1, on the website.
- More than three months up to five years: every citizen is entitled to reside in any other EU country, as long as she/he fulfils one of the following conditions: 1) either the migrant works or is self-employed, 2) or has a healthcare insurance and is sufficient resources for themselves ad their family not to become a burden on the social assistance system of the host Member State, 3) or is a student meeting the same requirements (healthcare insurance and sufficient resources).
- Five years or more: if a migrant has resided lawfully in the host state for a period of five years, he and his family have the right to permanently reside in the host state. The 'five year rule' is the most commonly used right to obtain a permanent residence permit (Art. 16, Directive 2004/38/EC, 2004). However, there are some other ways that may lead to the grant of a permanent permit, such as when a migrant worker has reached the age of retirement, became permanently incapable to work, or lives in the host state while working in another (Ar. 17, Directive 2004/38/EC, 2004).

Schengen Area

A related issue here is the Schengen Area. While in fact this Area emerged separate from the European Union, it has a considerable effect on the free movement of persons. Dating back to 1985, the BENELUX, Germany and France signed the Schengen agreement. The most important result of the agreement is the removal of all border controls at their common borders. Furthermore, the countries of the Schengen Area share a unified approach towards external border surveillance, harmonized rules on Asylum seekers, and cooperation in the field of police and law enforcement.

Gradually, the Schengen Agreement was incorporated in EU law, especially by the Treaty of Amsterdam in 1997. It needs to be noted here that on the one hand, some EU countries opted out from the Schengen agreements, such as the UK and Ireland. On the other hand, there are non-EU countries that participate in the Schengen Area, such as Iceland, Norway and Switzerland. In short, the Schengen Area facilitates the free movement of persons in the greater part of the EU and beyond, by abolishing common border controls. However, the zone was heavily tested in 2015 during the refugee crisis: the ongoing stream of refugees put a heavy burden on the countries with borders closest to conflict regions. Next to that, due to the Paris attacks, the question was raised whether the zone was safe enough for open borders. After all, once inside the zone, not only people with peaceful intentions could freely cross the borders: apparently, terrorists could do the same, as you can see in the news-item.

THE NATIONAL, 20 NOVEMBER 2015

Europe's Schengen zone called into question after Paris attacks

BY: JUSTIN VELA

The terror attacks in Paris and the influx of hundreds of thousands of refugees have European leaders looking to increase control over their borders, calling into question the continued existence of the Schengen zone.

The 26-nation area within Europe has no passport checks or other controls between its internal borders, allowing travellers to move across countries with ease.

But this Friday, interior ministers from European Union states meet in Brussels to discuss the future of the zone, with France pushing for tighter border controls. This could see Schengen, a historic attempt at a unified Europe with free movement of people and goods, effectively disbanded after only two decades of existence.

The agreement, named for the town in Luxembourg where it was signed, was implemented in 1995. It applies to an area stretching from Finland all the way to Hungary on Europe's southern frontiers. Greece is also a member, though it is separated from the rest of the countries by the Balkans.

All this being said about the free movement of persons, it is time to focus more on the business aspects of this freedom: the free movement of workers, as stipulated in Article 45 TFEU, and the free movement of the self-employed, as recognized in Article 49 TFEU.

Free movement of workers

Of course, one crucial element of the free movement of workers is the free movement of persons, as described above. Next to that, Article 45 TFEU stipulates the...

> '... abolition of any discrimination based on nationality between workers of the Member States as regards employment, remuneration and other conditions of work and employment.'

This right is further specified in Regulation 1612/68, 1968. In fact, this regulation prohibits discrimination in the access to employment, and discrimination while being employed (Barnard, 2010). In both cases, direct and indirect discrimination are prohibited. An example of direct discrimination of access to employment is given in example 7.6. While an example of indirect discrimination during employment is given in example 7.7.

It needs to be noted here that there is one important exemption to the prohibition of discrimination. When people are employed in the public service sector, discrimination on the grounds of nationality might be allowed. For instance, it does not contradict the TFEU when a major or the head of a police department should have the nationality of the country he works in (Art. 45 (4) TFEU).

EXAMPLE 7.6

Ohé! French Seamen

The French law (the Code Maritime) stipulated that aboard of a merchant or fishing ship, certain key-posts aboard should be reserved to persons with a French nationality, while the rest of the crew should have a ratio of French people of three to one foreigner. The European Court of Justice ruled that the French law was in violation with the free movement of workers, as stipulated in Article 29 TFEU and Regulation 1612/68. After all, the law directly discriminated other EU citizens in their access to work in the maritime sector. (ECJ, Case 167-73, 1974)

EXAMPLE 7.7

Teaching foreign languages in Italy

Six foreign language assistants at the University of Venice and Parma were unpleasantly surprised that based on Italian law, their contracts could not be renewed. A Presidential Decree stipulated that '...the contracts referred to in the first paragraph [concerning the appointment of foreign-language assistants] may not be extended beyond the academic year for which they are concluded and may be renewed every year for a maximum of five years'. Remarkably, the law did not restrict the renewal of employment contracts to other university staff members or teachers. The foreign law teachers that were affected by the Presidential Decree were all European citizens, but not Italian. In principle, the Presidential Decree would also apply to Italian citizens who work at a University as foreign-language assistant. However, in practice, only 25 per cent of all foreign language assistance had Italian nationality, and therefore, mostly foreign workers were affected by the Decree. Therefore, the European Court of Justice considered that this law was indirectly discriminative towards nationals of other Member States, and in violation of the free movement of workers. (ECJ, Cases *C-259/91*, C-331/91 and C-332/91, 1993)

Also for self-employed people, the free movement of persons is crucial. Next to that, a self-employed person will need to be able to establish himself in another Member State to pursue his economic activity. In other words, a self-employed person might need to set up the necessary infrastructure in another EU Member State to participate in economic activities. For instance, it might be necessary to run an office or other kind of establishment in the host country. Therefore, Article 49 recognizes the freedom of establishment. This right has two main components: the right to have access to self-employment in the host country, and the right to effectively exercise this right once established in the host country. Direct and indirect discrimination is prohibited. Sometimes, the court even goes beyond the concept of discrimination, and simply assesses whether the rules of a Member State hinder or restrict the enjoyment of this right, regardless a potentially discriminatory nature. Examples can be found in the case 'don't mess with lawyers' (example 7.8). It needs to be noted here that exceptionally, the court accepts a barrier to trade when the measure is proportionate and needed to protect the public interest, as we can see in the Gebhard case.

Freedom of establishment

EXAMPLE 7.8

Don't mess with lawyers

The case of Reyners: direct discrimination

Jean Reyners, a lawyer with a Dutch nationality, wanted to practice law in Belgium. While the lawyer received his doctorate degree at a Belgian university and has lived there for years, he was excluded from practicing his profession because he was Dutch. A Belgian law stipulated that lawyers in Belgium should have the Belgian nationality. Originally, likewise laws existed elsewhere in Europe, since some countries considered the profession of lawyer an authoritative profession, related to the public sector. However, the European Court of Justice ruled that legal professionals did not at all exercise any official authority, and therefore, the freedom of establishment should be guaranteed. In this case, the Belgian law was therefore considered a direct form of discrimination against the Dutch national (ECJ, Case 2/74, 1974).

7

The case of Gebhard: hindering access to a market

A lawyer with the German nationality set up an office in Italy, so he could help his Italian clients from there. The lawyer, Reinhard Gebhard, was regularly hired by the German speaking population of northern Italy. However, while practicing his profession, he made use of the Italian equivalent of the word solicitor: 'Avvocato'. While he was entitled to use such a professional title under German law, he was confronted with a suspension to pursue his professional activities of the Milan Bar Council. Under Italian law, a lawyer should be registered at the bar before using the title 'avvocato'. However, in Germany, mr. Gebhard was already registered as a lawyer, and had earned all necessary qualifications to practice his profession. While a host country may uphold their own laws and regulations on self-employed people regarding their knowledge and qualifications, they should in principle not hinder the access to that market. They may only uphold such a hindering measure when it complies with very strict conditions, such as the principle of non-discrimination, being justified by reasons of general interest, and suitable and proportional to reach its legitimate purpose. Besides that, Member States should recognize equivalent diplomas and qualifications earned in other Member States. Considering all this, the court ruled that the Italian rule violated the freedom of establishment, because it was an unnecessary hinder for mister Gebhard to access the Italian market for lawyers (ECJ, Case C-55/94, 1995).

Article 49 does not only apply to self-employed persons, but also to legal persons. So, the freedom of establishment also applies to companies. This is further specified in Article 54 TFEU, that stipulates that:

> 'Companies or firms formed in accordance with the law of a Member State and having their registered office, central administration or principal place of business within the Union shall, for the purposes of this Chapter, be treated in the same way as natural persons who are nationals of Member States.'

Also here, the right can be narrowed down to equal access to markets in other EU Member States through establishment, and equal treatment once established. Member States may not directly nor indirectly discriminate companies, nor hinder or restrict the enjoyment of this right. This had far-reaching consequences, since this practically allows companies to set op agencies in other Member States, just to make use of more favourable rules in that state, as you may see in example 7.9. Exceptionally, the court accepts a barrier to trade when the measure is proportionate and needed to protect the public interest.

EXAMPLE 7.9

The Centros case

How to circumvent Danish company law

Two Danish nationals owned a company that was registered in the UK. However, they never conducted business in Great Britain, nor was it their intention to do so. After being lawfully registered in the UK, the Danish owners wanted to register a subsidiary establishment in Denmark. Their hidden agenda was questionable. Under UK law, there were no minimum capital requirements to set up a private limited company. Under Danish law, one needed to invest at least 200.000 Danish Kroner (that is, under Danish law of 1991). Setting up a business in the UK therefore was a way to circumvent the Danish minimum capital rule. After all, the subsidiary establishment in Denmark would then technically be a UK company, set up in compliance with the UK law. In response to this, the Danish authorities refused to register the secondary establishment of the company, because it would constitute a violation of Danish law, since the minimum capital requirement was not met.

However, the two Danish owners appealed against this decision, and held that the Danish authorities should register their Danish establishment. They argued that their British company should enjoy unhindered freedom of establishment in Denmark. Since according to both UK and Danish law, the nationality of the company is determined by its originally registered (in this case therefore the UK), the European Court of Justice could only agree with the Danish owners, and the Danish authorities had to register the subsidiary establishment (ECJ, Case C-212/97, 1999).

The free movement of services

While in essence, the free movement of service is separately regulated in EU law, there is a strong connection with the before mentioned freedom of establishment. After all, service providers (e.g. a dentist, a physiotherapist, an ICT consultant, a conductor, a medical expert, a financial advisor) may need to establish themselves in another EU country to be able to offer their services. The difference between the freedom of establishment and free movement of services is that in case of the first, a service provider crosses the border and establishes himself on a more permanent basis in the other country. Trade barriers to this establishment are forbidden. In case of the latter, the service provider crosses the border from one EU Member State to another to provide the service. There is no permanent establishment involved. Trade barriers to the providing of such services are forbidden. Therefore, these are two different kinds of freedoms, although they could both be used in the context of the providing of services.

Article 56 TFEU stipulates the freedom to provide and receive services in the EU. This means that both the service provider and the service receiver may invoke this freedom, as long as one of them is crossing a EU border, and experiences a trade barrier as a result of national measures. Also here, the Court has ruled that direct and indirect barriers to providing of services is prohibited, as well as the hindering of services providing in general. Furthermore, also here, the Court may accept a barrier to trade when the measure is proportionate and needed to protect the public interest. An example of direct discrimination and a justified barrier to trade can be found in example 7.10.

7

EXAMPLE 7.10

Well insured in Germany
A German law stipulated that for the provision of an insurance, the insurer should be established and properly authorized in Germany. This law was disputed in a case in which the Commission and Germany were the primary parties, but both opponents were widely supported by several EU Member States. From this we can deduce that the matter was quite delicate. The German rules created a barrier to trade for insurers from other EU Member States, since they had to spend significant resources to be established and authorized in Germany.

The Court considered that the requirement to be established in Germany in order to be able to provide for the insurance was in direct violation of Article 56 TFEU. After all, such a requirement would make the free movement of services rather meaningless, and a direct discrimination of insurers from other EU Member States. German insurers are naturally already established in Germany, while the insurer from another EU country would have to realise establishment first before being able to provide the services.

However, regarding the authorisation, the Court ruled in favour of Germany. After all, proper authorisation could be necessary to effectively supervise the insurance agencies that operate on the German market. Insurances are products that have large effects on the consumer's wellbeing, especially when the insurer is irresponsible in managing their financial reserves. This has always been a tricky issue: insurers offer insurances for liabilities in the future that are unknown today. Bad reserve management may put the consumer at risk when they want to make use of their insurance. Therefore, the Court considered that the German authorisation requirement did not violate the free movement of services and was deemed necessary for the protection of the consumer. As long as the German legislation on this was not disproportional to realise this legitimate goal, there was no breach of Article 56 TFEU (ECJ, Case 205/84, 1986).

The free movement of capital
In a true free economy, the financing of economic activity is not restricted to country borders. For this reason, Article 63 TFEU prohibits restrictions on the free movement of capital and payments. This includes for instance the sales of mortgages, investments in real property and the purchase of shares of a company (EJC, Cases C-222/97, C 302/97 and C-367/98). Not surprisingly,

the free movement of capital is greatly linked to the creation of the monetary union (Barnard, 2010). Since the introduction of the Eurozone, the free movement of capital truly evolved to an important freedom within the European context. After all, the monetary policies are automatically harmonized due to the centralized organization of the Euro. Consequentially, factors as fluctuating exchange rates cannot result in trade barriers anymore. The European Court of Justice considers that next to direct and indirect discrimination in this field, as well as any measures that hinder the free movement of capital. Trade barriers may be justified when proportionate to realize a legitimate goal in the protection of public interest. An example of a restriction to the free movement of capital that could not be justified can be found in example 7.11.

EXAMPLE 7.11

The Scientology Church and cloudy investments

In France, a domestic law established a system of prior control regarding foreign investments. This practically means that each foreign investments needed to be authorized by the French government, before the transaction could be made. According to the French government, this was necessary to protect the public interest of France. After all, once a foreign investment is made, it is usually very hard to block the investment in retrospective. This way, criminal money can easily flow outside the country without proper prior control.

The system of prior control was successfully contested by the Scientology Church, established in France. *In casu*, the Church planned to invest in their UK trust fund. The European Court of Justice recognized the need to protect the public interest of France, but considered a general – unlimited – system of prior permission a violation of Article 63 TFEU. Therefore, the French law constituted an unjustifiable restriction of the free movement of capital (ECJ, Case C-54/99).

7

7.2.2 Harmonization of law

Next to the realization of the four freedoms, the European laws and policies on economics have been harmonized profoundly in order to ban trade barriers. In law, this is done on two levels, by so-called primary and secondary legislation:

- Primary legislation are the treaties that are signed and ratified by the EU Member States. The most important document for now is the Treaty on the Functioning of the European Union (TFEU). The TFEU lays down the general fundaments of European economic integration.
- Secondary legislation are the laws produced by the European legislature, based on and authorized by the primary legislation. Secondary law is more detailed and further specifies the primary law. These laws are produced by the European legislature, and consist mostly of regulations, directives, decisions, recommendations and opinions (Art. 288 TFEU).

The interaction of primary and secondary law was already explored in the previous section when we discussed the right to free movement of workers: while the core right is recognized in the TFEU (in particular Article 29), the right is further specified in Regulation 1612/68, 1968.

However, the different types of secondary legislation need some further explanation.

Regulation

A regulation is legislation that applies within the European Union without the interference of national parliaments.

Traditionally, this is the strongest and most powerful legislative act of the European Union. The law applies when adopted by the European legislature, and all Member States should act in compliance with the regulation. There is no involvement of the national parliaments, so on country level, there is no say in how the state should comply with the regulation.

Directive

A directive is legislation in which a certain goal or principle is adopted that should be implemented by the EU Member States the way they see fit.

So, in essence, the European legislature sets a goal, a target or expresses a principle in a directive. Member States enjoy a margin of discretion as to how to implement the directive. This then results in the fact that while the same goals, targets or principles are realized in each EU Member State, the method to realize them may differ per state. This implies an active role of the national parliaments, who are bound to implement the directive before a given deadline. However, this does not mean that when a Member State fails to implement the directive, or does not implement the directive on time, the content of the directive is meaningless. On the contrary, when the provisions of the directive involved are specific enough, they most certainly have direct effect, and may be invoked by any European citizen. Otherwise, the harmonizing effect of a directive could potentially be blocked by a Member State by simply refusing to implement its content. See for instance the Italian case described in example 7.12.

EXAMPLE 7.12

Bankruptcy in Italy: where's the money!?
Andrea Francovich, Danila Bonifaci and 33 other employees had a very bad day. Back in 1983, they had lost their job due to the bankruptcy of their employer, CDN Elettronica SnC, seated in Venice. Unfortunately, the company owed them months of unpaid salary before the bankruptcy was declared. As if matters weren't bad enough, in 1989, the liquidators claimed that the awarded money to ex-employers was simply gone, and therefore, no compensation was awarded.

However, a European Directive was adopted in 1980 (the Insolvency Protection Directive), in which at least a minimum level of protection was recognized for employees in case of bankruptcy. After all, Article 3 of that directive stipulates that all Member States to ensure the payment of outstanding claims resulting from contracts of employment in case of bankruptcy. The directive should have been implemented on 23 October 1983. However, apparently, the Italian government failed to do so, since the ex-employees were not paid.

While it would probably make no sense to sue the former employer (there was no money left), Francovich and the others decided to take a bald step and instead sue the Italian government. After all, if the Italian government would have implemented the directive in time, they would probably have been paid the money they were entitled to.

The European Court of Justice decided that the applicable articles of the directive were specific enough for direct application, and therefore, they could successfully be invoked by citizens. In this case, this means that the Italian government had to pay a compensation for the salary the company owed the former employees. (ECJ, cases C-6/90 and C-9/90, 1991)

Decision

A decision is legislation that only applies to an individual case.

This could for instance be the decision to fine a company for not complying with European competition rules, or decide on a position taken by the European Union in international affairs.

Recommendations and opinions

7

Lastly, there are the legally non-binding recommendations and opinions. In essence, they are what the word implies: a recommendation or opinion on how something should be done or understood. In practice, the commission adopts recommendations on various issues they work with in preparation of forming new laws and policies. The other European institutions usually adopt opinions, in which they wish to communicate their view on European matters. While behind the scenes, such documents may play an important role in the preparing of new laws and policies, they have no legal effect.

The European legislature uses secondary legislation particularly to harmonize economic standards in the European Union, to further facilitate free trade. After all, when the rules of the game are equal to competitors, they can compete fairly. This is perfectly in line with the idea of a free market economy. An example in which the European legislature uses secondary legislation – in this case a directive – to harmonize national laws can be found in case study 7.2 on the website.

7.2.3 Competition law

To realize a free market economy, it is necessary that not only Member States act in compliance with its principles. Also companies should behave themselves, and live up to the principles of free trade. One of them is fair competition. To this end, the TFEU and secondary legislation establish three main rules that apply to companies in the context of fair competition: the prohibition of cartels, the prohibition to abuse a dominant position, and rules on concentrations.

The prohibition of cartels

In essence, Article 101 TFEU prohibits cartels. These are usually agreements or practices that have the same effect: distorting fair competition. This certainly requires some further explanation.

Distortion of competition

First, we need to clarify what the distortion of competition then is. Article 101 TFEU gives plenty of examples. They include:

- The fixing of purchase or selling prices (see for instance the 'paint it black!' case);

- The limitation or control of production, markets, technical development, or investment to only a few (see for instance the 'An overkill of synthetic fibres' case);
- The sharing of markets or sources of supply;
- Applying dissimilar conditions to the same transactions with other trading parties, thereby placing them at a competitive disadvantage;
- Forcing the other party to accept contractual terms with obligations that are not related to the actual contract.

Cartel

Second, we need to specify the form of a cartel, which is usually an agreement or concerted practice. An agreement between economic entities implies that at some point it can be proven that the involved parties willingly gave their consent to distort fair competition through joint action. This can be done by a classic written agreement, but may also follow from evidence that secret meetings have been held to facilitate the cartel. However, this consent or intention of parties to participate in a cartel will not always be that easy to prove. After all, those involved will mostly try to disguise their illegal activities. To this end, the law also prohibits the so-called consorted practises. The commission, in assessing whether companies violate Article 101 TFEU, consider the result and consequences of the behaviour rather than their intensions. See example 7.13.

EXAMPLE 7.13

Paint it black!

Dyestuff is a pigment material that is used in the production of paint. In the early seventies, something strange happened in the dyestuff industry. On the same day, in various EU countries, competing dyestuff producers increased their prices with approximately ten per cent. While the Commission could find little evidence that the involved manufacturers made an agreement to distort the market by fixing prices, their behaviour unmistakably revealed that there was some kind of concerted practice. The commission concluded that the behaviour of the companies was in violation with Article 101 TFEU. (ECJ, Case 48/69, 1972)

Undertakings

Third, we need to establish who can violate the prohibition to Cartels. It is not without reason that in wordings of the Article, the concept 'undertakings' is used. This is explicitly a broader concept as for instance the word 'company' or 'firm'. In essence, all entities in society that at some point employ economic activity have to act in compliance with Article 101 TFEU. This therefore also may include non-profit organizations or government agencies, when they offer products and services that are in competition with private undertakings. For instance, a government institute running employment agencies or a harbour participates as an economic entity, and is bound to Article 101 TFEU.
Furthermore, also associations of undertakings are bound to article 101 TFEU. This means that also branch and industry associations should comply with the prohibition to cartels.

Fourth, there are exemptions to the prohibition of cartels. The Commission may exempt certain individual cartel agreements when they fulfil all the following criteria:

Exemptions

- improve the production or distribution of goods or contribute to technical or economic progress;
- it benefits the consumer;
- the cartel must be indispensable to realize the intended goals;
- the cartel must not distort competition substantially.

An example of such an exemption can be found in the 'an overkill of synthetic fibres' case (example 7.14).

EXAMPLE 7.14

An overkill of synthetic fibres

In 1984, the Commission granted an exemption to Article 101 TFEU to several producers of synthetic fibres. The market was well known for its overcapacity, resulting in an overload of products that could not be sold. The involved produces agreed to limit their production (which would normally be in violation with Article 101 TFEU). The Commission considered that this would end the overcapacity of the producers, and instead, the companies could allocate their resources to stabilize their organization, invest in their strengths and product innovation, instead of offering products. This particular agreement would not substantially distort the markets for it would leave a sufficient grade of competition intact. Furthermore, the consumer would eventually benefit, since the agreement would lead to a healthier market with on the long term more product innovation. (European Commission Decision 84/380/EEC, 1984)

Also, the commission may exclude certain cartels in general from Article 101 TFEU. Such exemptions are granted for instance in the automobile sector and the licensing of patents. In the markets, vertical agreements between producer and retailer may to a certain extent limit or divide the markets to gain more profit (see for instance: Commission Regulation 330/2010).

Lastly, the commission will usually not fine any cartels whose impact on the market is insignificant. As a rule of thumb, the European Court of Justice decided that in case of a horizontal cartel, the market share should be no more than 10 per cent, and in case of a vertical cartel no more than 15 per cent. A horizontal cartel is between undertakings in the same product stage, such as in the cases 'paint it black!' and 'an overkill of synthetic fibres'. A vertical cartel is between undertakings in different product stages, such as a producer to a retailer (European Commission notice C-368, 2001).

The abuse of a dominant position

Article 102 TFEU prohibits the abuse of a dominant position. Also here, further explanation is required.

First, we need to specify the meaning of this abuse. Article 102 lists possible abuses, and for the greater part resembles the list used in Article

Abuse

101 TFEU. The main difference between 101 and 102 is that in the first, the distortion of competition is realized by agreements or behaviour between competitors. In case of the latter, the abuse of a dominant position stems from a strong power position on a market of one or more companies. However, it is not unusual that companies are fined for violating both Article 101 and 102 at the same time.

According to Article 102, abuse may include:
- the fixing of purchase or selling prices;
- the limitation or control of production, markets, technical development, or investment to only a few;
- applying dissimilar conditions to the same transactions with other trading parties, thereby placing them at a competitive disadvantage;
- forcing the other party to accept contractual terms with obligations that are not related to the actual contract.

Dominant position

Second, we need to assess what a dominant position is. For the record, it is not forbidden to be successful. This means that an undertaking may have a dominant position, or even be a monopolist, as long as it does not abuse this position.
In General, the European Court of Justice defined the meaning of a dominant position in the famous Hoffmann-LaRoche case (ECJ, 85/76, 1979). In this case, the Court concluded that when an undertaking – or a group of undertakings – could independently act on a market, there is a dominant position. This means that the undertaking(s) holding the dominant position can autonomously regulate prices, supply, and other trading conditions while their competition is unable to influence these factors.
In general, it is assumed that when an undertaking holds a market share of 50 per cent or more, there is unquestionably a dominant position (Jones & Sufrin, 2011a).

Relevant market

Third, therefore, we need to know what the relevant market is. After all, in determining whether or not an undertaking can behave autonomously, one usually needs to know the size of the market. It makes quite a bit of difference if the market is a banana market, or a fruits market in determining the power position of an undertaking (ECJ, Case 27/76, 1978). This issue has always been a complex one. Roughly, the commission determines two aspects of the relevant market: a product aspect and a geographical aspect.

The product market is usually defined by considering whether or not a product has substitute products in practice. The Commission uses different techniques to determine this product market. One of these techniques is the infamous small but significant and non-transitory increase in price-test (SSNIP-test). In essence, the commission calculates what the effects would be when the price of one product (say, bananas) increases. When this results in a sales increase of substitute products (say, apples), the product market is not the banana market, but has a wider scope. If not, the product market is merely the banana market. However, such methods are not uncontested. In practice, this leads to endless debates between undertakings and the commission. Undertakings usually believe the commission has a too narrow view of their market. On the other hand, the Commission usually believes the undertaking has a too wide understanding of their market. An example of this can be found in the case 'What are tyres?' (example 7.15).

The geographic market may also influence the market size of an undertaking. For instance, undertakings that produce television shows in a particular language operate in the geographic market where this language is used or where the programmes are broadcast. Furthermore, some undertakings operate in only a few EU Member States. Then, naturally, the geographic market is restricted to those countries only.

EXAMPLE 7.15

What are tyres?

Michelin v. the Commission

On several occasions, the Dutch establishment of tyre seller Michelin was accused of abusing its dominant market position. The accusation included an obscure bonus system for dealers and different payment periods to customers. The major part of the dispute however was about the determination of the market. According to Michelin they had no dominant position at all, and therefore could not violate Article 102 TFEU. Michelin considered that they operated on the tyre market in general, and on this market, they faced substantial competition. However, the Commission disagreed, and considered that the tyre market for retreated tyres was different from that of replacement tyres. Most importantly, the supply channels and demand was different. After all, replacement tyres were simply sold by truck dealers, where retreat tyres were typically a service offered as an after sales service. On both markets, the Commission established that Michelin had a dominant market share, and accordingly, violated Article 102 TFEU (ECJ, Case 322/81, 1983 and Case T-203/01, 2003).

Concentrations

When two formally independent undertakings become one economic entity, this might have undesirable effects regarding free competition. For instance, an enormous power block is created that de facto makes fair competition impossible. While the opinion on the desirability of large concentration on the European markets differ (Jones & Sufrin, 2011b), the European legislature adopted the so-called 'merger regulation' (European Council Regulation 139/2004, 2004). This regulation authorizes the Commission to review a concentration against the principles of fair competition.

Concentration

> A concentration is the result of two or more independent economic entities that merge into one.

According to the regulation, a concentration can be a merger, a takeover, and a joint venture. In case of a merger, two or more previously independent undertakings merge into one. In case of a takeover, one undertaking purchases another undertaking. In case of a joint venture, two or more undertakings cooperate on a lasting basis and *de facto* function as an autonomous economic entity. Please note here that not all joint ventures therefore fall under the scope of the merger regulation: only those that are long-lasting and function as if they are an undertaking itself. See for instance example 7.16.

EXAMPLE 7.16

Japanese machinery

In 2002, three Japanese companies (Toray, Murata and Teijin) selling synthetic fibre machinery installed a joint venture on the European markets to combine their efforts in the development, production, marketing and sales of their products. The joint venture was named TMT Machinery Inc. The Commission considered that this joint venture would fall under the scope of the merger regulation. After all, the joint venture was long lasting, and operated as an autonomous economic entity on the european market. However, in this particular case, the Commission decided that the joint venture would be no treat to the principles of fair competition. (European Commission, Case COMP/M.2763, 2002)

In essence, those undertakings that are planning to create a concentration need to inform the European Commission prior to its realization. However, this is only necessary when the concentration has a so-called 'community dimension'. This means that it should potentially affect the cross border trade between EU Member States. So, if the concentration only has effect on the markets of one Member State, the Commission has no jurisdiction. Instead, possibly, the national competition authorities may have jurisdiction to review the proposed concentration.
If there is this cross-border effect, a community dimension is assumed to exist when:

- the combined worldwide turnover of all undertakings involved exceeds the threshold of 5.000 million euros;
- the turnover within the European Union of at least two of the involved undertakings exceeds the threshold of 250 million euros (European Council Regulation 139/2004, Art. 1).

If the intended concentration falls under the aforementioned category, the commission will start an investigation and decide whether this concentration is:

> 'a concentration which would significantly impede effective competition in the common market or in a substantial part of it...'(European Council Regulation 139/2004, Article 2 (3))

The reviewing methods of the Commission greatly depend on the situational factors, such as market seize, relevant market, expected impact on markets and remaining competition. An example of a proposed concentration that was blocked by the commission can be found in the press release. In this case, the express company UPS planned to acquire TNT Express.

30 JANUARY 2012

Mergers: Commission blocks proposed acquisition of TNT Express by UPS

BY: THE EUROPEAN COMMISSION

The European Commission has prohibited under the EU Merger Regulation the proposed acquisition of TNT Express by UPS. The Commission found that the take-over would have restricted competition in fifteen Member States when it comes to the express delivery of small packages to another European country. In these Member States, the acquisition would have reduced the number of significant players to only three or two, leaving sometimes DHL as the only alternative to UPS. The concentration would therefore have likely harmed customers by causing price increases. During the investigation, UPS offered to divest TNT's subsidiaries in these fifteen countries and allow the buyer to access its intra-European air network for five years. The Commission carried out an in-depth assessment, including a market test where customers and other interested parties were consulted. However, these remedies proved inadequate to address the identified competition concerns.

7.3 The organizational structure of the EU

European Council

On the highest level, there is the European Council. This body is composed of all (political) heads of the EU Member States. The Council convenes normally four times a year on high-level summits. During these summits, the general direction of European policies are discussed and established. However, technically, this body does not adopt laws, but instead is responsible for pointing out the general direction of European integration.

Law making

On a day to day basis, the European Commission, the Council of Ministers and the European Parliament are involved in law making. In short, the European Commission initiates the law making process while the Council of Ministers together with the European Parliament actually produce the law.

European Commission

The European Commission is the highest executive organ of the EU. They enforce European law by slapping fines on those who do not obey EU law. For instance, when a company violates competition law, the Commission may fine them accordingly. Next to that, the Commission supervises and allocates the EU budgets. Lastly, the Commission has the exclusive right to initiate law. This means that the Commission proposes new laws that can be adopted by the Council of Ministers and the European Parliament. While the Council and Parliament are the actual lawmaker, they cannot act without the initiative of the European Commission. The Commission is composed of 28 commissioners, one from each Member State. However, it is assumed that the Commission is a true supranational body that transcends national politics. A commissioner is appointed for a five-year term.
In a manner of speaking, the Commission represents the EU in itself.

Council of Ministers

The Council of Ministers is composed of a representative on the ministerial level of each EU government. The Council meets in at least ten different configurations, depending on the topic that is discussed. Usually, the minister or state secretary of each Member State that is responsible for the

debated topic will attend the Council. Therefore, when the matter concerns external relations, the responsible ministers of foreign affairs of each Member State will attend the Council's meeting. In rather complex procedures the Council drafts and adopts new legislation together with the European Parliament. Next to that, the Council adopts the EU budget, together with the European Parliament. Furthermore, the Council is responsible for the foreign policies and the closure of agreements between the EU and other entities.
In a manner of speaking, the Council of Ministers represents the governments of the EU Member States.

European Parliament

The European Parliament is directly elected by the European Citizens. The 751 parliamentarians therefore represent most of the political flavours in each Member State. In the course of time, serious cross-border political blocks have emerged. For instance, amongst others, the Christian Democrats, the Socialists, the Conservatives and the Liberals have teamed up on European level. Members of the European Parliament (MEPs) are appointed for a five-year term.
Their core responsibility is to draft and adopt – together with the Council of Ministers – new legislation. Next to that, the Parliament elects the Commission President, and approves of the other commissioners. Furthermore, the Parliament adopts the EU budgets, together with the Council of Ministers.
In a manner of speaking, the European Parliament represents the European citizens.

7

The European Court of Justice will be discussed in the next section, for it relates to dispute settlement. In the context of law making, it is important to notice here that the Court has played a grandiose role in the forming of EU law, since it has a final say in the interpretation of EU law.

FIGURE 7.2 The main EU institutes & law making

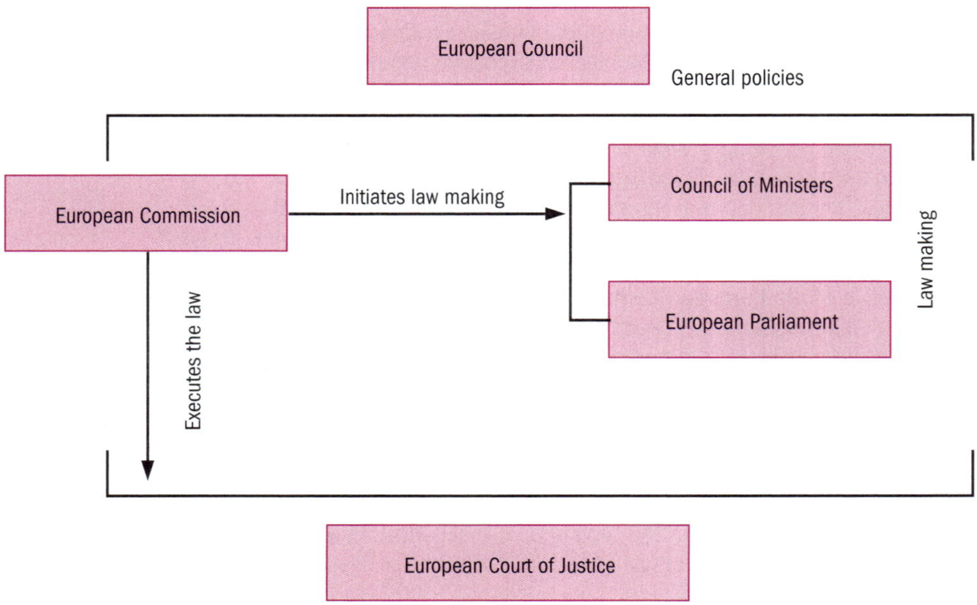

There are more EU institutions that play a role in the governance of the European Union. Examples are the European Central Bank, especially of importance in the context of the monetary union, and the European Court of Auditors, controlling the EU budgets. They will not be further discussed in this chapter.

European Central Bank

European Court of Auditors

Figure 7.2 shows a schematic overview of the EU Institutions in the context of law making.

7.4 Dispute settlement

European Court of Justice

The profound role of the European Court of Justice in EU law was already discussed above on several occasions. The Court is a true supranational court of the European Union, and has a final say on the interpretation of EU law. A case in which the meaning of European law is disputed can be brought before the European Court of Justice directly or indirectly through a preliminary procedure.
The most important matters that appear directly for the European Court of Justice are the following:

- The European Court of Justice is competent to rule in matters against a national government, brought before the Court by the Commission (Art. 226 TFEU) or another EU Member State (Art. 228 TFEU). While the first occurs regularly, the latter is a rarity. Plenty of examples in which the Commission initiates the procedure were discussed above, such as the Keck et Mithouard, the Zhu and Chen and the Gebhard cases (example 7.4, case study 7.1, and example 7.8).
- The European Court of Justice is competent in matters against a EU institution. For instance, when a Member State considers new EU legislation or an act of EU institution in violation with EU law. An example can be found below in the newspaper item. Although it does not follow directly from this article, the following is at stake: the European Court of Justice annuls a decision of the European Commission to allow third countries to store private data in compliance with their laws, and not with European Union law. This annulment had serious consequences for big online companies such as Google, Apple and Facebook.

THE WALL STREET JOURNAL, 6 OCTOBER 2015

EU Court Says Data-Transfer Pact With U.S. Violates Privacy

BY: NATALIA DROZDIAK AND SAM SCHECHNER

The European Union's highest court on Tuesday struck down a trans-Atlantic pact used by thousands of companies to transfer Europeans' personal information to the U.S., throwing into jeopardy data traffic that underpins the world's largest trading relationship.

In a victory for privacy advocates, the European Court of Justice ruled that national regulators in the EU can override the fifteen-year-old 'Safe Harbor' pact used by about 4.500 companies, including Apple Inc. and Alphabet Inc.'s Google, because it violates the privacy rights of Europeans by exposing them to allegedly indiscriminate surveillance by the U.S. government.

Preliminary ruling

Indirectly, the European Court of Justice produces preliminary rulings on the request of national Courts. The idea is that on a national level, European law should be applied in a similar way. To this end, the national courts may request the European Court of Justice to rule on the interpretation of European law when this is disputed in a national procedure (Art. 267 TFEU). When the national court is a court of last instance however, the court is obliged to submit the preliminary question. This way, European law is ultimately also applied similarly in the national courts.
We have seen plenty of examples of such rulings, such as the famous Van Gend and Loos, COSTA v. ENEL, Dassonville and Cassis de Dijon rulings (examples 7.1, 7.2 and 7.3).

Summary

- Originally, the European Coal and Steel Community, European Atomic Energy Community and the predecessors of the European Union were installed in the aftermath of the Second World War, as a means to mutual dependence and peace.

- The law of the European Union is characterized by its supranational law. This means that:
  - European law is directly applicable;
  - European law is superior to national law.

- In the European Union, the concept of free trade is organized in three main areas.
  - the four freedoms (free movement of goods, personnel, services and capital);
  - harmonization of law;
  - competition rules.

- The free movement of goods implies a ban on all fiscal and quantitative restrictions to trade.

- Fiscal restrictions implies the ban on custom duties (Art. 30 TFEU) and discrimination in using national taxation (Art. 110 TFEU).
  - The ban on custom duties implies that all import and export duties are forbidden, as well as all charges that have a similar effect. The only exception to this is charges for services provided for by Member States or inspections required by the European legislature.
  - The ban on discrimination in using national taxation means that national taxes may not be abused to disfavour foreign products over domestic products.

- Quantitative restrictions implies direct quotas and measures having equivalent effect (Art. 34 and 35 TFEU).
  - Quota to trade rarely occur, and when they do, they can only be justified using Article 36 TFEU.
  - Measures having equivalent effect may be distinctively applicable: the measure only applies to imported or exported products, and therefore hinders trade. They can only be justified using Article 36 TFEU.
  - Measures having equivalent effect may be indistinctively applicable: the measure applies to all products, but in practice discriminates against import or export products.
    - Such measures are prohibited when it concerns product requirements. The only exception to this is when a Member State invokes a rule of reason or Article 36 TFEU.

    - When the measure concerns a sales modality, a Measure Having Equivalent Effect that is indistinctively applicable are not in conflict with EU law, as long as all market participants are equally affected by this standard.

- ► The scope of the free movement of persons is considerably broadened by the introduction of European Citizenship. Consequentially, all European citizens and their families enjoy the right to move and reside freely within the European Union. The Schengen Area consequents in the removal of border controls between EU members, and thus contributes to the free movement of persons.
  - The free movement of persons furthermore implies the free movement of workers and the right of establishment for self-employed persons.
  - The free movement of workers (Art. 45 TFEU) means that direct and indirect discrimination in the access to employment and during employment is forbidden. There are exceptions in the public sector, where the nationality of a person may be a relevant factor.
  - The freedom of establishment (Art. 49 TFEU) implies the right to have access to self-employment and the right to effectively exercise this right in the host country. This means that direct or indirect discrimination as well as any measures that hinder the enjoyment of this right are prohibited. This right also applies to companies (Art. 54 TFEU). Exemptions are justified when needed to protect the public interest.

7

- ► The free movement of services (Art. 56 TFEU) includes the freedom to provide and receive services in the EU, when either the provider or the receiver crosses a EU border in the process. Direct and indirect discrimination are forbidden, as well as any measures that hinder trade. Exemptions are justified when needed to protect the public interest.

- ► The free movement of capital (63 TFEU), strongly linked to and facilitated by the introduction of the monetary union, implies a ban on all direct and indirect discrimination, as well as any measures that hinder this freedom. Exemptions are justified when needed to protect the public interest.

- ► In the EU, economic legislation is greatly harmonized by primary and secondary EU Legislation.
  - Primary EU Legislation are the treaties, most importantly the TFEU.
  - Secondary EU Legislation are regulations, directives, decisions, recommendations and opinions.
    - A regulation is legislation that applies within the European Union without the interference of national parliaments;
    - A directive is legislation in which a certain goal or principle is adopted that should be implemented by the EU Member States the way they see fit;
    - A decision is legislation that only applies to an individual case;
    - Recommendations and opinions are legally non-binding documents.

- ► There are three main rules in competition law: the prohibition to cartels, the prohibition to abuse a dominant position, and merger and rules on concentrations.

- A cartel is an agreement or concerted practice between undertakings or associations of undertakings that distorts fair competition.
  - An undertaking is an entity that employs economic activity in the EU.
  - The Commission may grant an exemption to this ban when the cartel is beneficial to the economy or has an insignificant effect.

- An undertaking has a dominant position when it can act autonomously on their relevant market.
  - The relevant market has a product and a geographic element.
  - The product market is mostly determined by analysing the existence of substitute products.

- A concentration can be a merger, a takeover or a lasting joint venture. When the involved undertakings exceed certain thresholds in turnover, the planned concentration has to be approved by the European Commission.

- The European Union has several institutions that govern the Union.
  - The European Council adopts the general policies and direction of the EU.
  - The European Commission initiates lawmaking and is the main executive body.
  - The European Council and Parliament produce the laws.
  - The European Court of Justice rules in matters of conflict regarding the interpretation of EU law.
    - The Court rules directly in cases between EU institutions and/or Member States;
    - The Court rules indirectly by a preliminary procedure in cases brought before a domestic court.

Practice questions

7

Open questions

7.1 Parma (Italy) is famous for their Prosciutto di Parma (Parma ham), a local raw ham. In the city of Parma, farmers producing Parma ham are increasingly confronted with competition. Ham producers from Germany, the Netherlands and France seem to be able to offer the product for a much lower price compared to the traditionally crafted Parmaham. Even from the South of Italy, some producers seem to successfully compete with Parma. This even results in the strange situation that in the city of Parma, the local products lose market share, and are replaced by competing ham products. Where Parma ham encompassed a market share of 85 per cent in 2010, this share is now decreased to 45 per cent. Especially the foreign producers seem to be successful on the local Parmesan market: they now hold a market share of 50 per cent. The Major of Parma decides to interfere, and adopts a new regulation. From now on, all ham that is sold consisting of more then 10 per cent of rest-material (other parts of a pig than the backside of which ham usually retrieved from), the product falls in a different tax category: instead of the usual 6 per cent VAT, the seller has to charge 12 per cent. This regulation seems to work: in the spring of 2015, Parma ham regained a market share of 60 per cent, ham from other parts of Italy (that are usually also traditionally produced, and therefore not consist of rest-material) takes a share of 20 per cent. The foreign products now encompass a market share of 20 per cent.

Do you think the Parmesan regulation is in accordance with EU Law? Please explain and refer to the relevant legislation.

7.2 The Spanish Civil Code stipulates the following provision:
'In case of the sale of goods to persons acting outside their profession or trade (consumers), the pricing in a shop should indicate the gross price and the national tax separately.' A French company is not amused. They have 100 establishments in France, and 30 in Spain. However, they have a joint shop lay-out, and the coordination of the shops designs – including the pricing – is centrally and uniformly organized. The consequence of the Spanish rule is that they have to adjust the pricing of their Spanish shops, which is very costly: from now on it is not possible to centrally organize the shop pricing for all their shops. They decide to sue the Spanish government, for they believe the new rule in the Civil Code is in contradiction with European law on the free trade of goods.

Do you think the Spanish rule is in compliance with EU law? Please explain and refer to the relevant legislation.

A well-known company, Microsoft, agrees to deliver software to six producers of food production machines. The software makes it significantly easier for food business operators to maintain a HACCP system (necessary for hygiene checks). Microsoft agrees to only deliver the software to the six producers. The machine producers, having a European market share of 17 per cent, increase the prices of their machines within a period of two months with 6 per cent. No evidence can be found of any written agreement between the producers in which this price increase has been regulated. It is however remarkable, that the producers deliver the Microsoft software for free to their clients (the food business operators), when they buy a machine. This software appears to reduce the clients' HACCP costs with almost 10 per cent. There is no obvious relationship between the purchase of a machine, and the software that is now automatically delivered together with the machines. It can be demonstrated in the annual financial reports that the six machine producers transfer 3 per cent of the additional turnover that is generated from the increases in price as tax free gifts to a research fund owned by Microsoft. The complex system looks roughly like this:

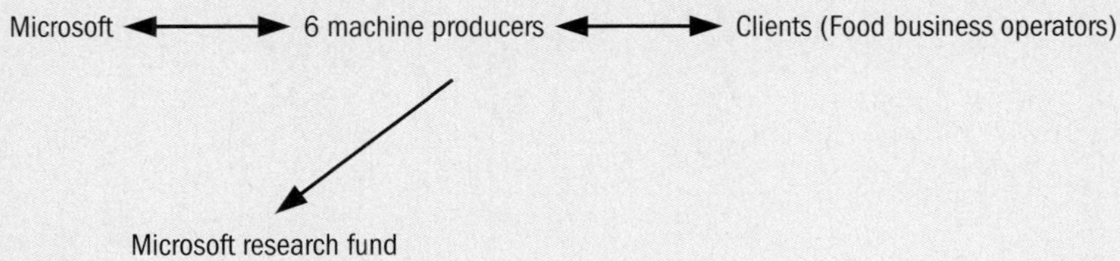

Competitors of the six producers are complaining, because they would like to have similar software, which simply seems to be unavailable, while other programmes do not even come near the efficient effect of the Microsoft software.

7.3 Do you think the behaviour of Microsoft is in accordance with Article 102 TFEU? Please explain thoroughly.

7.4 Do you think the behaviour of the six machine producers is in accordance with Article 101 TFEU competition law? Please explain thoroughly.

Essay question
More than once, the European Court of Justice played a very important role in defining European Union Law. In which case do you think the Court played the most dominant role in shaping EU law? Please write an essay in which you explain the main facts of the case, and why you think this case represents the most important landmark case of the Court.

Multiple choice question

7.1 If we would compare the TFEU with the GATT, we would conclude that Article 36 TFEU would be functionally equivalent to:
a Article I GATT
b Article X GATT
c Article XX GATT

7.2 In the European Union, the following institution has the exclusive right to initiate new law:
a the European Council of Ministers
b the European Parliament
c the European Commission

7.3 The Schengen zone guarantees:
a the freedom to reside anywhere in the zone, for at least three months
b the free movement of workers
c the free movement of services

7

7.4 Abraham is an Italian resident, and supplied services in Germany. He feels however discriminated by the German laws that apply to the service he delivers. In his support, Abraham should invoke:
a Art. 45 TFEU
b Art. 49 TFEU
c Art. 56 TFEU

PART 3
Business law

This part is a good starting point to become knowledgeable about how business law is organized in different regions of the world. These are mostly national concepts of law that are quite similar within the legal families. Most important is usually the distinction between common and civil law solutions to business challenges. However, in this part we will also discuss other concepts, such as Islamic law and traditional law solutions.
The topics we explore are contract law (chapter 8), liability law (chapter 9), labour law (chapter 10), company law (chapter 11), privacy law (chapter 12), intellectual property (chapter 13) and private international rules (chapter 14).

I DON'T SEE 'SEX' IN THIS CONTRACT...
BECAUSE THAT'S NOT LEGAL!
Sandor

8 Contract law

In this chapter, we will explore the law on contracts. First, the forming of a contract will be discussed. We will focus on the prerequisites for closing a valid contract and the exact time an offer or acceptance will have legal effect. Then, we will consider the content of a contract: in most legal systems there is contractual freedom, but this freedom is not unlimited. Next, we will explain the form of a contract: while there is mostly considerable freedom as to the form, the law may prescribe a particular form for certain types of contracts. Then, there might be factors that affect the validity of a contract, which may lead to a void or voidable agreement. These factors are portrayed in detail. To continue, we will briefly address the matter of performance according to a contract. And finally, we will discuss several international attempts to create a uniform legislative approach towards contract law, which might be used by businesses.

8.1 The forming of a contract

Contracts are at the core of doing business. Usually, one party promises to deliver a product or provide for a service in exchange for a certain reward.

Contract

> A contract is an agreement between two (or more) parties, in which the contracting parties promise to do something in exchange for something in return.

8

A contract is the result of an offer that is accepted. This means that two legal actions – the offer and the acceptance of the offer – are required to conclude a contract. However, mostly, it is assumed that 'just a promise to do something' is not enough for being a legally binding offer or acceptance. The law mostly requires something beyond a mere promise.

In this context, two matters need to be addressed:
- What are the prerequisites to form a valid contract?
- When does an offer or acceptance have legal effect/is legally binding.

8.1.1 A valid contract

In most legal systems, the difference between 'just a promise to do something' and a valid contract is clarified by law.

Determinability

It is widely assumed that an offer should be specific enough to consent to. After all, how can a vague promise be enforced by law? The requirements for such determinability vary per legal system. For instance, in Sharia law, a widely used principle is that the object of a contract must be precise regarding the essence, quantity and price (Bakar, 2003). The Dutch Civil Code stipulates that:

> 'The obligations to which parties subject themselves under the agreement, must be determinable.' (Art. 6:227 Dutch Civil Code)

A similar provision can be found in the French Civil Code (Art. 1108). The Civil Code of Laos is even more specific, stating that: 'The objective, price, and period for performance are necessary components of all types of contracts' (Article 11, Presidential Decree No 41/PO).

In the negotiation process, an offer that is not specific enough to be the basis of a valid contract, is often considered as an invitation to do business. In example 8.1, the message of Edward is hardly an offer, since it is not specific about the product nor the price. It will come as no surprise that the message of Samantha is much closer to a sound offer, since it is much more specific on the product, the price, the potential period and place of performance.

EXAMPLE 8.1

Selling drums

Edward wants to sell his drum equipment. To do this, he posts a message on an online second hand sales forum. He posts the following message: 'For sale: second hand Sonar Plus drum kit, only mildly used, against any reasonable offer.'

Samantha sells a similar drum kit. She post a message on the same website:
'For Sale: second hand Sonar Plus drum kit, only mildly used. Colour: Stain Blue. Included: snare stand and snare drum (14 inch), bass drum, double tom stand, tom (10 inch), tom (12 inch), floor tom (14 inch), three cymbal boom stands, crash cymbal (12 inch), crash cymbal (14 inch) ride cymbal (18 inch), high hat (14 inch) and high hat stand. Price: 5.000 U.K. pounds. Available: anytime. Place for pick up: London, Downtown Street 1402'

Next to the determinability of a contract, 'just a promise' is different from a valid agreement in terms of the main characteristics of a contract. Not all promises, how specific they may be, are automatically subject of a contract. A contract can only be used to lay down a particular type of promise. For instance, to agree with a bunch of friends to have a drink in a bar tonight at 8 pm may be quite a specific agreement. However, an average Court will probably be quite amused when one of the agreeing friends will sue the other for not showing up. There is something special about the promises made in a contract. This 'special' characteristic of a contract is understood differently around the world, although two main approaches can be distinguished: a common and a civil law approach (Farnsworth, 2006).

Common law

In the common law approach, a contract should comply with the doctrine of consideration. For instance, the Malaysian Contracts Act stipulates that: **Consideration**

> 'All agreements are contracts if they are made by the free consent of parties competent to contract, for a lawful consideration and with a lawful object, and are not hereby expressly declared to be void.' (Article 10, Contracts Act 1950)

In a traditional understanding, this means that a contract is per definition a so-called *quid quo pro* agreement: one exchanges something for something else. A contract therefore is a promise in exchange for a promise. In other words: there must be something in it for both parties.

> Consideration is the principle that in a contract something of legal value must me exchanged for something else of legal value. **Consideration**

There are two things that need to be in consideration here.
First, the promise should represent something of legal value. This could be money, property, the delivery of a service, ownership etcetera. Therefore, a gift is a one sided promise for nothing of legal value in exchange, and therefore would not be a contract between the donor and the receiver. Furthermore, elements as love and affection will not play a role in the consideration theory. If a father gives his house to his daughter driven by love and affection (and one symbolic dollar), there is usually no consideration, as you may see in the example 'Love and affection in Michigan: a gift in disguise'.

Second, the value in itself does not necessarily have to be fair or in balance with the counter promise. As long as at least something of legal value is offered in exchange, there is consideration. Even three empty chocolate bar wraps could fulfil this requirement, as we can see in example 8.2.

EXAMPLE 8.2

Three chocolate wraps for a record

Nestlé, a company that sells amongst other chocolate bars, ran a remarkable promotion campaign in the early sixties. When someone would send three empty chocolate bar wraps and a postal order for 1 shilling and 6 pennies, Nestlé would send you a record for free. On this record, there

was a song of which the copyrights were owned by a record label named Chappel. In the UK Copyright Act, it was stipulated that the copyright owner should receive at least 6,25 per cent of the regular retail sales price of a record.
In this case, the main question that was raised was whether Nestlé was indeed selling those records as a retailer, or merely giving them away for free for promotional purposes. In case of the first question, Nestlé would have to pay 6,25 per cent of the normal sales price of such a record. In case of the latter, the copyright protection for Chappel would not apply, and Nestlé could just give away those records without paying royalties to the copyright owner.

The House of Lords (UK) ultimately ruled that Nestlé used the records to increase their sales. Consequentially, despite the low 'retail' price of three wraps and a postal order, the records were used to add value. Therefore, this low price was still part of consideration between Nestlé and its customers. The result was that Nestlé had to pay 6,25 per cent of the normal – market conform – retail price of the records to Chappel (House of Lords, UK, 1960).

In the United States and Australia, the English consideration theory is transformed in the direction of the so-called 'bargain theory'.

Bargain theory

The bargain theory implies that consideration exists when the promise and return promise are bargained for.

This means that there is consideration when one promise is bargained for the other. This theory emphasizes a causal link between two promises. This means that the two parties in a contract must psychologically consider the one promise as a counter performance for the other.
When for instance someone voluntarily cleans someone else's house, and that person decides to give a bottle of wine to express his thanks, there is no bargaining. While in essence the two performances may have a legal value (a exchange of a service and property), they are not considered as counter-performances by the involved parties. After all, the house was cleaned and the bottle of wine was given voluntarily, without a legal obligation to do so. The person cleaning the house could also have decided to do something else, say, letting the dogs out. The person offering the wine could have given nothing, or offer a cup of coffee instead. Things would have been different though when the two parties would have agreed that one person would clean the house in exchange for a bottle of wine. In that case, a bargain was made, and therefore there is consideration. A likewise situation can be found in example 8.3. In essence, the one dollar was paid to fulfil the formal requirement of consideration, but not as a counter performance for the ownership of the house.

In other words; where in the UK understanding of consideration the focus lies on performances of legal value, the U.S.A. and Australian understanding pays more attention to the bargaining element, connecting the two promises.

EXAMPLE 8.3

Love and affection in Michigan: a gift in disguise

William Fisher lives with his mentally ill daughter Bertha Fisher in their house in Michigan. One day, the Father promises to 'sell' the house to his daughter while he continues to pay the mortgages for the house, so that Bertha has a place to live and has some property in case her father would die. Bertha's brother gives her one dollar and tells her to give that to their father as payment for the house. Unfortunately the father died shorty after the sales of the house. His trust fund refuses to pay the mortgages, as the father had promised. Consequentially, Bertha sues the fund to enforce the promise made by her father.

In last appeal, the Supreme Court of Michigan holds that there is no consideration between Bertha and her father. It is obvious that the payment of one dollar does not represent the actual value of the house. However, the value of the payment was never under dispute: if that would be the result of actually bargaining, there would be consideration. Valuing property after all is a subjective consideration, not an objective one.

The court doubted that the house was truly bargained for in the first place. Considering the circumstances, the payment was purely made to fulfil the legal requirement of consideration (*quid pro quo*). It was not truly part of a 'deal' that was closed in which the dollar was considered by the seller as actual payment for the immovable property. As a matter of fact, the Court considered that this sale was a gift in disguise, and could therefore not be legally enforced. Bertha argued that she gave her father love and affection, and that out of this love her father wanted to sell the house. So, in essence, the one dollar was not the only thing that was part of the bargain. The Court held that this argument was not convincing: love and affection are of no legal value, and therefore cannot be part of the consideration. (Supreme Court of Michigan, 1904)

There is one big deficit in the theory of consideration and the theory of bargain: as we have seen above, one-sided promises are in principle never enforceable. However, this might lead to quite some undesirable situations. To this end, in most common law countries, the principle of promissory estoppel was introduced.

Principle of promissory estoppel

> The principle of promissory estoppel implies that a one sided promise is enforceable when the promisor should reasonably expect the promisee to rely on the promise.

This is quite a mouthful. Consider a case in which one person promises something while the receiver of that promise promises nothing in return. Technically, the promise will never result in consideration, and therefore will not be enforceable by the receiver of that promise (the promisee). However, the promisee may rely on this promise, and as a result of that promise act differently compared to a situation in which the promise was not made. If this is something the promisor could reasonably expect, the principle of promissory estoppel may correct the rather indiscriminate approach in the

consideration or bargain theory. In such a situation, a court may decide that the promise, one sided as it is, will be enforceable after all.
For instance, in example 8.4, Timothy's parents could reasonably expect Tim to rely on the gift of 15.000 euros. As a result of this promise, Timothy signed a sales contract to buy the house he bargained for. In the absence of this promise, he would probably not have done such thing. When applying the principle of promissory estoppel, Tim could hold his parents to their promise. After all, the parents could reasonably expect him to rely on their promise, and Tim would suffer serious financial damage when his parents would not live up to their promise.

EXAMPLE 8.4

The evil parents of Timothy

Timothy wants to buy a house. At the age of 26, he still lives at his parent's place, which is a true disaster. He desperately wants a place of his own. After a long search, he finds out that the perfect house for him is for sale: the house is completely renovated and he could start living there immediately. He tries to negotiate a price with the owners that is affordable for him. Unfortunately, the lowest sales price the owners want to offer him is 200.000 UK pounds. After consulting his financial advisor, he finds out that he can get a mortgage of 185.000 UK pounds.

Lucky for Timothy, his parents promise to give him the missing 15.000 pounds. Happily, Timothy agrees to a contract with the sellers and expresses his will to pay 200.000 UK pounds for the house. The transfer of the house is scheduled one month later.

However, in the meanwhile, Timothy starts dating a girl: Samantha. Not really the type of girl Timothy's parents expected as their future daughter in law. The parents do not like this situation at all, and threaten to withdraw their previous offer to give Timothy 15.000 UK pounds as long as he is still dating Samantha. Timothy is in love, and does not want to give in to his parents. He continues dating Samantha. Simultaneously, poor Timothy is in some serious trouble, because he cannot fulfil his promise to the sellers of the house due to the missing 15.000 UK pounds.

Civil law

In civil law systems, there is no such thing as a consideration theory. Instead, there is usually a strong emphasis on the willingness of the contracting parties to be bound to the agreement. This is also referred to as 'contractual intention'. The main question therefore is whether a promise to do something equals the intention to be legally bound by that promise.

A fine example of this can be found in the Dutch Civil Code:

> 'A juridical act requires the will (intention) of the acting person to establish a specific legal effect, which will (intention) has to be expressed through a statement of the acting person.' (Article 3:33 Dutch Civil Code)

This means that a valid contract is the result of two parties expressing their will to be bound by their promises. Therefore, the intention and the expression of that intention must be the same. If there appears to be a difference between the expression of a promise and the intention to be contractually bound by this, the legal act is considered to be invalid. In example 8.5, the will of Suzy is not in conformity with what she declares. Therefore, based on Article 3:33 of the Dutch Civil Code, the offer is invalid and has no further legal consequences.

EXAMPLE 8.5

Suzy sells her city bike part 1

Suzy wants to sell her city bike. Her friend, Winny, is interested in buying the bike. The estimated value of the bike is 1.000 euros. Suzy sends an email to Winny in which she offers the bike for 10 euros. To her shock, she made a typo, and missed two '0'-s in her message.

As we have seen, the contractual intent plays no significant role in the common law systems. As long as one promise is an exchange for another, or there is a causal link between these promises as a result of a bargain, there is a valid agreement. In a common law country therefore, Suzy is bound to deliver the bike to Winny. In the Dutch system on the other hand, she would not be bound by her offer. However, when applying this principle permanently, this would create quite some uncertainty in doing business. After all, one can always claim that he communicated something else than intended. To add some balance in negotiation processes, and protect the other party from invoking Article 3:33 Civil Code too often, another Article was adopted.

> 'Towards him who has interpreted another person's statement or behaviour, in accordance with the meaning that he reasonably could give to it in the circumstances, as a statement with a certain content of this other person addressed to him, cannot be appealed to the absence of a with that statement corresponding will (intention).' (Art. 3:35 Dutch Civil Code)

The consequence of this Article is that when a party could reasonably expect the declaration to be in conformity with the will of the other party, this other party cannot invoke Article 3:33 Civil Code. In other words, Article 3:35 protects against a too generous usage of Article 3:33 Civil Code. In the case 'Suzy sells her city bike part 1', there is quite a huge difference between the estimated value of the product and her sales price. In such a situation, Winny should not be surprised that Suzy made a typo, and cannot reasonably assume that Suzy's declaration was an accurate expression of her will. For this, the financial gap between the estimated value and sales price is simply too big.
However, this would be different in the follow-up case 'Suzy sells her city bike part 2' (example 8.6). In this case, the sales price is not so far away from the estimated value of the bike. The price is in other words quite reasonable considering the value of the product. In such a case, the protection of Article 3:35 Civil Code can easily be invoked. Winny should be

able to rely on a reasonable offer, and may therefore reasonably expect the declaration to be in conformity with Suzy's will. Whether or not Suzy truly misspelled it is not an issue here: her offer can lead to a potentially reasonable deal. In this case, Article 3:35 protects against the misuse of Article 3:33.

The principle of reasonableness

Both Articles have one aim: guaranteeing the principle of reasonableness. Article 3:33 protects Suzy against an unreasonable deal, where Article 3:35 protects Winny against unreasonable usage of Article 3:33 of the Dutch Civil Code. It is interesting to note here that in the common law systems, this principle of reasonableness hardly plays a role in determining the validity of a contract. In contrast, in the civil law countries this is exactly the core issue.

EXAMPLE 8.6

Suzy sells her city bike part 2

Suzy still wants to buy her city bike. As we know, the estimated value of the bike is 1.000 euros. It is the intention of Suzy to sell her bike for this amount of money. She therefore sends another message to Winny. Unfortunately, in her haste, she misspells again, and by accident writes that she is willing to sell the bike for 950 euros.

8.1.2 The time an offer or acceptance has legal effect/is legally binding

In the negotiation process, it is important to know until what time an offer can be revoked without consequences. Furthermore, it is important to learn when an acceptance has legal effect, because from that moment onwards, the contracting parties are in agreement. Roughly, there are three distinct approaches in law that regulate all this: the Anglo/American model, the Romanistic model and the Germanic model (Zweigert & Kötz, 1998a).

EXAMPLE 8.7

Justin Bieber: baby, what do you mean?

Jainy is a Dutch teenager who is completely in love with the music (and of course, the looks of) Justin Bieber. Therefore, she desperately wants tickets for a concert of the handsome Canadian singer. One of her classmates – Sigrid – happens to be so fortunate to possess such tickets. Unfortunately, the classmate is unable to attend because of a holiday, and is willing to sell the tickets. On the 16th of December 2015, Sigrid makes a phone call to Jainy and informs her that she is willing to sell the tickets (two in total) for a sum of 200 euros. She also informs Jainy that she needs a reply within 48 hours, because she may also be able to sell the tickets to her niece from Canada, who will arrive to the Netherlands in a few days.
Jainy wants to consult her parents first before she agrees to Sigrid's offer, so she decides not to respond immediately. The next day, on the 17th of

December 2015, Jainy sends a whatsApp message to Sigrid in which she informs her that she agrees with her offer. However, Jainy has no internet included in her phone service contract, so she relies on the school's Wi-Fi. The Wi-Fi network was down for maintenance between 09:00 and 13:00hrs. Therefore, while the message was irrevocably sent to Jainy's smartphone at 10:00hrs, the message was displayed on Sigrid's smartphone at 13:00hrs, the moment the Wi-Fi network was up and running again.

Anglo/American model

The Anglo/American model originates in the UK and is widely applied in the common law countries. In this approach, an offer is revocable until accepted. Furthermore, the receiver of the offer may accept the offer once the offer is arrived until the moment the offer transpires. When this moment is not specified in the offer, it is usually accepted that an offer is valid for a reasonable period, which is something that will ultimately be determined by a court in case of a dispute. While in the Anglo/American model an offer seems to have a non-committal character once the other party has sent the message in which he accepts the offer, a legally binding contract is established. Therefore, the moment at which the party sending the acceptance has no control over the message anymore, or when it was sent, is decisive. Due to this last element, this model is also referred to as the postal theory or mailbox theory, since the contract is valid from the moment the acceptance was sent.

In example 8.7 this would mean the following. On the 16th of December 2015, the moment the phone call is made between Sigrid and Jainy, an offer was made. This is a fact because Jainy received the (oral) offer at that specific time. However, Sigrid's offer can be revoked at any time until either Jainy accepts the offer, or the consideration period transpires (and there is no more offer). On the 17th of December, at 10:00hrs, Jainy sent her acceptance, and a legally binding contract therefore exists. It is irrelevant that Sigrid only receives this message at 13:00hrs, since Jainy has no control anymore over the message since 10:00hrs.

However, it needs to be noted here that this postal theory was originally developed a long time ago in British courts in a time when people would send such messages through postal services (the first case dates back to 1818: Adam v. Lindsell). Currently, in most common law systems, the usage of modern communication means is integrated. For instance, in Australia, the postal theory merely applies to traditional post. In case of modern communication means such as email and smartphone communication, the moment at which the message was received is decisive (See for instance: House of Lords, 1983, Brinkibon v. Stahag Stahl und Stahlwarenhandelsgessellschaft mbH). Applied to the case of Justin Bieber, this would mean that Jainy and Sigrid would have a valid agreement at 13:00hrs instead of 10:00hrs.

Romanistic model

The Romanistic model originates in France, and is applied in those countries that used the French Civil Code as a model to their own, such as Italian law. The Romanistic model holds a middle ground between the Anglo/American model and the Germanic model. The offer is not as non-committal as the Anglo-American model. In the Romanistic approach, an offer is revocable until accepted. However, when the offeror revokes the offer before the offer expires, the other party may claim damage compensation. After all, the counterparty may have had reasonable expectations that the offer could lead to a valid contract. The offer can be accepted from the moment the offer was received. The offer expires at the time as is stated in the offer, or in the absence of that, within a reasonable period which will eventually be established by a court. A contract is legally valid when the offering party is aware of the fact that an acceptance has been sent. There is some debate about the exact time of this moment in French law. The Italian legislature quite simply assumes that when the acceptance was received, there is a valid agreement (Zweigert & Kötz, 1998a).

In example 8.7 the Romanistic model would result in the following. A legally binding offer was made during the phone call at 16 December 2015. From that moment onwards, Jainy may accept the offer within 48 hours. If Sigrid decides to revoke the offer within that period, Jainy may demand damage compensation from Sigrid. After all, missing Justin Bieber's concert is surely a small disaster for a true 'Belieber'. The acceptance of the offer occurs on December 17, at 13:00hrs, since it was received by Sigrid at that moment.

Germanic model

The Germanic model originates in Germany, and is applied in those countries that used the German Civil Code as a model to their own, such as the Netherlands, Portugal, Greece, and with some modifications, Japan. In the Germanic model, the offer is in principal irrevocable. This means that an offer may not be revoked until the offer transpires. In the absence of a specified date, a reasonable period applies. This means that an offeror has to take in consideration that the offer may be accepted, and therefore will be bound by the offer he made. An offer has legal effect when received by the other party. In the same line, the acceptance is generally considered to be effective when it is received by the offeror. Therefore, upon the receival of acceptance, a valid agreement is made. For this reason, the Germanic model is sometimes referred to as the 'reception theory'.

In example 8.7. the Germanic model would result in the following: a legally binding offer was made during the phone call at 16 December 2015. From that moment onwards, Jainy may accept the offer within 48 hours. During that period it is impossible for Sigrid to revoke the offer, and she is bound to perform in accordance with the offer when Jainy choses to accept the offer within these 48 hours. On December 17, at 13:00hrs, the contract is valid, since Sigrid received the acceptance at that moment.

The Chinese contract law combines elements of the Anglo/American and the Germanic model. In essence, an offer may be revoked before the acceptance is sent. This is in accordance with the Anglo/American model. However, when the offeror includes a time limit for the acceptance, the offer may not be revoked until this period transpires. The latter approach resembles the Germanic approach (Art. 18-19 Contract Law of the People's Republic of China).

8.2 The content and interpretation of a contract

In most legal systems, the contracting parties are in principal free to choose what they agree upon. However, contractual freedom is never completely unlimited. Three main exemptions are commonly apparent in most legal systems.

- Consumers are additionally protected since they are considered a 'weaker' party compared to a professional business;
- In line with this, General Terms mustered by a business should not be unreasonable;
- A contract may never have the aim of violating (mostly penal) laws.

For example, the Russian Civil Code recognizes contractual freedom in Article 421:

'1 The citizens and the legal entities shall be free to conclude contracts. Compulsion to conclude contracts shall be inadmissible, with the exception of the cases, when the duty to conclude the contract has been stipulated by the present Code, by the law or by a voluntarily assumed obligation.
2 The parties shall have the right to conclude a contract, both stipulated and unstipulated by the law or by the other legal acts.
(...)
4 The contract terms (provisions) shall be defined at the discretion of the parties, with the exception of the cases, when the content of the corresponding term (provision) has been stipulated by the law or by the other legal acts.' (Article 421)

The primary message here is that contracting parties are free to choose what the content is of their contract, with some exceptions. As we read this provision carefully, we can conclude that the freedom of contract means:

'• The freedom to enter into a contract.
• The freedom to choose the contracting party.
• The freedom to determine the content of the contract.' (Oda, 2012)

However, the Russian Civil Code therefore restricts contractual freedom on three grounds.
First, there are exemptions when a contract is a so called 'public contract'. A contract is 'public' when the selling party is a professional organization whose core activities are to sell products or services. This is per definition the case when the organization is a retailer. The company or organisation using this type of contract may not refuse to sell their products or services to someone, and should offer those under the same conditions. This includes the sales price (Article 428, Russian Civil Code).
Second, there are exemptions when one of the parties uses a standard form contract, the so-called 'contract of affiliation'. This type of contract usually is a 'take it or leave it' type of standardized contracts. These are often used in business to consumer contracts. It is after all quite unusual when a consumer wishes to renegotiate the general terms of a supermarket when purchasing groceries. However, the Russian Civil Codes recognizes that the other party has the right to renegotiate such contracts when the contractual terms deprive this party of his usual rights, restricts liability of the user of such contracts or is in general unreasonable to the other party (Article 428, Russian Civil Code).

Third, not surprisingly, a contract may not violate the law (Article 422, Russian Civil Code).
A tasty example of this principle in another legal system, the U.S.A., can be found in the 'Cowboys for Angeles' case (example 8.8).

EXAMPLE 8.8

Cowboys for Angels

Is sex with an escort legal in the U.S.?

Prostitution is forbidden by law in almost all States of the U.S.A. The only exemption to the rule is the State Nevada, in which in some counties, brothels are legal (please note, NOT in Las Vegas!). This means that per definition, prostitution in some shape or form will be practiced in illegality in the U.S.A. This also means that prostitution contracts are illegal, since contracts in the United States may not violate the law: a principle that has been developed in a wide array of case law.
Now, in most states there is loophole to still have paid. An escort agreement seems to circumvent the prohibition to prostitution. Take for instance the website http://cowboys4angels.com. On this website, women can engage in a contract with a male escort. The handsome, muscled boys are well mannered, academically educated and excel in all kinds of competencies that appeal to women. Examples of the latter are martial arts, poetry, massage and dancing. As the website puts it:
'Cowboys 4 angels knows that a real woman's needs go beyond the physical aspect when it comes to men. It is more of receiving genuine attention and engaging in activities with a safe, charming, non-judgmental gentleman with whom you can be yourself, discover and learn new things, and most importantly enjoy your time together in a safe and discreet environment.'

Sex with Jax?

When a women desires to enter into a service contract, a fee is paid per hour, day, weekend, or even an entire week. For instance, an intimate date with Jax – a world traveller, model and fitness expert – one pays a two-hour rate of 750 U.S. dollars. Is there sex involved? Officially, no. After all, this can never be part of the contract since it is Illegal. Jax provides his services mostly in Last Vegas, and in this city, paid sex is illegal. Therefore, the website states that:
'A legal and legitimate escort company offers personal services strictly for the time and companionship of its employees. Consequently, Cowboys 4 Angels does not contract for sexual services and we are never compensated for sexual services.'

A romantic spark

However, the site urges that if there is a romantic spark between the service provider and the woman in question, there is nothing wrong with that. When, occasionally, sex is the result of that, this is a consequence of two adults consenting to make love to one another. This has nothing to do with the contract, of course. So, while technically, the user of the website pays for genuine companionship, sexual intercourse may result from this. The latter is unpaid for and not covered by the contract. The usage of this 'loophole' in law explains why in practice it is a crime to pay a prostitute for his services, and hardly punishable when this is done in the context of an escort contract.

8.3 The form of a contract

The principle of contractual freedom does usually not only extend to the content of a contract. Also regarding its form, it is normal to enjoy a significant amount of freedom. For instance, the Contract Law of the People's Republic of China stipulates:

> 'The parties may, when making a contract, use written form, verbal form or any other form.' (Article 10)

Oral contracts

This means that generally, the main rule is that contracting parties choose the form of their contract. This also means that in principle, oral contracts have the same legal weight as written contracts. Practically however, the evidence that an oral agreement exists will be harder to deliver than in the case of a written agreement. Therefore, when the sum or content of the contract becomes more serious, contracting parties will most likely prefer a written agreement. However, oral contracts are everyday's business. For instance, ordering a drink at a bar, purchasing something in a supermarket, catching a ride with a cab or ordering food in a restaurant usually do not require written contracts. This is because they are daily actions and usually have a limited impact on someone's life.

Written contracts

However, it is quite common that exemptions are made for particular type of contracts that are of a specific nature. Mostly, such contracts are about the larger things in life. For instance, in Germany, contracts can always be concluded orally, except in particular cases. For instance, the sale of immovable property must be recorded in written form by a notary (Art. 311 (b) German Civil Code). Furthermore, when a lease contract is concluded orally for longer than one year, it is considered to be valid indefinitely, while a written lease contract is valid for the period that is agreed upon (350 German Civil Code). Also, a suretyship provision in a contract must always be in a written form (Art. 766 German Civil Code). Notably, in most common law countries, a sales contract is sometimes required to be in a written form. For instance, the U.S. Uniform Commercial Code stipulates that a sales contract for the price of 500 U.S. dollars or more should be in written form (Section 2-201).
It is furthermore not uncommon that in case of a written agreement, the contract should be written in (or translated to) the native language of the country in which the contract has legal effect. For instance, in Brazil, the language of a contract is to the discretion of the contracting parties. However, the contract should be Portuguese to be accepted as evidence in a Court (Art. 157, Brazilian Code of Civil Procedure).

It needs to be noted here that there is a difference between the legal requirement of the form of a contract and practical desirability. While most legal systems allow a great deal of freedom regarding the form of a contract, there is a serious problem with evidence in case of an oral agreement. Therefore, it might be advisable to use a written agreement when things got more serious than buying groceries or ordering a drink. For instance, in the early nineties, a long established practice in Hollywood was seriously questioned as a result of a court case between an actress and a film producer. In Hollywood it has been quite normal to informally agree on film roles, while in this case, the oral nature of the deal between the actress and the film producer caused quite some difficulties for both sides (Reeves, 1994).

8.4 Factors affecting the validity of a contract

While a contract may be formed and agreed upon in conformity with the law, there might still be reason to doubt its validity. This is mostly so when there are special circumstances that result in a certain unfairness, and consequentially affect the validity of the contract. While these factors differ per legal system, some are quite generally recognized by law. We can subdivide these factors in internal and external factors. In case of internal factors, the unfairness is created by something that happens in the sphere of the disadvantaged party. In case of external factors, the unfairness is created by something external to the disadvantaged party.

If one of those factors is apparent, the consequence might be that the contract is null and void, or voidable. In the first case, the contract is a nullity, and has never existed by law. In the latter case, the contract was lawfully concluded but one of the parties appears to be disadvantaged, and therefore may rescind the contract.

Null and void

Null and void means that a contract has never existed by law, as a result of a factor affecting the validity of a contract.

This means that the contracting parties have no choice but to accept the fact that their contract never existed. The consequence is that both parties will have to undo all they have done so far in fulfilling the obligations of the contract as if the contract never existed.

Voidability

Voidability means that a contract that is lawfully concluded may be rescinded by the disadvantaged party as a result of a factor affecting the validity of a contract.

This means that one contracting parties may choose to rescind the contract due to the unfairness he suffers. The disadvantaged party has to actively communicate that he rescinds the voidable contract. The consequence is the same as in a contract that is null and void: the parties will have to undo all they have done so far in fulfilling the obligations of the contract. While technically the contract did exist, its legal effect is reversed in retrospective.

It needs to be noted here that legal systems deal with such issues differently, and even use a different terminology that is difficult to translate to English. The above explained terms are a general starting point that appear in most legal systems. For instance, the Civil Code of the Philippines makes a more subtle distinction between contracts that are rescissible, voidable, unenforceable and void and inexistent, as you can see in example 8.9.

EXAMPLE 8.9

Contracts in the Philippines

In the Philippines there a four different types of factors that affect the validity of a contract: those factors result in either rescissible, voidable, unenforceable or void and inexistent contracts (Art. 1390-1422 Civil Code of the Philippines).

In case of a rescissible contract, one of the parties must be disadvantaged and therefore has a choice to rescind the contract. An example is a contract concluded on someone's behalf in his absence, while the contract obviously leads to a loss for the represented person.

In case of a voidable contract, it is not necessary that a party is disadvantaged, but he still has the choice to annul the contract. An example is a contract in which a mentally ill person or a minor is a contracting party, or contracts in which the consent of a party is vitiated by mistake, violence, intimidation, undue influence or fraud.

In case of an unenforceable contract, the contract is prevented from having any legal effect beforehand. An example is a contract conducted by two minors or two mentally ill persons. Another example is a contract in which someone represents someone else without the latter's consent.

In case of an inexistent contract, the contract is null and void, and therefore never existed. An example is a contract that violates the law, or a contract which has an object that does not exist yet.

Internal factors affecting the validity of a contract

Legal capacity

In most legal systems, for certain individuals, their legal capacity to conclude contracts is restricted. This is due to the fact that they are considered to be, or should be, incapable to close a contract. This is usually the case with minors and mentally ill people. In some legal systems, people who agree to a contract that are under influence of alcohol or drugs may also rescind the contract. Furthermore, in some legal systems, the capacity to conclude contracts of prisoners is restricted.
Regarding minors, the Lithuanian Civil Code stipulates for instance that:

> 'A transaction shall be voidable if formed by a minor under fourteen years of age, except in cases where the minor within the limits imposed by his age and in accordance with this Code and other laws of the Republic of Lithuania, may enter into transactions alone to satisfy his ordinary and usual needs.' (Art. 1:84 (1) Civil Code of Lithuania)

In this article, the legislature tried to create a balance of interest. On the one hand, minors should not be able to be part of contracts. On the other hand, if this would mean that they cannot buy anything, this would not be very realistic. Therefore, the article basically starts from the assumption that a child (under fourteen years of age) cannot engage in transactions, except when this is something you might expect to happen at a certain age, and the transaction relates to the usual daily needs of the child involved. So, a ten year old girl can buy some candy or other groceries without a problem. On the other hand, when the ten year old child would book a holiday, it will without a doubt lead to a voidable contract. In that case, the parents or legal guardian of the child will have the right to rescind the contract.

Unilateral mistake

A person may make a mistake in concluding a contract. This mistake may be one sided, so that only one of the two contracting parties errs in the interpretation or understanding of the contract. This is also called a unilateral mistake. As we have seen above, in section 8.1.1., in civil law countries, the intention and expression of someone's will to be bound by a contract should be similar. When they are different, there might be a mistake, as we have seen in the case of 'Suzy sells her city bike'. In the example (8.5 and 8.6), Suzy errs in her communication, and offers her bike for a price that is obviously too low compared to the estimated value of the bike. The Dutch law that is used in the example stipulates that such a one-sided mistake results in a contract that is null and void (Art. 3:39 Dutch Civil Code). While in common law countries the courts are usually not so keen on accepting a unilateral mistake as a reason for voiding a contract (Zweigert & Kötz,1998b), it does happen when it is obvious that the other party could or should have known that the disadvantaged party made a mistake, as you can see in the classic British case 'Hairy skins from Argentina' (example 8.10).

EXAMPLE 8.10

Hairy skins from Argentina
A unilateral mistake

Colin & Shields, a London based enterprise, agreed to sell 30.000 hair skins from Argentina to the Beelgian trader Louis-Levie Hartog. In the contract, Collin & Shields mistakenly state the sales price per pound instead of per piece. As a result, the skins would be sold at a price of one third of the average sales price that is normal in this sector. Of course, Mr Hartog wants the deal effectuated, since the sales price is extremely favourable to him. However, the British High Court ruled that Mr Hartog very well knew that Colin & Shiels made a mistake, since during the oral negotiations the price was always discussed per piece, and not per pound. Therefore, the contract was declared void, since Colin & Shields could rightfully claim they made a unilateral mistake (High Court, Britain, 27 June 1939).

The power of an individual or company to conclude contracts may be restricted by law or by the statues of a company. This is especially relevant when an individual represents a company and closes a contract with another party. After all, when representing a company, the company representative will usually not have a 'carte blanche' to conclude contracts with other parties purely on his own discretion. Mostly, the statues of the company will specify to what extent its representatives will have the power to bind the company to contracts. When the company representative exceeds his power, the contract may be invalid. In Russian law for instance, when a person exceeds power granted to her/him, the contract is voidable. However, the other party may not have known the limitation of the power of the company representative, and rely on its apparent authority. Such authority may sometimes be deduced from the representative's behaviour. When a company representative drives a company car, uses company papers and has a company business card, it is most likely that the representative may sell things on behalf of the company. In law, we call this ostensible authority, since the powers of the representative reasonably appear from the circumstances. Therefore, as stipulated in the Russian Civil Code, a contract in which a company representative exceeded his/her powers may only be rescinded when the other contracting party knew or should have known this (Art. 173 and 174 Civil Code of the Russian Federation). An example in which this played an important role can be found in the case 'A super-loan by Superbank' (example 8.11). To this end, it may be recommendable to publicly publish the representation rules of a company (for instance through a chamber of commerce) to avoid any misunderstanding about the powers of a company's representative.

Ostensible authority

EXAMPLE 8.11

A super-loan by Superbank

A public limited company in Russia wished to rescind a contract in which part of the companies possessions were pledged to the bank as security for a loan of 230 million Rubbles. The company involved was a Technological Trade Centre in the south eastern Oblast Amur. The company director had concluded this contract on behalf of the company while it was not authorized to do so by the shareholders. However, the Director had falsified a document that showed he held a majority of the company's shares, suggesting that he was fully authorized to conclude the agreement. The bank (Супербанк, or 'Superbank') was not amused when the company rescinded the contract, and demanded that the company would comply with the contract.

In the end, the Supreme Commercial Court ruled that the bank could not reasonably suspect that the document used by the company director was falsified, nor was there any reason the bank should have known this. The main motivation for this was that the bank at the time of concluding the contract had no means to find out which shares were owned by what shareholder. As it turned out, the company was bound to comply with the obligations set forth in the agreement (Supreme Commercial Court, Russian Federation, 11 February 1997).

External factors affecting the validity of a contract

Something might happen external from the disadvantaged party that causes her/him to consent to a contract. When this is an unfair factor, the contract may be null and void or voidable. These factors are in most legal systems an equivalent to bilateral mistake, misrepresentation, or duress. It needs to be noted here that different terms are used per legal system, although the phenomenon is in essence similar.

Bilateral mistake

8

A bilateral mistake occurs when both parties of a contract are mistaken regarding the nature or content of a contract.

This means that both parties had a different understanding regarding the nature or content of the contract compared to the actual nature or content. In common law systems, one usually distinguishes between a common mistake and a mutual mistake. In case of the first, the contracting parties are mistaken in a similar way, as we can see in example 8.12. In case of the latter, contracting parties are mistaken in different ways, as you can see in example 8.13.
It needs to be noted that the phenomenon of a bilateral mistake is typically a common law construction. In civil law countries, provisions on contractual intent usually suffice to solve these kinds of matters. However, equivalent legislation on the bilateral mistake does appear occasionally in civil law countries. For instance, the Dutch Civil Code stipulates that there is a so-called fundamental mistake:

> '...if the opposite party, at the moment on which the agreement was entered into, had the same incorrect assumption as the mistaken party, unless he could have believed that the mistaken party, if this party had known the mistake, still would have entered into the agreement.' (Art. 6:228 (1)(C) Dutch Civil Code)

EXAMPLE 8.12

Ward's Will

Ward possesses an automatic grass mower, which he permanently lends to his nephew Bryan. Unfortunately Ward dies. His wife, Charlotte, is willing to sell the automatic grass mower to Bryan for a friendly price of 25 U.S. dollars. What both Bryan and Charlotte do not know however, is that Ward in his will declared that Bryan will be the new owner of the grass mower, and not Charlotte. In essence, Bryan bought something he already possessed.

EXAMPLE 8.13

Freddy the Farmer and the tricky tractor

Freddy is an old farmer, and is on the eve of his retirement. His son, Ferdinant, will run the farm in the near future. As a surprise, to mark this important new step in the life of Ferdinant, Freddy wants to buy him an agrimotor. At the wholesale for agrimotors, Ferdinant is advised by their sales-manager, Ginny. On her advice, he buys the latest model of a Massey-Harris agrimotor. To be sure the machines does everything an average tractor does, he specifically asks Ginny. She responds that this machine is brilliant, and even does a lot more.

At home, Ferdinant could not be happier with his new agrimotor. He proudly drives his tractor in town, to show his latest machinery. Unfortunately, he is fined by the local police officer. As it appears, Ferdinant does not have a driver's license yet. While for the average agrimotor this is not required, this particular type is so advanced that the law demands its driver to hold a driver's licence. Freddy feels deceived by Giddy, who after all told him the agrimotor had the characteristics of an average tractor. Gidy for her part, had no idea Freddy's son was only 17 years old and did not have a driver's license.

A rather particular form of a mistake is the mistake caused by the other party. This is called misrepresentation.

Misrepresentation

Misrepresentation occurs when the disadvantaged party is mistaken regarding the nature or scope of a contract while this is caused by the action of another party.

Please note that 'action' of another party may also be the absence of action, such as not telling that a product has a certain defect.
In British law, three forms of misrepresentation exist: innocent, negligent and fraudulent misrepresentation (Mulcahy, 2008). In all three cases, the misrepresenting party provides false information about the contract, and therefore will lead to a voidability of that contract. The difference lies in the state of mind of the party causing the misrepresentation.

- In case of fraudulent misrepresentation, the misrepresenting party is dishonest on purpose.
- In case of negligent misrepresentation the misrepresenting party is not necessarily dishonest, but certainly negligent in providing information about the contract.
- In case of innocent misrepresentation, the misrepresenting party is not dishonest nor negligent, but provides for false information nevertheless.

You can find an example of all three types of misrepresentation in the case 'the clumsy car seller' (example 8.14).

Usually, in civil law countries, such a subtle subdivision in types of misrepresentation does not exist. In general, cases of innocent and negligent misrepresentation can be solved by applying the general provisions in which contractual intent is a prerequisite for a valid contract. After all, one will hardly have the contractual intent to purchase a car with a malfunctioning engine. Mostly however, fraudulent misrepresentation is regulated separately, but mostly under a different name, such as 'deceit'. For instance, the German Civil Code stipulates that:

> 'A person who has been induced to make a declaration of intent by deceit or unlawfully by duress may avoid his declaration.' (Art. 123 (1))

EXAMPLE 8.14

The clumsy car seller

Chang is a salesmen of second hand cars. A lady, Jia, enters his showroom, and appears to be interested in a Ford Fiesta, built in 2008. Chang assures Jia that the engine block has been renewed, and therefore, the car will last for another decade without too much problems. This convinces Jia, and she purchases the car. After a couple of months, the car engine malfunctions. She hires an engineer to make the necessary repairs. This engineer is a bit surprised to see that the original engine is still in the car. It seems that the engine was never renewed!

Scenario 1 (fraudulent misrepresentation): Chang knew very well that the engine block was never renewed, but deliberately lies to Jia about this.

Scenario 2 (negligent misrepresentation): Chang normally renews the engine block of all cars he resells. However, he is not sure whether he renewed the engine of this particular car. He assumes that he probably did so, and informs Jia that without hesitation the engine block was renewed.

Scenario 3 (innocent misrepresentation): Chang usually hires an engineer to renew the engine blocks. The engineer assures him that he renewed the engine block, but in truth failed to do so. Chang relies on the information of his engineer, and has no idea that the engine block has not been renewed.

As we have seen in the provision of the German Civil Code, there is another factor that may affect the validity of a contract: duress.

Duress

Duress is the situation in which a party consents to a contract under threat.

This threat could be violence, but also other forms of putting someone under pressure, such as blackmailing. In the news article concerning the Italian politician, his personal assistant was clearly afraid of him, and feared the consequences if she would not sign the labour contract. At that time, the politician was already under investigation for other cases of extortion. This is a rather obvious example of duress.
In some legal systems, there are related legal constructions that recognize the voidability of a contract in which someone was put under a certain unfair pressure and consented as a result of this. For instance, in English law, the concept 'undue influence' is used when one person abuses his power position over the other in the conclusion of a contract. Examples in which this may occur are in relationships in which one has power over the other, such as in in the relation employer – employee, guardian – child, doctor – patient.

Undue influence

Another example would be the concept of 'abuse of circumstances', as we can find in the Dutch Civil Code:

Abuse of circumstances

> 'Abuse of circumstances is legally present when someone who knows or should have known that another person might be induced to perform a juridical act because he is under the influence of particular circumstances, like a state of emergency, dependency, thoughtlessness, an addiction, an abnormal mental condition or inexperience, nevertheless has stimulated this other person to perform this juridical act, although what this someone knew or should have known, should have refrained him from doing so.' (Art. 3:44 (4)

When applied to the case of the Italian politician, both the concept of undue influence and abuse of circumstances might be apparent. In the first case, due to the power relation between the politician (employer) and his personal assistant (employee). In the latter due to the fact that the personal assistant had lost her job and had to look after her ill mother. It is rather easy to make use of these circumstances and lure her into the disputed contract.

INTERNATIONAL BUSINESS TIMES, 19 DECEMBER 2013

Italian Politician Included Weekly Sex in Personal Assistant's Job Contract

BY: UMBERTO BACCHI

An Italian councillor has been accused of requiring that his personal assistant sign a contract of employment that demanded she have sex with him at least once a week. The 32-year-old assistant of Luigi De Fanis, 53, was required - by contract - to spend time with the central Abruzzo region's councillor for culture at least once a week and 'make love,' La Repubblica newspaper reported.

Due to the extra work load, the woman was reportedly entitled to a €36.000 wage on top of her yearly salary.

'The councillor was obsessed by me,' the mother-of-one told detectives. 'He forced me to sign it. I couldn't say no. I was afraid.' (...)

Italian councillor Luigi De Fanis allegedly demanded sex from his personal assistant. The councillor elected with Silvio Berlusconi's former People of Freedom (PDL) party, offered the woman a job as his assistant when she had to quit her full time job in health care and find a new occupation to look after her ailing mother, she said. The additional job requirements followed shortly after.

8.5 Performance of the contract

Of course one would like to make sure that the other party sticks to the agreement. To this end, in some legal systems, the principle of good faith is recognized. This means, amongst others, that the contracting parties have the responsibility to deal with one another in an honest and fair way. This of course includes the fulfilling of their obligations in good faith towards one another. We already say in chapter one that this legal principle is widely used in the Common Law countries. But also in other legal systems, the principle is widely recognized (Mackaay, 2011).

Principle of good faith

However, the principle of good faith is not always respected. Then, how do you bind someone to a contract when the other appears to be unwilling or unable to perform? One general rule of an almost universal scope is that in case of non-payment: it is ultimately possible to request the authorities to seize and sell property of the debtor in order to settle the payment. However, this is not so useful in case of other kinds of obligations, such as the delivery of goods or performance of services. Legal systems deal with such obligations in different ways. As Zweigert and Kötz already observed, it is in civil law countries usually possible to enforce performance of such duties through the courts. For instance, the German Civil Code stipulates that in the case of the sales of goods:

> 'If the debtor is to surrender a movable asset or a number of specific movable objects, the court-appointed enforcement officer is to take them away from the debtor and to physically submit them to the creditor.' (Art. 883, German Code of Civil Procedure).

Of course, this article is only helpful when performance is still possible. If the product involved is of a limited durability, the product was intended for a special occasion (say, a wedding suit), or the product was destroyed, things are different. It will be obvious that the delivery of (what's left of) the product will not lead to fulfilment of any contractual obligation. In that case, a suitable damage compensation will be awarded to the disadvantaged person. This does not necessarily have to be equal to the sales price already paid, but may also compensate for the damage suffered for the fact that the good was not delivered (Art. 280, German Civil Code).

In contrast, in most common law systems, the preferred approach is to grant damage compensation immediately instead of enforcing the particular contractual obligation (Zweigert & Kotz, 1998c).
Although it is certainly not the case that in each legal system, a contract is considered to be a final agreement that is ultimately bounding. Take for instance India, where a contract is considered part of the process of doing business. Do not be surprised that your Indian counterparty wishes to renegotiate terms of a closed contract when circumstances have changed, or expect a certain degree of flexibility in the interpretation of the contractual terms. It is more important that business partners build a relationship based on mutual trust than performing in compliance with the exact wordings of the contract (Katz, 2008).

Please note that the particularities of contractual liability will be further explored in chapter 9.

8.6 International contract law

To overcome the differences between legal systems, and most of all, to make international trade run more smoothly, several initiatives have been undertaken to unify the law of contracts. This is done with regard to the content of international contract law, and with regard to the form of international contracts.

Substance

UNIDROIT principles

CISG

Regarding the substance of international contract law, notable examples are the UNIDROIT principles of international commercial contracts, and the UN Convention on Contracts for the International Sales of Goods (CISG). Both documents offer one set of contract rules in the international B to B markets. Furthermore, the International Chamber of Commerce has developed standard rules that regulate the liability between sender and receiver during international transport in a B to B contract. These rules are so-called International Commercial Terms (INCOTERMS).

INCOTERMS

Such documents might be applicable as a result of international private law rules, or as a result of the deliberate choice of contracting parties. This will be further explored in chapter 14.

These international provisions are often a result of negotiating between different legal systems, and therefore contribute to the unification of contract law. It also has an effect the other way around: they may serve as a source for inspiration in the forming of new national legislation. For instance, the UNIDROIT principles were carefully studied by the Japanese legislature in preparation of their reform of the Civil Code in 2009, and some of its principles are now adopted in Japanese law (Uchida, 2011).

Form

Also regarding the form, attempts to facilitate international trade through unifying forms were undertaken. For instance, the International Chamber of Commerce adopted ICC Model Contracts: single formats that can be used in different kinds of B to B settings, if the contracting parties choose to use it (www.iccwbo.org).

ICC Model Contracts

Summary

- A contract is an agreement between two (or more) parties, in which the contracting parties promise to do something in exchange for something in return.

- A contract is a result of two legal actions: an offer and the acceptance thereof.

- Not all promises are a part of a contract. The law further specifies which promises are suitable for a contract.

- It is a universal rule that the obligations of a contract should be determinable;

- In common law systems, the doctrine of consideration applies:
  - Consideration is the principle that in a contract something of legal value must be exchanged for something else of legal value.

  In the U.S.A., this principle is transformed to the bargain principle:
  - The bargain theory implies that consideration exists when the promise and return promise are bargained for.
  - The principle of promissory estoppel corrects undesirable effects of the above theories, and implies that a one sided promise is enforceable when the promisor should reasonably expect the promisee to rely on the promise.

- In civil law systems, there is a focus on contractual intention instead.

- There are three approaches in law regarding the time at which a legal act has legal effect.
  - The Anglo/American model originates in the UK and is widely applied in the common law countries. In this approach, an offer is revocable until accepted. Furthermore, the receiver of the offer may accept the offer once the offer is arrived until the moment the offer expires.
  - In the Romanistic approach, an offer is revocable until accepted. However, when the offeror revokes the offer before the offer transpires, the other party may claim damage compensation.
  - In the Germanic model, the offer is in principal irrevocable. This means that an offer may not be revoked until the offer transpires.

- In principle, there is contractual freedom. This freedom is usually restricted in three ways:
  - Consumers are additionally protected since they are considered a 'weaker' party compared to a professional business.

- In line with this, General Terms mustered by a business should not be unreasonable.
- A contract may never have the aim of violating (mostly penal) laws.

► In principle, contractual freedom also extends to the form of a contract. Special types of contracts however may be subdue to rules requiring a specific contract form.

► There are factors that may affect the validity of a contract, and may lead to a contract that is null and void or voidable.
- Null and void means that a contract has never existed by law, as a result of a factor affecting the validity of a contract.
- Voidability means that a contract that is lawfully concluded may be rescinded by the disadvantaged party as a result of a factor affecting the validity of a contract.

► Factors affecting the validity of a contract could be internal and external.
- Internal factors are:
  - Restrictions to legal capacity, such as minors, mentally ill people, people who are under influence of drugs or alcohol, prisoners, and company representatives who exceed their power.
  - A unilateral mistake.
- External factors are:
  - A bilateral mistake, and in particular misrepresentation, which occurs when the disadvantaged party is mistaken regarding the nature or scope of a contract while this is caused by the action of another party. Examples are fraudulent, negligent and innocent misrepresentation.
  - Duress, which is the situation in which a party consents to a contract under threat.
  - Undue influence, when one person abuses his power over the other party.
  - Abuse of circumstances.
- In the performance of a contract, the principle of good faith can be applied.
- In civil law countries, it is mostly possible to enforce performance through the courts.
- In common law countries, this is mostly not possible, and the courts usually resolve non-performance by granting damage compensation to the disadvantaged party.

► Internationally, several initiatives have been undertaken to unify the law of contracts.
- This is done with regard to the content of international contract law, such as the UNIDROIT Principles, the CISG and INCOTERMS.
- This is done with regard to the form of international contracts, such as the ICC model contracts.

Practice questions

Open questions

8.1 Ward Bernaerd is a very successful lawyer. One day, his niece calls him in panic: her employer holds her to an article in their employment contract that forbids her to start her own business within one year after she quits her job for the employer. Bernaerd successfully defends her in court, and the court declares the provision null and void, since it would put a disproportional burden on the employee.
In the meanwhile, Bernaerd is renovating his house, and is in need of a furnisher. Coincidently, the husband of Bernard's niece is a furnisher, and he offers his services for free. After all, Bernaerd helped his wife winning the court case, and did not accept any money for that. Bernaerd is positively surprised, and thanks the husband for his generosity.

Considering UK and U.S. law, would you consider this a contract?

8.2 Considering the case in question 8.1, would there be a contract based on civil law?

8.3 Xena sends a text message to Javi in which she writes that she is willing to sell her law textbook for 4 euros. Actually, she intended to ask 40 euros but misspells. Finally, she purchased the book for 120 euros. Javi is aware of this, but agrees nevertheless.

What would be the legal consequences of this considering UK law?

8.4 What would be the legal consequences of the case mentioned in question 3 considering civil law?

Essay question

Lu sends an offer to Wang, in which it is stated that she wants to sell her piano to her for 22000 Chinese yuan. The offer is sent through email on the 5th of October, and received by Wang on the same date. In the offer, it is explicitly stated that the offer is valid until the 9th of October. The 8th of October, Wang agrees to the offer, by sending an email. Unfortunately, the mail got stuck in the hub, and enters Lu's mailbox on the 9th of October. That morning however, Lu had cancelled the offer, and explained that she sold the Piano to someone else.

Consider the Anglo/American model, the Romanistic Model and the Germanic model. What would be the legal consequences of the above facts considering the acceptance and cancelation of the offer? Write an essay in which you compare the consequences in each model.

Multiple choice questions

8.1 Dana sells her car. She knows very well that the engine should be replaced any moment now, for it is used up. However, when she sells the car to Anna, she tells her that she recently renewed the engine block.

8.2 In UK law, this type of misrepresentation would be called:
a Fraudulent misrepresentation
b Negligent misrepresentation
c Innocent misrepresentation

8.2 Voidability means:
a that a contract has never existed by law, as a result of a factor affecting the validity of a contract
b that a contract has never existed by law and may be rescinded by the contracting parties
c that a contract that is lawfully concluded may be rescinded by the disadvantaged party as a result of a factor affecting the validity of a contract

8.3 In case of non-performance, common law courts usually:
a focus on damage compensation
b focus on enforcing the proper performance of the contract
c focus on rescinding the contract

8.4 Contractual intent is typically:
a a common law phenomenon
b a civil law phenomenon
c an example of a universal legal principle

FOO
D. GROHL
FOO FIGHTERS
Sandor

9 Liability law

In law, there are several ways to hold someone liable for harm that is inflicted. Liability may emerge from a contract due to a breach of contract, and the resulting damage thereof. Obviously, not all liability can be traced back to an existing contract. There is also liability outside the scope of a contractual relation. Such liability can be subdivided into fault based liability and strict liability. In case of the first, the culpability of the perpetrator is a central issue. In case of the latter, culpability plays no role, and instead the law attributes liability to someone for practical reasons or because it is fair.

9.1 Contractual liability

As we have seen in the previous chapter, contracting parties do not always do as they have promised. This means that the party who did not receive the promised performance will be disadvantaged. All legal systems have incorporated some legal way to settle this discomfort, albeit in different ways. It needs to be noted here that in this context both the terms 'non-performance' and 'breach of contract' are used. Currently, they are used internationally as interchangeable concepts, although the first finds its origin in civil law systems, while the latter originates from the common law jargon.

In brief, civil codes inspired by the civil law legal family usually adopt a legal remedy to enforce fulfilment of the obligations of a contract as a primary legal remedy. In common law systems, there is a stronger emphasis on damage compensation rather than demanding the specific performance that was agreed upon. Islamic law also focuses on damage compensation, but in a more restricted way. However, it needs to be noted here that practically, the approaches tend to mingle increasingly (Katz, 2006). It is not without reason that in international unification documents, such as the CISG and the UNIDROIT Principles, a mixture can be found, in which both enforcement of the obligations and damage compensation as a primary remedy can be found (Can Aksoy, 2014).

9.1.1 Civil law

An example of a civil law solution is provided by the Japanese Civil Code, inspired by the German Civil Code. The code stipulates the following in Articles 414-415:

'414. 1. If a debtor wilfully does not perform his obligation, the creditor may make a demand for compulsory performance to the court; except where the nature of the obligation does not admit of it.

When the nature of an obligation does not admit of compulsory performance, if the subject of the obligation is the doing of an act, the creditor may demand the court to have It done by a third person at the debtor's expense;

415. If a debtor does not perform the obligation in accordance with its real meaning, the creditor may claim compensation for any damage caused thereby. The same is the case if the debtor becomes unable to perform for any cause attributable to him.'

In fact, the Japanese Civil Code adopts a threefold approach towards non-performance. First, the party that does not perform according to the contract can be enforced by law to do so. If that appears to be impossible, the non-performing party should pay the costs of a third party to perform on his behalf. If that appears to be impossible, damage compensation can be awarded to the disadvantaged party.

Likewise approaches can be found elsewhere, predominantly in most German or French inspired civil codes. The general approach seems to be that:
- When performance is impossible, damage compensation is awarded;
- When performance is still possible, performance can be demanded within a reasonable time. When justified, additional damage compensation can be awarded;
- When performance still does not occur, damage compensation can be awarded.

THE GUARDIAN, 13 JULY 2010

Jennifer Lopez may face $40m lawsuit for cancelling concert

BY: SEAN MICHAELS

Jennifer Lopez may be sued for up to $40m (£26,5m) after pulling out of a concert in northern Cyprus. Although booked for a concert in the island's Turkish-occupied north, the U.S. singer cancelled her appearance last week, citing the 'political realities' of the region.

But according to the owners of the resort where Lopez was to perform, politics matter much less than the fine print of the singer's contract. 'The cancellation ... is not covered by any clause in the contract she signed with us,' insisted Murat Bozoglu, CEO of the Istanbul-based company.

(...)

While the $220m resort seemed like an attractive prospect, Lopez seems to have neglected the delicate geo-political situation in Cyprus. Turkey has held the north of the island since a 1974 invasion, displacing about 200.000 Greek-Cypriots and unilaterally claiming sovereignty for the region.
(...)
'After a full review of the relevant circumstances in Cyprus, it was the decision of her advisers to withdraw from the appearance,' read the statement on Lopez's website. 'Jennifer Lopez would never knowingly support any state, country, institution or regime that was associated with any form of human rights abuse.'

Consider the case of Jenifer Lopez. Obviously, Lopez is in breach of the contract, since she will not perform at the hotel as was promised. However, the exact circumstances may lead to different outcomes in applying this civil law approach to contract law, as we can see in examples 9.1 and 9.2.

EXAMPLE 9.1

Civil law: impossibility

Jennifer Lopez was invited to perform on a special celebration day that embarks the 10th anniversary of the hotel. For the occasion, the hotel organizes a grand celebration on a particular date. However, on the festive day, Lopez does not show up. In this case, it would make no sense when the hotel would demand to still perform on a later day: this would be pointless, considering the special celebration. It is in other words impossible for Lopez to still fulfil her obligations based on the contract.

Impossibility

In case of impossibility, it is normally so that the non-performing pays damage compensation to the disadvantaged party. This is not only the sum of money that reflects the value of the agreed performance, but additionally also damage that was caused by the non-performance. In the case of Jennifer Lopez (example 9.1), this could be the fact that the hotel sold tickets or rooms to their clients who wanted to see Lopez perform and want their money back, the costs of additional personnel hired by the hotel on that particular date, or reputational damage suffered by the hotel.

Most civil law systems however make an exception when the impossibility is a result of a so-called 'force majeure'. These are extraordinary things that in the course of normal business normally do not happen, such as a natural disaster, a terrorist attack, a fire, or a hurricane. When as a result of this a contracting party is unable to perform, she or he is usually excused for not performing. After all, one could usually not foresee such events, nor can they be blamed for it. This would be the case when Lopez could not arrive on Cyprus due to extreme weather, or a violent conflict that erupts on the island as a result of the political tensions. In that case, it will not be possible for the owner to demand any damage compensation. Instead, the contract will be terminated, and none of the parties will have any obligations towards one another. An example of such a provision in civil law is provided in the French Civil Code (Art. 1148):

> 'There is no occasion for any damages where a debtor was prevented from transferring or from doing that to which he was bound, or did what was forbidden to him, by reason of force majeure or of a fortuitous event.'

EXAMPLE 9.2

Civil law: performance is still possible
Jennifer Lopez was invited to perform on a certain – random – date, but does not show up for the reasons stated in the news article. The hotel may demand that she will perform on a later date, within a reasonable period. After all, performance is still possible and could lead to the fulfilment of Jenifer's contractual obligation. However, the delay in her performance may have caused damage, which may need to be compensated by Jennifer.

Performance is still possible

Considering example 9.2, in a civil law approach the promised performance may be demanded by the disadvantaged party. After all, the performance is still possible. Situations in which this occurs are usually when a contracting party did not perform satisfactory in view of the other party, or the performance was delayed. The first would be the case when Jenifer Lopez would appear on stage as promised, but as drunk as a lord, singing horribly. The latter would be the case she did not show up on the promised date, and did not perform at all. In both cases, a decent performance may be demanded by the other party: the hotel. In the meanwhile, there is damage due to the non-performance of Jennifer. The hotel may demand Jenifer to compensate for this, in wait for her performance. While in this case, additional damage compensation will be more obvious; there are many cases in which this will hardly be necessary. In a simple case in which payment was overdue, or goods not delivered on time, simply paying or delivering will settle the issue most of the times.

In many legal systems, it is required to formally inform the other party that he is in breach of contract, and why. It is mostly required to do this in written form. In this letter, you demand the fulfilment of the obligation within a certain period. The formal notice is mostly a prerequisite for any further legal actions. In Germany, this type of letter is called a 'mahnung', and in French law this is called a mis en demeur. Only when the non-performing party does not fulfil the obligation as promised within the reasonable time communicated in the letter, additional legal action can be taken, such as terminating the contract. This is demonstrated quite clearly in the CISG (Art. 47 (2)):

> 'Unless the buyer has received notice from the seller that he will not perform within the period so fixed, the buyer may not, during that period, resort to any remedy for breach of contract. However, the buyer is not deprived thereby of any right he may have to claim damages for delay in performance.'

This means that all damage compensation that is caused by the delay in performance may always be demanded afterwards.

9.1.2 Common law

In Common law approaches, the solution to a breach of contract is slightly different. The focus is not so much on enforcing the promised performance, but rather on determining the damage compensation that should be paid. For example, the Indian Contract Act Stipulates in Article 73:

> 'When a contract has been broken, the party who suffers by such breach is entitled to receive, from the party who has broken the contract, compensation for any loss or damage caused to him thereby, which naturally arose in the usual course of things from such breach, or which the parties knew, when they made the contract, to be likely to result from the breach of it.'

In general, it is not so relevant why the contracting party is in breach. Personal motives or incapability do not play a significance role. Neither does it make that much of a difference whether or not fulfilment of the obligations is still possible. Not performing is not performing, and therefore damage compensation is rewarded. This would mean in example 9.3 that Lopez is liable for the salary spent on Bieber's performance. After all, these were the costs of replacing Lopez with a similar type of act at the last moment. Since Jenifer does not show up, these are the consequences.

To avoid these rather drastic forms of liability, it is not unusual to negotiate a so called 'force majeure clause' in the contract itself, so that both contracting parties may rescind the contract when such event occurs, without the need to pay a (completely unforeseeable) damage compensation. Considering example 9.4, this would mean that Lopez may terminate the contract, and there is no ground for any damage compensation. This means that the hotel will have to pay Bieber's salary.

EXAMPLE 9.3

Common law: a breach of contract

Jennifer does not show up due to the fact that her flight was delayed. This is a result of extreme weather conditions in the major part of Europe. Since the Hotel celebrates their 10th anniversary on this particular night, Justin Bieber, who coincidentally spends his holiday in that hotel, is hired as a replacement for Jennifer Lopez. This is to guarantee that the hotel's clients may attend a top international act that is comparable to Jenifer Lopez on this particular night. Unfortunately, Bieber's salary is a bit higher compared to Lopez. The result is that the hotel had to spend €12.000 more on the concert than was estimated.

EXAMPLE 9.4

Common law: a force majeure clause

The same happened in scenario 3. However, in the contract between the hotel and Lopez, the following clause was negotiated:

'Neither party to this agreement shall be liable for failing to perform or delay of performance, if delay is caused by circumstances or events outside their reasonable control, which shall include but not be limited to industrial action, acts of God, terrorism, civil commotion, refusals to grant licences or permissions.'

9

Also, it is quite normal to include a clause in the contract that determines the sum of money (or a maximum amount) to be paid in case of breach of contract beforehand. Damage compensation will be paid nevertheless, even when the other contracting party did not suffer any real damages. The added value of such a clause though is that the contractual consequences will be more foreseeable. An example can be found in the same Indian Contract Law (Article 74):

> 'When a contract has been broken, if a sum is named in the contract as the amount be paid in case of such breach, or if the contract contains any other stipulation by way of penalty, the party complaining of the breach is entitled, whether or not actual damage or loss or proved to have been caused thereby, to receive from the party who has broken the contract reasonable compensation not exceeding the amount so named or, as the case may be, the penalty stipulated for.'

To conclude, also in common law systems, it is usual to send a formal notice to inform the other party he is in breach of contract. In the common law family this is known as a 'breach of contract notice' or a 'notice of breach'. For instance, the U.S. Uniform Commercial Code (§ 2-607 (3) (a)) stipulates in the case of the sales of goods that:

> 'the buyer must within a reasonable time after he discovers or should have discovered any breach notify the seller of breach or be barred from any remedy.'

9.1.3 Islamic law

In Islamic law, the traditional fiqh teaches us that a breach of contract may only result in a financial compensation that equals the price paid in exchange for the promised goods or services. This is so understood in at least two important legal schools of Islam: the Hanafi and the Shafti'i. This means on the one hand that enforcing fulfilment of the contract as is possible under civil law systems is not an option. It also means that additional damages such as the loss of income, paid interest to finance goods, or image damage are in essence not compensated. However, it needs to be noted here that in most modern understandings of Islamic law – most notably in Jordan, Kuwait, and the United Arab Emirates, the traditional approach is increasingly complemented by Western concepts of damage compensation (Saleh, 1989). Although interest as a loss will hardly be compensated, which is in line with the principles of Islam.

9.1.4 The CISG

In the Convention on Contracts for the International Sale of Goods, a compromise was found between especially the civil and common law approach: the disadvantaged party may choose between demanding the specific performance or damage compensation (Article 45 from the perspective of the buyer and 61 from the perspective of the seller). However, choosing one of them explicitly does not prevent claiming the other. This means that in the case of Lopez, the hotel does not have to wait to demand damage compensation before Lopez was given the opportunity to perform (Katz, 2006).

9.1.5 Other remedies

To encourage the performance of the other party, there are two more or less generally accepted additional legal remedies: suspense of the performance, and the retention of title clause.

Suspense of performance

When it becomes obvious that the other party will not perform as agreed in the contract, the disadvantaged party may choose to suspend his own performance.
For instance, the CISG stipulates in Article 71 that:

> 'A party may suspend the performance of his obligations if, after the conclusion of the contract, it becomes apparent that the other party will not perform a substantial part of his obligations as a result of: (a) A serious deficiency in his ability to perform or in his creditworthiness; or (b) His conduct in preparing to perform or in performing the contract.'

Considering example 9.5, it would be perfectly justifiable when Royal Cars would recall their cars while they are still on transport, and suspend the delivery of the goods until Car Land regained their creditworthiness. However, the other way around, it would be quite questionable if Car Land would suspend payment due to the fact that Royal Cars put only 29 out of the 30 cars on transport, thereby not completely fulfilling their obligation as agreed in the contract. After all, one could hardly say that delivering 29 out of the 30 cars is not performing 'a substantial part' of the agreement.

EXAMPLE 9.5

Cars

Royal Cars Ltd (supplier) and Car Land Ltd (retailer) concluded a contract in which Royal Cars promises to deliver 30 brand new in exchange for a sum of 150.000 pound. On the 1th of March 2016, Royal Cars puts 29 cars on transport (one car incidentally appears to be forgotten). If all goes well, they will arrive at Car Land on March 5th. However, on March 3rd, Royal Cars finds out that Car Land is in some serious trouble, and most likely will lose their creditworthiness soon. The company appears to have failed paying some other suppliers the last couple of days.

Another option in this context is to include a retention of title clause.

Retention of title

> A retention of title clause means that the ownership of supplied goods will transfer from the seller to the buyer at the moment of payment instead of delivery.

Practically, this would mean in Cars' case that Royal Cars Ltd could rest assure that they would not suffer from a possible bankruptcy of Car Land after the delivery of the cars. After all, while the cars may have been delivered and therefore in the physical possession of Car Land, they are still in the legal possession of Royal Cars. Only when Car Land pays the agreed sum, the legal possession will transfer. Therefore, when Car Land would go bankrupt between the delivery of the cars and the scheduled payment of these cars, Royal Cars may confiscate the cars, and keep them out of the bankruptcy estate.

9.2 Non-contractual liability

Not all liability stems from a breach of contract. Liability may also result from non-contractual relations. Everyday, people interact. Sometimes, this interaction results in damage. For instance, someone is violent and injures someone else. Or someone fails to press the break of a car in time and causes a traffic accident. The general idea is – simply put – that if someone causes damage to another, the causer of the damage is bound to pay for it. In essence, there are two types of non-contractual liability. In the first type, the causer of the damage should pay for the damage because he is to blame for it. This is called fault-based liability. In the second type, the law prescribes that someone should pay for damages, regardless whether he is to blame for it. This is called strict liability.

9.2.1 Fault-based liability

Around the world, there are many approaches towards fault-based liability. However, we can distinguish two major starting points: a general approach and a specific approach. Some legal systems have implemented one general rule on fault-based liability that covers the entire subject. This approach is usually mustered on the European mainland (most notably France and Germany), and all legal systems that were inspired by these systems. The other starting point is that the law prescribes different types of specific fault based liability. This approach can be found in the common law systems, in which different types of the so-called 'torts' are used.

The general approach

On the European mainland, the French and German Civil Codes have always been leading, and most other civil law systems were greatly inspired by one of them. The French rules on fault-based liability can be found in Articles 1382 and 1383 of the French Civil Code, where the most relevant German provisions are Articles 823 (I and II) and 826 of the German Civil Code. The wordings and content of these Articles differs, but there are some general features that can be distinguished:

- One needs to violate a rule or right;
- One needs to be culpable for this violation;
- There must damage;
- There must be a causal link between the violation of the rule or right and this damage.

Below, we will briefly explore these features in both the French and German legal system.

Violation

To be liable, one needs to violate a certain rule or right. It needs to be noted here that such a violation can be established by someone's action, but also by not acting. Acting and not acting are even specified in two separate Articles in the French Civil Code (the before mentioned 1382 and 1383). So being ignorant, negligent, or not taking precautionary measures that lead to damage to someone else may also lead to the violation of a rule or right.

In French law, this violation is referred to as a 'faute'. There are several ways to establish a 'faute'.
First, there is a faute when someone violates a written standard which results in damage to someone else.
For example, when someone causes a traffic accident, the Highway Code is usually violated (the driver may have driven too fast, or may not have kept enough distance).
Second, there is a faute when someone does not act the way a decent man should act. All French people should act as a good, just and cautious person.
For example, if someone acts without proper caution and this results in damage, there is a faute. This is the case when someone is visiting your place, does not pay attention as to where he walks, and as a result breaks your very expensive Chinese vase.
Third, if someone is convicted for a crime, and in committing that crime damage was caused, there is per definition a faute.
For example, when someone rapes someone else, and in committing the act, physical and psychological damage was caused, the perpetrator is liable for this damage.
Fourth, there is a faute when someone abuses its rights.
For example, when a neighbour plants very high trees on his ground with the sole purpose to irritate the other neighbour who now cannot enjoy the sun in her garden anymore, there is a faute. After all, the neighbour planting the trees abuses his right to land ownership.

In German law, the violation of a rule or right is referred to as a 'tadbestandswidrigkeit'. One violates a rule or right in several ways.
First, there is tadbestandswidrigkeit when one violates someone's protected right.
For example, when you violate the right to ownership by causing damage to property, or violate someone's right to physical integrity by causing injuries.
Second, just like the French 'faute', the violation of a written standard that results in damage will lead to tadbestandswidrigkeit.
For example, when someone lights a cigarette in a forest where it is forbidden to smoke due to fire risk, and as a result a wild fire erupts, causing injuries to others and damage to property, there is tadbestandswidrigkeit.
Third, when someone behaves unethically. This means that someone behaves in a manner that is generally considered to be in conflict with decent morality. This type of tadbestandswidrigkeit includes the abuse of a right, as we have seen in the French faute, but is also frequently used in the context of unfair economic behaviour, such as distorting competition by creating a cartel.
For example, two major companies establish a cartel, and as a result, a third competitor faces bankruptcy.

Culpability

Violating a right or rule in itself is not enough for being liable under fault-based liability. One also needs to be blamed for this. The legal word for this is culpability. In both the French and German legal system, culpability is assessed using an objective test. The question is raised whether a reasonable person could foresee the risk he took by violating the rule or right, and what this person could reasonably do to avoid the violation to happen. The question is not raised whether the plaintiff in question did indeed foresee the results of his action, or would be able to avoid the violation to happen. The latter would be a subjective test, which is hardly relevant anymore in both legal systems. Therefore, in example 9.6, in situation 4, it would not matter much if Claire had truly no idea that throwing a brick against a window would indeed break the window. What matters is if a reasonable thinking person would be able to make that assessment. If the answer is yes, and Claire still throws the brick, she is culpable.

9

Applying an objective test however will also lead to discussion. For instance, what are consequences that a reasonable person may foresee? Should Claire understand that there is a chance that in a living house someone might sit next to a window, and might be hurt by the brick thrown through this window (situation 1)? Or should Claire seriously take into consideration that in the house highly sensitive explosions are stored (situation 2)? Most likely, situation 1 will fall within the scope of what a reasonable person should foresee, while this is doubtful in situation 2. In each specific case, a court will have to apply the objective test and decide on the issue of culpability.

The only exception to applying an objective test in German law is when the violator would be a minor or mentally ill. In such cases, the German law applies a subjective test, and the question is raised whether Claire could foresee the consequences of her actions. In example 9.6, situation 5, in German law the conclusion will probably be that a six year-old child will not be able to foresee the consequences of throwing a brick through a window. In French law, the objective test is still used, but the parents of the child are strictly liable for the behaviour of the child. Therefore, although the child will be judged against 'adult' objective standards, it will never have to pay damage compensation in practice (Van Dam, 2013a).

A violator of a rule or right is not culpable when he can invoke an excusing circumstance. Both the French and German legal systems excuses such as self-defence, the defence of the interest of others, or an emergency situation. This means that in example 9.6, in situation 3, Claire is not culpable for throwing the brick. After all, she does so to save Charles. It would be rather peculiar if Charles would sue Claire for the broken window after being saved by her.

EXAMPLE 9.6

I threw a brick through a window

Claire (24 years old) throws a brick through the window of Charles's house.

Situation 1: A few weeks ago, Charles broke Claire's heart. In retaliation, Claire now breaks Charles's window. She did not see however that the mother of Charles was sitting besides that window, and is now seriously injured.

Situation 2: A few weeks ago, Charles broke Claire's heart. In retaliation, Claire now breaks Charles's window. She did not know that Charles secretly stores very sensitive explosives in his living room, because he is planning to sell them on the black market. As a result of the brick, the explosives do what they usually do: explode. The entire block (including the houses of Charles's neighbours) is vanished.

Situation 3: There is a fire in Charles's house. Claire throws a brick though his window to clear the path to save him.

Situation 4: Claire seriously believes that a brick cannot damage a window, and therefore, just to scare Charles a bit, throws the brick towards the window. Unfortunately, the window breaks as a result of the impact.

Situation 5: A few weeks ago, Charles broke Claire's heart. In retaliation, Claire now breaks Charles's window. Claire is not 24 but 6 years old.

Damage

The mere violation of a rule or right for which someone is to blame will not lead to any liability. After all, for claiming damages, we need actual damage that can be claimed. When someone holds someone else's smartphone and accidently drops it, but the smartphone remains entirely intact, there is no way this could lead to any damage compensation. This is a simple example, in which it is obvious there is no damage. However, things might be more complicated. What if you say something bad about someone else on social media, hurting the feelings of the other, and damage his good name? The damage in this case is much less visible, but may have serious consequences for the person whose reputation was damaged. French and German law deal with this issue differently.

In French law, the award of damage compensation is for the major part to the discretion of the courts, since the law remains silent on the exact determination of damage ('dommage'). The case law in France is quite casuistic and not so consistent when it concerns the granting of damage compensation. The main reason for this is that the French Court of Cassation will not receive appeals on the amount of damage compensation, and leaves this to the lower courts to decide. Any unifying effect of a central court is thereby absent (Van Dam, 2013b). However, what the court rulings have in common though is that:

- There should be actual damage.
- The damage should be suffered in a legitimate context. This means that damage resulting from illegal interest cannot be compensated. For example, you cannot claim damage compensation if someone damages the car you drive in when it appears that this car is not even yours, but borrowed from a friend.
- The damage should be very likely (the courts use the word 'certain'). This is obviously the case when something is damaged, or when there is physical injury. However, if someone is injured and is jobless, it is

uncertain whether the injured person loses one or more chances to find a job in the period of injury. The possible economic loss is therefore less certain, and the French courts will show less enthusiasm to compensate such uncertain damages.
- The damage must be suffered personally. One cannot demand damage compensation for the damage inflicted on someone else. However, the suffering of someone else may also cause damage to others: when someone is killed, the relatives may demand compensation damage since they suffer from their grief.

In Germany, the Civil Code is much more explicit in what kind of damages may be compensated. The restoration of damage, additional damage, economic damage and intangible damage are separately regulated. The general rule (in both contractual and non-contractual liability) is that:

> 'A person who is liable in damages must restore the position that would exist if the circumstance obliging him to pay damages had not occurred.' (Section 249, German Civil Code)

So, in essence, the violator of the rule or right should pay for all costs that are involved with restoring the situation to before the violation occurred. So when you break someone else's car, you are bound to pay for the repair. However, when the restoration leads to an impossible or disproportionate burden for the violator, fitting damage compensation may be awarded (Section 251 German Civil Code). In example 9.7, one could argue that it would place a disproportionate burden on Mo to get a new hand signature of a celebrity. This would probably involve flying around the world and stalk the lead singer of the Foo Fighters for a while. In this case, Mo will surely buy a new record for Chris, though the hand sign will not be restored or renewed: instead damage compensation will be rewarded. While this burden is disproportionate, think about a case in which the hand signature belonged to a popstar that already passed away. In that case, restoring or renewing would truly be impossible.

EXAMPLE 9.7

The Foo Fighters and the lost vinyl
Chris is happy to possess a hand signed vinyl record of the Foo Fighters which was hand signed by their lead singer, Dave Grohl. Mo borrows this record to impress a girl who happens to be a huge Foo Fighter fan. At some point, the record gets lost, and Mo cannot find it anymore. Chris wants a new one, and insists that it should be hand signed by mister Grohl himself.

Additionally, when restoration seems to be inadequate to compensate for the damage, additional damage compensation may be awarded (Section 251 German Civil Code). For instance, when you damage someone else's care, and as a result of the damage the insurer is not willing to insure the car under the same conditions as before. Now only restoring the damage will not compensate for the higher insurance costs for the owner of the car. Therefore, these additional costs may also be compensated for.

The above does not include non-financial damages. They are separately recognized in the German Civil Code. Section 252 recognizes damage compensation for lost profits. Furthermore, Section 253 recognizes specific categories of intangible damage. These include the (non tangible) consequences of injury to the body, health, freedom or sexual self-determination. Other forms of non-tangible damage compensation were not recognized for a long time. However, in case law, another type of damage compensation seems to emerge which compensates for reputation damage, as you can see in example 9.8.

EXAMPLE 9.8

The Herrenreiter and sexual potency

A German pharmaceutical company, well known for their products that increase sexual potency, was sued by a famous German brewer and amateur show-jumper (Herrenreiter). The pharmaceutical company had used a photograph of the brewer while he was show-jumping on the back of a horse in promotion of one of their products. The link between sexual potency and riding a horse was quite suggestive, and the amateur show-rider had never given any permission for this picture to be used. Since the brewer was quite famous in Germany, and accordingly his good name was damaged by this commercial, he demanded damage compensation for reputation damage.

The German legal system would originally allow damage compensation up to the amount of income the Brewer would potentially receive when he would allow his picture to be used. However, the German Court of Appeal awarded much higher damage compensation in a broad interpretation of the German Civil Code in conjunction with the German Basic Law. Since Article 1 and 2 of the German basic Law protect the human dignity and personal freedoms, the Court considered that in this case, higher damage compensation was justified, since these two fundamental rights were violated by the commercial. Since this verdict, non-financial damage in the field of image or reputation damage has been accepted widely in the German Courts (Bundesgerichtshof, 1995).

Last but not least, the damage must be a result of the violation of the rule or right. Imagine someone damages your car, and you are so angry that you throw your smartphone through the room. In that case, we have to conclude that there hardly is any causality between the violation to property by damaging your car, and the damage to the smartphone. **Causality**

The specific approach

In the common law systems, the starting point of non-contractual liability is not centrally organized, but is built around precedents in case law that deals with specific types of liability. This approach dates back to the 12th century, in which the English writ system was introduced. In essence, the complaints of people who wanted to sue one another were submitted using standardized types of 'writs' that would reflect the particular nature of the complaint. Nowadays, these specific types are called 'torts'.

Writ system

Tort

While this tort law is traditionally build around case law, increasingly also legislation is used. For instance, all States of Australia have uniformly adopted a law on defamation, regulating the tort of defamation (Rolph, 2008). Consequentially, when someone inflicts intentional harm on someone's reputation by spreading false statements, the victim can claim damage compensation under this tort.

The different types of tort are slightly different in each common law system, although the general features are pretty much the same. In general, a distinction can be drawn between intentional and unintentional torts.

Intentional torts

In intentional torts, someone intentionally injures someone or damages property. There is usually a very direct link between the intentional action and the damage done. In the Canadian system of tort law (except Quebec, in which a civil law system is implemented), there are at least four main types of intentional torts: trespass to the person, trespass to land, nuisance and defamation. Only recently, in some states, a new tort is added: the invasion of privacy, for instance in Ontario, (Court of Appeal for Ontario, 2012). However, this tort is not widely accepted.

Trespass to the person

> Trespass to the person is the interference with a person's body or freedom.

This tort is composed of several more specific tort types, which includes assault, battery, false arrest and false imprisonment. In the case of assault, someone is threatened but not physically harmed. In the case of battery, someone is actually physically harmed. In the case of false arrest and false imprisonment, someone is deprived of his freedom for unjust reasons. This could be done by a public authority, but also by a fellow citizen (for instance, kidnapping).

Trespass to land

> Trespass to land is the entering of someone's land without permission of the owner.

This means that when someone enters your house without your permission, you might sue this person for illegally violating your domain. For instance, when a tenant stays in a house while he did not pay the rent, the landlord may sue the tenant for trespass to land. After all, he stays in the house without permission. Another example is when a hunter shoots game on the territory of a farmer without his permission. It is therefore not even required that actual damage is done, purely the violation in itself is cause of financial compensation. However, normally, the tort of trespass to land coincides with the damaging or violation of property on that land, and consequentially, higher damage compensation will be awarded. The classic example is the burglar who breaks a window to enter the house, and steals property.

Nuisance

> Nuisance is the use of property in such a way that it substantially interferes with the use of someone else's property.

Examples of nuisance are the making of noise in the middle of the night so that neighbour cannot sleep, and therefore cannot enjoy the comfort of their house. Another example is keeping pets without taking proper care of their hygiene, and as a result, the neighbours are confronted with smell and other hinder that interferes with the enjoyment of living in their house.

Defamation

Defamation is the inflicting of harm on someone's reputation by spreading false statements.

An example of defamation can be found in the news item 'False abuse accusations against teachers "on the rise".'

CBC NEWS, CANADA, 24 APRIL 2012

False abuse accusations against teachers 'on the rise'

BY: MARK GOLLOM

Teachers across Canada are having their reputations ruined as increasing numbers get falsely accused of abusing their students, or acting inappropriately with them, experts say.
'We are getting more and more "teacher-talk" evidence and teacher narratives that clearly indicate that false accusations are on the rise,' Jon Bradley, associate professor of education at McGill University, told CBCNews via email.
'Active parents are making things, in some cases, very difficult,' he said.
University of Ottawa faculty of education professor Joel Westheimer told CBC's Ottawa Morning that incidents of false allegations used to be fairly rare in both Canada and the United States.

Unintentional torts

Tort of negligence

In unintentional torts, someone is negligent, and as a result is to blame for the damage done. Therefore, unintentional tort is usually referred to as the tort of negligence. It is generally accepted that this tort consists of three elements:

- there is a duty of care;
- this duty is breached;
- the breach results in damages.

The Canadian Supreme Court has specified that in determining whether someone has a duty of care, an objective test is used: if a reasonable person could foresee that his action or not acting would result in damages, there is a duty of care to avoid the damage (Supreme Court of Canada, 1999). If this does not happen, this duty is breached. Below, when U.S. product liability is discussed, negligence is explained in further detail.

Defences

For each type of tort, the courts have developed defences that may be invoked by the committer of the tort in his defence. For instance, in defence for battery, one could invoke self defence, or consent of the victim. Another example in defence of negligence is when the victim was also negligent, and the damage would have been avoided if the victim would fulfil his own duty of care. Think about a motor cyclist that does not wear a helmet: when someone else cause a traffic accident and the cyclist suffers serious head injuries, the victim is partly to blame for this due to not wearing a helmet.

It needs to be noted here that there are significant differences in the type of damages that may be awarded under tort law systems compared to the civil law systems. The most notable types of damage compensation are compensatory damages, nominal damages and punitive damages.

Compensatory damages

Compensatory damages are the damages awarded to compensate for the actual loss that results from the tort. These include the punitive damage. More measurable matters such as the costs of restoring, repairing and economic loss. They are referred to as special damages. However, in common law systems it is quite normal to award on top of that a less defined, more general, sum of money to compensate for the grief, pain or discomfort that is suffered. They are referred to as general damages.

Nominal damage

Furthermore, there is nominal damage. This is damage that is awarded while there is no actual damage. However, the mere fact that someone committed a tort is in itself a ground for a (small) damage compensation. For instance, when someone enters your land without your permission, but does not cause any damages, nominal damage compensation may be awarded. This also means that actual damage, as is the case in civil law systems, is not necessarily a prerequisite for damage compensation in common law systems.

Punitive damage

Also, there is the concept of punitive damage. This is a sum of money awarded to the victim of the tort with the sole purpose to punish the violator, and deter her/him from doing it once more. These kinds of damages are usually unheard of in civil law countries, and originate from penal law. Generally, such damage is not randomly awarded, and only plays a role in serious offences in criminal law (Supreme Court of Canada, 2002).

In figure 9.1 you may find a schematic overview of the most important torts and damages.

FIGURE 9.1 A schematic overview of torts and damages under common law systems

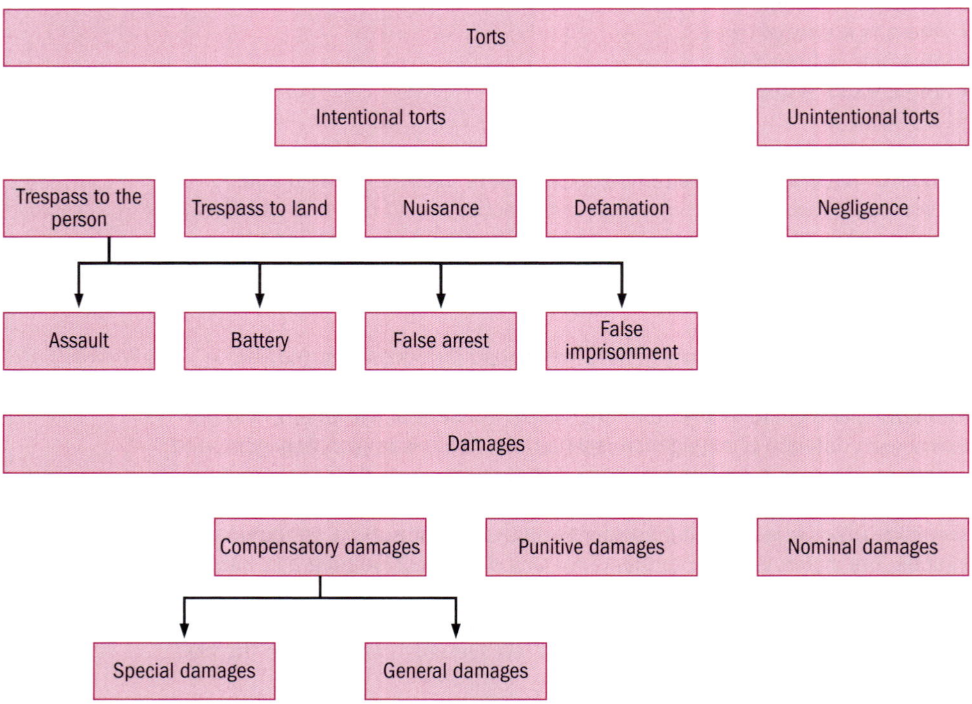

9.2.2 Strict liability

It is not always very practical or desirable to require evidence of the fact that someone is 'to blame' for caused damage.
When a manufacturer produces a defective product that causes injuries to some of their consumers, it is very hard to figure out which employee or which manager in what stage of the production process made a mistake and is therefore to blame for the damage. Instead, it is much more practical to simply agree that manufacturers are responsible for their products, and have to pay for any damages caused by the defective product. It would put a disproportionate burden on the victim of the malfunctioning product to require evidence of some sort culpability of company.

When a pet, say a dog, bites a random passer-by and causes injury, someone has to pay for the damage. Since one usually cannot sue a pet, it seems only reasonable to sue the owner of the pet. However, it is mostly impossible to proof that the owner of a pet is culpable for the pet going wild and biting the victim. Therefore, the law may create this liability by using the concept of strict liability. The owner of a pet is then always liable for its behaviour, regardless the circumstances.

The European Product Liability Directive

A fine example of strict liability for defective products can be found in European Law, to be precise in Council Directive 85/374/EEC. The core idea is stipulated in Article 1, that reads: 'The producer shall be liable for damage caused by a defect in his product.'

However, this seemingly simple sentence needs some further clarification. A couple of questions need to be answered:
- What is a product?
- Who is producer?
- When is a product defect?
- For what damage can the producer be held liable?

Product

In answer to the first question, Article 2 helps us out. Products covered by this directive are all movables, with the exception of agricultural products and game. So, this means that immovable property and agricultural products are not covered by this directive.

Producer

Furthermore, Article 3 further clarifies what a producer is. This is first, not surprisingly, the manufacturer of an end product. However, also the producer of the raw materials or component parts may be held liable when the defect is caused by their creation.
Furthermore, any retailer that puts his name on the product is considered to be as liable as a producer. This is usually the case of a house brand: while the name on that product is not the name of the manufacturer, it is the only name known by the consumer. Therefore, the seller of his own house brand is just as liable as if he were the real manufacturer.
To conclude, any agent that imports products from outside the European Union is liable as if being a manufacturer. After all, outside the EU, the consumer is confronted with different rules, and will not necessarily benefit from the consumer protection that applies in the entire EU zone. Therefore, the consumer should be able to hold the company liable that imports the malfunctioning product.

Article 6 specifies when a product is considered to be defective:
'1 A product is defective when it does not provide the safety which a person is entitled to expect, taking all circumstances into account, including:
 (a) the presentation of the product;
 (b) the use to which it could reasonably be expected that the product would be put;
 (c) the time when the product was put into circulation.
2 A product shall not be considered defective for the sole reason that a better product is subsequently put into circulation.'

Presentation

The presentation of the product is essentially what the manufacturer communicates on the package, information leaflet or manual, as we can see in example 9.9. From this, the end user may deduce what the product should – or should not – be used for, or what the limits are of the products capacity. The consumer is then informed about the (im)possibilities of the product, and cannot use this against the manufacturer in a later stage. Especially in the pharmaceutical industry, information leaflets will inform the user of the medicine of all possible side effects that may be caused by the medicine. Consequentially, the consumer was informed and cannot hold the manufacturer liable when suffering from one of these side effects. To illustrate, manufacturers of most contraception drugs will eagerly inform you that taking the pill will not necessarily guarantee that you will not get pregnant. In 9.10, a clear example is provided in which the presentation of the product led to product liability. After all, when the manufacturer puts on the package a note saying 'Nespresso machine compatible' it is very surprising that the cup ruins the entire machine.

Reasonable usage

The use which could be reasonably expected is another criteria that determines the defectiveness of a product. However, the term reasonable is quite a subjective concept. In practice, the European courts will consider whether the average, reasonable thinking person would consider a certain usage of the product as normal. On the one hand, a manufacturer should produce products that meet reasonable expectations. When a consumer buys a chair, he may reasonably expect that it is possible to sit on it without breaking the chair. On the other hand, one cannot expect a manufacturer to take into account the sheer stupidity of an individual. Take someone who puts her cat in a microwave to dry up, or irons his jeans without taking the jeans off. It is unlikely that these people will be able to successfully invoke product liability against the manufacturer of the microwave or iron.

Age of product

The third criterion is the time in which a product was put into circulation. One may simply have higher expectations of a brand new car, than a second hand car that is twenty years old. If the engine breaks in case of the first after two miles of driving, the product is definitely defective. However, the same cannot be said in case of the second hand car. In line with this, the second paragraph of Article 6 – just to be sure – adds that the mere fact that products have been improved in the meanwhile will never lead to the conclusion that the old product is therefore defective, or does not perform what can reasonably be expected.

EXAMPLE 9.9

The ethical coffee company

A slight miscalculation

A Suisse company produces coffee cups that are compatible with the famous Nespresso coffee machines. However, when placed in the Nespresso machine, the cup seems to stagnate in the machine. The pin penetrating the cup is not strong enough to fully sting the cup. The result is that most of the coffee pulp and cup material gets stuck in the machine, preventing any further use of the devise. It seems that the designer of the cup made a miscalculation, and therefore the cups are not only useless in the machine, but also damage the devise beyond repair.
I bought these cups in 2011 in a local supermarket in my hometown, called the Plus Market. The damaged Nespresso machine was recently purchased for 120 euros. The defective cups were bought for 4 euros per package.

Legal remedies manufacturer

While the Directive in itself focuses on providing consumers with legal remedies to facilitate them in holding a manufacturer liable for defective products, Article 7 provides for some legal remedies for the manufacturers. If the manufacturer can invoke one of the provisions laid down in this Article, he is not liable for the defective product. For instance, manufacturers are excused from product liability when they can prove that they did not put the defective in circulation. Imagine a thief steals 20 bikes from a producer while they were unfinished, and sells them illegally to a retailer. The consumer who eventually buys the bike from the retailer might suffer damage due to the defectiveness of the unfinished bike. However, they will not be able to successfully sue the manufacturer, since he did not put these bikes into circulation.
Another remedy is when the manufacturer can prove that the defect that caused the damage did not exist at the moment the product was put into circulation. When the owner of a smartphone accidently drops it in the loo, the product will turn out to be defective. Damage may include the loss of a lot of data. However, it is not very likely that the manufacturer is liable for the clumsiness of the end-user. In practice, this remedy is often used in the smartphone branch. While smartphone providers are rather generous in their warranty period of their products, the reality is that it is often hard to prove that a defect is indeed caused by the manufacturer, and not by the daily usage of the owner of the product. An example of this approach can be found in the sample of the Huawei Warranty articles that apply in the EU (example 9.10).
Another important remedy is the situation in which the state of scientific and technical knowledge at the time when the product was put into circulation was not such as to enable the existence of the defect to be discovered. In other words: if even the smart brains of mankind did not know something was damaging, then a manufacturer cannot be held liable for that. Famous examples are the usage of asbestos in immovable property, or the smoking of cigarettes. There was a time when it was not known that these products could be lethal to men. The major court suits on product liability of such products focus on the period in which the damaging effect was discovered, but the manufacturers did not yet warn for its consequences.

EXAMPLE 9.10

Huawei Warranty in the EU
An example

'1 The warranty lasts and is provided in accordance with the respective local laws, as standard for a period of twenty-four (24) months for the host unit, six (6) months for the battery and charger, and three (3) months for the earphone from the date of purchase of the product ("Warranty Period"), and is only applicable if you have purchased the Product in a member state of European Union, Iceland, Norway or Switzerland.
(...)
5 This Warranty does not cover damage resulting from:
 1 Normal wear and tear of the equipment.
 2 Defects and damages due to the equipment being used other than in a normal and customary manner.
 3 Any unauthorised disassembly, repair, alteration or modifications being carried out.
 4 Misuse, abuse, negligence or accident howsoever caused.
 5 Defects or damage arising from improper testing, operation, maintenance, installation, or any alteration or modification.
 6 Defects or damage due to spillage of food or liquids, corrosion, rust or the use of wrong voltage.
 7 Scratches or damage to plastic surfaces and all other externally exposed parts that are due to normal customer use.' (http://consumer.huawei.com, 2016)

Burden of proof consumer

In essence, the consumer suffering damage from a defective product needs to prove three things, as is stipulated in Article 8: the damage, the defect and the causal relationship between defect and damage. This can be quite simple: when a cab driver gets injured due to a malfunctioning break, it will not be so hard to prove the damage, the defect and the causal link between the two. However, the more indirect the consequences, the harder it will be to prove all three prerequisites. When this cab driver as a result of the accident becomes afraid of driving cars and is psychologically unfit to work, it will be more difficult to prove that there is a causal relation between the malfunctioning break and the psychological damage and loss of income of the driver.

Damage compensation

When it is proven that the manufacturer is liable for a defective product, one needs to establish the scope of this liability. In general, Article 16 stipulates that the EU member states may adopt a maximum liability of damage compensation of a defective product, but that maximum may not be lower than 70 million euros. For instance, in Germany this is 85 million euros (Art. 10 German Product Liability Act), while in the UK there is no maximum for damages resulting from product liability (O'Neil, 2011).
Article 9 specifies what kind of damage should be compensated by the manufacturer. First, that is all damage caused by death or by personal injuries. Second, this is result damage with a threshold of 500 euros.

Result damage

Result damage is the damaged to other products intended for private usage, caused by a defective product.

This means that other products than the defective product are damaged as a result of the defect, and these products are also in the sphere of normal consumer usage. Would it be products for professional use, the product liability would be in the B to B context, and therefore outside the scope of this directive. In the case of the 'Ethical Coffee Company' the result damage is the Nespresso machine, which was demolished by the defective cup. However, since the damage only amounts to 120 euros, it is not covered by the EU product liability directive. Would it have been 600 euros, I could claim the full result damage directly from the Ethical Coffee Company. The threshold therefore only distinguishes who should pay the damage, and does not mean that only the damage that exceeds 500 euros should be paid by the manufacturer.

Now, as to the damage compensation, the above applies to all EU Member States. However, three questions remain. First, who pays for the result damage below 500 euros? Second, who compensates for the defective product? And third, to what extent is it possible to demand non-material damage compensation such as psychological damage or loss of income? These issues are not covered by the EU directive, and therefore fall under the discretion of the national legal systems of the EU.
With regard to the first two questions, the general approach seems to be that the retailer is liable for these costs. So, the retailer where the product was bought should compensate for result damage below 500 euros, and is bound to repair, renew or compensate for the product that is defective. With regard to the third question, compensation for non-material damage is diversely regulated amongst the EU Member States. It is not uncommon that for a claim for non-material losses, an additional claim is required based on the more regular tort acts, which usually involves fault-based liability. A more detailed example of how this might work can be found in case study 8.1, 'product liability in Finland', available on the website.

Product liability in the U.S.A.
In the common law oriented countries, product liability is constructed in the tradition of torts, rather than explicitly embedded in written standards. However, also here, product liability is mostly a form of strict liability.

For instance, in the U.S.A. there are three major approaches in product liability: the negligence theory, the strict liability theory, and the breach of warranty theory. The last two approaches show characteristics of strict liability.

Negligence theory

The negligence theory is the oldest approach in product liability, and should be classified of a form of fault based liability. In short, the theory implies that a victim of a defective product has to prove that the manufacturer breached a duty of care towards the consumer. In essence, it means that when a manufacturer could reasonably foresee that the product would lead to damages suffered by the consumer, the manufacturer is liable. This is especially the case when mistakes were made in the product design, the manufacturing process, or the warning instructions on the product. If these mistakes result in actual damage of the consumer, the manufacturer is liable for breaching his duty of care towards the consumer.

In obvious cases, it will not be so hard to find evidence that the manufacturer is liable under this negligence theory. When the wrong paint is used for baby furniture – containing poisonous chemicals – every reasonable man will understand that this is a serious flaw in the design of a product. When a baby becomes ill as a result thereof, the negligence theory will not be so difficult to apply. In the context of unsafe manufacturing processes, the same goes for a pre-packaged food supplier, in which one of the packages is not vacuum as a result of a mistake during the manufacturing. The consumer may become ill after consuming the food that is not well packed. A last example is when the warning notice on medication fails to inform the consumer that using the drug may affect driving skills, and one of the users of the medicine causes an accident in traffic.

All these cases are pretty straightforward, and will in practice turn out to be easy to prove using the negligence theory. However, when products become more complex, or the manufacturing is outsourced by different sub-contractors, it will not always be easy for the consumer to prove that the manufacturer breached his duty of care. Therefore, in the 70ies, in both case law and legislation, a new concept was introduced: that of strict product liability.

Strict liability theory

The strict liability theory leaves out the culpability part that can still be found in the negligence theory: it is not relevant whether or not a manufacturer could reasonably foresee that a product would be defective as a result of breaching a duty of care towards the consumer. Instead, the courts will use two types of tests to figure out whether or not a product is defective. The first test is the consumer expectation test. The question then is raised whether the average consumer would reasonably expect a certain usage or characteristics of the product. If that is the case, and the product does not meet these reasonable expectations, the product is defective.

The second test is the risk-utility test. In this test, the question is raised whether the utility or the possible risk of the product is bigger. When utility outweighs the risk, the product may be dangerous but not defective. For instance, a certain medication with dangerous side effects may be the only way to cures someone. In that case, the utility outweighs the possible risks. The other way around, when the possible risks outweigh the utility, the product is definitely defective. Courts in the U.S.A. even use a formula to determine this: the so called hand furmula (Owen, 1997). In brief, it means that the probability of the damage is maximized with the actual damage. If this amount exceeds the costs of taking measures (for instance altering the design, or issuing a warning), there is no product liability. Such a formula is for instance frequently used in the many cases against football helmet manufacturers. The probability of damage as a result of the usage of the helmet is maximized with the damage suffered by the victim. Mostly, the damage in such cases is quite serious (in example 9.11 the victim is half paralyzed) and will therefore usually exceed the costs of the manufacturer to redesign the product so that the helmet is safer. In the U.S. the risk-utility test is mostly preferred over the consumer expectation test. The first is relatively easy and neutrally measurable, while the concept of consumer expectation is rather vague and subjective (Twerski, 2009).

EXAMPLE 9.11

Butting heads and breaking bones
It is remarkable how many law suits were held in the U.S.A. against the manufacturers of football helmets. A notable example is the case of Greg Stead, who was injured during a football match at his high school in Florida, in the early seventies. During the match, Stead was hit in the spine by another player, who was wearing a Riddell helmet. As a result, Stead suffered serious neck injuries – even quadriplegia – and consequentially had to spend the rest of his life semi-paralyzed in a wheel chair. In the end, the football helmet manufacturer – Riddell – was sued. The plaintiff held that if the helmet was thus designed that being hit by the product could lead to quadriplegia, there must be a design mistake. The Supreme Court of Florida agreed, and Riddell was held liable for the damage on the basis of strict liability. In compensation, the plaintiff was awarded a sum of 5.3 million U.S. dollars. This court ruling opened the floodgates, and since then numerous successful claims were filed against helmet manufacturers for all kinds of injuries. (Supreme Court of Florida, 1975)

Breach of warranty theory

Lastly, there is the breach of warranty theory. In short, this means that a product should be able to do as is specified by the manufacturer. In practice, this means that whatever the manufacturer communicates regarding the product, or what can be reasonably deduced from this falls within the scope of this theory. This could be explicit, such as written statements on the package or package leaflet, promises made in advertisements, or warranty clauses in the contract. Examples are that a product will last for a certain period, can be used for particular ends, or will lead to particular results when used. This could also be implicit (the so called implied warranty), when it can reasonably be deduced from what the manufacturer communicates about the product. This is mostly understood as the reasonable expectations a consumer may have when using the product. For instance, one should be able to use a chair to sit on, and consume a candy bar without getting sick. The advantage of this theory is that a consumer does not really have to prove the defect of a product, but rather that a product does not do what the warranty clause suggests. The disadvantage is that mostly, the damage compensation awarded is not as high compared to the other two approaches.

Summary

9

- There is contractual liability and non-contractual liability.

- In contractual liability, there are different approaches.

- The civil law systems have in common that:
  - When performance is impossible, damage compensation is awarded, except when a force majeure is invoked;
  - When performance is still possible, performance can be demanded within a reasonable time. When justified, additional damage compensation can be awarded;
  - When performance still does not occur, damage compensation can be awarded.

- The common law systems there is a strong focus on monetary damage compensation.
  - It is not unusual to agree on a clause excusing the contracting parties from performance in case of a force majeure;
  - It is not unusual to agree on a clause that determines the amount of money that is to be paid in case of non-performance beforehand.

- In Islamic law, traditionally, breach of contract may only result in a financial compensation that equals the price paid in exchange for the promised goods or services. In a modern understanding of Islamic law, this concept is somewhat broadened in the direction of civil or common law.

- The CISG offers a compromise between especially the civil and common law approach.

- Next to contractual liability, contracting parties may invoke other legal remedies to support their claim. These are most notably the suspense of performance and the retention of title.
  - Suspense of performance means that when it becomes obvious that the other party will not perform as agreed in the contract, the disadvantaged party may choose to suspend his own performance.
  - A retention of title clause means that the ownership of supplied goods will transfer from the seller to the buyer on the moment of payment instead of delivery.

- Non-contractual liability can be subdivided in fault based liability and strict liability. In the first, culpability plays a profound role. In the latter, culpability plays no role for liability is determined by the law.

- In fault-based liability, there are two major approaches: the civil law approach (general) and the common law approach (specific).

- In the civil law approach, mostly inspired by the French and German Civil Code) there is a general fault based liability provision. In this provision it is specified that:
  - One needs to violate a rule or right;
  - One needs to be culpable for this violation;
  - There must damage;
  - There must be a causal link between the violation of the rule or right and this damage.
- In the common law approach, fault-based liability is developed by the courts as so called 'torts'.
- Most notably, there are the following standard tort types:
  - Intentional torts: trespass to the person (assault, battery, false arrest and false imprisonment), trespass to land, nuisance and defamation.
  - Unintentional torts: negligence (there is a duty of care; this duty is breached; the breach results in damages).
- For each tort, defences are developed that may be invoked by the defendant.
- There are different types of damage compensation that may be awarded. These include compensatory damage, nominal damage, and punitive damage.
  - Compensatory damage is the damages awarded to compensate for the actual loss that results from the tort.
  - Nominal damage is the damage awarded to compensate the mere fact that someone committed a tort is in itself, regardless the existence of actual damage.
  - Punitive damage is the damages awarded to the victim of the tort with the sole purpose to punish the violator, and deter her/him from doing it once more.

► In strict liability, the law regulates who is liable for what damages, regardless the element of culpability. An example of strict liability is product liability.

- In Europe, product liability is regulated in Council Directive 85/374/EEC.
  - A products are all movables with the exemption of agricultural products and game.
  - A producer is a manufacturer, the retailer who puts his name on the product, any agent that imports products from outside the European Union.
  - A product is defective when it does not provide the safety which a person is entitled to expect.
  - The producer is liable for all damage caused by death or by personal injuries, and the result damage with a threshold of 500 euros.
- In the U.S.A., there are three approaches in product liability.
  - In the negligence theory, a victim of a defective product has to prove that the manufacturer breached a duty of care towards the consumer (fault-based liability).
  - In the strict liability theory, culpability is left out as a prerequisite, and the courts will apply the consumer expectation test or the risk-utility test to establish product liability.
  - In the breach of warranty theory, a product should be able to do as is (explicitly or implicitly) specified by the manufacturer.

Practice questions

9

Open questions

Bauer, a professional Dutch singer, buys a new microphone. Unfortunately, the microphone cannot stand the awful sounds of his singing, and as a result explodes. The costs for medical treatment are 400 euros. The instruments of Bauer's band are also damaged (450 euros), and the microphone must be replaced (800 euros). The microphone was produced by a Japanese based company 'Microsblode', and sold by the Belgian company 'Musicmaker'.

9.1 Who can Bauer sue for damage compensation based on the Council Directive 85/374/EEC of 25 July 1985? Please, refer to the relevant articles.

9.2 If U.S. law would be applied, how would the case discussed in question 1 then be solved?

9.3 Clarissa is the owner of a bar. She has to open a cellar hatch to replace beer barrels. The hatch is in a corridor that is frequently used by clients, because the restrooms are located at the end of this corridor. Tricky thing however is that the hatch is just around a corner, and therefore not quite visible. Normally, an employee would close the hatch when working below, but Clarissa forgets since she does not regularly perform this duty, being the owner herself. The result is dramatic: one of the customers falls into the hatch opening, and breaks a leg.

If you would apply the civil law approach in fault-based liability, how would you assess the liability of Clarissa.

9.4 If common law would apply in the case of question 9.2, how would you assess the fault-based liability of Clarissa?

Essay question

Sylvia hires a contractor to isolate the shed in her backyard. She plans to make a small studio in which she can practise with her guitar without her neighbours complaining about the noise. She is after all a professional guitarist. The contractor is confident he can do the job. When the isolation is finished, the shed looks wonderful, but unfortunately the sound is as loud as if there was no isolation, and Sylvia cannot use her shed for the purpose she intended.

Write a short essay in which you compare the legal actions Sylvia would probably take if common law, civil law and Islamic law would apply.

Multiple choice questions

9.1 In case of non-performance, the CISG allows the disadvantaged party:
a to first demand performance
b to immediately claim damage compensation
c to choose between option a and b

9.2 A 'retention of title' clause means that:
a when it becomes obvious that the other party will not perform as agreed in the contract, the disadvantaged party may choose to suspend his own performance
b the ownership of supplied goods will transfer from the seller to the buyer on the moment of payment instead of delivery
c a contracting party is entitled to rescind the contract at anytime

9.3 Trespass to the person is:
a an intentional tort
b an unintentional tort
c no tort at all

9.4 Which element is not an issue in strict liability?
a violation of a right
b culpability
c a causal link between the violation of a right and damage

DELL
WELCOME TO
ELL
D
Sandor

10
Labour law

When countries industrialize, labour law can protect the interest of employees. In this chapter, we will first explore the causal relation between industrialisation and the emergence of labour law. Then, we will explain how labour law is developed on a global level. Furthermore, we will discuss how different legal systems facilitate the realization of proper labour conditions. In this light, we will focus on the nature of labour contracts, the duration of such a contract, minimum wage, labour conditions, non-discrimination rules, the right to organize and collective bargaining, and social security systems.

10.1 The industrial revolution and the emergence of labour law

Labour law is not a very old legal subject. It is inextricably linked to the industrial revolution, which started around 1760 in England, and initially spread throughout Western Europe, North America and Australia. Before that time, in these regions, the concept of working for someone else was always in the sphere of either involuntary work (such as slavery) or in the form of apprenticeship, a journeyman or in a master/servant relation. Those who were self-employed worked as a free craftsman, and the only legal organization was a system of so called guilds, in which labour related aspects of those who were in the employment of these craftsmen were discussed and (loosely) regulated (Finkin, 2006).

However, the industrial revolution changed societies significantly. Both in a positive and negative way.

In a positive way, it was now easier to produce products on a large scale and offer them for a lower price. In that sense, the industrial revolution led to an increase in creativity, ideas and scientific progress (Trinder, 2013). However, there were also some troublesome side effects. The first was that the working class moved from the countryside to the greater cities. This is called urbanisation. After all, making a living in the country side was next to impossible, since the bigger factories were producing far lower costs than craftsmen in the country side. The problem was however that the cities could not house all these inhabitants, and therefore 'slums' were built at the borders of these cities, where people lived in poor conditions. The second consequence was that as a result of industrialization, people lost their jobs since machines took over manpower. This led to an ever-increasing income gap between the company owners and the working class. The third effect was increasing damage to the environment. For the first time in history, mankind was confronted with the boundaries of mass production, including the effects of using fossil fuels and pollution. For employees this meant that they had to work in an unhygienic environment (Trinder, 2013, Wernaart, 2015a). It is not surprising that in this context, that the so-called 'social question' or 'labour question' was raised, addressing the wellbeing of employees (Finkin, 2006).
Simultaneously, the monarchs in Europe began to lose their powers and these countries became increasingly more democratic. The result was that the working class in the early 20th century had an increasing political influence on law making.
As a result, the legal position of employees was gradually strengthened through law in several fields. The issues dealt with can be sub grouped in recognizing proper labour conditions, the right to organize and collective bargaining, and the adoption of social security standards.

Elsewhere in the world, countries industrialized considerably later, though also here, there seems to be a link between industrialization and the creation of labour laws. This is especially the case in the so-called Newly Developed Countries, such as the BRIC countries (Brazil, Russia, India and China), the Asian tigers (Taiwan, Singapore, South-Korea and the former Hong Kong) and more recently the Arab Emirates, Malaysia, Turkey and South Africa. Of course, the context differs from the European context.

Asian industrialized countries

The Asian industrialized countries mostly share a colonial past, in which concepts of law were already exported from Europe. Furthermore, the ongoing trend of globalization played a significant role in the debate on labour law in Asia. On the one hand, companies gladly made use of the more flexible labour standards in the upcoming Asian economies. However, these standards would usually have been considered inadequate in the countries of origin of these companies. An example of this can be found in the case 'Dell and the ICT Hell' (example 10.1). On the other hand, the creation of international labour law in the period after the Second World War had some influence in the adoption of labour laws. This was most notably done by the International Labour Organization. As a result of its work, labour laws have been adopted in the entire region (Sankaran, 2007).

Islamic industrialized countries

In Islamic countries, the context is different: also here, industrialization is a trigger to adopt labour laws, and these laws are usually inspired by European concepts for various reasons (including a colonial past). However, in Islamic countries, lawmakers attempt to unite principles of Islam, which are God given, with codified labour standards founded on a European model, which are usually secular (Zulfiqar, 2007). Established labour principles in Islamic law, deduced from religious texts such as the Qu'ran are for instance the right to a fair wage, good employership (the employee should be treated as a member of the family), and the right to a share in the profit of a company.

EXAMPLE 10.1

Dell and the ICT Hell

The world's largest ICT factories can be found in Shenzhen City, China. In 2013, the Danish human rights watchdog published a report in which the labour conditions within these factory walls was criticized (Stracke et al. 2013). The information substantiating the report was gathered by conducting risky under-cover operations, since the Chinese authorities were not quite cooperative in gathering the relevant data. The report focused on the supplying factories for the American based ICT company Dell, although similar conclusion can be drawn for the suppliers of other ICT companies such as Apple, Samsung, HP, IBM, Fujitsu, Lenovo, Acer, Sony and Toshiba.

Poor labour conditions

Examples of the poor labour conditions are plenty. For instance, employees were bound to work over hours. Not only because they were forced to by their superiors, but also due to the fact that the salary of a 40 hour working week was inadequate to make a living. Furthermore, the work comes down to very long days of extremely boring production line work. Also, the employees were forced to work with dangerous materials without proper protective measures, and were intimidated during work: employees had to ask permission to assume another working position. Next to that, the employees usually live near the factory, and are housed *en masse* in very small rooms (mostly 8 to 12 employees per room). If an employee wants to quit the job, he risks not being paid for the previous period. During the summer season, a lot of youngster are also employed in these factories, as an 'intern'. However, in practice, they simply participate in the production line work, while their school receives a financial compensation for this (DanWatch, 2015).

Dell

Dell stated on several occasions to share the concerns expressed by DanWatch. For instance, in their annual Corporate Social Responsibility Report, they state that:
'According to Verisk Maplecroft's Human Rights Risk Atlas, the information and communications technology industry manufactures in some of the highest-risk countries in the world. Challenges like excessive working hours, insufficient transparency and violations of freely chosen employment standards are systemic and not specific to any one company. Dell continually works to eradicate these and other issues' (Dell, 2015).
Up to now, DanWatch holds that Dell is not living up to their own expectations, and keep pressing their suppliers to lower their prices, instead of improving the labour conditions of the Chinese employees.

10.2 International labour law

Since the emerge of international institutions after the Second Wold War, also on an international level, labour standards were adopted by organizations such as the United Nations and the affiliating International Labour Organization.

IVCESCR

Within the UN framework, the International Covenant on Economic, Social and Cultural Rights (IVCESCR) was adopted in 1966, which recognizes many rights for workers. On top of that, a specialized agency was installed, with the aim to protect and promote labour rights in the world: the International Labour Organization (ILO). This organization has drafted many thematic conventions to improve the recognition of employees' rights that may also serve as a source for inspiration for domestic labour laws. Furthermore, the ILO offers its services in the international arena as a consultant and supervisor in the field of labour law. For instance, the ILO supervises the implementation of the Bangladesh Accord, to improve the position and safety of employees in the garment industry.

ILO

European Social Charter

Also on a more regional level, labour law is internationally embedded. For instance, the European Social Charter is a European treaty in which economic, social and cultural human rights are recognized. Its wordings were greatly inspired by the ILO conventions, and have an explicit focus on labour law. The Charter recognizes for example the right to safe and healthy working conditions (Art. 3), the right to a fair remuneration and a decent living standard (Art. 4), the right to organize (Art. 5), and the right to collective bargaining and to strike (Art. 6), the right to social security (Art. 12) and the right to benefit from social welfare services (Art. 14). Equivalent treaties can be found elsewhere in the world, such as the American San Salvador Protocol, the African Banjul Charter, and the Arab Charter on Human Rights.

The legal effect of such treaties is in de hands of its Member States. On an international level, some rather ineffective complains procedures were installed as a compromise between those who wanted the rights to have an explicit effect, and those who consider these rights as a reference point for the adoption of domestic policies. On a national level, it is up to the courts to enforce such rights. However, this is not always easy, and pretty much depending on the kind of monism or dualism that exists in the Member State (Wernaart, 2013a). An example of how international labour standards may have legal effect in its Member States can be found in case study 10.1 'Clumsy ministers and clever courts', available on the website.

10.3 Proper labour conditions

In different areas law can be adopted to protect employees against their employers. These areas are most notably rules on the nature of a labour contract, the duration of a contract, minimum wage, labour conditions, non-discrimination, the right to organize and collective bargaining, and social security.

10.3.1 The nature of labour contracts

In most legal systems, an employment contract is a special type of contract. Where on the one hand the general principles of contract law apply, there is usually something special about a labour contract. Mostly, on top of normal contract law, being an employee gives access to certain rights and guarantees.
Examples (depending on the legal system) could be paid maternity leave, pension rights, sick leave, the right to benefit from social benefits, or paid holidays. Furthermore, being an employee one could benefit from collective bargaining and participate in trade unions. Lastly, being employed by someone usually results in a certain stability regarding someone's income, securing the livelihood of the employee. However, there are also other ways in hiring labour force than concluding an employment contract.
A company or employer may also hire self-employed people. They are also called flex-workers, casual workers, contractors, atypical workers, temporary workers or freeters. What they have in common is that they are mostly hired for a particular task or short period as an external employee, and when this task or period is completed they leave the organization. They are therefore not an employee, and do not enjoy their 'special status'. They have to take care of such things by themselves, which sometimes puts them in a more vulnerable position. It is therefore important to be clear on which workers are employees, and which workers are self-employed, because it makes quite a difference for the worker involved, as we can see in example 10.2.

EXAMPLE 10.2

Casualization in Nigeria

In Nigeria, labour law is most noticeably regulated by the Nigerian Labour Act (1990). The Act offers some basic protection for employees.
For instance, the employee should be paid in a legal tenure, and (with some exceptions) not in kind (Art. 1). Also, the employee should be paid, even if the employer has no work for her/him (Art.17) , and during illness up to a maximum of twelve days (Art. 16). Next, an employee has a right to a break when he works six hours or more a day (Art. 13), and has a right to a holiday of a week when he works for more than twelve months for the employer (18). Furthermore, an employee has the right to join a trade union, and may not be fired due to trade union membership (Art. 9).
It is remarkable however that the law remains silent on the legal position of casual workers, nor does it define the difference between an employee and a casual worker. Economic crises since 1986 created a strong demand for more flexibility on the labour market. As a matter of fact, employees were fired en mass, and replaced by casual workers: a phenomenon called casualization. As a result, the companies could cut in their costs and become more competitive. While the percentages are hard to verify, some suggest that in 2012 in most economic sectors, approximately 60 to 97 per cent of the Nigerian workers were casual workers (Fapohunda, 2012). These workers received a considerable lower wage, had little labour rights, could not become a member of a trade union and could be fired instantly. This of course reflects the arguments against casualization. However, some are more optimistic, and point out that as a result, companies in some sectors are more competitive, and as a result, there is more employment (Kalejaiye, 2014).

The legal problem seems to be that Nigerian law nor practice does not draw a line between an employment contract and a causal worker. Even if a casual worker works for years at the same company in the same position, there is no legal remedy to the worker that could help her/him to get the status of an employee. The only provision that might help a bit is article 7 of the Labour Act. This Article stipulates that the employer should inform the employee within three months after the beginning of the worker's period of employment about the status and nature of the labour contract. At least, this suggests that the worker knows what he is up to.

Sometimes, there is a thin line between being an employee or a self-employed person. In Germany, there are at least four types of labour relations that are relevant in this context. One could work as an employee, as an employee-like person, as an executive staff member or as self-employed (Zenker, 2014). This means that there are some shades of grey between employee on the one hand, and self-employed on the other. German law offers different kinds of protection to each.

Employee

In German case law, an employee is defined as someone who is obliged to work for an employer based on a private contract, and the relationship with the employer is of personal subordination. This suggests that the employee is an integrated person in the organization of the employer, and the employer stands hierarchically above the employee. The latter means that the employer may give direction to the work done by the employee, and the employee has to – within the boundaries of the labour contract – obey these directions.

Employee-like person

In case of an employee-like person, the worker is free to determine his own work within the organization, and is not considered to be integrated in the organization of the employer. There is no hierarchy between this worker and the employer. On the other hand, the employee-like person is to a certain extend economically depending on the employer, since he works for 50 per cent or more for the same organization. The employee-like person is not as protected as the employee. For instance, the rules on dismissal in Germany do not apply to them, which means they are easily fired. On the other hand, they do have access to the labour courts, and may commence litigation before this specialized body.

Executive staff member

In case of an executive staff member, they might work in employment comparable to an employee, but have a managerial function. Due to this, they practically act as an employer. As a result, the protection for employees only partly applies to executive staff members.

Self-employed person

A self-employed person is not in a hierarchical relation with an employer, and free to organize his activities as they see fit. Furthermore, they usually work for an organization only to complete a specific job, task or period, and then move on the next. They are therefore not economically depending on one employer only. There is hardly any protection for the self-employed under German labour law.

Contracts of service

In the common law legal family, an employment contract is often referred to as a contracts *of* service, where a labour contract with a self-employed is named a contract *for* service. However, in practice, this difference is not always so easy to establish, especially when labour relations are undefined, flexible or unclear. In the Irish legal system, the courts have developed several tests to determine the nature of the labour contract: the control test, the integration test and the economic reality test (Daly & Doherty, 2010).

Contract for service

When applying the control test, the court will assess to what extent the employer is able to exercise control over the day to day activities of the employee. The test therefore establishes whether or not there is a hierarchical relation between the employer and the worker. This is a useful test in jobs where it is clear that a 'superior' gives direction to his personnel on a daily basis, but less useful in professions where employees enjoy a great deal of freedom in determining their daily activities.

Control test

Another test is the integration test, in which the courts will assess to what extent the worker forms an integral part of the organization of the employer. To illustrate: an accountant who works 40 hours a week for a bank permanently, will pass the integration test, while an accountancy advisor, who advises the frequently though irregularly, will not. This test is rather useful in case of a worker who enjoys a great deal of freedom in his daily work, but seems to work rather permanently for the organization. When the contractual status is unclear, the integration test may help her/him out, and it will turn out that he is an employee. However, this test is less useful in the context of sub-contractors. While they may be in a hierarchical relation with a superior in the organization, and work for that organization on a more permanent basis, it is clear that he is not an employee.

Integration test

The last test is the economic reality test. In applying this test, the courts assess who bears the financial risks in performing the job: the organization or the worker. In practice, the application of the test might include elements of the control test and/or the integration test, as we can see in example 10.3.

Economic reality test

EXAMPLE 10.3

Ready Mixed Concrete

Mister Latimer owns his own truck, and uses this truck exclusively to transport concrete to customers of Ready Mixed Concrete (RMC) ltd. Latimer had a labour contract in which it remained rather unclear whether there was a contract of service or a contract for service. In the end, the nature of the labour relation was disputed before the English High Court of Justice.
The court considered several facts that appeared from this particular labour relation. The most important circumstances were that firstly, Latimer owned his own truck, but used equipment of the concrete company. Next to that, he wore a company uniform and the company logo was printed on the car. Furthermore, Latimer was allowed to appoint a driver in his absence, and determine his own working hours, driving routes and holidays. The court, using an economic reality test, concluded that considering all these facts, the labour relation appeared to be more a contract for services than a contract of services. The fact that Latimer enjoyed a great deal of freedom in his work (element of the control test), used his own truck, and as a self-employed person appeared to bear all the financial risks for this truck and his own employment, were decisive (The High Court of Justice of England and Wales, 1968).

10.3.2 Duration of the contract

One possible way to protect or guarantee a permanent income for employees is to manage the expectations regarding the duration of an employment contract. Most legal systems balance between two extremes.

Employment-at-will doctrine

On the one hand, there is the employment-at-will doctrine, meaning that an employee can be fired or can quite the job at any time for any reason. As we can see in example 10.4, in the U.S.A. this approach is mustered for a long time in American labour law. On the other hand, there is the assumption that when an employee is in the employment of an employer, this job is a lifelong position. In other words: the contract is for an indefinite period. This is the starting point in Sweden, as we can see in example 10.5. In both approaches, exemptions are build in that offer more protection to employees in the employment-at-will approach, or create more flexibility for employers in the 'indefinite contract' approach.

EXAMPLE 10.4

At will employment in the U.S.A.

In the U.S.A. labour agreements are considered as 'normal' contracts that govern a private relation. That is, the relation between the employer and the employee. The idea is that the government should not interfere with such private relations, since individuals should be entirely free to conduct their own business.

In a landmark ruling, the Supreme Court of Tennessee (1884) held that: 'Obviously the law can adopt and maintain no such standards for judging human conduct; and men must be left, without interference to buy and sell where they please, and to discharge or retain employees at will for good cause or for no cause, or even for bad cause without thereby being guilty of an unlawful act *per se*. It is a right which an employee may exercise in the same way, to the same extent, for the same cause or want of cause as the employer. He may refuse to work for a man or company, that trades with any obnoxious person, or does other things which he dislikes. He may persuade his fellows, and the employer may lose all his hands and be compelled to close his doors; or he may yield to the demand and withdraw his custom or cease his dealings, and the obnoxious person be thus injured or wrecked in business.'

Exceptions

Ever since, this is the starting point in American labour law. However, in some states, exceptions to this principle are accepted (Hackstock & Heyroth, 2002; Muhl, 2001; Summers, 2000).

The first is the public policy exception. This means that a dismissal of an employee may not contradict the public policy of the state. For instance, some rights of employees are publicly protected, such as the protection of whistle-blowers and the duty to notify public authorities about criminal activities within a company. If an employee is fired for such a reason, the dismissal will be illegal.

The second well-known exception is the implied contract. In some labour relations, it becomes obvious that the employee may reasonably expect that his employment will not be terminated 'at will'. This could be deduced from the companies written policy not to fire employees when they function

properly, or from oral statements of the employer that the employee may expect to be hired for a particular (or indefinite) period.
A third exception is that all U.S.A. citizens should comply with federal laws. For instance, in the U.S.A., discrimination on gender, disability and age are forbidden at the Federal level. A dismissal that seems to be discriminatory is therefore illegal.
Fourth, in some states the principle of good faith and fair dealing is recognized, which means that an employer may not fire an employee without a valid, legal reason. Especially when they have been employed for a long time. Since this principle restricts the employment at will doctrine considerably, it is not widely accepted.

EXAMPLE 10.5

Permanent employment in Sweden
The starting point of Swedish labour law has always been that an employment contract was for an indefinite period. Until today, this is still the general approach in law.
During several reforms however, it became more accepted to hire employees for a definite period. First, fixed term contracts were only allowed for specified situations or in certain sectors. This eventually evolved to a general rule in which a fixed term contract was allowed in all situations and all sectors (In Swedish law called 'alva'). However, there are some 'rules of the game' both contracting parties should stick to. First, both contracting parties should clearly consent to the fixed term. Second, the fixed term cannot exceed the threshold of two years. Third, when an employee works for an employer longer than two years in a period of five years time, the contract is assumed to be an employment contract for an indefinite period (Adlercreutz & Nyström, 2010).

10.3.3 Minimum wage

Another matter is that of the minimum wage. In some countries, a minimum wage is adopted to protect employees. The idea is that an employee should be entitled to a certain life standard that a minimum wage should at least guarantee. This entitlement is then established by law, and it is not possible to deviate from this minimum standard by a collective or individual agreement. The matter of a minimum wage has always been a delicate issue in politics, and its advantages (for instance: Card & Krueger, 2015, or Eyraud & Saget, 2005) and disadvantages (for instance: Friedman, 2014) are heatedly debated. Both 'camps' use an impressive arsenal of statistics and innovative methodology. However, their conclusions could not be more different.

Arguments in support

Those who support the idea of a minimum wage usually refer to the consequences of industrialization, in which companies try to produce for the lowest possible cost in a 'race to the bottom'. In this race, they cut in the costs of wages, which go down unrestrictedly, due to the fact that there is plenty of labour force, and fewer jobs as a result of the fact that machines replace the manpower. When one would enforce a minimum wage, the working class will most likely spend more money, the economy will improve, and even more jobs will be created. Another effect is that due to the creation of more jobs, the government will have to spend less on social security systems, which encourages the economy in itself. Furthermore, people with a guaranteed minimum income will lead to innovation, for jobs that are not worth paying the minimum wage will disappear and replaced by more efficient or clever processes. Those who are used to working in such jobs will be more motivated to continue studying.

Arguments against

Those who oppose the idea of a minimum wage refer to the fact that employers are forced to hire personnel for an amount that may exceed their market value. IN other words: an employee earns more than supply and demand would dictate. This leads to economic obstruction, the loss of employment, and as a result, more people who depend on social benefits. Another effect of a minimum wage is that at some point, the consumer price will go up, since the company is bound to pay a higher price for production costs compared to a situation without the minimum wage. When consumer prices go up unnecessarily, sales will drop, and the economy is yet again obstructed.

In general, the existence of a minimum wage in itself is probably not a guarantee for an adequate income. There are countries with a minimum wage set by law in which the law is not properly enforced, and as a result the effects are marginal, which is shown in the example of Afghanistan (example 10.6). There are also best practices of countries without a minimum wage in which the average income is relatively high, such as the Scandinavian model (example 10.7). A condition for a market driven minimum wage that is not controlled by a legislature seems to the existence of powerful trade unions.

EXAMPLE 10.6

Minimum wage in Afghanistan

The minimum wage for government employees in Afghanistan is determined by law. A government worker that is hired under an employment contract should earn 5.000 Afghanis per month. There is also a minimum wage for the atypical governmental worker: 6.000 Afghanis. A minimum wage for private sector workers was only established for atypical workers: 5.500 Afghanis. For employees in the private sector, no minimum law exists.
In practice however, the law is hardly maintained. According to the U.S. human rights watchdog Humanrights.gov, 'the labor ministry had only 20 inspectors for 34 provinces, and the inspectors had no legal authority to enter premises or impose sanctions for violations. Resources, inspections, remediation, and penalties for violations were inadequate and insufficient to deter violations.' Next to that, a majority of the work in Afghanistan is done informally, meaning that there is no 'official' contract between the worker and the employer. As a result, a significant part of the Afghani workers work in the illegality, even beyond the control of these inspectors' (humanrights.gov, 2014).

EXAMPLE 10.7

The Scandinavian model

No minimum wage

In Norway, Sweden, Finland Denmark and Iceland, there is no minimum wage fixed by the law. Instead, a minimum wage is negotiated per sector, between employers and the labour/trade unions. Minimum wage therefore is out of the hands of the legislature, and entrusted to the process of collective bargaining. This means that in the Nordic countries, the labour unions always have played an important role in the adoption of labour agreements (Andersen, 1996). This is also reflected in the high participation rate of employees in these unions. For instance, in Iceland, 85 per cent of the employees is a member of a trade union (Icelandic Confederation of Labour, 2010). In Norway and Finland the trade unions even have an executive role, and oversee the enforcement of these agreements. A similar approach can be found in Iceland, where the trade unions have the role of inspector, and thoroughly inspect whether the salary and working conditions of employees are in line with the collective agreements. Interestingly, the wages in the Nordic country are relatively high compared to other European countries who have adopted a minimum wage by law (Eldrig & Alsos, 2012).

10.3.4 Labour conditions

One aspect of labour law is the entitlement of employees to proper labour conditions. The concept 'proper conditions' is rather differently understood around the world, and furthermore may be different per sector. In the newspaper item we see legal reforms in New Orleans, aimed to protect bar employees and musicians against the unhealthy effects of working in an environment with continuous cigarette smoke. In case study 10.2, available on the website, we see the attempts of the United Arab Emirates to improve the dreadful labour conditions of migrant workers.

THE NEW YORK TIMES, 22 APRIL 2015

New Orleans Bars Issue Last Call for Smoking

BY: CAMPBELL ROBERTSON

Just after midnight, it became illegal to smoke in bars in New Orleans.

Las Vegas, Philadelphia and several other large cities have not totally banned smoking in bars, according to a count kept by the American Nonsmokers' Rights Foundation. But New Orleans, home of bars that never close and beers ordered to go, was one of those places where people assumed a smoking ban would never fly.

(...)

In late fall, LaToya Cantrell, a City Council member, introduced a concrete proposal against smoking. After multiple revisions, the council unanimously approved a smoking ban ordinance several months later, but not before heated discussion over public health and lost revenues, and what all this meant for the identity of New Orleans.

10.3.5 Non-discrimination

The principle of non-discrimination is generally recognized as an important element of labour law. It is the core principle of most UN human right treaties, as well as ILO conventions. Furthermore, most constitutional law stipulates the prohibition to discriminate.

Discrimination

Discrimination is the unequal treatment in similar cases based on irrelevant factor.

However, it is not always easy to properly define discrimination, and enforce non-discrimination in practice. The problem lies in what is considered to be an irrelevant factor. The understanding of the word 'irrelevant' may be different. According to the ILO, discrimination based on race, colour, sex, religion, political opinion, national extraction or social origin are such irrelevant variables (ILO Convention 111, Article 1). Furthermore, it is observed by the ILO that increasingly, age, sexual orientation, HIV/AIDS status and disability, are protected under anti-discrimination laws (ILO, 2007).

In essence, there are three types of discrimination: direct, indirect and positive discrimination. Please note that the concepts of direct and discrimination were also discussed in the context of international economic cooperation, in chapters 6 and 7.

Direct discrimination

Direct discrimination is to explicitly disadvantage someone based on an irrelevant factor.

An example of this can be found in the website sample discussing the Wal-Mart policy towards same-sex couples regarding spousal health insurance coverage. Such a health care insurance can be obtained through an employer, and also covers the health care of the partner of the employee. Until 2014, this coverage was not accessible for same-sex couples, also when married. That would be a form of direct discrimination, considering the fact that same-sex marriages were recognized in Massachusetts. After all, this seems to suggest that sexual preference is considered an irrelevant factor for different treatment. Since 2014, the company changed its policy, and all couples (married or unmarried, same sex or traditional) are now covered.

● www.USnews.com

Wal-Mart Sued for Alleged Anti-gay Discrimination

A lesbian couple says unfairness cost them $150.000

The nation's largest private employer is being sued for alleged discrimination against same-sex couples.

A Massachusetts lesbian couple on Tuesday announced the lawsuit against Wal-Mart, and they're asking a judge to certify it as a class-action to allow them to represent others.
Jaqueline Cote and Diana Smithson say Wal-Mart's pre-2014 policy of denying benefits to same-sex couples – unless required by state law – cost them at least $150.000 in medical bills.
The couple formerly worked together at Wal-Mart and married in 2004, when Massachusetts became the first state to allow same-sex marriage. They tried unsuccessfully to enrol Smithson in Wal-Mart's spousal health insurance coverage from 2008, when she left the company to care for Cote's mother.
Smithson developed ovarian cancer in 2012, and the couple is seeking to recoup costs incurred through Jan. 1, 2014, when the company expanded coverage to all married and unmarried couples.
By: Steven Nelson 14 July 2015

Indirect discrimination

Indirect discrimination is when a non-discriminatory standard or practice disadvantages someone based on an irrelevant factor.

An example of indirect discrimination can be found in the Italian Mailman case (example 10.8)

EXAMPLE 10.8

The Italian Mailman
A case of indirect discrimination
Mr Giovanni Sotgiu is an Italian national, and an employee of the German Postal Service. When he was recruited for the company, he lived with his family in Italy. Because he works a long distance from home, he received a special allowance on top of his normal wage. However, Mr Sotgiu finds out that his colleagues who lived in Germany at the time of recruitment, also work a long distance from home and received 10 Deutsche Mark, while he only receives only 7,50DM. As it appears, the regulation on these allowances makes a distinction between employees residing in Germany (regardless their nationality) at the time of recruitment, and those who did not. The first are awarded a greater allowance compared to the latter category of employees.

Mr Sotgiu feels discriminated based on his nationality, and sues his employer. The German Postal Service held that there was no discrimination, since the regulation involved did not make a distinction based on nationality but on place of residence at the time of recruitment (which was not forbidden by any European law).
The European Court of Justice however, disagreed. The Court ruled that employees who are recruited abroad usually do not have the German nationality, and those who are recruited in Germany will most of the time be German. While the regulation in itself indeed does not discriminate based on nationality, it will have the practical effect of doing so. After all, the regulation will result in the fact that most of the time foreigners are disadvantaged compared to German nationals (ECJ, Case 152/73, 1974).

Positive discrimination

Positive discrimination is to explicitly advantage someone who is disadvantaged based on irrelevant factors.

Law and policy makers might choose to adopt measures to counter existing discrimination of a particular group. One of the means to do so is to require preferential treatment of the disadvantaged group. This phenomenon is called positive discrimination. An example of this is the fact that women are usually underrepresented in the board of directors of companies. Some countries have therefore implemented a so-called woman quota to guarantee that a certain percentage of board members will be female. Such a policy is widely debated, and the media reports differently on the success of such a quota (as we can see in the two news items). However, research seems to suggest that implementing a woman quota has only a limited effect on the encouraging of equal pay and equal job opportunities between men and women (Bertrand et al. 2014).

THE TELEGRAPH (UK), 13 JANUARY 2015

Proof that women in boardrooms quotas work

BY: LAUREN DAVIDSON

Introducing quotas to boost the number of women in corporate boardrooms is working, according to a new global index from Catalyst, the non-profit organisation for women in business.

Norway, the first country in the world to mandate that women account for 40pc of its board seats, tops the ranking of 20 countries across three regions, with 35,5 per cent female representation on the boards of its OMX-listed companies.

France, which gave its companies until January 2017 to reach the 40 per cent quota, is far ahead of its 20pc interim target with women accounting for 29.7pc of board seats, closing in on Finland's 29,9 per cent.

Companies listed in Stockholm have women in 28,8 per cent of their board seats, ranking Sweden fourth on Catalyst's census.

(...)

The wider picture is less rosy, however.

At the bottom end of Catalyst's table, with 3,1 per cent, Japan's female boardroom representation is less than a tenth that of Norway's.

And despite the lengths taken by a handful of countries to legally mandate a fairer gender balance in boardrooms, not one has yet to fulfil this allocation.

THE NATIONAL POST (CANADA), 14 JANUARY 2015

Norway, France and Finland tried to help women by using quotas on corporate boards. It hasn't worked.

BY: JESSICA GROSE

There's a persistent gender divide in the upper tier of most industries in the United States. The magic number seems to be just under 20 per cent - that's the percentage of women who are equity partners in law firms (17 per cent), in Congress (18, per cent), and on the boards of S&P 500 companies (19,2 per cent). A new report from the research arm of Catalyst (...) compares the number of women on boards in the U.S. with the number of women on boards in several other countries, with the takeaway being that we're failing here. The top three countries for women on boards are Norway, Finland, and France, where the percentage of female board members ranges from 29,7 per cent to 35,5 per cent. Not coincidentally, these three countries also all have government-mandated quotas for women on corporate boards. At least in sheer numbers, the quota system seems to be working. But, despite what the Catalyst report highlights, it looks like a greater number of women on boards hasn't actually translated to big improvements for women working for those corporations. And that's because focusing on executive-board bean counting is not enough.

10

10.3.6 The right to organize and collective bargaining

As we have seen above, the industrial revolution led to a society in which employees were greatly depending on employers. After all, industrialization led to a shortage of jobs, and a surplus of labourers. This placed the well-organized employers in a power position that could easily lead to exploitation and other unfair practices. To offer some counterweight to the power position of employers, the right of employees to use their collective strength is recognized in most industrialized countries. This includes the right to form Trade Unions, the right to collective bargaining, and the right to jointly strike. In the example 'the slaves of Dubai' we have seen that a prohibition to use such collective employee strength contributes to weakening the position of employees, especially in newly developed or industrializing regions. In the example of 'the Scandinavian model' on the other hand, we have seen how trade unions might contribute to setting important labour standards such as a minimum wage.

The right to collective action by employees played a significant role in the garment industry of Bangladesh since 2013. While the absence of effective legal protection of employees created a competitive advantage for many Bangladeshi companies, the poor working conditions in the end could only lead to a disaster. When the building of Rana-Plaza collapsed in April 2013, all stakeholders, some intrinsically, some pushed by the public opinion, wanted to improve the situation (Wernaart, 2015b). On the one hand, this was done by self-regulation to which all the involved stakeholders consent: the Bangladesh Accord. On the other hand, legal reforms in labour law were

Bangladesh Accord

implemented by the Bangladeshi government. The most important changes were the involvement of employees in assessing the safety of their working place, and lowering legal barriers to participate in Trade Unions, as we can see in example 10.9.

EXAMPLE 10.9

The collapse of the Rana-Plaza building

The Bangladesh Accord and legal reforms

In Bangladesh, over 4 million people work in the garment industry. The country is attractive for foreign company due to the low labour wages. After all, the minimum wage in Bangladesh in the garment industry is 5.300 Bangladeshi Taka (BDT) per month in full employment. This is approximately 67 U.S. dollars. For a long time, the poor labour conditions of Bangladeshi workers in the garment industry was criticized by many Non Governmental Organizations (NGOs). Especially the low wage and the harsh and dangerous working conditions were contested. On the 24th of April 2013, a nightmare came true: a huge factory building (the Rana-Plaza building) collapsed and as a result more than a thousand employees died. This changed everything.

Big brands that had outsourced their production in that building were now publicly named and shamed in their home countries, and massively a call for action was made. This resulted in a landmark agreement between the involved companies, international and local employer and employee organizations, and quite a lot of NGOs. This so-called 'self-regulation' aimed at strengthening the position of employees. The ILO serves as a neutral forum in which the implementation of this accord can be discussed by the various stakeholders.

Key elements of this agreement were that from now on neural inspectors would check the safety of the working conditions, employees are trained and educated in how to enforce their rights, employees are actively involved in creating a safer environment, employees may not be fired when they blow the whistle about an unsafe workplace, and both employers employees are equally represented in a supervisory body that oversees the implementation of this accord (Accord on Fire and Building Safety Regulations in Bangladesh, 2013).

In the same period, the government of Bangladesh amended its labour laws (Bangladesh Labour (Amendment) Act, 2013) to strengthen the position of trade unions. Before these reforms, the names of trade union leaders were communicated to their employers when a new Trade Union was registered. This had a deterrent effect on potential Union leaders. This obligation is now removed from the Bangladesh labour law. Furthermore, trade unions are now allowed to consult experts in the context of collective bargaining (Art. 202a, Bangladesh Labour Act 2013), which potentially strengthens their bargaining position. These amendments certainly had some effect, since in the last half of 2013, 152 new labour unions were registered, with a total of 29156 members (ILO, 2014). On the other hand, the labour reforms were criticised, since according to the ILO they only partly addressed the Labour issues in the country. (UN 2013)

10.3.7 Social security standards

Due to various reasons, an employee may not be able to make a living for himself and his family anymore. Causes could be sickness, disability, old age, maternity, the death of a family member, or simply losing a job. States usually regulate a system of social benefits to create a safety net for those individuals. Such a system of social benefits is then designed to secure that an employee is unable to provide for their – and their family's – basic needs. Furthermore, one could also argue that a social security system is developed to facilitate those who make use of it to find a fitting job that enables them to provide for themselves without the help of social benefits (Pennings, 2012).

As we can see in example 10.10, social security can be financed by withholding money from the employees' wages, obliging employers to pay a sum per employee, or using tax revenue.

EXAMPLE 10.10

The social security system of Mexico

The current system of Mexico was established in 1942, and since then frequently amended. In general, the funds of these social benefits are collected by withholding salary of the employee, paid for by the employer directly, or funded by the government. The type of social benefits can be classified under the categories sickness and maternity, death and disability, day-care, old age, occupational risks and housing (PWC, 2015).

In case of illness, most healthcare costs are covered. When due to illness an employee cannot work, 60 to 100 per cent of the salary is paid by the government, while sometimes employers pay for the difference between the normal wage and the contribution of the government (depending on the applicable Collective Agreement). This also applies to absence during maternity.

When an employee is permanently disabled, a minimum of 35 per cent of his average wage will be compensated by the government. This percentage is increased when people depend on the income of the disabled person (for instance, an additional 10 per cent per child or depending parent, and 15 per cent for a husband or wife). When an employee dies, his relatives will receive a percentage of his pension. This is normally 90 per cent of this pension when a husband or wife dies, where an orphan will receive 20 per cent.

When an employee is at the age of 65, she or he may retire. During his career the Retirement Savings Systems withholds 2 per cent of the wages, and the Old Age System withholds 3,15 per cent. These combined should guarantee the retired employee a decent pension. The exact sum of the pension depends on the way the retiree chooses to be paid, and what kind of an arrangement is made.

A fixed percentage of the employee's wage is withheld to insure the professional against occupational risks. The percentage depends on the risk category of the profession. In Mexico, there are five so-called 'risk clauses' in which a profession is represented. The percentage paid for this insurance varies between 0,5 and 7,5 per cent of the employee's wage. For example, an accountant would approximately pay 0,5 per cent, while a miner would pay 7,5 per cent.

The Constitution of Mexico stipulates that most employers should provide for housing of their employees. To this end, 5 per cent of the normal wage of an employee is contributed to a fund. This fund may be used by the employer to buy a house, repair a house, or pay of a mortgage.

Summary

- Labour law emerged as a result of the industrial revolution.

- Industrialization led to three social challenges: urbanisation, a growing income gap and environmental damage.

- As a result of these challenges, as well as increasing political influence by the working class in especially Europe, the wellbeing of employees was addressed in a legal context.

- On a global level, labour standards were adopted within the United Nations, including the International Labour Organization.

- On a regional level, labour standards were adopted by regional human right bodies, such as the American San Salvador Protocol, the African Banjul Charter, the Arab Charter on Human Rights and the European Social Charter.

- To protect the interest of employees, countries may adopt rules on the nature of a labour contract, the duration of a contract, minimum wage, labour conditions, non-discrimination, the right to organize and collective bargaining, and social security.

- An employment is a special contract. Usually, such a contract gives access to certain guarantees and stability for the employee. This is not so in case of a self-employed person. Therefore, it is important to clearly define the nature of the labour relation.

- In German law, a distinction is made between an employee, an employee-like person, an executive staff member and a self-employed person. In this order, their legal protection is reduced.

- In common law systems, a distinction is made between contracts of service and contracts for service. The first represents an employee contract where the latter assumes the labour is done as a self-employed person. To draw a line between the two, courts may apply the control test, the integration test and the economic reality test:
  - When applying the control test, the court will assess to what extent the employer is able to exercise control over the day to day activities of the employee.
  - When applying the integration test, the courts will assess to what extent the worker forms an integral part of the organization of the employer.
  - When applying the economic reality test, the court will assess who bears the financial risks in performing the job: the organization or the worker.

- One possible way to protect or guarantee a permanent income for employees is to manage the expectations regarding the duration of an employment contract. Most legal systems balance between two extremes:
  - There is the employment-at-will doctrine, meaning that an employee can be fired or can quit the job at any time for any reason.
  - The assumption that when an employee is employed, this job is a lifelong position.

- In some countries, a minimum wage is adopted to protect employees. Arguments against a minimum wage suggest that it works counterproductive, where arguments to support it conclude that it has a stimulating effect on the economy.

- The concept 'proper labour conditions' is differently understood around the world and may be different per sector.

- The principle of non-discrimination is generally recognized as an important element of labour law.

- Discrimination is the unequal treatment in similar cases based on an irrelevant factor.

- There are three types of discrimination: direct, indirect and positive discrimination.
  1. Direct discrimination is to explicitly disadvantage someone based on an irrelevant factor.
  2. Indirect discrimination is when a non-discriminatory standard or practice disadvantages someone based on an irrelevant factor.
  3. Positive discrimination is to explicitly advantage someone who is disadvantaged based on irrelevant factors.

- To offer some counterweight to the power position of employers, the right of employees to use their collective strength is recognized in most industrialized countries. This includes the right to form Trade Unions, the right to collective bargaining, and the right to jointly strike.

- States usually regulate a system of social benefits to create a safety net for those employees who cannot provide for themselves or their families. This is especially the case of sickness, disability, old age, maternity, the death of a family member, or losing a job.

Practice questions

10

Open questions

10.1 Karl runs his sole proprietorship, and is specialized in advising organizations on Lean Management. He is hired by BMW for a period of already 5 years, as an external expert. His advisory role for BMW takes up to 80 per cent of his entire workload, and even 90 per cent of his income. He advises the management board, so he does not really have a superior within the BMW organization.

What would be the legal employment relation between Karl and BMW according to German law?

10.2 Consider the case in question 10.1. What would be the legal employment relation between MBW according to common law?

10.3 Before the industrial revolution in Europe took off, child labour was never really an issue. Could you imagine why this was an issue all of a sudden after the industrialization of the European countries?

10.4 In this chapter, various opinions about a woman's quota are portrayed. Do you think such a quota is desirable and would work? Please explain.

Essay questions

In the U.S.A. the employment-at-will doctrine is embraced. From the perspective of the employee there are positive and negative aspects to this doctrine. Write an essay in which you analyse the pros and cons, and write your own conclusion.

Multiple choice questions

10.1 A British farmer is in need of employees to harvest asparagus. However, she does not want a Polish migrant to work for his business. She therefore requires people who apply for the job to pass an English writing test. The result is that only British people apply for his job, out of which she hires two employees.

This is an example of:
a direct discrimination
b indirect discrimination
c positive discrimination

10.2 The Kafala system is in essence:
a a system of sponsorship between a company and an expat
b a system of payment on behalf of expats
c a system of creating jobs for expats

10.3 The right to strike is part of:
a the right to self-determination
b the right to social security
c The right to organize and collective bargaining

10.4 In the Scandinavian model there is:
a no minimum wage fixed by law
b no minimum wage fixed by collective bargaining
c a minimum wage fixed by international treaties

TO DIE
FOR!
KKGGGG!...
Sandor

11 Company law

In this chapter we will explore different legal forms to run a business. First, we will discuss unincorporated forms, such as the sole proprietorship and the partnership. Then, we will focus on incorporated forms, such as the private and public limited company. To continue, some special legal forms will be highlighted, such as the foundation, the company limited by guarantee, the Societas Europaea and concerns.
Differences in flexibility in company law between legal systems may result in regulatory competition. Therefore, two examples of such competition will be discussed.
To conclude, foreign companies may be subdue to further regulations compared to domestic entrepreneurs. We will briefly explore this issue in the last section.

11.1 The legal form of a company

One can run a business in different legal forms. The choice of a legal form is important, because it determines how the business must be established and run, and who is liable to what extent for business debts.

In general, there is a difference between unincorporated and incorporated companies. In the first case, the company is composed of natural persons, while in case of the latter case the company has a separate legal identity.

Unincorporated company

> An unincorporated company is composed of natural persons and has no separate legal identity.

As a matter of fact, these natural persons *are* the company. This also explains why in most legal systems the liability of these natural persons is unlimited. After all, when that which you are goes bankrupt, you go bankrupt.

Incorporated company

An incorporated company is composed of shares owned by natural or legal persons but has its own legal identity.

People or other companies may own an incorporated company by obtaining shares. However, the owned company has a legal identity of its own. This explains why in most legal systems the liability of the owners is limited. After all, when that which you own goes bankrupt, you only lose that which you own, but nothing more.

It is important to note here that due to the historical development of company law, it is quite normal that the applicable rules on unincorporated companies can be found elsewhere than the rules on incorporated companies. Unincorporated companies exist as long as trade exists, and have always been regulated in the sphere of normal contract laws. For instance, a general partnership is usually founded on a private agreement between two or more partners who share their resources to do business. Such rules usually have a long history, and its origin may even date back to the Roman Empire. In contrast, incorporated companies are a product of the industrial revolution, and have emerged since the adoption of the French Commercial Code in 1807. The need was felt to create legal constructions to protect investors and society against the consequences of bankruptcy of such big undertakings (Hopt, 2006).

11.1.1 Unincorporated companies

The main characteristic feature of an unincorporated company, as stated above, is that the company is no separate legal entity. Instead, the owners are the company. As a result of that they are personally liable for any company debt.

Personal liability

Personal liability means that the individuals of which the company is composed are unrestrictedly liable for any company debts.

This means that liability reaches beyond the scope of what is invested in the company, and may affect all private means of the members of the company.

Sole proprietorship

The simplest form of an unincorporated company is that of a sole proprietorship, also known as a sole trader.

Sole proprietorship

A sole proprietorship is a legal form of an unincorporated business that is composed of one individual who is personally liable for the company's debts.

In general, it is mostly relatively easy to set up a sole proprietorship. In comparison to other legal forms, there are only a few prerequisites to register this legal form, if there are any at all.
For instance, in Sri Lanka, one has to register a sole proprietorship at a Provincial Council in the Registrar of Business Names, but only if the name of the business is different than the name of the owner. It needs to be

noted here however that only a citizen of Sri Lanka may set up a sole proprietorship: a foreigner is obliged to incorporate his business.
The added value of this type of business is that there are hardly any formalities involved, and it is therefore quite easy to set up the business. In terms of taxation, the business is not considered as a separate legal entity, and therefore all income earned by the business is considered income tax, and dealt with accordingly. In other words: there is no separate tax obligation on behalf of the business.
The disadvantage is that the owner of the one-man company is fully liable for the business, and all its debts. This liability may also involve the property and means of the business owner's family members under certain circumstances. This is especially the case when the owner is married to someone in full patrimony: the property and means of the couple are considered as one, which may be used to settle the business debts. An example of this can be found in the case 'Wedding Pie Store' (example 11.1).

Employees

The fact that a business is a sole proprietorship does not mean that the business may only be run by one individual. The legal form only says something about the ownership, and not necessarily about employment. This means that a sole proprietorship may hire employees. In practise, the amount of employees will be limited, since it will mostly be more convenient to choose another legal form for the company when the business grows. A very common phenomenon in the Small and Medium Enterprise world is that a husband or wife owns a sole proprietorship and hires a family member to work on behalf of the company. In the U.S.A. it is even possible to co-own the business in a so called 'husband-and-wife-sole proprietorship'. Technically, the husband and wife can choose to be a qualified joint venture. The consequence is that the International Revenue Service (the Federal tax agency) will not consider the couple as a partnership, but as two sole traders (Joint Committee on Taxation, 2007).

Husband-and-wife-sole proprietorship

EXAMPLE 11.1

Wedding Pie Store to die for

Oni runs her own sole proprietorship called Wedding Pie Store, and uses the slogan 'to die for'. She mainly sells homemade wedding pies. Unfortunately, one day she uses the wrong ingredients, and instead of milk she puts cyanide in one of her pies. As a result, the groom of the wedding dies horribly in front of his very recent wife. The relatives of the groom sue 'Wedding Pie Store' and want an enormous damage compensation for the loss of their family member.

In court, the larger part of the claimed sum is awarded, and 'Wedding Pie Store' has to pay 6,5 billion Indian rupee. The means Oni allocated for her company are insufficient to pay this sum. Therefore, she has to sell her car, and most of her non-essential personal belongings such as jewellery, ICT and multimedia tools, and some furniture to pay off the debt. Furthermore, since she is married in full patrimony, also her husband's car and expensive watches are sold to settle the debt.

Please note that this legal form is in some legal systems also referred to as a 'one man business' (for instance in the Netherlands). However, the same term is used in other legal systems to refer to a private limited company owned by one shareholder (for instance India). Therefore, in this book we avoid using this name.

The partnership

One could choose to combine their strength in terms of funding, know-how, talent and capabilities. This can be done by establishing a partnership.

Partnership

> A partnership is a legal form of an unincorporated business that is composed of more than one individual who are personally liable for the company's debts.

For instance, the Russian Civil Code stipulates that:

> 'The participants of the general partnership shall jointly bear the subsidiary responsibility by the partnership's obligations with their entire property.' (Chapter 4, Article 75 Civil Code of the Russian Federation)

Usually, there are different types of partnerships. In South Korean law, we see a perfect example of the most common types of partnership.

General partnership

First, there is the general partnership, called the Hapmyung Hoesa.

This legal form is used for medium and small companies in which the partners play a very active role in the organization of the company. In South Korea, the nature of the business is not relevant: all kinds of activities can be conducted jointly through a Hapmyung Hoesa, whether it is a cooperation amongst professionals, or a collaboration to sell products.

In some legal systems however, a distinction is made between partnerships for professionals (such as lawyers, medical experts, financial advisors etcetera) and commercial activities. This is the case in Germany, where there is a distinction between a professional partnership (Partnerschaftgesellschaft) and a commercial partnership (Offene Handelsgesellschaft).

Now, back to the Korean Hapmyung Hoesa. The relation between the partners is usually regulated by a partnership contract. The Korean Commercial Act basically stipulates what the rules are when things are not regulated in such a contract. Most importantly all partners are authorized to manage the company, and represent the company externally. In a partnership contract however, this authority can be limited to some of the partners, and the scope of their authority may be specified. For instance, as we can see in the case 'Dress your Wedding', the partners may agree on a threshold of money that each partner may spend on behalf of the company, or exclusively restrict company representation to one or more partners in case of certain legal actions. Please note however that this partnership contract is mainly a contract that governs the relation between the partners. External parties are not bothered too much by its content. When one of the partners exceeds its competency and this cannot reasonably be known by the third party, the legal consequences will be borne by all the partners. This phenomenon has been discussed in chapter 8 in the context of ostensible authority. In this light, the Korean Commercial Act stipulates that any restriction placed on the authority of a partner may not be asserted against a third person acting in good faith (Art. 209). In the case of the wedding dress company (example 11.2), in situation 1, this means that all partners are liable for the purchase

of the Porsche, even though Javiera violated the partnership contract. This liability is towards the third party selling the Porsche. However, after the matter with the third party is settled, it could very well be that Fransisca and Constanza sue Javiera for breaching the partnership contract.
In case of damage cause by one of the partners on behalf of the company to a third party, all partners are jointly liable (Art. 210 Commercial Act of Korea). This means that the third party who suffers the damage may claim the full damage compensation from any of the partners. The same goes for the settlement of a debt on behalf of the company. The suffering party therefore does not have to claim equal parts of the sum from the partners one by one, but may just demand payment of the full some by any of the partners. When the company assets prove to be inadequate to pay the damage compensation or the debt, the partners are personally liable (Art. 212 Commercial Act of Korea), and their private means could be used to pay the damage compensation or debt. In the case of the wedding dress company, this means that in situation 2, the three partners will have to use their private means to settle the debt.

Figure 11.1 shows a schematic overview of a general partnership

FIGURE 11.1 A general partnership

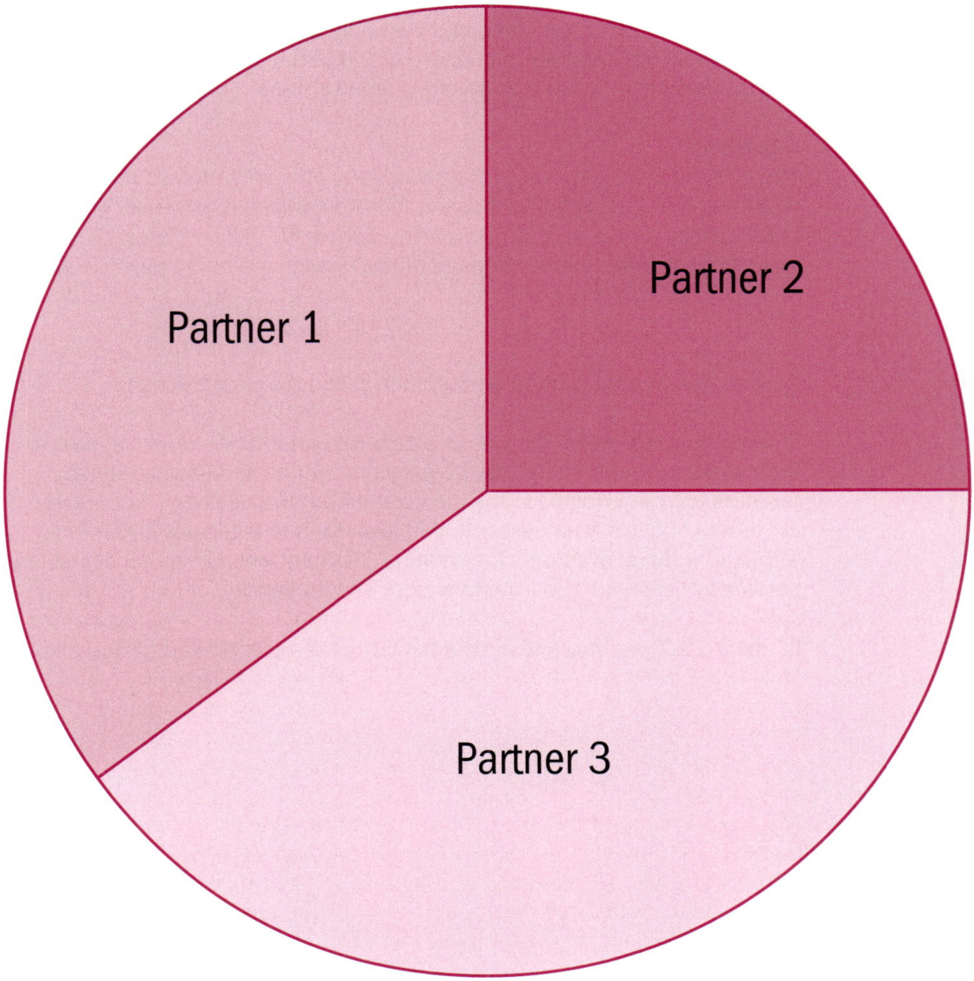

EXAMPLE 11.2

Dress your wedding

Fransisca, Constanza and Javiera are a general partnership 'Dress your Wedding'. They sell chic but affordable modern wedding dresses. Business is good and therefore they decide to invest in their own real estate in Valparaiso. Since then, business is even better than before. The general partnership is established in a partnership contract. Several aspects of their business are regulated in this contract. For instance, the partners are not allowed to spend more than 680.000 Chilean pesos per week on behalf of the company without the consent of the other partners. Furthermore, Fransisca and Constanza invest 200 million Cilean pesos each, while Javiera invests her know-how instead of money. After all, she knows everything about fashion, and has a very strong network in the wedding scene. Also, the partners agree that due to her skills and know-how, only Javiera may represent the company in case of purchasing wedding dresses. Furthermore, it is agreed that the partners get a salary of 14.000 pesos per month when the net profit exceeds 42.000 Pesos. If the profit is lower, this sum will be divided by the three partners in equal proportion. When the profit is higher, it will be used for new investments.

Situation 1

One day, Javiera has a mood swing and impulsively buys a brand new Porsche on behalf of the company. The costs are 175 million Chilean pesos. The Porsche seller is unaware of the partnership contract, and cannot reasonably know that Javiera's representation authority is limited.

Situation 2

The ladies did not pay one of their suppliers, not even after a formal notice of a breach of contract. The dresses that were supplied however have all been sold by 'Dress your Wedding'. The debt is 80 million Chilean Peso's. The company unfortunately does not have enough means to pay this debt.

11

Limited partnership

Second, there is the limited partnership, called the Hapja Hoesa.

In fact, the same rules apply as in a general partnership. However, next to the normal partners, there may be partners with limited liability. These partners are not involved in the management of the business, but merely contribute financially. In essence, this legal form is a general partnership with one or more investors. The 'normal' partners who run the business are personally liable, but the investors enjoy limited liability.

In figure 11.2 you may find a schematic overview of a limited partnership.

FIGURE 11.2 A limited partnership

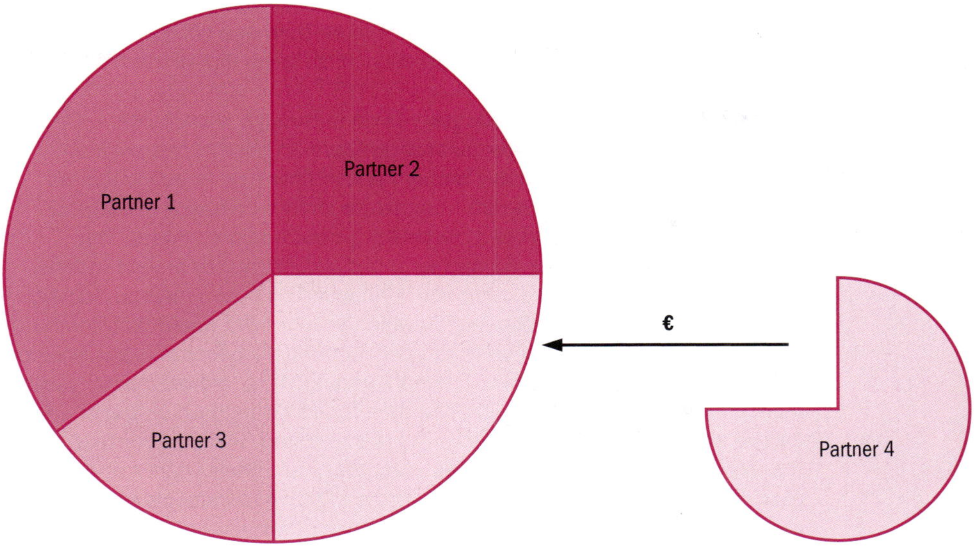

11.1.2 Incorporated companies

An incorporated company has several main characteristics. Cahn & Donald (2011) distinguish five main features:

- A company is a legal personality, and has therefore the same rights and duties as a natural person.
- There is limited liability. This means that the shareholders may at the most lose their investment in the company in case of bankruptcy, nothing more. This also means that the board of directors in principle is not liable on behalf of the company. This is the reason why an incorporated company is also referred to as a limited company.
- There are transferable shares: shareholders may sell their share in the company to someone else. This can be in a private transfer, or through stock exchange.
- There is a centralized board of directors, who govern the company on behalf of the shareholders.
- The ownership of the company is shared amongst the shareholders, in proportion to the value of the share.

Two aspects here are of particular importance. First, one may separate ownership from managing the company. This is done in case of both the private and public limited companies. In contrast, as we have seen above, this is not the case in a limited partnership, a general partnership or a sole proprietorship.

Management board

A limited company has its own managing board that operates separately from their shareholders. Please note that this is mainly the legal structure, in which there is a group of owners (shareholders) that appoint on their behalf a board of directors (a management). This does not necessarily mean that the shareholders may not appoint themselves as managing board. Shareholders appointing themselves as management board is, due to the private nature of the company, much more common in case of a private limited company. In case of a public limited company it is rather unusual, and sometimes even undesirable. After all, a shareholder in the public domain will usually hold shares of more than one company. Being a member of the board of one of them may cause a conflict of interest.

Second, the financing of the company is done through shareholders. One may limit the financing to internal shareholders (in case of the private limited company) or raise many through public financing (a public limited company). The essential feature of a private limited company is that the shares are privately owned by a particular group of shareholders. This means that shares are not funded by public means, but by private means. In contrast, a public limited company is financed by public means. Actually, it is a legal form of 'crowdfunding' in which anyone who would be interested may buy a share of the company and consequentially become a shareholder. This explains the name 'public' limited company. This 'crowdfunding' can be facilitated by using a stock exchange as a forum through which the shares can be sold and bought by anyone who is interested. Please note that only a small percentage of public limited companies sell their shares at a stock exchange. However, since it are usually the bigger multinationals who do so, the value of their shares and the performance of our economies are usually inextricably linked, and therefore an indicator of economic growth (or the opposite).

Private limited company

A private limited company is in some legal systems also referred to as a limited liability company. An example of this is South Korea, where the Korean name of a limited liability company is used: the Yuhan Hoesa. Another example is the Spanish the Sociedad de Responsabilidad Limitada (S.R.L.).

Yuhan Hoesa

In Korea, the Yuhan Hoesa is understood as a hybrid company form that finds middle ground between a partnership and a limited company. This legal form has the characteristics of a partnership, but the partners are limitedly liable, as in a limited company.
The owners in a Yuhan Hoesa are involved in the daily affairs of the company, and run the business actively. Furthermore, the shares of the partners cannot be transferred without the consent of at least 75 per cent of the other partners, and there can only be a maximum of 50 partners. These are important differences compared to the rules for a public limited company, and contribute to uphold the character of a small or medium partnership. This legal form of a company is often used in case of a family business.

Sociedad de Responsabilidad Limitada

In case of the Spanish Sociedad de Responsabilidad Limitada (S.R.L.), the shareholders are not necessarily involved in the daily affairs of the company. They appoint a management board, which could consist of at least one director, with a maximum of 12 board members. Just like the Korean Yuhan Hoesa, there are significant legal restraints to transfer shares of a Sociedad de Responsabilidad Limitada to another shareholder. Therefore, also this form is suitable for small and medium enterprises or a family business. However, the S.R.L. is also sometimes used as a legal form by foreign entrepreneurs. The reason for the latter is that the legal requirements to set op a S.R.L. are not as complex as the requirements to set up a public limited company. For instance, the minimum capital to register this business form is 3.000 euros. To register a public limited company, 60.000 euros is required (of which 25 per cent must be available immediately at the moment of registering).

Figure 11.3 shows a schematic overview of a private limited company.

FIGURE 11.3 A private limited company

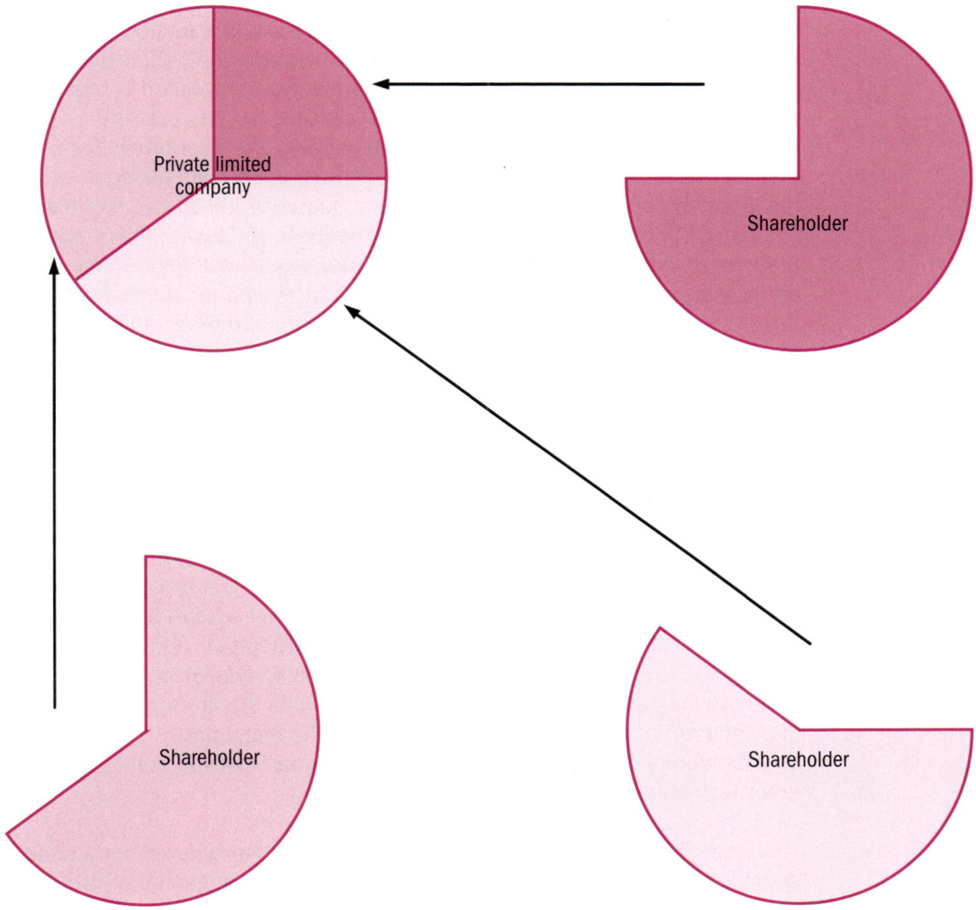

Public limited company

A public limited company is the legal form used for bigger companies which are financed through public means. The shareholders of such a company could be anyone, or any organization. There are differences per region as to what kind of shareholders a company has. For instance, in the U.S.A. and the UK, shares are owned by individuals, whereas in the European mainland it is more common that banks, investment funds or other organizations own a company. In India, it is more common that families own public limited companies, where in China the state plays a more fundamental role as a major shareholder (Crane and Matten, 2015). A public limited company may sell their shares on stock exchanges, but it is usually not required to do so.

The largest multinationals of course do sell their shares at stock exchanges.
Examples of public limited companies are the Korean Chusik Hoesa and the Spanish Sociedad Anónima.

Chusik Hoesa

In the Korean Chusik Hoesa we see a very clear distinction between management and ownership. The shareholders are not involved in the day to day decision-making processes, and have appointed a management board on their behalf to do so. Mostly, the general ideas, principles and rules that apply within the company are written down in a founding document, usually referred to as 'articles of incorporation'. The exact relationship between the shareholders and management board is mostly specified in this document. In general however, we can say that the shareholders can exercise influence through their power to appoint or dismiss a management board, and through their general meetings in which the shareholders have a say in the general, fundamental direction of the company. During the so-called 'ordinary meetings' the shareholders adopt the annual financial statement and make decisions about their share, such as the payment of dividend, or the increase of the amount of shares. During the 'extraordinary meetings', the shareholders are authorized to discuss whatever is in the articles of cooperation. This might lead to an amendment to these articles. It will be not surprising that these kinds of decisions do not relate to the day to day functioning of the company, but rather relate to the more general direction.

In the context of a public limited company, it is not unusual to appoint a supervisory body that audits the performance of the board of directors on behalf of the shareholders. After all, the bigger the organization, the more diverse the composition of the shareholders may be. It is than not always possible to regularly check whether the management acts in the interest of the shareholders, in line with the articles of incorporation. To this end, Korean law requires each public limited company to appoint at least one statutory auditor (Park, 2011). This auditor checks the performance of the management and reports to the shareholders. In his capacity as statutory auditor, he may attend board meetings and request that the management reports to the auditor about certain decisions.

Spanish Sociedad Anónima

The Spanish Spanish Sociedad Anónimashows us that one will need to be serious to establish this kind of a business. A minimum capital of 60.000 euros is required. However, it needs to be noted here that only 25 per cent of this amount needs to be available at the moment of incorporation. Also here, the shareholders exercise their power through ordinary and extraordinary meetings, comparable to the Chusik Hoesa. To make sure that decisions are indeed in order to adopt a decision, at least 25 per cent of the shareholders should participate in the voting. When the decision involves an amendment to the articles of incorporation however, 50 per cent should vote. In the later case, two thirds of the attending shareholders should agree on the amendment.

Figure 11.4 shows a schematic overview of a public limited company.

FIGURE 11.4 A public limited company

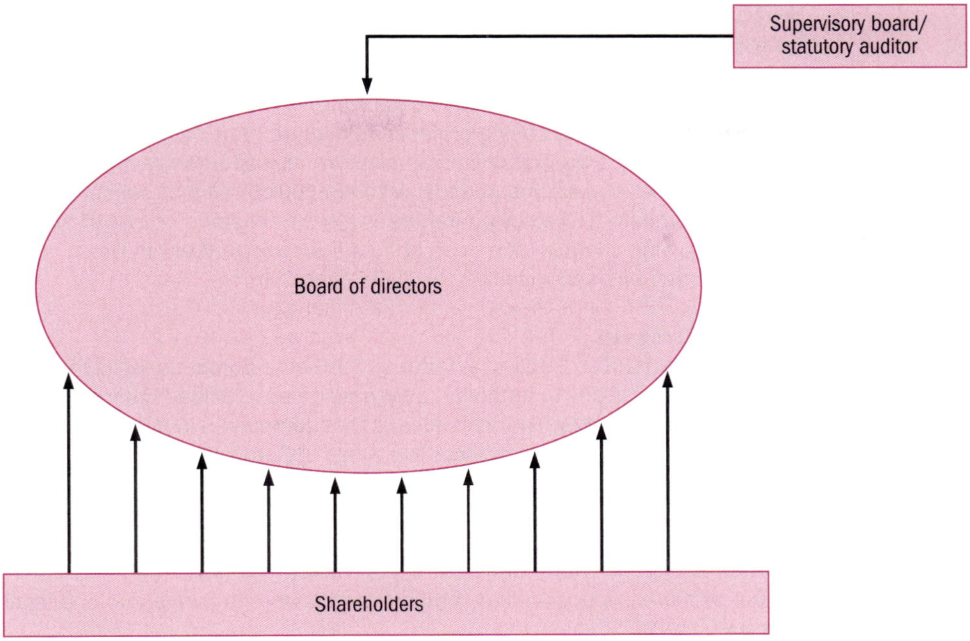

11.1.3 Special legal forms

Some legal forms of a business do not fall under the 'usual' categories as discussed in section 11.1, but are worthwhile exploring. In this section therefore we discuss the foundation, the company limited by guarantee, and the Societas Europaea and concerns.

Foundation

Sometimes one would need a legal form in the pursuit of a social goal. Amongst others, a foundation could be used. The concept of a foundation has different meanings throughout the world. In Norway, for instance, a foundation is composed of predominantly financial means that are to be used for a defined (social) purpose. These means usually result from gifts and donations, and are controlled by the foundation. The foundation as such does not have any shareholders, as in a limited company, but is most certainly a separate legal personality. As a result, the controllers of the foundation are not personally liable for any possible debts. Please note, that it is not forbidden to make profit through a foundation. However, given the fact that a foundation has no shareholders and is funded by donations and gifts, the main motive will mostly be to realize a social goal. In Norway, a foundation must be registered in the Foundation Register, and are supervised and controlled by the Norwegian Foundation Authority (Foundation Act of Norway, 2001). The economic power of foundations should not be underestimated. It is not unusual that banks or multinationals invest significantly in a foundation as a part of their corporate social responsibility programme. Next to that, massive donations by private individuals to tackle a certain problem or find a cure for a disease results in huge organizations, in size and management comparable to a multinational company.

Company limited by guarantee
A variation to a limited company is thecompany limited by guarantee. In essence, the shareholders do not necessarily invest in the company in the form of stocks, but instead promise to be liable for a certain amount of money in case of bankruptcy. This company form is mostly used for companies outside the trading profession, and are more likely to be used in case of non-profit organizations. Examples are charity organisations, schools and health care institutions (Minkang, 2006). In that sense, the goal of a company limited by guarantee might be the same of that of a foundation. This company form can be found amongst others in Great Britain, Hong Kong and Nigeria.

Societas Europaea
In Directive No 2157/2001 of 8 October 2001, the European legislature created the possibility to establish a European public limited company: the Societas Europeae(SE). The main idea is that companies in different legal systems can run their affairs under the wings of one single European company form. The SE can be installed in four situations (Art. 2, Directive 2157/2001):

- An existing public limited company with subsidiary establishment in another Member State of the European Union.
- Two or more existing limited companies who want to merge into one legal entity: the SE.
- Two or more public limited companies in different Member States of the European Union who wish to enter in a joint venture. The joint venture is then registered as a SE.
- Two or more limited companies who establish a holding company for their national companies in the form of an SE.

To set up a Societas Europeae, a minimum capital of 120.000 euros is required (Art. 4, Directive 2157/2001), and the legal structured is entirely governed by European law. This unique legal form can be used to form European concerns amongst companies without the necessity to overcome legal barriers between countries.

Joint venture
Sometimes, two or more businesses want to join the forces for a particular project. Usually, a joint venture is a temporary cooperation between companies to share a certain expertise or resources in the expectation of joint profit (Killing, 2013).
Joint ventures can be used for research purposes, for instance when several automobile producers develop a new engine block together, or when a pharmaceutical company wants to make use of another company's patent in order to develop a new medicine. A joint venture may also be used to do business abroad without the need to set up a subsidiary establishment in the other country. Instead, a company could set up a joint venture with an existing company in that country. In example 11.3, we see a joint venture between a coffee producer and a service caterer.

The participating companies could use a legal form to form the joint venture, which will most likely be a limited company, in which the participating companies own the shares.

However, it is not always necessary to create an entire new legal entity for such an adventure. In that case, the involved companies might sign a joint venture agreement. In essence, the joining companies keep their own legal form, and allocate part of their resources or know-how to contribute to the joint venture, in compliance with the joint venture agreement. In the agreement, it is regulated what resources will be allocated to the joint venture, how the profit will be divided, how the joint venture will be managed, and how the settlement of possible debts will be arranged. The joint venture in itself is then not a legal form, but an agreement between two legal forms.

EXAMPLE 11.3

Nespresso Café

Combining coffee & catering

In 2015, Nespresso set up a joint venture with food caterer Do&CO in Vienna. Through this joint venture, both companies want to combine the high quality coffee produced by Nespresso with the operational expertise and know-how in the food service business industry by Do&CO. In essence, Nespresso delivers the product, and DO&CO is responsible for the catering in the so-called 'Nespresso Café' (Nestle, 2015).

Concerns

A shareholder is not necessarily a natural person, but could also be another company, a bank, the state or an investment fund. As a result, companies can own companies, especially in the case of public limited companies. A company owning more companies is mostly referred to as a holding company. The chain of companies that relate to one another in terms of ownership is called a concern. For instance, the Dutch company Ahold is a holding company for famous brands such as Albert Heijn, Bol.com, Etos and Gall & Gall. In each case, Ahold owns a majority of the shares of the listed companies, as we can see in figure 11.5.

FIGURE 11.5 A concern

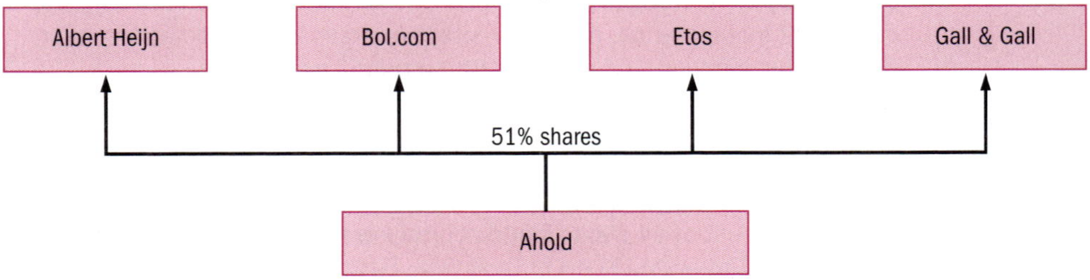

11.2 Regulatory competition

Legal systems have different grades of flexibility in company law. In case of the larger public limited companies it may make a difference in which country the company is registered. Within the United States of America, for instance, public limited companies have registered en masse in the State Delaware, since this state offers the most flexible company laws, as we may see in example 11.4.
Also regarding taxation, there might be regulatory competition. It is no secret that the Netherlands is a tax haven for many multinationals, as we may see in the news item. This attracts a lot of companies who are registered in the Netherlands, but do not necessarily employ business activities in that country. Such companies are also called 'mailbox companies'. Some consultancy companies even specialize in advising wealthy people or companies on how to use legal constructions in other countries to make use of more flexible tax laws. In April 2016, the Panemese consultancy company Mossack Fonseca made the worldwide headlines by accidentally leaking the names of their clients: the so-called Panama Papers. This resulted in a global discussion on the ethics of 'tax avoidance'. While in essence, these kinds of constructions are not necessarily illegal; they most certainly are morally questionable.

EXAMPLE 11.4

Delaware companies

In the U.S., the company law in the State of Delaware has been one of the most attractive law systems for business for a long time. Since the existence of limited companies, there has been a certain competition amongst the U.S. States in attracting the most companies by adopting company laws that are favourable to businesses. This competition seems to be won by Delaware. For companies there are four reasons to register as a Delaware company: easy registering, flexible and advanced laws, a specialized court system, and the broad application of Delaware law elsewhere in the U.S.

First, it is relatively easy to register a foreign company in the state. After all: 'Any person, partnership, association or corporation, singly or jointly with others, and without regard to such person's or entity's residence, domicile or state of incorporation, may incorporate or organize a corporation under this chapter (Section 101, General Corporation Law)'.

To establish a company, one only needs a registered office address and a registered agent in that state, but does not necessarily have to do business in Delaware (Section 131-132 General Corporation Law). As a result, more than 50 per cent of all public limited companies in the United States are registered in Delaware (State of Delaware, Department of State, 2015).

Second, in Delaware, company law is known to be of a high quality, advanced, and flexible (Black, 2007). The Legislation focuses on reducing regulations that at some point interfere in doing business on the one hand, and promotes regulations that facilitate smooth business on the other. For instance, under Article 102 (b)(7) of the Delaware Corporation Law, a company may limit or restrict liability of their managers. This was a direct response to the fact that in the absence of such a rule, businesses were confronted with high costs for liability insurances for their management. It is also noteworthy to mention that it is an informal tradition in Delaware that the legislature will consult the Corporation Law Section of the Delaware Bar Association before adopting any company law. This means that those lawyers that work daily with company legislation can comment and advise on new company laws.

Third, the Delaware Court system is famous for its Court of Chancery, having jurisdiction in company law matters. This court has produced very detailed and specialized case law on almost all provisions of Delaware company legislation. As a result, the court is at the forefront of giving direction to the development of U.S. company law. Unlike most other courts in Delaware, this Court is a court of equity, meaning that it delivers judgement without a jury, but with trained and educated judges only (www.courts.delaware.gov, 2015).

Fourth, as a result of the fact that a majority of the U.S. based companies is now a Delaware company, most other U.S. States have incorporated the Delaware company laws in their own legal system. This means that in practice, Delaware company law is now applied in the entire United States (Cahn & Donald, 2010).

THE ECONOMIST, 10 OCTOBER 2015

Corporate tax avoidance

Still slipping the net

On a roundabout near one of the main roads into Amsterdam sits a drab office block, which is home to hundreds of multinationals–on paper. Intertrust, the firm whose flag flutters outside, provides registration for local subsidiaries of the big companies, and other ancillary services. But many of those multinationals have a minimal physical presence there.

(...)

The Netherlands, and other low-tax havens such as Ireland and Luxembourg, have attracted much criticism from other countries for the legal loopholes they leave open to encourage such tax avoidance by big corporations. The three countries attract a huge amount of foreign direct investment (see chart), but much of it flows back out again, with the money ultimately financing factory-building and the like in another part of the world. By routing such investments via tax havens, multinationals can save on a variety of taxes, perfectly legally. The havens say that all they are doing is providing a business-friendly climate. But critics, including the United States Senate and the European Commission, say they are undermining the global tax base and helping big firms to avoid paying their fair share.

11.3 Foreign companies

When someone wants to run a business in another country, the entrepreneur will not always have the luxury to choose between all the legal forms of a company. As we have seen above, the law of Sri Lanka for instance does not allow a foreigner to run an unincorporated form of a business. When a foreigner wants to set up a new enterprise in Sri Lanka, it should be an incorporated business (Central Bank of Sri Lanka, 2012). In general, therefore, it will not be surprising that foreign entrepreneurs will mostly use an incorporated form to run a business abroad.

Another issue arises when an existing company wants to do business in another country. Usually, legal systems also regulate how foreign businesses may conduct economic activities in their country. To stick to the example of Sri Lanka: a foreign company may choose to set up an establishment in Sri Lanka. This is done to register as a so-called 'Overseas Company'. Another option is to limit your business activities by doing business without a permanent physical establishment, but being represented in Sri Lanka to facilitate business. This is then called an 'off-shore company'. Both must be incorporated company forms.

Summary

- One can run a business in an unincorporated or incorporated legal form.
  - An unincorporated company is composed of natural persons and has no separate legal identity.
  - An incorporated company is composed of shares owned by natural or legal persons but has its own legal identity.

- In unincorporated legal forms, the individuals of which the company is composed are unrestrictedly liable for the company debts. This is called personal liability.

- The simplest form of an unincorporated company is that of a sole proprietorship, also known as a sole trader.
  - A sole proprietorship is a legal form of an unincorporated business that is composed of one individual who is personally liable for the company's debts.
  - Usually, there are only a few prerequisites to set up a sole proprietorship.
  - The business is not considered as a separate legal entity, and therefore all income earned by the business is considered income tax.
  - the entrepreneur running a sole proprietorship may hire employees.

- A partnership is a legal form of an unincorporated business that is composed of more than one individual personally liable for the company's debts.

- There are different types of partnerships: the general partnership and the limited partnership.

- In some legal systems, the general partnership is subdivided in a professional and a commercial partnership:
  - In a general partnership, the partners play an active role in the organization of the company.
  - The internal affairs of a partnership are usually regulated in a partnership contract. This includes rules of spending and representation on behalf of the partnership.
  - In case of damage or debt, all partners are jointly liable.

- In a limited partnership, the same rules apply as in a general partnership. However, next to the normal partners, there may be partners with limited liability. These partners are not involved in the management of the company.

- An incorporated company has five main features:
  - The company is a legal personality.
  - There are transferable shares.
  - There is a centralized board of directors.
  - The ownership of the company is shared amongst the shareholders, in proportion to the value of the share.

- In a private limited company, the shares are not easily transferrable.

- In a public limited company, the shares are publicly transferrable. This could be done at stock exchanges.

- A foundation is used as a legal form to realize a social goal that does not necessarily relate to profit.

- A company limited by guarantee can also be used for social purposes: the shareholders agree to be liable for a certain sum in case of bankruptcy.

- The Societas Europeae is a European public limited company.

- A joint venture is a temporary cooperation between companies to share a certain expertise or resources in the expectation of joint profit.

- Companies can own other companies, and establish a concern of companies.

- Different grades of flexibility in company law leads to regulatory competition.

- When an entrepreneur wants to set up a business in another country, he may have to act in compliance with additional rules and regulations. Most likely, the entrepreneur will have to use an incorporated legal form.

Practice questions

Open questions

11.1 Min-Jun and Seo-Jun are normal partners in a Hapja Hoesa (limited partnership), named 'I nongdam ibnida'. Their rich aunt, Jo-Woo, promises to invest 13.000 South Korean Won (SKW) in their company. She does not participate in any management decisions however, and merely wants a return on investment. In their partnership contract, it is stipulated that Min-Jun and Seo-Jun have to agree on all purchases that exceed the threshold of 2.000 SKW. One day, Seo-Jun purchases a new cleaning machine on behalf of 'I nongdam ibnida' for a sum of 3.000 SKW. The selling company does however never receive any payment. The sales manager decides to visit the establishment of 'I nongdam ibnida', and is received by Min-Jun. As it appears, Min-Jun was never consulted for the purchase of the cleaning device, and has no idea. The manager of the selling party demands immediate payment from Min-Jun, if need be out of his own private assets. Min-Jun is not amused, and is wondering what to do.

To what extent can the sales manager indeed demand Min-Jun to pay the sum? Please explain.

11.2 Would it make any difference if the sales manager was aware of the partnership agreement of 'I nongdam ibnida'?

11.3 Bad tidings are coming for 'I nongdam ibnida'. It seems that the company is not able to pay their creditors anymore. As a result, the company is declared bankrupt.

To what extent are the partners liable for the debt?

11.4 Please explain the main differences between a private and public limited company?

Essay question

As discussed in the chapter, regulatory competition may lead to the phenomenon that companies try to register in the country with the most flexible or favourable rules. Results are the so-called 'Delaware company' and the 'panama papers'. Write an essay in which you describe the possible positive and negative effect of this, and conclude with your own opinion on the matter.

Multiple choice questions

11.1 Running an unincorporated company leads to:
a personal liability
b limited liability
c fault based liability

11.2 Which option is incorrect?
A sole proprietorship
a has no employees
b does usually not have a separate obligation to pay tax
c can usually not be registered by a foreigner

11.3 Which of the following companies will not be able to set up a Societas Europeae?
a An existing public limited company with subsidiary establishment in another Member State of the European Union
b Two or more private limited companies in one Member State of the European Union who want to do business in another Member State
c Two or more public limited companies in different Member States of the European Union who which to enter in a joint venture

11.4 A foundation:
a may not make profit
b does not have a profit aim
c has a primary goal to make profit

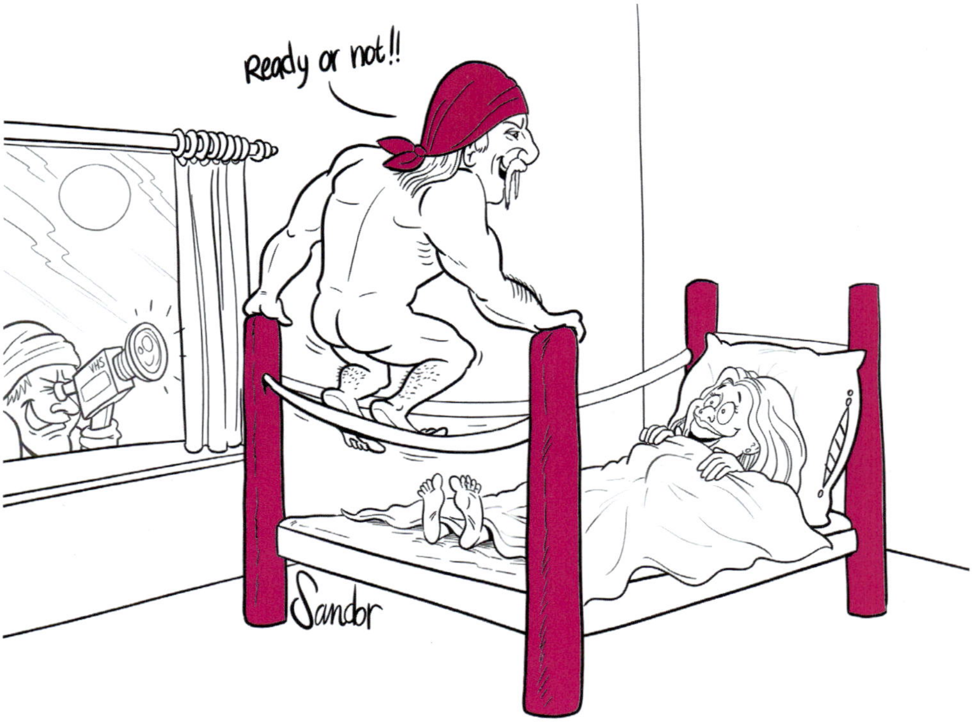
Ready or not!!
VHS
Sandor

12 The right to privacy and data processing

The right to privacy is an internationally recognized fundamental right. In this chapter, we will first discuss the difficult position of this right in relation to other (fundamental) rights. Then, we will explore how the right to privacy – especially in private legal relations – is organized in the U.S.A. and in the EU. However, it is not always easy to make sure foreign controllers of personal data act in compliance with your national laws. Therefore, lastly, we will discuss some jurisdiction challenges in this context.

12.1 Privacy: a clash of rights

The idea that someone should have the right to live in privacy is widely accepted. On the global level, this right is – for instance – recognized in the International Covenant on Civil and Political Rights, Art. 17:

'1 No one shall be subjected to arbitrary or unlawful interference with his privacy, family, home or correspondence, nor to unlawful attacks on his honour and reputation.
2 Everyone has the right to the protection of the law against such interference or attacks.'

As simple as this may sound, it is not always easy to determine the limitations of this right. After all, people cannot live in full privacy: exceptions are necessary in order to realise other rights. For instance, if I would write an extensive book about Justin Bieber in which I would like to reveal all kinds of new gossip about his private life, we can be quite sure that he would consider this a violation of his privacy. On the other hand, if I would not be able to publish the book, my right to freedom of speech, as well as my right to benefit from my Intellectual Property Right would be seriously restricted. Somewhere, the law has to draw a line between those conflicting interests.

This right affects both the public and private relations in society. In the public sphere, the question will mostly be to what extent the government may interfere with somebody's right to privacy to protect public security, morality, or health. This is rather obvious when the police kicks in a door to arrest a notorious criminal. In sacrifice of the criminal's privacy, the government may punish her/him for crimes committed in the past, and perhaps prevent her/him of committing crimes in the future. It becomes a bit more complicated when a government as a precaution tracks everyone's internet behaviour, including emails, in order to track potential terrorists.

In the private sphere, other issues play a role. In labour law relations for instance, the question arises to what extent the private activities and beliefs of an employee may play a role in the labour relation with the employer. To what extent for instance may the sexual preference play a role in hiring new employees? When the employer finds homosexuality offensive, is it then his good right to use sexual preference as a selection criterion. After all, it is his company, and everyone has freedom of speech and is free to have their own opinion about such matters. Or is this a private matter that is not the employer's business? Similar dilemmas can be observed in the sphere of political preference, or religious beliefs. Another matter is activities of the employee in the private sphere that do not relate to the job in itself. In the news item we see an example of a teacher who was fired after performing in an adult movie. While in essence performing in the movie was done outside the sphere of education, the school considered that teachers have an educational role in general, and performing in an adult movie cannot be a part of that role. In each legal system, privacy laws will help us in drawing the line between the privacy of the employee on the one hand, and the interest of the employer on the other hand.

THE DAILY MAIL (UK), 4 MAY 2015

Czech teacher who moonlighted as a porn star sacked after pupils discover her explicit videos and parents complained (Steel, 2013)

BY ELAINE O'FLYNN

A Czech teacher who auditioned to appear in a porn movie has been fired, after her gobsmacked pupils found the video online.

The unnamed teacher has now allegedly claimed she was drugged by filmmakers after footage from the casting was shared on the internet.

The 35-year-old mother of two, from the town of Ceska Lipa in the northwest of the Czech Republic, made the 40-minute video for a porn site after she travelled to Prague for a casting call.

She is filmed telling the interviewer she is into fitness, has two children and is separated, before she starts rubbing oil over her naked body and having sex with a man on camera.
Pupils are her school discovered the film online and began sharing it, before a parent came across the incriminating clip and informed the school.
(...)
Appalled headteacher Petr Jonas added: 'As soon as we learnt about this we had no other choice than to say goodbye to her.'

In the context of private law, consumer data is a difficult issue. On the one hand, companies would like to know as much as possible about their potential customers in order to offer them the most suitable products for the best price. On the other hand, this may lead to practices that data is gathered about consumers while they do not always know exactly who is processing that data, and what will be done with that data. This data can be retrieved from the behaviour of consumers online, which may be monitored by cookies or social media websites. Personal data of consumers is valuable to companies, as shown in example 12.1.

EXAMPLE 12.1

How much is your personal data worth?
In 2013, the Financial Times published a report in which industry pricing data was analysed (Steel, 2013). Amongst others, the Financial Times concluded that in general, companies are willing to pay 0,0005 U.S. dollar for general information about a person including age, gender and address. This means that per 1.000 persons, 0,50 U.S. dollars is paid on average for such type of information. However, when the information becomes more detailed, or the target group more specified, the amount companies are willing to pay goes up. For instance, data about potential car buyers will yield 0,0021 U.S. dollars (that is 2,11 U.S. dollars per 1.000) and companies pay 0,11 U.S. dollars per person when it is a pregnant woman. Most popular seems to be very particular information about someone's health condition: companies pay up to 0,26 U.S. dollars per person for this type of data.

Considering that online, data about millions of people is stored in structural and unstructured ways (so-called Big Data), and every day this incredibly huge amount of data grows rapidly, there surely is a lot of money to be earned in selling personal data to companies for marketing purposes.

Another issue in the private law sphere is the revealing of sensitive information about someone without his consent. This could be done in the media by news agencies, but also by individuals on social media. In essence, by publishing information about someone, they make use of their freedom of speech, which includes freedom of the press. This may however result in a violation of someone else's right to privacy.

Freedom of speech

There are obvious cases in which it is generally accepted that the right to privacy should prevail over the right to freedom of speech. When a French

tabloid decides to publish nude pictures of the Duchess of Cambridge (Kate Middleton) after a paparazzi photographer spent hours invading the private territory of the royal couples' holiday location, it will be beyond doubt that the privacy of the Duchess prevails (Jones, 2012).
The situation is more delicate when the police decide to publish an (anonymized) video of suspected criminals, and social media users are able to track and trace those suspects, publicly naming and shaming them. Especially when the data of one of the subjects appears to be incorrect and leads to an innocent man, as we can see in example 12.2. This case happened in the Netherlands, in which suspects are hardly ever revealed to the public to protect their privacy until they are proven guilty. This would have been somewhat different in the U.S.A., where the freedom of speech and the press is sometimes favoured over the right to privacy (Reza, 2005).
Another edgy matter is when the then-leader of the IMF, with quite a questionable past in such matters, is accused of raping a hotel employee. In all corners of the world, the press assumed that he was more or less guilty, while in the end the Supreme Court of New York dismissed the indictment and considered the hotel maid's story very incredible (Supreme Court of New York, 2011). Despite this verdict, the man involved had to resign from his position and, next to that, had to reassess his ambition to run for president in France.

EXAMPLE 12.2

Head kicking caught on camera a social media witch hunt

On January 4th 2013, a group of eight friends went to a bar in Eindhoven, the Netherlands. The boys spent the night dancing and drinking beer. On their way home, they come across a lonely man, and it appears that the eight, out of the blue, start beating up this unfortunate traveller. At least one of the friends is extremely aggressive, and keeps kicking against the head of the man while he lies down on the street, unconscious.

However, the brutal deeds were caught on a surveillance camera, and the Dutch authorities try to catch the perpetrators by spreading the video through social media. The faces of the group of eight are blurred, so they are unrecognizable for those who do not know them personally. Social media users responded furiously to this video. While there is the usual fighting during each night out, it is unusual that it is caught on camera, and spread through social media. Especially the fact that eight boys almost randomly start beating up an unknown passenger, and continue kicking for so long, fuel the public outrage. The video went 'viral', resulting in a true social media witch-hunt.

Clever social media users were able to remove the blurred pixels and so the 'eight from Eindhoven' were clearly visible for everyone. Finding out their names now was relatively easy, and a Dutch media website decided to publish not only their names, but also their phone numbers. Since then, the boys were named and shamed in public. A fact that the court that ruled in the matter even took into consideration and lowered the sentences (Court of 's-Hertogenbosch, 2013).

The media site did not really check their sources twice, for one of the phone numbers belonged to a namesake of one of the boys, and had nothing to do with the entire affair. Unfortunately, this namesake, running his own business, received several death threads on his phone, and saw a dramatic decrease in his clientele (Kamp, 2013).

All in all it will be clear that privacy laws are amongst the most delicate ones because they regulate a very important fundamental right, and simultaneously, may result in a violation of other very important rights when applied too drastically. The right to privacy clashes regularly with other fundamental rights.

12.2 Privacy laws around the world

In this section, we will discuss the privacy laws in the U.S., which are not centrally organized, and the privacy laws in the EU, which are.

12.2.1 The U.S.A.

In the U.S.A. there has always been some reluctance against governmental interference in private matters. This partly explains why in the U.S. there is at most constitutional protection for individual privacy rights against the government. However, for any other protection in the field of privacy, one has to turn to other sources of law. First, there is tort law as developed by the courts, which basically protect citizens against direct and obvious violations of privacy. However, the more subtle cases in which companies process personal data in big proportions in order to get more insight in how to approach their customers falls usually outside the scope of the torts. For this, we have to turn to federal and state statutes, of which the latter are not surprisingly rather different per state. These Statutes do not regulate privacy as a general concept, but rather deal with specific matters or topics of privacy (Levin & Nicholson, 2005).
In this section, we will first explore the U.S. constitutional protection of privacy. Although this protection only regulates public legal relations, some legal concepts – such as the reasonable expectation of privacy – are also used in private relations in the sphere of tort law. Then, we will shortly focus on some federal laws regulating specific aspects of privacy. In this discussion, we will focus on an area in which public and private legal relations seem to overlap in law: the privacy of internet behaviour. Last, we will discuss the various torts that protect privacy in private legal relations.

The U.S. Constitution

The first thing that immediately stands out when studying the U.S. Constitution is that there is no general recognition of the right to privacy. This is in strong contrast with one of the 'competing' human rights: the right to freedom of speech: This right is firmly embedded in the First Amendment to the Constitution. It gives an impression of the importance of freedom of speech in the U.S.A., and possibly how such a right relates to the right to privacy. After all, lower legislation that at some point harms the right to freedom of speech will be declared unconstitutional by the Supreme Court, while this remains to be seen when the right to privacy is involved.

Freedom of speech

In illustration: several attempts by the federal legislature to restrict or ban explicit adult material in the sphere of child porn, and restrict the access of minors to explicit materials were declared unconstitutional by the Supreme Court. The reason for this was that they were too broadly formulated, and therefore potentially have a broader coverage than strictly necessary to protect the wellbeing and privacy of children. This could result in restricting freedom of speech regarding those expressions who are – as a side effect – forbidden by these laws but do not directly contribute to the protection of children. An example of a landmark case can be found in 'the free speech of pornography' case (example 12.3). While such a case might seem bizarre in the eyes of someone who is more interested in morality than in adult movies, the example should be understood in a more principal context: the idea that people should be able to express what they want is highly valued, even when it may offend people, as long as it is not against the law. The law should be in line with the Constitution, and every inch that restricts the freedom of speech more than necessary to comply with the Constitution is undesirable.

EXAMPLE 12.3

The free speech of pornography

The Child Pornography Prevention Act (CPPA) of 1996 broadened the scope regarding the kind of child porn that was banned on the U.S. markets. This includes 'any visual depiction, including any photograph, film, video, picture, or computer or computer-generated image or picture, that is, or appears to be, of a minor engaging in sexually explicit conduct'. Due to this broad description, some Californian porn producers were afraid to lose substantial parts of their income, because their main productions would from now on be illegal. Previously, only pornographic expressions dirextly involving children were forbidden. Now also virtual child pornography and productions in which adults acted or dressed like minors were forbidden. This 'shady' branch in the porn business appeared to be quite large, and therefore some of the porn producers united in the Free Speech Coalition to stand their ground.
According to them, of course children should never be harmed in producing pornography. However, the restriction in the CPPA was so broad, that it covered also legitimate alternatives to child porn. Such a restriction would violate their freedom of speech, and is therefore unconstitutional. After all, while it is the business of the government to protect the privacy of children, it is not of the business to protect anything more than that.
In the end, the Supreme Court had a similar view on these affairs, and declared the CPPA unconstitutional (U.S. Supreme Court, 2002).

Fourth Amendment

The most explicit reference in the Constitution is the Fourth Amendment, in which citizens are protected against unreasonable searches and seizures by the government:

> 'The right of the people to be secure in their persons, houses, papers, and effects, against unreasonable searches and seizures, shall not be violated, and no warrants shall issue, but upon probable cause, supported by oath or

affirmation, and particularly describing the place to be searched, and the persons or things to be seized.'

Expectation of privacy

The central question that follows from this constitutional protection is when people may have a reasonable expectation of privacy, and therefore a government may not intrude into this privacy. In other words: when a citizen has a reasonable expectation to be private, a government may not in principle interfere with this privacy, unless it is authorized by special means such as a search warrant in case of suspicion of criminal activities. The word 'reasonableness' is a rather flexible concept and may be understood differently. It makes quite a difference if a court would consider whether the individual in question feels he is in a private situation, or whether people in general think that in such a situation, someone should be able to be private. The first is called a subjective test, while the latter is called an objective test.

In a colourful chain of case law, the U.S. Supreme Court clarified the exact meaning of this reasonable expectation of privacy. According to their own doctrine, the Supreme Court mostly first applies a subjective test to establish whether the individual involved feels that his privacy is violated, and then reviews this against what society in general would think about that: the objective test (U.S. Supreme Court, 1967). It is however debated to what extend the subjective test truly adds value to case law, and whether it is really used any further than just a formal consideration (Kerr, 2015). Amongst others, the Supreme Court recognized the following locations as private areas: someone's home, or temporary place of residing, such as a hotel room; a business office; designated areas in public places which are intended to offer privacy, such as a restroom; someone's property, such as a trunk, a briefcase, or someone's luggage; the content of correspondence, the content of someone's smartphone, and to a certain extent a car.
The Court also specified what situations are not protected under the Fourth Amendment. These include virtually all public areas (Slobogin, 2002). For instance, people should reasonably expect that in public areas, there are surveillance cameras, and when people drive a car, their route is not a secret (Supreme Court, 1983). The main consideration appears to be that the usage of modern technology merely replaces the more traditional governmental ways of inspecting the public domain, such as police surveillance.

The fourteenth amendment

The above mentioned case law mostly relates to what places or things would fall under the constitutional protection of the right to privacy. In these cases, the Court predominantly gives an interpretation of the Fourth Amendment. However, the right to privacy has more constitutional components than that. For instance, the Fourteenth Amendment recognized the right to liberty, which encompasses privacy aspects in the sphere of family life and self determination. For instance, the Court has declared state laws unconstitutional that violated the right to choose the type of school you prefer (1923), the free choice to use contraception or not (1965), the right to terminate medical treatment (1990), and the right to express your sexual preference (2003).

State constitutions

It needs to be noted here that a general right to privacy is recognized in the Constitution of some of the U.S. States themselves. Currently, this right is explicitly recognized in ten U.S. States, and will be protected by their supreme courts. For instance, the Constitution of California (Art. 1 section 1) stipulates that:

> 'All people are by nature free and independent and have inalienable rights. Among these are enjoying and defending life and liberty, acquiring, possessing, and protecting property, and pursuing and obtaining safety, happiness, and privacy.'

Federal laws

As we have seen above, the Constitution only offers a limited and quite fragmented protection regarding the right to privacy. In Federal laws, some aspects of privacy are further regulated. Also here, privacy is regulated topic by topic, instead of a general approach. Where the Constitution only regulates certain aspects of privacy in the relation between the government and its citizens (public law), federal laws regulate both public and private law aspects but always in separate acts.

Regarding privacy laws in the public domain, there is first a general Privacy Act (1974) that basically requires government employees to collect only the private data of citizens when it is proportionate to its legitimate goal. This means amongst others that the government should obtain the data preferably directly from citizens, and use only the information that is absolutely necessary. Furthermore, there are specialized laws on various topics, such as the Driver's Privacy Protection Act, protecting personal data of motor vehicle records stored by state authorities, and the Family Educational Right and Privacy Act, protecting the data of students in educational records.

The privacy of internet behaviour

In the context of ICT and data protection, there are federal laws around three main topics: the privacy of communication, the privacy of financial information, and the privacy of medical records (Wu et al. 2011). Especially the first – privacy of communication – is a controversial issue.
In general, it is recognized that the content of email correspondence is a private affair and is protected by the Fourth Amendment. However, this is not always the case when email addresses are used for public affairs (working for the government) or in the employment of an employer. In both cases it is quite common for the government or a private employer to notify the employee through terms of use that their internet behaviour may be monitored. In such a case, the employee has no reasonable expectation of privacy regarding the contents of his email correspondence (U.S. Court of Appeals, 4th circuit, 2000).

Furthermore, when emails are stored by an Internet Service Provider, the protection of its content is significantly weakened after 180 days: when this time transpires, it is much easier for authorized government employees to access the content of these emails (Thompson & Cole, 2015). However, in case of suspected terrorism, the possibilities to gather digital information – including the content of digital communication – are much broader as a result of the so-called Patriot Act (2001).

In the Electronic Communications Privacy Act, a prohibition to install pen registers or trap and trace devises without a courts permit is included. However, Internet Service Providers are excepted from this prohibition when tracing internet traffic is necessary to protect the provider or users of the provider from unlawful or abusive use of the service provider. This may sound a bit cryptic, but in practise this mostly means that ISPs do track and trace who sends mailings to whom in order to find and eliminate spam or fishing messages.

Also here, the concept of 'reasonable expectation of privacy' is assessed by the courts in ruling on disputes that relate to internet privacy. The general idea is that where the content of emails is private, the information about the addressees of your emails, volume of the internet traffic of an ISP user, and the IP addresses of websites that are visited are not. The main motivation for this approach is that internet users voluntarily give that information to a third party – the Internet Service Provider – and therefore cannot expect this information to be private. For instance, a U.S. Court of Appeals held that:
'The government's surveillance of e-mail addresses also may be technologically sophisticated, but it is conceptually indistinguishable from government surveillance of physical mail. In a line of cases dating back to the nineteenth century, the Supreme Court has held that the government cannot engage in a warrantless search of the contents of sealed mail, but can observe whatever information people put on the outside of mail, because that information is voluntarily transmitted to third parties.' (U.S. Court of Appeals -9th circuit, 2007)

12

Tort law and the right to privacy
In private legal relations, besides the few laws that protect particular aspects of privacy, tort law is used to enforce the right to privacy. In general, the tort that relates to privacy is referred to as 'invasion of privacy'. In fact, four types of invasion of privacy can be found in the U.S. case law: intrusion on seclusion, appropriation, public disclosure and false light. Al four cover a particular aspect of privacy. What they have in common is that in all invasion of privacy cases the reasonable expectation of privacy is the leading concept.

Invasion of privacy

> Intrusion on seclusion applies when someone intentionally intrudes the privacy of someone else.

Intrusion on seclusion

This tort is the most commonly used in the context of privacy. Four main elements should be considered (Illinois Appellate Court, 1986).
First, the intrusion must be unauthorized. When you voluntarily give someone access to your mailbox and that person comes across data you would rather not share with others, there is no intrusion. When someone takes control of your computer from a distance and uses your webcam to make photographs, there obviously is.
Second, a reasonable person should find the intrusion objectionable. That is most certainly the case in the Miss Teen U.S.A. example. However, what to think of a teacher posting a selfie on Instagram with his students on the background? In each case, the court would have to draw the line between objectionable and acceptable.

Third, the intrusion should concern a private matter. When Jake Shears (lead singer of the Scissor Sisters) decides to undress on stage during a live performance, he is clearly not in a private setting. The audience will not be accused of intruding his seclusion. However, when he would do such thing at home, and a journalist who stands outside uses a very strong lens to capture this moment, it is a private matter. However, quite a lot is considered to be public, as we have seen above in the context of the U.S. Constitution. For instance, when an undercover journalist recorded what an employee in an open workplace was saying, this was considered to be in a public space. After all, the employee should know that everything he said could potentially be overheard by any of his colleagues, including an undercover reporter (Supreme Court of California, 1999). Also, when a newsmagazine published the picture of an open casket during a funeral of a diseased soldier, this was considered to be a public matter, since the relatives of the soldier opened the funeral for anyone who wished to attend (Federal Court of Appeals, 2007).
Fourth, the intrusion results in some form of suffering. In essence, this prerequisite is met when the victim of the intrusion experiences discomfort as a result of that intrusion, and is in court cases not always thoroughly discussed.

CNN, 26 SEPTEMBER 2013

Arrest made in Miss Teen U.S.A. extortion case

BY: GREG BOTELHO

A college student was arrested Thursday for allegedly hijacking the webcams of young women – among them reigning Miss Teen U.S.A. Cassidy Wolf – taking nude images, then blackmailing his victims to send him more explicit material or else be exposed.
Jared James Abrahams, a 19-year-old computer science student from Temecula, California, surrendered on Thursday to the FBI on federal extortion charges, the agency announced. Authorities say he victimized young women surreptitiously, by taking control of their computers then photographing them as they changed out of their clothes.
His arrest came six months after a teenager identified in court documents as C.W. alerted authorities. She has since publicly identified herself as Cassidy Wolf, the recently crowned Miss Teen U.S.A. She touted news reports of her alleged tormenter's arrest on her Twitter feed.

Appropriation

Appropriation applies when someone uses someone else's name or likeliness without permission for commercial purposes.

In some states, the tort of appropriation is also referred to as the right of publicity. After all, this tort protects people's commercial rights regarding their name or likeliness. Think about the usage of the image of the late Bob Marley or a likeliness of the teenage mutant hero turtles on t-shirts without the consent of the relatives of Marley, or the trademark owner of the turtles. The tort of appropriation protects such celebrities or well-known figures against the commercial exploitation of their name or image against their will, or the will of their trademark holders (Hylton & Goldson, 1996). As we see in example 12.4, the tort of appropriation is regularly used in disputes between celebrities and tabloids that write about them.

EXAMPLE 12.4

A fistful of dollars

In 1997, the famous actor Clint Eastwood sued the National Enquirer for using his name and image in a promotion campaign for the latest edition of the magazine. In the magazine, it was suggested that the tabloid held an exclusive interview with the movie star, discussing all kinds of personal details. In fact, the interview never took place, and the article was a fake fabric of quotes taken from other sources. Eastwood claimed that his reputation was damaged, because he would never allow a tabloid to interview him exclusively. Furthermore, the tabloid used his image and name to promote the sales of this particular edition without his consent. Eastwood won the case, and was awarded 150.000 U.S. dollars damage compensation on top of the claimed attorney costs (Federal Court of Appeals, 1997).

In this case, the entire article as published by the National Enquirer was considered to be a violation of Eastwood's privacy. The main reason for this seemed to be that the tabloid claimed to have had en exclusive interview with Eastwood, which was not true. In other cases, the content of such articles was never considered to violate the privacy of celebrities due to their newsworthiness, and freedom of the press. However, using the image of celebrities to promote the sales of such tabloids has always been considered to cross the line (Belmas et al, 2016).

Pubic disclosure

> Pubic disclosure applies when someone publicly discloses private fact of someone else.

A claim based on the tort of public disclosure is composed of the following elements.

First, the information that is disclosed should be publicly disclosed. In general, disclosing private facts about someone on a website, a blog, social media or a newspaper is public disclosure. Yelling something in a crowded street is not.

Second, the information should be private. This means that the information should be unknown to the public before the disclosure.

Third, the information should be offensive to a reasonable person. These generally include information about someone's sexual orientation or activities, medical history, or financial affairs. For instance, in on case, a girl suffers from a rare disease in which she cannot stop eating but simultaneously keeps losing weight. Reporters from a magazine called Time invaded the hospital, took pictures of the hospitalized girl without her consent, and published an article about her disease, using her name, also without her consent. This was considered to be a violation of privacy by the Missouri Supreme Court (1942).

Fourth, the information should not be newsworthy. This is to protect the free press. In general, it is assumed that well-known figures such as celebrities are newsworthy, even when it relates to information that would be private for 'normal' people, such as someone's sexual orientation or sexual life. However, a recent verdict of the Circuit Court of Florida seems to restrict the unlimited freedom of speech of the press when it concerns private facts of celebrity, as we can see in the newspaper item. However, the publisher of the disputed sex tape of Hulk Hogan decided to appeal the verdict, so we will have to await the ultimate decision in this case.

SKYNEWS, 22 MARCH 2016

Hulk Hogan Wins Extra $25m In Sex Tape Case

A jury awards additional punitive damages worth $25m (£17,3m) to the wrestler over a sex tape posted on Gawker's website.

Hogan was awarded $115m (£79,5m) last week after a **Florida jury found Gawker violated his privacy** by publishing a video of him having sex with his former best friend's wife in 2012.
Gawker has indicated that it will appeal against the initial verdict.
The case pitted arguments over a celebrity's right to privacy in the internet age against the freedom of the press, which is protected in the U.S. Constitution.
Hogan's lawyers noted that he was unaware the encounter was being filmed when it took place over a decade ago and that the footage was not newsworthy. (...)
Hogan, whose real name is Terry Bollea, testified that he still suffered from the humiliation of the video going viral.

It was alleged that Gawker's value increased by $15m (£10,4m) after the post, although the website contended that it made $11.000 (£7.600) in advertising revenue.
Gawker's lawyers, meanwhile, called into question whether the sex tape was a stunt and pointed out it had already appeared on at least two other websites.
(...)

To conclude, the tort of false light, or defamation, was already discussed in chapter 9 in the context of liability law, and more specifically, tort law. Just as a reminder, the definition of defamation is as follows:

Defamation

> Defamation is the inflicting of harm on someone's reputation by spreading false statements.

12.2.2 The EU

In the European Union, the protection of privacy is centrally regulated. From may 25th 2018 onwards, Regulation 2016/679 will regulate the privacy protection of individuals in private legal relations, where Directive 2016/680 will regulate this protection in public legal relations. Both will replace the 'old' directive on data protection (Directive 95/46/EC), which

applies until these dates. Privacy law in the EU is therefore in transition. The new legislation was deemed necessary to improve the legal position of citizens towards the protection of their personal data, to simplify existing legislation, to catch up with modern developments, and to contribute to a digital single market (European Commission, 2016). In this section, the newest legislation will be the starting point. We will focus on the Directive 2016/679, since the public legal relations have a very limited overlap with the private legal relations. This was already the case in the 'old' Directive, and even more so now that the European legislature decided to regulate these legal relations in two distinct laws.
The EU Regulation and Directives are intended to give a more specific effect to human right treaties to which the EU members are also a Member State, such as Article 8 of the European Convention for the Protection of Human Rights and Fundamental Freedoms.

Processing personal data
Not all the procession of data falls under the protection of Regulation 2016/679. Only personal data is protected. Article 2 of the Regulation defines personal data as 'any information relating to an identified or identifiable natural person'. This means that the data involved leads directly or indirectly to the identification of an individual. In case of direct identification it is not that complex: usually the name of an individual is then involved, and we know who the data subject is.

Direct identification

However, also a combination of data that does not directly reveals the identity of the data subject may also fall under the protection of this regulation. In case of indirect identification the data involved does not explicitly identify the data subject. However, the data will ultimately lead to the identification of a person. This could be for instance due to the fact that the combination of data can only lead to one individual. Think about mentioning a job of which there is only one (the quality manager of a certain department). Not using the name directly does not really cover whose identity is involved. Think also about registering someone's zip code, age, brand car, amount of children and marital status. Probably this combination of data will only lead to one individual each time. Think furthermore of collecting data you cannot use in such a way that it leads to identification of a person, but is intended to be used by someone else who can, such as in example 12.5.

Indirect identification

EXAMPLE 12.5

Tracing truant students
George is tired of the busy traffic of students in his street, especially because they seem to go the nearest bar instead of college. Therefore, he decides to take pictures of students that pass by during college hours but go the wrong direction, and keeps track of the exact time and date the photographs were taken. While he has no idea who these students are, he passes the photographs to the school the students belong to. The Dean of that school now most certainly knows who these students are and will probably have a grim chat with them.

The mere fact that you have access to data does not fall under this Regulation. The Regulation only applies if one uses that data in some way. In the terminology of the Regulation, this is called 'processing'. The Regulation defines collecting as an operation that is performed on personal data. Examples are the collection, recording, organisation, structuring, storage, adaptation or alteration, retrieval, consultation, use, disclosure by transmission, dissemination or otherwise making available, alignment or combination, restriction, erasure or destruction of data.

Processing

In practice this simply means that as long as there is only access to data, the Regulation does not apply. Only when something is done with that data, the Regulation should be taken into consideration.

In the terminology of the Regulation (Art. 4), a distinction is made between a controller, a processor and a recipient. It needs to be noted here that the Regulation for the major part holds the controller responsible for lawful data processing.

Controller

The controller is the one (natural or legal person) who determines the purposes and means of the processing of personal data. For instance, in the WhatsApp case (example 12.8.), WhatsApp Inc. is considered to be the controller, and therefore ultimately responsible for the data processing.

Processor

The processor is the one (natural or legal person) who actually processes the personal data on behalf of the controller. For instance, the company hiring a market research agency to conduct a market research in which personal data is used is the controller. The market research agency is the processor. It needs to be noted here that the controller and the processor could be the same institution. When a company has its own market research department, the company is both controller and processor.

Recipient

A recipient is the one (natural or legal person) to whom the personal data is disclosed. This could be an analytic agency that analyses data collected by a processor on behalf of a controller.

Principles

In general, data procession should at all times be in compliance with several basic principles. The most important principles are listed in Article 5 of Regulation 2016/679. These are: the principle of lawfulness, fairness and transparency; purpose limitation; data minimisation; accuracy; storage limitation; integrity and confidentiality; and accountability.

Lawfulness, fairness and transparency

The principle of lawfulness, fairness and transparency means firstly that data procession should at all time be in compliance with European and domestic legislation. When data procession constitutes a violation of law, it is not in compliance with the Regulation. Examples can be found in the sphere of illegal methods of data collection, such as secretly filming people in a private setting, stealing data, or forcing someone to provide for data. Secondly, it means that a data subject should be made aware of the data processing, and understand what will happen with the personal data. In the example of Amazon.com (example 12.6) you may find an example of a practice in which it could be questioned whether this is in compliance with the idea of fairness and transparency. At least the data subject should be aware of the fact that his data is processed before the processing occurs, not after.

EXAMPLE 12.6

Amazon.com

The conditions of use for Amazon.com, which include their privacy policy, state that when a customer visits the website, he is automatically subject to their conditions of use. The exact wordings are:
'Welcome to Amazon.com. Amazon Services LLC and/or its affiliates ("Amazon") provide website features and other products and services to you when you visit or shop at Amazon.com, use Amazon products or services, use Amazon applications for mobile, or use software provided by Amazon in connection with any of the foregoing (collectively, "Amazon Services"). Amazon provides the Amazon Services subject to the following conditions...' (www.amazon.com, 2016).

However, you can only know this when you've already visited their web shop. This leads to the remarkable situation in which a data subject is informed about the fact that whatever he does on the website is monitored and used after part of this data is already processed. After all, it seems questionable whether it is fair and transparent when rules apply to people while they cannot be aware of this from the beginning, nor consent to it.

12

Purpose limitation

The principle of purpose limitation means firstly that data is collected for specified, explicit and legitimate purposes. In other words, data should not be processed in the pursuit of vague purposes. When a website communicates to process data about 'internet behaviour' for 'analytical purposes', this is simply not explicit enough. Secondly, data should not be further processed in a manner that is incompatible with this legitimate purpose. This means that data that is processed for one specific purpose may not be processed for another purpose that was not known on the moment of processing. For the second processing, a separate legal basis is required. An example can be found in example 12.7.

EXAMPLE 12.7

Funky furniture

A web shop selling furniture processes the name, address and bank account of a data subject for the purpose of sending orders to this client. Before storing this data, each customer is required to consent to this data processing. However, it appears that the same data is also sold to other parties for marketing purposes. This practice will not be in compliance with the principle of purpose limitation.

Data minimisation

The principle of data minimisation implies that the processed data should be adequate, relevant and limited to what is necessary in relation to the purposes for which they are processed. This means that if a legitimate goal can be realised without processing personal data at all, this should be done without using that data.

It also means that data procession should be proportionate to the legitimate goal. The WhatsApp case (example 12.8) provides a good example of this: also data of non-WhatsApp users were processed by WhatsApp, while this was not necessary to realise their legitimate purpose. In earlier legislation, this is also referred to as the principle of proportionality.

Accuracy

The principle of accuracy means that personal data which is processed should be accurate and, where necessary, kept up to date. Sometimes, inaccurate or old data may be in conflict with the interest of the data subject. When a financial advisor for instance stores incorrect income data of a client, this client might end up with an unfortunate mortgage.

Storage limitation

The principle of storage limitation means that the data must be kept in a form which permits identification of data subjects for no longer than is necessary for the purposes for which the personal data are processed. For instance, storage of customer data is usually considered to be no longer necessary when the time in which legal claims regarding the contract can be brought before a court transpires. This is different in each legal system, but will usually be around two to three years. Another example is the storage of video tapes from surveillance cameras. If no theft or other crime takes place, the content of the video tapes should be deleted as soon as possible.

Integrity and confidentiality

The principle of integrity and confidentiality means that personal data must be processed in a manner that ensures appropriate security of the personal data. The more sensitive the personal data is to the data subject, the more safety measures are expected. Surely, safety measures failed in the case of Ashley Madison, as we can see in the news item.

THE INDIAN EXPRESS, 19 AUGUST 2015

Ashley Madison hacked: Here's why the website for 'cheating spouses' got targeted.

AshleyMadison, a website to help 'cheating spouses find a fling online', has been hacked by a group called The Impact Team, which has threatened to post user information online if the website is not shut down.
AshleyMadi.com is owned by Avid Life Media (ALM), a Toronto-based firm. ALM also owns other dating sites like Cougar Life and Established Men. AshleyMadison has been around since 2001 and claims to have over 37 million users.
So why did AshleyMadison get hacked? According to the hackers, a part of the reason appears to be $20 fee that AshleyMadison would charge its users if they wanted their profile deleted completely. The hackers, who broke into the site, revealed that the data of even those who had paid the fee was still very much present.
The hackers also leaked maps of internal company servers, employee network account information, company bank account data and salary information. The Impact Team has also accused ALM of running a prostitution ring with the website called Established Men which aims to connect rich men with attractive girls.

The principle of accountability basically means that at any time, the controller is responsible for the data processing, and liable for any violations of privacy laws.

Accountability

Justification

Next to acting in compliance with the principles discussed above, each and every data processing should be justifiable. This means that the controller should be able to justify the data processing invoking one of the justification grounds as stipulated in Article 6. Article 6 of Regulation 2016/679 is almost identical to Article 7 of the old Directive 95/46/EC. In essence,

> 'a the data subject has given consent to the processing of his or her personal data for one or more specific purposes.'

Consent should be given actively by the data subject, and not passively. Therefore, on EU websites, the user will always have to 'tick the box' when agreeing to a privacy policy or general terms. This is also referred to as a 'click-wrap agreement'. The opposite, in which consent is assumed to be given when a consumer visits a website or makes use of a service, is called a 'browse-wrap agreement'. The example of Amazon.com (example 12.7) would fall under this category. In the EU such an agreement, when it leads to the procession of personal data, is illegal.

> 'b processing is necessary for the performance of a contract to which the data subject is party or in order to take steps at the request of the data subject prior to entering into a contract.'

When someone places an order at a web shop, the company will have to make use of at least the name, address and information regarding the customers bank account to deliver the order properly. If not, it is simply impossible to fulfil the contractual obligations of the company towards the consumer. The same applies to sending a quotation or invoice. However, the contractual obligation must be towards the data subject, and not towards a third party. An example of a violation of this principle can be found in example 12.8.

EXAMPLE 12.8

What's app?!

The California based company WhatsApp Inc. launched a worldwide communication app in 2009. The application can be downloaded on most smartphone types, enabling their users to send text-messages, but also photos, videos and sound fragments to other WhatsApp users. The app initially costs 0,89 eurocents when using an I-phone, but no costs are charged for the sending and receiving of messages after the paid download. One of the conditions for downloading the app is that the users give WhatsApp access to their digital address book. This includes the addresses of people who do not use the app, and who are unaware of the fact that this company is processing their personal data.
In a joint research conducted in 2013, the Canadian and Dutch data protection authorities concluded that this practice was a violation of Canadian and Dutch privacy laws (College Bescherming Persoonsgegevens, 2013).

Jurisdiction

A first matter of dispute was the applicable law. After all, in their general terms, WhatsApp chooses Californian law as applicable to all their contracts, as you can read here:
'You agree that: (i) the Whatsapp Service shall be deemed solely based in California; (ii) the Whatsapp Service shall be deemed a passive server that does not give rise to personal jurisdiction over Whatsapp, either specific or general, in jurisdictions other than California; and (iii) that you agree to subject to the jurisdiction of California in the event of any legal dispute. (...) Any claim or dispute between you and Whatsapp that arises in whole or in part from the Whatsapp Service shall be decided exclusively by a court of competent jurisdiction located in Santa Clara County, California.'

Furthermore, WhatsApp holds that: 'If you are a user accessing the WhatsApp Site and Service from the European Union, Asia, or any other region with laws or regulations governing personal data collection, use, and disclosure, that differ from United States laws, please be advised that through your continued use of the WhatsApp Site and Service, which are governed by California law, this Privacy Policy, and our Terms of Service, you are transferring your personal information to the United States and you expressly consent to that transfer and consent to be governed by California law for these purposes.'

Therefore, WhatsApp disputed the authority of the Canadian and Dutch data protection authority.
In the Netherlands, the Data Protection Act is considered as mandatory law, and cannot be deviated from by means of a contract. The Dutch authority held that WhatsApp specifically targets the Dutch market. This can be demonstrated by the fact that WhatsApp has a Dutch FAQ site, and encourages the providing of Dutch language information about their service. Therefore, the App should act in compliance with Dutch – and thus also European – privacy laws. While in disagreement with this reasoning, WhatsApp eventually changed its policies, as we will see below, in line with the European Data Protection Directive 95/46/EC.

Principles

The Canadian and Dutch data protection authorities concluded that to provide the service, it was not necessary to also process the personal data of non-WhatsApp users. Until that time, WhatsApp did not offer the possibility for its users to make a selection of telephone numbers they wanted to communicate with through WhatsApp. It was in essence an 'all or nothing' agreement in which either no agreement was possible, or all personal data stored in the digital telephone book was processed by WhatsApp. However, it would be an easy adaption to offer the possibility of the user to select telephone numbers instead of using the entire phone book. Therefore, the authorities concluded that WhatsApp violated the principle of proportionality.

Justification

Furthermore, the Canadian and Dutch data protection authorities held that no justification could be found to process the personal data retrieved from the address books of app users who are not a user of this service.

First of all, the Dutch authority held that the non-WhatsApp users did not give their consent in any way to this kind of data processing. They do not even know their data is being processed, nor what the purpose is of the processing.
WhatsApp argued that the processing of digital address books was necessary to perform their obligations based on the service contract they have with WhatsApp users. After all, how can WhatsApp connect users of their service with one another without being able to determine which of someone's contacts is a fellow WhatsApp user? As it seems, indirectly WhatsApp invokes the current Article 6 of Regulation 2016/679, section b. However, such an argument will always fail, since the non-WhatsApp users are not a part of any contract with WhatsApp, and therefore their personal data can never be used when this is necessary to perform contractual obligations with WhatsApp users.
Also, the Dutch watchdog concluded that no evidence could be found that WhatsApp could otherwise justify the processing of this kind of data based on any of the sections of the Dutch equivalent of Article 6 of Regulation 2016/679.

Response WhatsApp
In 2015, the Dutch data protection authority reported that WhatsApp, as a result of their previous research, has changed its approach towards the data of non-WhatsApp users. While it remains technologically impossible to offer the service of the app without storing data of non-users, this data is now separately stored from the data of WhatsApp users. Furthermore, the data of non-users is 'hashed' (transcripted) in such a way that it is almost impossible to be used any further. The hashed data is furthermore only accessible by a very limited amount of technicians. According to the Dutch authority, this practice is now in compliance with the relevant privacy legislation (College Bescherming Persoonsgegevens, 2015).

'c Processing is necessary for compliance with a legal obligation to which the controller is subject.'

This is different per legal system. An example that applies to all EU countries is that any data controller is obliged to inform the competent authorities when during their data procession criminal facts are discovered.

'd Processing is necessary in order to protect the vital interests of the data subject or of another natural person.'

When someone looses consciousness and a doctor tries to figure out someone's blood type to save her/him, of course this is a legal proceeding. Also when the data subject – who is unable to do so – did not given his consent.

'e Processing is necessary for the performance of a task carried out in the public interest or in the exercise of official authority vested in the controller.'

In some countries, the certification of cars is entrusted to companies. The certifier will have to process the personal data of the car owner and even send this to the competent state authorities as a result of their public task. In a way, in certifying the car, the company now acts as a semi-public organ.

> 'f Processing is necessary for the purposes of the legitimate interests pursued by the controller or by a third party, except where such interests are overridden by the interests or fundamental rights and freedoms of the data subject which require protection of personal data, in particular where the data subject is a child.'

This is the vaguest justification ground, and basically forms an 'etcetera'-type of ground. At any time, when the legitimate interest of the controller outweighs the privacy of the data subject, the controller may process the data. In other words: if a controller cannot justify processing data under sections a-e, he will have to try the more broader justification ground under f. In practice, such a claim will always have to be considered case by case by a judge. However, it is generally accepted that companies use customer data also to send them (personalized) advertisements once in a while. This is after all considered to be what companies normally do, while the privacy of their customers in not affected much more than it already was. For a company on the other hand, it is of a vital importance to keep in touch with their customers and inform them about their products or services. However, it needs to be noted here that the selling of personal data to third parties will never be considered as something that is 'normal', and to justify this, a company will have to use another justification ground.

Special data types
Regulation2016/679 specifies particular types of data that may not be processed at all, except in occasional circumstances. These data are data revealing racial or ethnic origin, political opinions, religious or philosophical beliefs, or trade union membership, and the processing of genetic data, biometric data for the purpose of uniquely identifying a natural person, data concerning health or data concerning a natural person's sex life or sexual orientation. In general, the controller of such data has to justify this kind of data processing based on one of the grounds listed in Article 9. These grounds are not as flexible as those listed in Article 6.

Data subject rights
The data subject has various rights towards the data controller. These rights are listed in Articles 16-21 of Regulation 2016/679. These rights include:
- The right to ratification of inaccurate data (Art. 16);
- The right to erasure of data when there is no legal ground for the processing (Art. 17, the so called 'right to be forgotten');
- The right to restrict data processing when data processing seems inaccurate, disproportionate or unlawful (Art. 18);
- The right to receive the data which is processed by the controller (Art. 20);
- The right to object to the processing of data (Art. 21).

The last right does not imply that a company at all time should recognize the objection. However, in the case of direct marketing activities, the company has to act in compliance with the objection, and stop processing data for such purposes. That explains for instance why in the EU all direct marketing emails have an 'unsubscribe' function.

12.3 Jurisdiction challenges

While a state may regulate the procession of data within its territory, it is harder to create enforceable rules for data processor operating from outside its borders. After all, in a globalized world, on a frequent basis data controllers process data of data subjects in other countries. But how do you make sure these controllers do not violate your own domestic privacy principles? There are several approaches.

According to Russian privacy law for instance, any organization, company or individual that stores personal data of Russian Federation citizens must do so on Russian territory. This means that when the data is in a physical form, it must be stored in Russia, and when it is in a digital form, it must be stored on a Russian internet service provider. Practically, this means when a foreign company stores and uses customer data, or data of potentials, this data must be stored within the Russian Federation. Automatically therefore, the data procession is subject to Russian law, and supervised by the Russian data protection authority Roskomnadzor. Foreign companies and institutions that seem to violate this rule have three days to comply after notification of the Roskomnadzor. When the violation continues, Roskomnadzor is – amongst others – authorized to block access to the websites of the violating party in the entire Russian Federation (Federal Law no. 242). This way, the Russian Federation can guarantee to a certain extent the compliance of foreign data controllers with their privacy laws.

Safe harbour principles

Another option is to make an agreement between countries in which privacy principles are harmonized. A famous example is the so-called 'safe harbour principles'. These principles would enable U.S. companies to process personal data of EU citizens in line with EU privacy laws (Commission Decision of 26 July 2000). However, in 2015, the European Court of Justice declared these principles as invalid. The direct cause for this was a lawsuit filed against the social media network Facebook (U.S. based), which did not adequately guarantee the privacy of its users in compliance with EU privacy rules (ECJ, Case C-362/14, 2015). A new agreement between the U.S. and the EU is expected, called the EU-US Privacy Shield (European Commission, 2016).

Summary

- ► The right to privacy is an internationally recognized fundamental right, and is often at the core of difficult legal issues in both public and private legal relations.
- ► In the U.S. privacy is not centrally organized.
- ► The U.S. Constitution does not recognize a general right to privacy, but protects elements of privacy in public legal relations.
- ► In the U.S. the right to privacy is in a tensed relation with the freedom of speech, in which there is a tendency to let the freedom of speech prevail.
- ► In especially the fourth and fourteenth amendment, elements of the right to privacy are constitutionally recognized, as well as in a handful of Federal laws.
- ► In general, the concept of the reasonable expectation to privacy is leading in privacy case law.
- ► A reasonable expectation to privacy is subjectively and objectively tested.
- ► In private legal relations, tort law is used to protect the right to privacy against one another.
- ► The invasion of privacy is composed of four different torts:
  - Intrusion on seclusion applies when someone intentionally intrudes the privacy of someone else:
    - The invasion should be unauthorized;
    - A reasonable person should find the intrusion objectionable;
    - The intrusion should concern a private matter;
    - The intrusion results in some form of suffering.
  - Appropriation applies when someone uses someone else's name or likeliness without permission for commercial purposes.
  - Public disclosure applies when someone publicly discloses private fact of someone else:
    - The information that is disclosed should be publicly disclosed;
    - The information should be private;
    - The information should be offensive to a reasonable person;
    - The information should not be newsworthy.
  - False light/defamation is the inflicting of harm on someone's reputation by spreading false statements.

- In the European Union, the protection of privacy is centrally regulated.

- Regulation 2016/679 will regulate the privacy protection of individuals in private legal relations, where Directive 2016/680 will regulate this protection in public legal relations.

- Regulation 2016/679 applies when:
  - The data concerns any information relating to an identified or identifiable natural person. This includes direct and indirect identifiability.
  - The data is processed.

- Regulation 2016/679 distinguishes between:
  - The controller, who is the one (natural or legal person) who determines the purposes and means of the processing of personal data;
  - The processor, who is the one (natural or legal person) who actually processes the personal data on behalf of the controller;
  - The recipient, who is the one (natural or legal person) to whom the personal data is disclosed.

- Regulation 2016/679 stipulates that data processing must be in compliance with the principle of lawfulness, fairness and transparency; purpose limitation; data minimisation; accuracy; storage limitation; integrity and confidentiality; and accountability.

- Regulation 2016/679 stipulates that data processing must be justified under one of the grounds listed in Article 6.

- Regulation 2016/679 imposes a stricter regime on the procession of sensitive data, which are data revealing racial or ethnic origin, political opinions, religious or philosophical beliefs, or trade union membership, and the processing of genetic data, biometric data for the purpose of uniquely identifying a natural person, data concerning health or data concerning a natural person's sex life or sexual orientation.

- Regulation 2016/679 recognizes the following rights of the data subject:
  - The right to ratification of inaccurate data;
  - The right to erasure of data when there is no legal ground for the processing;
  - The right to restrict data processing when data processing seems inaccurate, disproportionate or unlawful;
  - The right to receive the data processed by the controller;
  - The right to object to the processing of data.

- There are jurisdiction challenges when the data controller is foreign; there are various approaches to make sure these controllers do not violate your own domestic privacy principles.

12

Practice questions

12

Open questions

Please consider this sample taken from the privacy policy of www.donaldjtrump.com. The cookies are installed without the visitor's active consent, but the visitor is informed about the cookies on the website.

'... Cookies enable our website to keep track of your preferences and activities relating to the website. Our website creates session cookies for each visit in order to facilitate your visit. The session cookie transpires at the end of the session.

We use a third party service provider to send e-mails on behalf of us. There are no cookies in the e-mail. However, when an e-mail recipient clicks on a link to Trump website included in the e-mail, a persistent cookie is placed on the user's computer. This cookie is used to measure the effectiveness of our e-mail marketing efforts and better understand how our users navigate through the site. The cookie set by our service provider will remain on your hard drive 30 days after the last time you clicked on the coded link in the e-mail, or until you delete it.

We use third party service providers to serve and host our advertisements. These third parties use persistent cookies to track the number of times our site is accessed and whether the site was accessed from the advertisement. The cookies generated from the advertisements do not contain personally identifiable information and may remain on your hard drive three or more years unless deleted by you...'

12.1 Would you consider these terms in compliance with U.S. privacy laws? Please refer to relevant torts.

12.2 Would you consider these terms in compliance with EU privacy laws? Please refer to the relevant legislation.

A company sends its employees to a training. During this training, DNA material of the employees is taken and analysed. Based on the analysis it is possible to see what kind of hormones are apparent in the body of the employee, which says something about the probable characteristics. The results of this test are used to complete a psychological profile of the employee, which is used to facilitate the employee to improve his professional skills. The results are confidential, and only given to the employee and the employer. The employee is supposed to participate, as part of his job.

12.3 Would you consider this practise in compliance with U.S. privacy laws? Please refer to relevant torts.

12.4 Would you consider this practise in compliance with EU privacy laws? Please refer to the relevant legislation.

Essay question

Write an essay about U.S. and EU privacy laws in which you explain which approach you prefer and why: the decentralized U.S. approach, or the centralized European approach?

Multiple choice questions

12.1 The U.S. Constitution:

a only partly recognizes a right to privacy in the relation between the government and the citizen
b does not recognize the right to privacy
c only partly recognizes a right to privacy in the relation between the government and the citizen, as well as in private relations

12.2 In the U.S. addresses to which email or mail is sent:

a is not considered to fall under the scope of reasonable expectation to privacy
b is considered to fall under the scope of reasonable expectation to privacy
c is partly considered to fall under the scope of reasonable expectation to privacy

12.3 Publicly revealing private facts about someone could be illegal as a result of the following tort:

a Inclusion on seclusion
b Appropriation
c Pubic disclosure

12.4 A click wrap agreement:

a means that an internet user actively consents to written terms
b means that an internet user passively consents to written terms
c means that an internet user indirectly consents to written terms

HARRY
POTTER
BY
J.K. ROWLING
Sandor

13 Intellectual property

In this chapter we will discuss the various forms of intellectual property. One is able to own a creative idea, have a sole right to commercially exploit this idea, and is protected against others who might interfere with this right. In this chapter, we will discuss copyrights and its neighbouring rights, patents, the protection of semi-conductors, industrial design, breeders rights, the protection of a company name and trademarks.

13.1 The forms of intellectual property

When someone has a great idea and wants to exploit this idea economically, they want to prevent others from making use of this great idea. In law, this protection of creative work is done by intellectual property.

Intellectual property

I Intellectual property is the exclusive ownership of a creative work.

In essence, this means that the owner of the intellectual property has the exclusive right to determine what will happen with the idea. It could be that the owner just wants to make use of the idea all by himself. However, this kind of ownership can also be sold or licenced so that others (in return for payment) may also use the idea for their benefit. Not only natural persons but also companies can own intellectual property. As a matter of fact, in some sectors such as the ICT sector, the pharmaceutical industry or the food business sector, the majority of the companies property will consist of immaterial ownership: various forms of intellectual property.

For different kinds of creative works, there are different kinds of intellectual property. Each form of intellectual property has its own legal foundation, and therefore its own way of obtaining the ownership. A distinction is made between on the one hand copyrights and related rights, which are not necessarily intended for industrial usage and, on the other hand industrial property, which is intended for industrial usage. In this chapter we will discuss the most important forms of intellectual property, see also figure 13.1. These include copyright and related rights, which are the neighbouring rights, computer programmes and database rights. We will furthermore discuss the following industrial property rights: trademarks, company names, patents, industrial design and breeders rights.

Industrial property

FIGURE 13.1 Different forms of intellectual property

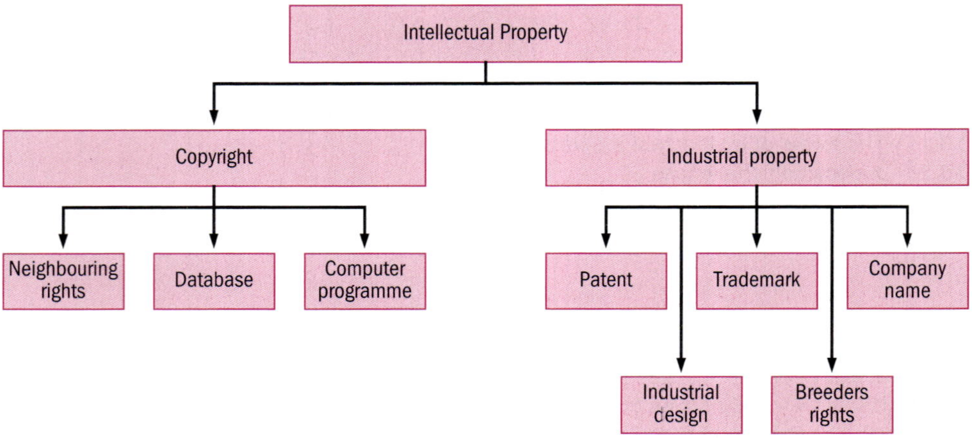

13.1.1 Copyrights and related rights

The oldest form of intellectual property is copyright. In international law, the Berne Convention is the most important agreement that generally regulates copyright law around the world. After all, with 171 members, this agreement has a wide reach. This convention defines the works that may be copyrighted as 'literary and artistic works' (Art. 2). While this sounds very artistic, its scope is rather broad and includes many issues that are not in the sphere of writing books or music. The same Convention gives us examples of what this literary and artistic work might be. This includes books, pamphlets and other writings, monologues, dramatic works, choreographies, music, films, drawings, photographic works, works of applied arts (maps, plans, illustrations etc), translations and adaptions to existing work, and collections of literary or artistic work.

The owner of a copyright is in principle the author. This can be a natural person or a legal person. When more than one author created the work, the ownership is usually shared. In general, the ownership of copyright can be split into two different rights: moral rights and economic rights.

Moral rights

The moral rights are usually considered to be independent from the economic rights, and imply that the author of work has the right to be

recognized as the author of the work, and has the right to object to any unwanted modification of the work. Article 6(bis) of the Berne Convention refers to the first as the right of paternity, while the latter is called the right of integrity. These rights cannot be sold, and are therefore intangible.
One will be recognized as the author when she or he delivered the creative achievement that established the work. While this does not mean that the author should physically create the work, the work should be observable in some shape or form. This means that first, it is the creative achievement that counts, and not the physical creation of the work. It is the architect who holds the copyright of the design of a building, and not the construction workers who physically built the building. Secondly, it means that one cannot own a copyright on mere thoughts. Work can only be copyrighted when it is observable, so that other people can see, hear, touch, smell or taste the work.
When someone is the author, she or he may reject to any unwanted modification of the work. This means that when someone slightly alters the work and publishes it under his own name, the original author may demand a full stop to this activity, and when needed claim damage compensation. An example of this can be found in the case 'Tanya Grotter and the Magical Double Bass' (example 13.2).

The are rights that may be exploited in order to gain profit from the literary or artistic work. These are usually – in some shape or form – subdivided into the right to reproduce, communicate and distribute. A fine example is provided in the Law of Mongolia on Copyright and Related Rights, Article 11. Besides allowing the author to modify his own work, and rent the work, the law recognizes that:

'12.2 The exclusive rights over the exploitation of his/her work shall include the exclusive rights to allow or prohibit the following activities:
- 12.2.1 reproduction of a work;
- 12.2.2 publication of a work;
- 12.2.3 distribution of a work (...)'

The idea is that these rights are transferrable. For instance, the author of a book will transfer the rights to reproduce and distribute to a publisher, since the average writer will not have a book press in his backyard. This transfer is then usually done in exchange for royalties when the book is sold by the publisher. The same applies to artists producing music, although nowadays music hardly results in physical products, as we can see in example 13.1.
When someone holds the economic rights to an artistic or literary work, he holds the exclusive rights to commercially exploit this work. Of course, this does not mean that this right is limited to one person or company: such rights can be owned by more right holders. To stick to the Harry Potter example: Rowling sold her story to multiple publishers around the world who are allowed to publish a certain translation of the book in a particular region. And Bruce Springsteen allowed various artists to record, perform, and sell their interpretation of his song 'Because the night'. However, when someone does not poses this right, the author or right holder (such as a publisher) may reject the distribution, reproduction and communication of the work by others.

EXAMPLE 13.1

Melodic Power Rock

The author of this book is the drummer of a melodic power rock band called 'the Seasons'. Since physically producing CDs is not very profitable these days, they decide to allow distribution and reproduction of their latest record through online channels only. They hire an ICT agency to take care of a smooth transfer of their rights to various streaming services. In essence, the streaming services are licenced to distribute the new songs on their website. In exchange for that, The Seasons will receive a (small) compensation per streamed song. Simultaneously, the songs are put on Youtube. While here, users may watch the song for free, Youtube may add advertisements to the videos when they become more popular. The more popular the videos get, the more compensation will be awarded to the copyright holder: the Seasons.

EXAMPLE 13.2

Tanya Grotter and the Magical Double Bass

Tanya Grotter is the main character of a series of novels written by the Russian author Dimitri Yemets. The first edition of the series was entitled 'Tanya Grotter and the Magical Double Bass'. The plot showed remarkable similarities with the first Harry Potter book (the Philosophers stone). However, the context of the story was transferred to a more Russian atmosphere. Noteworthy similarities were the fact that Tanya Grotter was born with a strange mark on her nose, was raised by non-wizards due to the fact that her parents were killed by an evil magician, Tanya studied at a school for witchcraft, and she usually played a game that closely resembles Quidditch. According to Dimitri Yenets, the books were intended to be a parody to the original Harry Potter series. However, the author of Harry Potter (J.K. Rowling) as well as her publisher disagreed.
Rowling and her publisher were planning to start litigation against Yemets in Russia, but were unable to succeed. Therefore, they decided to try to book the publication of the first translation abroad, which happened to be the Dutch translation in 2003. The Dutch court agreed that Tanya Grotter was a violation of the copyright owned by Rowling and her publisher. Especially the moral rights of Ms Rowling played a crucial role here, because she should have the right to resist any modification of her original work. As a result, the Tanya Grotter series is hardly available in any other language than the Russian.

There are however also limitations to copyright. First, not all creative ideas fall under the scope of artistic and literary work. It is generally accepted that one cannot own the copyright to facts and things that are generally known. For example: the fact that Charles the Fifth ruled France from 1515-1555 and was born in 1500 cannot be owned. The same applies to applied methods or systematic classifications. One cannot own the formula $A^2+B^2=C^2$ to calculate the circumference of a triangle, nor can one own the Alphabet or Periodic System. Furthermore, in most legal systems, codified standards and other official forms of legislation are considered to be public, and cannot therefore be owned privately.

Second, the author is not in all circumstances protected against the usage of his work. Most legal systems allow quotations of someone's work, as long as the author is named. This is often done in the press and academic writings. It is therefore fine to say that Martin Luther King said: 'I have a dream that my four little children will one day live in a nation where they will not be judged by the colour of their skin but by the content of their character'. Furthermore, the economic rights of copyright suggest that these should lead to profit. This also means that the non-profit usage of someone's work is no serious violation of the economic rights. Therefore, the usage of someone's work for educational or academic purposes, or in a private setting, is not always considered a violation of the right holder's copyright. For instance, the Copyright Law of Mongolia (article 24.1.8) allows '...to reproduce works for private use'. This means that when one purchases a study book, she or he may copy parts of this book to use the copy for studying in the train, without violating the author's copyright. Also, in some legal systems, making fun of someone else's work in the form of a parody is exempted from copyright protection. This means that movies such as Scary Movie, in which all kinds of existing horror scenes and characters are used, is not illegal. However, there is a thin line between a funny parody, and a bad attempt to steal someone else's work, as we can see in the case 'Tanya Grotter and the Magical Double Bass' (example 13.2).

As Copyrights is not an industrial right, and therefore not necessarily in the sphere of company ownership, an official registration of copyright as a prerequisite for ownership is usually not necessary. As long as the author has evidence that he is responsible for the creative achievement, the copyright will belong to her/him. However, this does not mean that in legal systems agencies are active who facilitate creating the evidence of authorship by opening the possibility to register your work.

Duration

Usually, a copyright is protected for a relatively long period. The TRIPS agreement recognizes a term of 50 years after the first publication (Art. 12), where in the U.S. this period may be up to 120 years (depending on the kind of work and author). In Europe, copyright is protected as long as the author lives, and for another 70 years after his death (Directive 2006/116/EC).

Related rights

In essence, two related rights are important to discuss in the context of copyrights: neighbouring rights and database protection. Both are – as the word already implies – related rights to the copyright, but not quite the same.

Neighbouring rights

> Neighbouring rights are the rights to the fixation of a unique interpretation or context to existing work.

With the term 'fixation' we basically mean that someone 'performs', 'produces', or 'broadcasts' existing work in a unique manner, and this manner is protected by neighbouring rights. The International Convention for the Protection of Performers, Producers of Phonograms and Broadcasting Organisations is one of the leading international treaties that recognizes such neighbouring rights for performers, producers and broadcasting companies. Each at some point do something with existing work, and the way they do this is protected.

A performer for instance performs a song based on his interpretation of the song; a producer finishes the song mixing the different aspects of the instruments in a way he finds the best balance, and a broadcasting company makes a radio programme in which songs are played in a manner and order, or discussed before and after, which is unique. Therefore, they are all protected by law, meaning that no one else may use their performance, production or broadcast without their consent. While they all did not necessarily create the work, and therefore this will not fall under the scope of copyright protection, their 'touch' on the existing work is now protected, as we can see in the case 'Heart performing 'Stairway to Heaven' (example 13.3).

EXAMPLE 13.3

Heart performing Stairway to Heaven

On December 2nd 2002, the great rock band Led Zeppelin was honoured at the Kennedy Center for their contribution to art and culture in the United States of America. It is a tradition that during this ceremony, colleague artists perform the songs of the honoured. In this case, amongst others, Ann and Nancy Wilson (members of the band Heart) performed the most famous song of Led Zeppelin: Stairway to Heaven. An incredible performance, ending with an entire orchestra and choir, drove the members of Led Zeppelin to tears. Not because it was that bad, but because it was unbelievably beautiful. Ever since, the interpretation of Ann and Nancy Wilson of the song went viral, and was downloaded, watched and shared many times. While of course Led Zeppelin has the copyright to Stairway to Heaven, the Wilson sisters own the neighbouring rights to their grand performance.

Database protection

Another related right is database protection. Sometimes one does not want to protect works itself, but rather the specific combination of works, or particular data filed in a database.

Database

> A database is a collection of independent works, data or other materials arranged in a systematic or methodical way and individually accessible by electronic or other means. (Art. 1, Directive 96/9/EC, 1996)

The European Database Protection Directive furthermore stipulates that not any random collection of data is subject to database protection. It should be data of which the owner should have done a substantial investment in either the obtaining, verification or presentation of the contents (Art. 7). This means that storing the weather report each day will hardly lead to a protected database since anyone could do that without that much effort. However, creating a customer database or a database of potential customers is not so easily done. Also all kinds of quantitative research, or big data analyses will not be that easy to collect. Especially in this sphere, one would like to protect such databases. While the contents of qualitative research, or a customer list will hardly be suitable for copyright protection, a company would not want a competitor to use their data.
A database does not only protect content that cannot be protected by copyright. It may also protect a collection of copyrighted material. In that case, the database owner does not necessarily own the copyrights, but the

right to the particular collection. For instance, the charts in which popular songs are listed is a particular database based on the sales, downloads and streams of songs. The owner of the database here does not own the copyrights to the songs, but does own the database protection: someone else may not publish these charts without permission.

13.1.2 Patents, semi-conductors, industrial design and breeders rights

Inventions can be protected. The same can be said about related industrial applications or creative designs, such as semi-conductors, industrial design and breeders rights.

Patents

The definition given in the European Patent Convention nicely demonstrates the key elements of what a patent is:

> 'European patents shall be granted for any inventions, in all fields of technology, provided that they are new, involve an inventive step and are susceptible of industrial application.'

The main characteristics therefore are that a patent should be an invention, new, involve an inventive step and are industrially applicable.
An inventionis therefore something industrial, which can be produced. That is very broad, and legislation usually focuses on defining what is not patentable, instead of what is. The Chinese Patent Law (2008) however gives us some more explicit idea of what an invention is:

Invention

> 'Inventions mean new technical solutions proposed for a product, a process or the improvement thereof.'

This means that usually, a discovery or a scientific theory or method are not patentable. So, one cannot patent the discovery of a new planet, or the healing power of a natural substance. One can however patent the technique used to discover the planet, or the technique used to produce a medicine with the healing substance as an ingredient. Furthermore, one cannot patent Pythagorean theorem but one can patent a device or product in which this theory is applied.

Furthermore, it is generally recognized that one cannot patent things that are contrary to public morality. It is therefore very unlikely that one will be able to patent weapons of mass destruction. However, it is not always easy to determine when a patent is contrary to public morality, because sometimes it depends on the usage of the invention rather than the invention itself. For instance, the well-known Haber-Bosch process is a patented technique to create ammonia from nitrogen. However, it can be used to create artificial fertilizers, but was also used in the horrific gas chambers of the Nazis during the Second World War.
Also, living things cannot be patented. The human body can never be patented, since that would imply that human species are owned by someone else. Therefore, the reproduction of body parts, or a cured individual cannot be patented. As to plant and animal species, the same applies, as we can see in the newspaper item. However, in some cases, artificial modification of plant species may be protected by breeders rights, as we will see below.

SCIENCE, 14 MAY 2014

No Patent for Dolly the Cloned Sheep, Court Rules, Adding to Industry Jitters

BY: KELLY SERVICK

Dolly the sheep enjoyed a brief and highly publicized life as the first mammal cloned from an adult cell before succumbing to lung disease in 2003 at age 6. But an attempt to patent Dolly, and lay commercial claim to animals produced by cloning, survived much longer. But that nearly 10-year-long saga also appears to have ended last week when a U.S. federal appeals court ruled against giving a patent to Dolly's creators.

(...)

In 2009, the Roslin Institute of the University of Edinburgh, where Dolly's creators Keith Campbell and Ian Wilmut made their discovery, received a U.S. patent on the method used to make her: somatic cell nuclear transfer (SCNT). But they had also submitted a second claim on the product: Dolly herself, and any other cattle, sheep, pigs, and goats produced using SCNT. The U.S. Patent and Trademark Office (PTO) turned down that application, however, citing a federal law that restricts the subject matter of a patent to exclude 'laws of nature, natural phenomena, and abstract ideas.'

13

Novelty

The invention should be a novelty. This means that a similar invention is not filed yet. Since the invention is usually considered as a solution to a technological problem, it is about the practical application of the invention that should be new. This also means that when the physical features of an invention differ, but the practical solution is the same compared to a previous registered patent, there is not much of a novelty. In the case Apple v. Samsung (example 13.4), you may find plenty of examples in which the novelty of patents was disputed between the two companies.

Involve an inventive step

The invention should involve an inventive step. Article 54 of the European Patent Convention (Art. 54) specifies that:

> 'An invention shall be considered as involving an inventive step if, having regard to the state of the art, it is not obvious to a person skilled in the art.'

This means that an expert in the field will not consider the invention as an obvious solution to the problem. A solution is obvious when it is not far enough from the 'state of the art' in a certain field of expertise.
This was the core of the issue between Apple and Samsung regarding the so-called 'slide to unlock' patent (see for more details, example 13.4). This technique was patented as a practical solution to the problem that a touch screen would keep functioning when someone would put the device in his pocket. By enabling a device to be unlocked only by a certain swipe, the problem has been solved. This technique was patented by Apple. However, Samsung disputed the fact that this patent would involve an inventive step, since similar techniques were already used in other contexts. This would mean that it would only be obvious to apply such a technique on a device like an iPhone, and could therefore not be patented.

Last, an invention should be susceptible to industrial application. This simply means that the invention 'can be made or used in any kind of industry' (Art. 57 European Patent Convention). This narrows down the scope of patents to actual products or applications within products. It also means that just 'looks' of a product, or any form of literary or artistic works are not patentable. After all, this is why we have designers rights and copyrights. It furthermore narrows down the scope to industrial use only. This is sometimes understood as that applications or methods in the medical sphere are not patentable. The Board of Appeal of the European Patent Office ruled in 1994 that a certain organic compound could not be patented for it appeared to have a contraceptive effect. The main reason was that the substance would be used by women in a private setting, not in an industrial one, and that therefore the effect of the compound could not be patented. It would have been different of course when a company would develop a product in which the compound was used: the product can be patented for it is industrially applicable in the sense that it can be produced on a large scale. However, the effect of the compound in itself is a natural effect, and is not industrially applicable (Boards of Appeal of the European Patent Office, 1994).
However, as we have seen above, these things are usually explicitly excluded by patent legislation, which makes the prerequisite of industrial application gradually losing its importance (Gielen et al. 2007).

Software patent

One important thing needs to be noted here however. There is a different understanding of the concept of industrial applicability in the U.S. and Europe when it concerns software. In the U.S. software is patentable, while in Europe, this is generally considered not to be industrially applicable (Guntersdorfer, 2003). The only way to patent software in Europe is when the software is such an integrated part in an industrial application, that the application would not be meaningful without the software. For instance, software to operate an industrial machine would be part of the patent for the entire machine.

EXAMPLE 13.4

Apple v. Samsung

Bad romance

In the telecom industry, industrial property rights are extremely important and the main competition tool for such companies. That is why there are so many court cases between the leading companies in the sector. For instance, Apple and Samsung are sworn enemies in the court room. Since 2011, Apple and Samsung are engaged in over 50 lawsuits around the globe in at least 19 countries and before some international tribunals. In this the so-called patent war, not only patents but also industrial design has been the subject of the court cases.

Amongst others, Apple and Samsung sued one another over important technological aspects of their devices, such as the so-called bounce back technique, 3d (and later versions) network settings, data synchronisation techniques, the adaptability of backgrounds to apps, media storage techniques, and video compromising techniques. Sometimes courts around the world had to rule in various infringements of patents at the same time, and had to conclude that both companies were violating one another's patents simultaneously. For instance, a South Korean court ruled in 2012 that Samsung violated Apple's patented bounce back technique, while Apple violated two patens related to wireless network. Both companies were awarded damages (Bonnington, 2012).

Slide to unlock patent
Another long lasting dispute between the two companies is the 'slide to unlock' technique. A smartphone will be automatically locked after not being used for a specified time. To activate the device once more, the consumer has to slide the screen in a particular manner. This technique is known in the U.S. as the 8,046,721 patent (the 721 patent in brief). The disputes concerning this patent perfectly demonstrate the capricious nature of patent issues on this level. Originally, a Californian District Court had ruled that indeed Samsung interfered with the Apple patent, but did not want to ban the involved Samsung products from the U.S. market. Instead, a sole monetary compensation was awarded to Apple. Apple appealed from this decision, and the U.S. Federal Courts of Appeals ruled that certain Samsung products indeed must be banned, but left it to the lower courts to concretize the particularities of that ban (U.S. Federal Courts of Appeals, 2015). However, the procedure lingered on, and ultimately, it was Samsung appealing against the decision of the lower court to ban Samsung products. In appeal, the same appellate court ruled that the disputed patent in itself was invalid, since it was not an original creative production. Instead, existing technology was used to construct the 'slide to unlock' technique. *In casu*, Samsung was able to find evidence that at least in two cases prior to the filing of patent 721 similar techniques were designed and widely discussed (U.S. Federal Courts of Appeals, 2016). Samsung claimed that it was an obvious technique, well known amongst ICT experts, and therefore not patentable. The exact slide to unlock technique after all was not so far away from the already known 'state of the art'.
Earlier, German, Dutch and UK courts had already doubted the validity of this patent, and decided not to award any damages in a similar case in Europe (Beiersmann, 2013).

Design
Not only patents were disputed between Apple and Samsung in the ongoing patent war. Also industrial design has been a continuous source for debate. Apple frequently accused Samsung of copying the looks of their smartphones and tablets, including the shape of the devices, as well as the colour combinations used in the display screens. During various court procedures around the world in 2011 Apple tried to demonstrate the violation of their design rights by showing comparing photocopies of the Samsung and Apple products (Kane & Sherr, 2011), but were later accused of tampering with the photos, making the devices more look a like than in real life. A U.K. Court even ruled that for this reason, Apple would have to pay all Samsung's fees paid for their defence in court (England and Wales Court of Appeal, 2012). In 2016, Apple tried Samsung before the U.S. Supreme Court for alleged copying of the backside of the iPhone (a rectangle with rounded corners). The more fundamental background of this

court case is whether such things as rounded corners indeed make a difference to the consumer and should therefore be protected. In lower court rulings, Samsung had to pay a fine for using Apple like rounds, which is estimated to be a big part of their profits on the disputed devices (Mullin, 2016).

Does it help?
The question can be asked whether any of the companies truly benefit from suing one another. First, they both lose and win cases, and the verdict of such cases are, as it seems, hard to predict. Furthermore, the side effects of such court cases may be undesirable for the companies. For instance, several times certain products were banned from national markets as a result of patent verdicts. Another example is that of an Australian Court case, in which Apple had to reveal the source code of their iPhone 4 to Samsung, in order to investigate a possible infringement with Samsung patents (Macari, 2011). It can be questioned whether the competing between two ICT giants should take place in a court room or on the markets.

Procedures to submit a patent are different in each country. However, through treaties such as the Patent Cooperation Treatyand the European Patent Convention, countries try to harmonize the content and the procedures of their patent laws. Some characteristics are more or less shared.
First, there is the so-called 'prior art search'. When one wishes to file a patent, the relevant patent agency will conduct a research to the prior art that relates to the patent. The goal is to find out if the invention is indeed a novelty, or perhaps already exists. The result of this search will be published in a 'prior art search report'. Such a report plays an important role in possible legal disputes between companies who claim that the patent of their competitor violates a patent of their own.
Second, when a patent is properly filed, the owner has guaranteed a monopoly in the commercial exploitation of that patent. This means that the owner may sue each and every company or individual that violates this patent for any commercial usage. In exchange for this monopoly position however, the patent must be publicly published. This means that everyone, including the competition, may learn about all the characteristics and technological applications of the patent. The idea is that a monopoly position may not interfere with technological progress. If a competitor is able to use what can be learned from the filed patent, and create something new based on that, it is not illegal. However, the new invention should be far enough away from the prior art (that is, the originally filed patent). For these reasons, not all companies choose to file an invention, and keep it a trade secret within their company, as you can see in example 13.5.
Third, a patent is not everlasting, but has a limited duration. As a result of the WTO TRIPS agreement (Art. 33), in most legal systems the duration of a patent is now 20 years. After that, there is no further legal protection of the invention.

EXAMPLE 13.5

Coca Cola

A trade secret

The original inventor of Coca Cola, John Pemperton, never patented his drink. Instead, the Coca Cola formula has always been a trade secret. Considering the value of the company, the trade secret is worth an incredible amount of money. However, to patent the formula would have too many negative side-effects for the Coca Cola Company. First of all, their closely guarded secret formula would be out in the open, allowing their competitors to test and alter the recipe. Second: a patent will transpire in the end (after 20 years in this case). This would mean that after 20 years, the Coca Cola competitors will be able to make use of the formula without paying anything to the original inventors.

The protection of semiconductors

The technology that relates to semiconductors or microchips is often highly advanced. Companies invest heavily in the development of new chips that lead to better operational machines. They appear in simple machines, such as a coffee machine, but also in high tech ICT technology, such as a smartphone, or a machine used to assemble cars.

The problem however is that it is not always easy to protect such a chip under traditional patent or copyright law. Especially the demand that something must be a novelty will sometimes be hard to proof. After all, the way a semiconductor is constructed is usually quite similar, while it is the exact way the integrated circuit of the semi-conductor is formed into a closed circuit that makes it work. Such a circuit is easily copied, and hard to protect using patent or copyright laws. Therefore, on the initiative of the U.S., since 1984, semi-conductors have their own Intellectual Property regime. In the U.S. this right is protected under the Semi-Conductor Chip Protection Act. Since then, most other industrialized countries followed this example (Hoeren, 2010). Japan followed in 1985 with their Law on the Circuit Layout of a Semiconductor Integrated Circuits, and In Europe, semi conductors are protected under Council Directive 87/54/EEC of 16 December 1986.

On an international level, the protection of semiconductors is recognized in Art. 35-38 of the WTO TRIPS-agreement. Article 35 specifies that:

> 'Members agree to provide protection to the layout-designs (topographies) of integrated circuits (referred to in this Agreement as 'layout-designs').'

This article clarifies what exactly is protected under semiconductor protection: the actual topography of the closed circuit. Through this circuit, energy flows so that the device of which the semi-conductor is part will actually function. When filing a chip for Intellectual Property protection, one will have to provide for a photocopy of the circuit. This will result in a sole right to commercially exploit the chip, and prevent competitors from copying of the semi-conductor. Due to the fact that the TRIPS-agreement specifies a 10 year term for such protection, most legal systems adopted this period in their national legislation.

Industrial design

In today's industries, not only the application of an invention, but also the looks of a product need to be protected. Think about the design of a bottle of Coca Cola, as we can see in example 13.6, but also the design of a car, a smartphone or a simple standing clock. For this, we have industrial design.
In the U.S. context, the phrase 'design patents' is also used in contrast to the term 'utility patent'. The later resembles a patent as we have discussed above, the first resembles industrial design.

EXAMPLE 13.6

Coca Cola and the female body

To make sure that the consumer would recognize a coca cola product from afar, a distinct shape was created to package the product. In essence, the Coca Cola bottle is supposed to resemble that of a female body. And if you really want to know, it is one body in particular: that of actress Mae West (Ryan, 2015).

Article 25 of the TRIPS-agreement recognizes that:

> 'Members shall provide for the protection of independently created industrial designs that are new or original. Members may provide that designs are not new or original if they do not significantly differ from known designs or combinations of known design features. Members may provide that such protection shall not extend to designs dictated essentially by technical or functional considerations.'

From this we can learn two things. First, this intellectual property protection is about industrial design. A design is not an invention, nor any other form of intellectual property right. It is about the shape of a product, which contributes to product recognition by the consumer.
Second, the design should be new or original. This means that the design may in practice not lead to confusion amongst a reasonable consumer. As we can see in the case Apple v. Samsung (example 13.4), on many occasions Apple accused Samsung of copying their designs, and as a result confused consumers about who the producer of the product would be.

Duration

The TRIPS Agreement recognizes the duration of designers right for at least ten years (Art. 26). In practice, most countries adopt a longer term. For instance, design patents in the U.S. may have a term of 15 years, while in the BENELUX, a maximum term of 25 years is recognized.

Breeders rights

As we have seen, plant species are usually exempted from patent protection, since one cannot own nature. However, sometimes new plant species are created by breeders who experiment or use particular techniques. This might result in stronger species, or species that are more tasteful/colourful etcetera. To reward the effort of a breeder in creating such a new species, breeders rights are recognized internationally.

Needless to say is that these rights predominantly play a role in the agricultural sector.

Internationally, breeder's rights are recognized in the TRIPS Agreement (Art. 27 (3) (b)), but not further specified. The International Convention for the Protection of New Varieties of Plants (UPOV convention 1991) instead seeks to harmonize the national legislation of its member states in this context. In the convention we can read that one can file a breeders right only when the new plant species is new, distinct, uniform and stable.

A plant species is new when a similar plant has not been filed earlier (Art. 6 UPOV Convention).

A plant species is original if 'it is clearly distinguishable from any other variety whose existence is a matter of common knowledge at the time of the filing of the application' (Art. 7 UPOV Convention). This prerequisite would therefore mostly prevent existing plant species to be owned by a company or individual. It should truly be a new species, as a result of breeding.

A plant species is uniform when the new species has clear and distinguishable characteristics (Art. 8 UPOV Convention). When as a result of the breeding process vague characteristics appear (the colour could be red, but also pink or blue), it is not uniform enough to file.

A plant species is stable when the breeding process leads to similar results (Art. 9 UPOV Convention). When breeding leads to ever changing characteristics in new plant species, it is not possible to file.

Duration

While it differs around the world, the duration of breeders rights is usually between 20 and 30 years.

Breeders rights have more than once been the core of heated debate about the justness of owning new plant species. As we can see in the news item, breeders rights may also result in filing long lasting traditional breeders methods. When this is done first by a powerful international company, local farmers may find themselves in a troublesome situation.

● www.newinternationalist.org

Battling the 'Monsanto law' in Ghana

This week, farmers in Ghana are on the frontlines of a battle. The national parliament is due to return from its summer break and first thing on the agenda is the government's Plant Breeders Bill. The proposed legislation contains rules that would restrict farmers from an age-old practice: freely saving, swapping and breeding seeds they rely on. Under the laws, farmers that use seed varieties claimed under new intellectual property rights by individuals and companies anywhere in the world risk hefty fines or even imprisonment.

According to the Ghanaian government and its corporate backers, the new laws would incentivise the development of new seed varieties and ensure crops are safe and saleable. Yet in recent months, farmers, campaigners, trade unions and faith groups have taken to the streets in the cities of Accra, Tamale and beyond. They warn that the bill would hand control of the country's seeds to giant corporations like Monsanto. They fear the laws would allow corporations to exploit farmers, capture profit and push GM seeds in to the country's food system. It's why campaigners have dubbed the bill 'the Monsanto Law'.
By: Chris Walker 20 October 2014

13.1.3 Trademark and company name

A company uses a company name to distinguish their company from other companies, and a trademark to distinguish their product from other products. So, for example, Apple is a company name, and iPhone a trademark; Nestlé is a company name, and Nespresso a trademark. Both company names and trademarks are important tools to get the attention of the consumer, and to make the consumer aware of whose product or service they are buying.

Company name

In this context, most attention usually goes to trademark protection. Therefore, we will only briefly touch upon the company name, and suffice with three important remarks about the protection of company names.
First, most companies also file their company name as a trademark, to be sure it is well protected.
Second, usually the registration of a company name occurs when registering the company in itself, usually at the involved Chamber of Commerce.
Third, it is generally accepted that a company name may not interfere with an existing trademark, and vise versa.

Trademark

A trademark aims to distinguish a product or service from competing products and services.
Article 15 of the TRIPS Agreement defines a trademark as:

> 'Any sign, or any combination of signs, capable of distinguishing the goods or services of one undertaking from those of other undertakings, shall be capable of constituting a trademark. Such signs, in particular words including personal names, letters, numerals, figurative elements and combinations of colours as well as any combination of such signs, shall be eligible for registration as trademarks. Where signs are not inherently capable of distinguishing the relevant goods or services, members may make registrability depend on distinctiveness acquired through use. Members may require, as a condition of registration, that signs be visually perceptible.'

So, what does this ling line mean exactly? In general, a trademark is something that is usually observable, and considering the examples provided in the article, graphically displayable. Think about a brand name, a logo, or a sign that people may recognize and therefore know that this particular product belongs to a certain company. To be exactly sure what can be protected under trademark protection, we will have to explore what the so-called absolute grounds for refusal are. Absolute grounds are reasons for a trademark agency to refuse the filing, and therefore, apparently, the sign is not eligible for trademark protection.

Absolute grounds

Most of all, a trademark should have a distinctive character. This means that it should be able to distinguish one product from another. Using a word that is generally used to refer to the type of products, or using characters that are generally used in daily life for all kinds of reasons, will probably not lead to trademark protection. Someone producing furniture will not be able to file the name 'furniture' as a trademark for his products. A simple circle, used in many different contexts, will probably also not be accepted as a trademark. There is a debate about registering a single colour as a distinctive feature. As we can see in example 13.7, this is in some situation possible, but not a standard course of action. In contrast: BP was unable to register their green shade of their logo as a trademark in Australia (The Guardian, 2014).

Furthermore, a trademark may not constitute something that is against the law, public order, or is immoral. Therefore, a hitman registering a trademark for his services will probably fail, as well as a criminal organisation involved in money laundry or human trafficking.

EXAMPLE 13.7

High heels in red

The litigation of Christian Louboutin

One of the more remarkable cases that relate to trademark protection is the protection of the colour red for the soles of stilettos. One of the distinct features of Christian Louboutin's designs is that the sole of the shoes are fully red. However, other brands, such as Zara, Dr. Adams Footwear and Yves Saint Laurent also produced shoes with a red sole, using a likewise shade of the colour. Court proceedings took place – amongst others – in Belgium, the Netherlands, France and the U.S. Central issue in these cases was the question whether it would be possible to own a colour as a trademark.

In the U.S., Louboutin sued Yves Saint Laurent for selling stilettos that were entirely red. According to Louboutin, the colour used was similar to the sole of their designs, and therefore constituted a violation of their trademark right. Yves Saint Laurent claimed that it should be impossible to claim a colour in the fashion industry, practically restricting all other shoe designers in their creativity and choice. In the end, a U.S. Courts of Appeals ruled that on the one hand, it is possible to own a colour as a trademark, as long as the consumer would associate that colour with the company. On the other hand, the court restricted the scope of the trademark to stilettos composed of a red sole while elsewhere other colours were used. This practically means that Louboutin indeed owns their colour as a trademark for the sole of stilettos, but also that Yves Saint Laurent is able to continue to sell their fully red pumps. After all, they are not covered by the trademark protection owned by Louboutin (U.S. Courts of Appeals, 2011).

The Benelux Convention on Intellectual Property recognizes a single trademark protection in Belgium, the Netherlands and Luxembourg. However, since all three Member States are also member of most other international trademark conventions, the content of the Benelux Convention gives a good impression of the possible nature and scope of trademark protection in general.
The scope of trademark protection is stipulated in Article 2.20 of the Benelux Convention. The Article distinguishes four grades of protection. In practice, it is up to the owners of the trademark to protect their trademark in court when they believe their rights are violated. Therefore, this type of protection is also referred to as 'relative grounds' to refuse using a trademark: they are not assessed before, but after usage.

Relative grounds

First, the owner of a trademark is protected against the use of a sign that is identical to the trademark for identical products. These are basically the 'fake' products. This would protect Rolex watches for instance against the usage of their name and logo (the crown) on watches that are fake.

Second, the owner of a trademark is protected against the use of identical or similar signs for products that are identical or similar. This is a broader category, in which a competitor uses a sign for likewise products that are not necessarily exactly the same. The case of Louboutin would be a good example, protecting the shoe producer against the usage of red soils by their competitors. While the design of the shoe will probably be different, and the colour red may also be of a slightly different shade, Louboutin has trademark protection for certain categories of stilettos. In general, the bottom line for a court will be whether the average consumer might be confused about the likeliness between the signs.

Third, the owner of a trademark is protected against the use of a sign that is identical or similar for completely other products. When the average consumer would link the two trademarks, and the original owner would suffer damage as result, the first trademark right is violated by the second. An example can be found in 'a case of erection' (example 13.8).

EXAMPLE 13.8

A case of erection

Blue pills and trademark protection

Viagra is a drug that stimulates the erection of the phallus, and is widely available. Sigra is a drug that maintains the erection of the phallus, and is available as description-only. However, both pills are blue, and have a similar looking shape. Besides that, the product name Viagra and Sigra shows some resemblances in sound. Viagra – who was there first – sued Sigra before a Dutch court, based on the Benelux Convention.
The Court in the end ruled that while the product in itself might be different, the consumer would unmistakably link the two due to the similarity in shape, colour and name. As a result of that, the Sigra drug was banned from the Benelux market (Dutch Local Court of Zutphen, 2004).

Fourth, there is some sort of 'etcetera' category. When one trademark at some point causes damage to another, the trademark of the latter might be violated where 'where use of the sign without due cause would take unfair advantage of or be detrimental to the distinctive character or the repute of the trademark' (Art. 2.20 Benelux Convention). This could be anything a company does to cause damage to another trademark. A vivid example can be found in the newspaper item, in which a beer producer – Bavaria – used clever guerrilla marketing to distract attention from the trademark of the main sponsor of the World Championships in South Africa, 2010.

THE GUARDIAN, 16 JUNE 2010

World Cup 2010: Women arrested over 'ambush marketing' freed on bail

Two Dutch women were released on bail today after facing charges that they organised the ambush marketing stunt that led to 36 orange-clad women being ejected from Soccer City earlier this week. The women were arrested under the Contravention of Merchandise Marks Act, which prevents companies benefiting from an event without paying for advertising. The 36 women were accused of being part of a campaign to promote a Dutch brewery. South African police arrested the two women at their hotel in the Johannesburg district of Roodepoort today, two days after they were questioned at the Holland versus Denmark game. They appeared at Johannesburg magistrates court and were released on bail of 10.000 rand (£900) each, with their next court appearance set for 22 June.

(...)

The women allegedly led the group of Dutch women who attended Monday's match at Soccer City wearing orange dresses paid for by the brewery company Bavaria. They said they were ejected from the stadium by Fifa's officials.

(...)

Anheuser Busch's Budweiser is the official beer for the tournament and world football's governing body fiercely protects its sponsors from brands which are not Fifa partners.

13

Duration In line with Article 18 of the TRIPS-agreement, the term of a trademark in most legal systems is seven years, and it is possible to renew the trademark protection indefinitely.

13.2 Jurisdiction challenges

While legal regimes of Intellectual Property mostly do not cross borders, companies and individuals who own Intellectual Property do. Therefore, some international attempts have been made to make international recognition and filing of intellectual property possible.

For instance, the Berne Convention establishes a Union for its members in which the copyrights of its citizens are respected. Article 6 of the Convention stipulates that:

> 'Authors shall enjoy, in respect of works for which they are protected under this Convention, in countries of the Union other than the country of origin, the rights which their respective laws do now or may hereafter grant to their nationals, as well as the rights specially granted by this Convention.'

This means that the author of this book, a Dutch citizen, should enjoy the copyright protection as regulated in the other 170 countries that are a member of this Convention. If a Canadian student would secretly copy and distribute this book in Canada, the Dutch author should be able to use the Canadian copyright legislation to protect his work, which was initially written and published in the Netherlands.

Priority right

The Paris Convention for the Protection of Industrial Property recognizes a priority right for the filing of a patent in one of its Member States (Art. 4). This means that when an inventor files a patent in any of the states, competitors are unable to file a similar or likewise type of patent for the period of one year. However, the protection is only limited to that period, when the inventor does not continue the procedure to obtain a fully recognized patent, the protection transpires. An example can be found in the case 'tissue engineered heart valves' (example 13.9).

EXAMPLE 13.9

Tissue engineered heart valves

Dr. Sanders is an expert in the field of tissue engineering. He is able to develop a technique that enables artificial heart valves to be accepted by a human body, and grow alongside this body. In practice, this means that especially children with malfunctioning heart valves may be helped by this technique, since they only have to undergo surgery once in their life in order to get the artificial, tissue engineered, heart valves. Until this invention, children with malfunctioning heart valves would have to undergo frequent surgery to get new artificial heart valves of different seizes, compatible with their ever growing body. The major part of his research was done in the Netherlands and Switzerland (Sanders, 2016).

Unfortunately, Dr. Sanders does not have the financial capacity yet to truly produce these heart valves, nor put his research into practice. To protect his industrial property, he files the application of his invention as a patent in the U.S.A. After all, the U.S. procedure is quicker and easier compared to the Dutch or Swiss. In the meanwhile, he tries to get enough investors to finance the true exploitation of his invention, and makes sure he continues the patent filing within the year. His competition is now prevented from filing likewise patents, and he has the time to realize financing the entire project.

Patent Cooperation Treaty

The Patent Cooperation Treatyresults in one single procedure to submit an international patent.
In fact, this procedure results in a centrally organized sum of separate national procedures to grant the patent: the patent will be submitted in each separate state, However, all the research that was necessary to

formulate the patent request has already been done, and will – if the submitter is lucky – be accepted by the national patent agencies.
On a more regional level, the European Patent Office, the treaty body of the European Patent Convention (EPC), created one single procedure to file a patent in all the Member States of the EPC. Also here, this procedure results in a centrally organized sum of separate national procedures to grant the patent. This is a practice that has been criticized for a very long time now. It is expected that in 2017, a so called Unitary Patent, will be recognized that would significantly simplify this rather complicated procedure. From then on, one single filing would result in the patent protection in major part of the European Union, without the need for any further national procedures. Furthermore, a Unified Patent Court will rule in matters of dispute.

Unitary Patent

Similar attempts can be found in the field of trademark protection. For instance, the Madrid Agreement (and its very important Protocol) creates a system in which a trademark can be filed with one procedure at once in all Member States. However, it needs to be noted here that this agreement and protocol does not have a universal scope: the Protocol has only 97 Member States, and the Agreement only 55.

Madrid Agreement

Summary

- Intellectual property is the exclusive ownership of a creative work.

- For different kinds of creative works, there are different kinds of intellectual property.

- A distinction is made between on the one hand copyrights and related rights that are not necessarily intended for industrial usage and, on the other hand industrial property, which is intended for industrial usage.

Copyrights and related rights

- Copyright relates to literary and artistic works.
  - The owner is the creator, who automatically holds the moral and economic rights.
  - Moral rights is composed of the right of paternity and integrity and cannot be sold;
    - the right of paternity is the right to be recognized as the author;
    - the right of integrity is the right to oppose unwanted modification to your work.
  - Economic rights are the rights to distribute, communicate and reproduce, and can be sold.
  - Limitations to copyright are that facts and things that are generally known cannot be copyrighted, nor methods or systematic classifications, or the law.
  - An author has to allow quotation of his work, reproductions for private use, and in some countries, parodies to his work.
  - The duration of a copyright depends on the legal system, and is somewhere between 50 years and 120 years.

- There are two related rights to a copyright:
  - Neighbouring rights are the rights to the fixation of a unique interpretation or context to existing work.
  - A database is a collection of independent works, data or other materials arranged in a systematic or methodical way and individually accessible by electronic or other means.
    The owner should have done a substantial investment in either the obtaining, verification or presentation of the contents.

Industrial rights

- A patent is any invention, in all fields of technology, provided that they are new, involve an inventive step and are susceptible of industrial application.

- Inventions mean new technical solutions proposed for a product, a process or the improvement thereof; excluded are usually discoveries or a scientific theories or method, living things, and things against public morality.
- A novelty means that a similar invention is not filed yet;
- An invention shall be considered as involving an inventive step if, having regard to the state of the art, it is not obvious to a person skilled in the art.
- Industrial application means that the invention can be made or used in any kind of industry.

► Procedures to file a patent are different in each legal system, but they have in common:
- A prior art search is done by the competent agency to establish the novelty of the invention.
- When a patent is properly filed, the owner has guaranteed a monopoly in the commercial exploitation of that patent. In exchange for this monopoly position, the patent must be publicly revealed.
- A patent usually has a duration of 20 years.

► Related to patents is the protection of semi-conductors.
- A semi conductor is a topography of integrated circuits, which should be new.
- The duration of semi-conductor protection is usually 10 years.

► Related to patents is the protection of industrial design
- Industrial design is about the shape of a product, and should be new and original.
- The duration of industrial design varies between 15 and 25 years.

► Related to patents is the protection of breeders rights
- To reward the effort of a breeder in creating such a new species, breeders rights are recognized internationally.
- A breeders right can be filed when the plant species is new, distinct, uniform and stable.
  - A plant species is new when a similar plant has not been filed earlier;
  - A plant species is original if it is clearly distinguishable from any other variety whose existence is a matter of common knowledge at the time of the filing of the application;
  - A plant species is uniform when the new species has clear and distinguishable characteristics;
  - A plant species is stable when the breeding process leads to similar results.

► A company uses a company name to distinguish their company from other companies, and a trademark to distinguish their product from other products.

► For a company name, the following things are commonly recognized:
- A company name is usually also registered as a trademark;
- Registration usually occurs when registering the company at the chamber of commerce;
- A company name may not violate existing trademarks and vice versa.

- ► Any sign, or any combination of signs, capable of distinguishing the goods or services of one undertaking from those of other undertakings, shall be capable of constituting a trademark.
  - This means that a trademark is observable, have a distinctive character and is not against the law, public order or immoral.
  - Trademark protection has the following scope:
    - The owner of a trademark is protected against the use of a sign that is identical to the trademark for identical products;
    - The owner of a trademark is protected against the use of identical or similar signs for products which are identical or similar;
    - The owner of a trademark is protected against the use of a sign that is identical or similar for completely other products;
    - When one trademark at some point causes damage to another, the trademark of the latter might be violated where use of the sign without due cause would take unfair advantage of or be detrimental to the distinctive character or the repute of the trademark.
  - The duration of a trademark is usually indefinite, and must be renewed once in seven years.
  - While legal regimes of Intellectual Property mostly do not cross borders, companies and individuals who own Intellectual Property do. Therefore, some international attempts have been made to make international recognition and filing of intellectual property possible.

Practice questions

Open questions

13.1 Ozzy Osbourne sings a version of a song of the band the Rolling Stones. The song was written by all four members of the Stones, who welcome the version of Osbourne, and agree that he records this and sells his version. Ozzy gives Sony Ltd permission to sell his version of the song. The original version of the Rolling Stones was sold on record by Decca records.

Please explain what (parts of the) copyrights are owned by Ozzy Osbourne, the Rolling Stones, and Decca records, based on the Council Directive 2001/29 EC? Please refer to the relevant articles.

13.2 John discovers that a certain plant species cures Psoriasis, a skin disease. He is furthermore able to cross the species with another plant, and as a result the curing power increases. He also develops a medicine that is easily producible, and writes an extensive paper about his wonderful cure.

How would you recommend John to protect his creativity in this case?

13.3 What is the main difference between a patent and a protected semi-conductor?

13.4 Cloey writes down the results of each match played the European Championships (football), and puts all this data in an excel sheet. She claims that she now owns the database right to this excel sheet, based on EU Directive 96/9/EC, 1996.

Is she right in her assumption? Please explain and refer to relevant legislation.

Essay question

In Europe, software is usually copyrighted, while this is patented in the U.S.A. Analyse both approaches, and conclude which of the two you prefer.

Multiple choice questions

13.1 In general, patent authorities around the world merely file patents. The only thing they normally check before filing is:
a Whether the patent is industrially applicable
b Whether an inventive step is involved
c Whether the patent is a novelty

13.2 In the Patent Cooperation Treaty, one procedure is recognized to file a patent internationally. This comes down to:
a One globally recognized patent
b One procedure to file the patent separately in each jurisdiction
c Various procedures to file the patent separately in each jurisdiction

13.3 A Dutch comedian makes fun out of an alcohol-free brand named 'Buckler Beer', produced by Heineken. As a result (which can be proven), the sales of this beer drop significantly.
Heineken may invoke:
a no Intellectual Property at all
b trademark protection
c company name protection

13.4 Which answer is incorrect: the moral rights of a copyright encompass:
a the right of paternity
b the right of integrity
c the right of justiciability

Sandor

14 Private international law

In this chapter, we will discuss the formal side of dealing with international legal disputes between private parties. To settle an international dispute, we need to know what court has jurisdiction, what law will be applied, and how a national verdict can be executed in an international setting. We will explore the concept of free choice regarding these matters between private parties, and private international rules that settle this in the absence of a choice. These rules can be substantive, and create new rules on an international level, or objective, and refer to national courts and law in an international legal dispute.

14.1 International legal disputes

Usually, the law does not cross borders, for it is – with the exception of international law of course – nationally determined. People however do cross borders. This leads to complex questions when two natural or legal persons from different nationalities end up in a legal dispute. In this book we have seen many examples of such occasions. Think of J.K. Rowling, suing the publishers of translations of Dimitri Yemets' 'parody' to her work, or think about Apple and Samsung suing one another in various countries, resulting in different verdicts across the world about similar topics. As we have seen, it might make a difference what the court rules in a dispute, and what law is applied by this court.

In essence, in an international legal dispute, there are three main questions that need to be answered.
First, we should determine what court has jurisdiction on the matter.
Second, we should determine what law should be applied by this court.
Third, we should determine how the verdict of the court can be executed. As we can see in example 14.1, a ruling of a court in a country is hard to apply to someone who is not in that country. In this case, Ming would probably need an Indian court to execute the Chinese verdict.

EXAMPLE 14.1

A court ruling made of China

Ming, a Chinese citizen, sues Laabh, who lives in India. Ming used to do business with Laabh, but in the end, it appears that Laabh delivered wrong, incomplete and malfunctioning products. Unfortunately for Ming, he already paid Laabh. As if matters weren't bad enough, as a result of the wrong delivery, Ming loses a significant part of his clientele. According to Chinese private international rules, Ming sues Laabh in a Chinese Court, because the contract was a Chinese business contract, and the characteristic performance of the contract was to take place on Chinese soil. The Chinese court, referring to the Civil Code of China, rules that Laabh has to pay damage compensation to Ming. Laabh is officially informed about this verdict, but does not feel the urge to pay. After all, it is very unlikely that the power of the Chinese court reaches beyond the borders of China. And Laabh sits comfortably in his home in Bombay...

In other words, we need to determine where to sue, based on what law, and how to make sure the other party acts in compliance with the verdict. The rules that answer these questions are usually referred to as private international law.
The problem is that most countries have their own reference rules regarding international legal disputes, which makes this field of law truly a maze. For instance, as we can see in the news item, Shell was sued in the Netherlands by (representatives of) Nigerian farmers for damaging their land. When Nigerian law stipulates that a company can be sued in the country where the disputed activities took place, the Dutch law stipulates that a company can be sued in the country where it is primarily registered. This means the legal systems draw different conclusions in the case where farmers would like to sue Shell as a result of an oil leak that happened in Nigeria. Such situations may lead to an incomprehensible stalemate, and are better avoided. In the end, what will count is whether a court has the power to guarantee the execution of a verdict. Since shell is registered in the Netherlands, the Dutch court may ultimately force the company to stick to its verdict. This could – if needed – be enforced by the police. This would of course be quite different when Shell would be located in Japan.

THE GUARDIAN, 18 DECEMBER 2015

Dutch appeals court says Shell may be held liable for oil spills in Nigeria

A Dutch appeals court ruled on Friday that Royal Dutch Shell can be held liable for oil spills at its subsidiary in Nigeria, potentially opening the way for other compensation claims against the multinational.
Friday's ruling overturned a 2013 finding by a lower Dutch court that Shell's Dutch-based parent company could not be held liable for spills at its Nigerian subsidiary.
The legal dispute dates back to 2008, when four Nigerian farmers and the campaign group Friends of the Earth filed a suit against the oil company in the Netherlands, where its global headquarters is based.
Judge Hans van der Klooster said the court had found that it 'has jurisdiction in the case against Shell and its subsidiary in Nigeria.'
Shell's Nigerian subsidiary, Shell Petroleum Development Company of Nigeria Ltd (SPDC), said in a statement: 'We are disappointed the Dutch court has determined it should assume international jurisdiction over SPDC.'
'We believe allegations concerning Nigerian plaintiffs in dispute with a Nigerian company, over issues which took place within Nigeria, should be heard in Nigeria,' it said.

There are some international initiatives to harmonize such rules, but these agreements are scattered and diverse. It is therefore recommendable to avoid proceedings based on such uncertain rules, and make use of the generally recognized contractual freedom. This means, amongst others, that the contracting parties may determine beforehand what court has jurisdiction and what law will apply in the event of a legal dispute concerning the contract.
However, since not all legal disputes are about contractual obligations, it is not always possible to make such a choice, and disputing parties are still depending on the complex system of private international law. We distinguish two types of private international law. First, there are rules that create new substantive law for an international setting. Second, there are agreements between countries stipulating reference rules. In such rules, a court or a legal system is prescribed in certain legal disputes. These kinds of rules are labelled as objective private international rules.

14.2 The free choice principle

In the context of a contract, it is generally recognized that the contracting parties have a free choice to determine what they agree upon. This free choice means two things. First, it means that the content of the contract – as long as it is not against the law – is a free choice. This has been discussed extensively in chapter 8. Second, it means that the contracting parties may agree on what will happen in case of a legal dispute concerning the contract. This means that contracting parties may promise to try mediation first, before actually going to court. This is usually a cheaper solution to settle a dispute, circumvents complex private international rules, and is aimed at solving a problem instead of winning a case. This also means that contracting parties may choose what court has jurisdiction and what law will be applied in their dispute. An example can be found in the case 'mediation first' (example 14.2).

EXAMPLE 14.2

Mediation first

In a business to business contract, a company from Germany closes a deal with a company in New Zealand. In their contract, three sections are included on private international law:

'23 In case of a legal dispute regarding this contract, both parties agree to actively try to settle the dispute by means of mediation first, before bringing the case to a court.

24a When mediation does not lead to a satisfactory result for both the contracting parties, the case will be brought before a commercial court in New Zeeland.

25a The competent court will use German law to settle the legal dispute referred to in section 24a.'

This freedom of choice is naturally not unlimited. After all, unlimited freedom could hypothetically mean that contracting parties select the legal system of the country with the most flexible rules in criminal law, and therefore justify practices that are in other countries considered illegal. Therefore, this contractual freedom is firstly restricted to private law only, and not to other branches of law. The other restriction is that freedom of choice may never lead to a violation of fundamental norms and values of a country, such as a violation of human rights (Kiestra, 2014).

As we can see in the news item, the Dutch woman used to the Dutch Penal Code, was unpleasantly surprised to be arrested after being raped in Qatar, since in their Penal Code, rape is considered a form of adultery and is committed by both the rapist and the victim. The Dutch penal system only considers the rapist a criminal. The Dutch women clearly could not 'choose' Dutch law in her case, or agree with her rapist on such things. The Penal Code in Quatar is not something that can be deviated from, since it does not regulate private legal relations but the relation between the state and the individual (public law). Next to that, the content is that of something that is considered as a fundamental principle in the country, based on Islamic law.

CNN, 13 JUNE 2016

Dutch woman jailed in Qatar after reporting rape convicted of 'illicit sex'

BY: SCHAMS ELWAZER AND PAUL ARMSTRONG

A Dutch woman who has been in jail in Qatar since mid-March after she reported being raped, has been found guilty of 'illicit consensual fornication' and being 'drunk in a public place.'

At a court hearing in Doha Monday, the 22-year old, whom CNN has identified only as Laura, was handed a one-year suspended sentence and placed on probation for three years for the sex-related charge, and fined 3.000 Qatari Riyals ($823) for being drunk outside a licensed location.

She'll almost certainly be deported immediately.

A Syrian man also appeared alongside her and was found guilty of the same crimes. He was sentenced to 100 lashes for the illicit fornication charge and a further 40 lashes for the illegal consumption of alcohol. As a Muslim he is not allowed to drink at all under Qatari law.

No mention was made of the rape accusation during proceedings. Neither defendant was present in court, in what was the third hearing in the case.

14.3 Substantive private international rules

Occasionally, countries try to avoid the complexities of applying private international rules from domestic legal systems by adopting treaties with substantive law. Such treaties basically create 'new' law that applies in international disputes, so that it is not necessary to use the law of any domestic legal system. We call such treaties substantive private international rules. Well known examples are the Convention on Contracts for the International Sale of Goods (CISG), INCOTERMS and the Inter-American Specialized uniform through bill of lading for the international carriage of goods by road.

The CISG applies to B to B contracts between two parties whose place of business is not in the same country and these countries are a member of the Convention. Besides that, if only one of the involved businesses is located in a Member State of the CISG, and private international rules dictate that the applicable law is that of the CISG Member State, the convention is still applicable (Art. 1). An example of the latter can be found in the case 'Applying the CISG' (example 14.3). However, contracting parties may exclude the CISG in their contract, and chose other applicable law instead (Art. 6). CISG

EXAMPLE 14.3

Applying the CISG

A company from San Marino is in a legal conflict with a company in South Africa. The matter of dispute is the interpretation of a sales contract. San Marino is a member of the CISG, South Africa is not. The businesses did not specify in their contract what law will be applicable in case of a legal conflict. The private international rules from both San Marino and South Africa point out that the law of San Marino should be applied in this case. As a result, the matter will be resolved by the competent court using the CISG.

The CISG provides for uniform rules in closing a sales contract. For instance, a choice was made for the reception theory when an offer or acceptance thereof is legally binding (art. 16 and 18 CISG). The Convention specifies the legal obligations of the seller and the buyer, and what remedies there are in case of non-performance for both parties. As discussed before in chapter 8, the choice was made to allow both for demanding performance and claiming damage compensation in case of non-performance.

INCOTERMS

In international business, in a B to B relationship, it is important to specify the exact liability of the sender and the receiver of goods during the transport. For this, the International Chamber of Commerce created the so called International Commercial Terms (INCOTERMS). The word INCOTERMS is a registered trademark of the Chamber of Commerce. In the most recent version of the INCOTERMS, 12 different INCOTERMS were adopted (or updated from previous versions). Occasionally, companies make use of the previous version that dates back to 2000. If this is intended, it is recommendable to make this abundantly clear in the sales contract.
In essence, three things are regulated through these INCOTERMS between the sender (seller) and receiver (consignee) of the goods:

- Who bears the costs for what part of the transport.
- Who is responsible for the relevant insurances, tax payments legal documents and permits during what part of the transport.
- Who bears the risk for the goods during what part of the transport.

14

In total, there are 11 different INCOTERMS. It is important to select the INCOTERM that suits your particular business relation and transport mode the best. INCOTERMS divide the responsibility regarding the above mentioned issues between the seller and the consignee. Of major importance is the so called critical point during the transport. This is a location or transport vessel, depending on the INCOTERM, on which the responsibility shifts from sender to consignee. First, we can distinguish four INCOTERMS that are specifically adopted for transport on ocean freights (FAS, FOB, CFR and CIF), while the others can be used for any kind of transportation. Second, it is possible to subdivide the INCOTERMS in grades of responsibility from full responsibility for the seller to full responsibility for the consignee, in which the critical point is gradually moving away from the seller. You can find an overview of this in example 14.4 and table 14.1.

EXAMPLE 14.4

A (really) short overview of the various INCOTERMS

For all kinds of transport

EXW (Ex Works): The seller delivers the goods in his own premises or another agreed place. From then onwards, he consignee is fully responsible for the transport.

FCA (Free Carrier): The seller delivers the goods to the carrier or another agreed place in the exporting country. From then onwards, the consignee is fully responsible for the transport.

CPT (Carriage Paid): the seller delivers the goods to the main carrier of the transport (the shipment in the exporting country). From then onwards, the consignee is fully responsible for the transport. However, the seller pays for the main transport.

CIP (Carriage and Insurance Paid): The seller delivers the goods to the main carrier of the transport (the shipment in the exporting country). From then onwards, the consignee is fully responsible for the transport. However, the seller pays for the main transport, and is bound to insure the value of the transport for 110 per cent.

DAT (Delivered at Terminal): the seller delivers the goods to the importing country (usually a port or an airport) and is therefore fully responsible for the main transport. However, from the moment of the delivery in the importing country, the consignee is fully responsible for the remainder of the transport in his own country, including all formalities of importing the goods.

DAP (Delivered at Place): the seller delivers the goods to the transporter in the importing country, and is responsible for all formalities of importing the goods. For the remainder of the transport, the consignee is responsible (which is hardly worth mentioning).

DDP (Delivered Duty Paid): the seller delivers the goods directly to the consignee. The only responsibility for the consignee lies with the unloading of the goods from the final transport.

For ocean freights only
FAS (Free Alongside Ship): The seller delivers the goods to the ship in the country of export. From that moment onwards, the consignee is fully responsible for the transport.

FOB (Free On Board): The seller delivers the goods on the ship in the country of export (and is therefore responsible for the shipment, but not for the transport). From that moment onwards, the consignee is fully responsible for the transport, including its costs.

CFR (Cost and Freight): The seller delivers the goods on the ship in the country of export, and bears the costs for the main transport. The consignee bears the risk for the main transport, and is for all else responsible for the remainder of the transport.

CIF (Cost, Insurance and Freight): The seller delivers the goods on the ship in the country of export, and bears the costs for the main transport. The seller also insures the goods during the shipment for 110 per cent. The consignee bears the risk for the main transport, and is for all else responsible for the remainder of the transport.

TABLE 14.1 The critical points during transport of the various INCOTERMS

Place seller	Agreed place in importing country	(Air)port in exporting country	(Air)port in importing country	Agreed place in exporting country	Place of Consignee
EXW	FCA	CPT/CIP	DAT	DAP	DDP
		FAS/FOB/CFR/ CIF			

International carriage of goods by road

Where INCOTERMS regulate the liability between sender and receiver, other international instruments regulate the liability of the carrier. For instance, in the America's, the Inter-American Specialized uniform through bill of lading for the international carriage of goods by roadspecifies the liability of the transporter. For instance, the treaty stipulates that the sender is liable for the payment of the freight and other legal costs that come with the transport, such as taxes (Art. 4). The carrier on its own behalf is liable for loss and damage to the goods during transport, and for a delay in the delivery (Art. 5). However, this liability for loss or damage should never exceed the actual value of the goods (Art. 6).
As to the court that may rule in matters of conflict based on this treaty, the courts of virtually all the involved countries have jurisdiction (Art. 11): that is the court in which the defendant has its habitual residence, or principal place of business, the court of the country in which the goods were sent, where the damage was done, or where the goods should have been supplied.

14.4 Objective private international rules

In bilateral or multilateral treaties, countries may harmonize their international private reference rules.

An extensive example can be found in the context of the European Union. Through a handful of regulations, a more or less coherent system of objective private international rules is created.
In essence, Regulation 1215/2012 (by some named the EEX Regulation, or Brussels I), deals with the first question in private international law: jurisdiction matters in civil and commercial proceedings.
The second question, that of the applicable law, is most importantly regulated in Regulation 593/2008 for contractual obligations and 864/2007 for non-contractual obligations. They are by some referred to as 'Rome I' and 'Rome II'. Another popular name for Regulation 993/2008 is the 'ECO Regulation'
The third question in private international law, how a verdict can be executed in another country, is dealt with in Article 39 of the EEX Regulation:

> 'A judgment given in a Member State which is enforceable in that Member State shall be enforceable in the other Member States without any declaration of enforceability being required.'

Therefore, the execution matter is not a real issue within the European Union, and all verdicts are enforceable throughout the entire EU territory, regardless the nationality of the court. This leaves us two questions that remain to be answered in case of an international conflict with a European

dimension: what court has jurisdiction and what law should be applied? While the wordings and structure of the relevant regulations are complex at first sight, the following step approach should work to solve private international issues in a relatively simple manner.
This web of objective private international rules is complex, but using the following step approach might clear things up a bit.

Step 1 Did the conflicting parties make a choice?
Both the EEX and the Rome Regulations recognize the principle of free choice. This means that private parties who are in a legal conflict may choose the jurisdiction (Article 25 EEX), and applicable law (Article 3 Rome I and Article 14 Rome II) that applies to their conflict. When this is done properly, there is usually no problem in this field, and it is a matter of bringing the case before the court that is agreed upon that will apply the law that is agreed upon. Usually, this is then the end of the story when it concerns private international law. Therefore, especially in contractual relations, it is wise and helpful to include these choices in the contract, so that in case of legal disputes there are no doubts about such things. Of course, it would be helpful to agree on the court and law in case of non-contractual obligations. However, in practice, such things happen unexpectedly, and people are already in conflict when such choices need to be made. The chance that a 'kind agreement' on such matters will be made is then usually smaller.

There are two things that need to be mentioned in the context of applicable law.
First, contracting parties do not necessarily have to choose a national legal system. They might also declare instruments of substantive private law applicable to their contract or case. An obvious example is the choice of INCOTERMS to regulate matters of liability during transport between sender and receiver.
Second, especially in the Rome I regulation, there is some additional protection for the 'weaker' party. This is especially so in a Business to Consumer relation, and en employer to employee relation. In such cases, the consumer or employee often has no choice but to accept the general terms of a consumer contract, or the conditions set by the employer. Of course both the consumer and employee agree to such things by signing the contract, but have in practice very little influence on the actual choice that is made. There is after all no real negotiation but a 'take it or leave it' offer by the stronger party: the selling company or the employer. Therefore, despite the choice that is made in such contracts, Articles 6 and 8 Rome I offer some additional protection to the consumer and employee. It is recognized that under certain circumstances, the consumer and employee may not be deprived of the legal protection they would normally have in the place where they live (consumer contract) or work (employment contract). An example is given in the 'smoking guitar' case (example 14.5).

EXAMPLE 14.5

Smoking guitars

Frederique, residing in France, buys a new guitar from a Spanish web shop. In the general terms of this web shop it is clearly stated that the Spanish law is applicable to all contracts closed with the company.

The guitar is delivered on time, and Frederique is quite eager to test his new instrument during one of his live performances. Unfortunately, there seems to be a defect in the product, because after two minutes of playing, the plug that connects the guitar to the amplifier explodes. Frederique is not hurt, but his guitar (worth 400 euros) is a smoking piece of wood.

According to Spanish law, the 400 euros should be paid for by the producer, and not by the supplier. The producer is a company situated in Germany, and not responding to any emails or phone calls. According to French law, the 400 euros should be compensated for directly by the supplier.
In this case, Frederique might use the law that is more favourable to him: French law. Despite the choice for Spanish law, the element of French law that is more favourable to the consumer will prevail, and so the consumer is additionally protected.

Step 2 Does a lex specialis apply?
When no choice of jurisdiction and/or law was made, one needs to establish whether the legal conflict falls under the scope of a specific law. In legal terminology, we call a more specific law a *lex specialis*, in contrast to a general law, which is a *lex generalis.* For instance, there are particular rules for consumer, insurance, transport, employee and immovable property contracts.

Considering the latter: Article 8 (4) and 24 EEX stipulate that a dispute over immovable property should be brought before the court of the country where the immovable property is situated. A similar reasoning can be found in Article 4 (c) of Rome I regulation, which stipulates that the law of the country in which the immovable property is situated applies.

Step 3 Use the lex generalis
If no choice of jurisdiction and/or law was made, and no *lex specialis* applies, one should turn to the general rules of the regulations.
In case of the EEX, these are Articles 4 and 7. Article 4 mainly stipulates that a person should be sued in his country of residence. Article 7 gives the plaintiff an alternate choice. For example, in case of a contract, the court of the place of performance may also have jurisdiction. An example of this can be found in the case 'no delivery' (example 14.6).

EXAMPLE 14.6

No delivery

A German company is in a legal dispute with a Finnish company. The dispute relates to a failure of the Finnish company to deliver goods, while the German company already paid for those goods. On top of that, the German company claims additional compensation damage for loss of income. In their contract, no choice of jurisdiction nor law was made.
Since this is a B to B contract, there is no *lex specialis* governing this relation. Therefore, to determine what court has jurisdiction, the German company will have to consult Articles 4 and 7 of the EEX. The conclusion is

that they can sue the Finnish company in their home country, based on Article 4 EEX. However, since the characteristic performance should have taken place in Germany (the delivery of the goods), the German company may also choose to sue the Finnish company before a German court.

In case of Rome I, Article 4 is a general rule that mainly stipulates that the law of the country of the service provider or seller of goods is applicable. In case of Rome II, the law of the country where the damage occurs is applicable (also, Article 4). An example of the latter can be found in the case 'a Belgian driver...' (example 14.7).

EXAMPLE 14.7

A Belgian driver...

A Belgian driver causes a traffic accident in Poland by damaging the car of a German. The conflicting parties do not agree on any legal choice regarding the jurisdiction or applicable law to their case. The Rome II regulation does not provide for a *lex specialis* for tort law. Article 4 of Rome II stipulates as a general rule that the law of the country where the damage was done applies. That means that whatever court has jurisdiction, this court has to apply Polish law.

When we go through these three steps, the jurisdiction and applicable law will always be found, as we can see in figure 14.1.

FIGURE 14.1 The European system of objective private international law

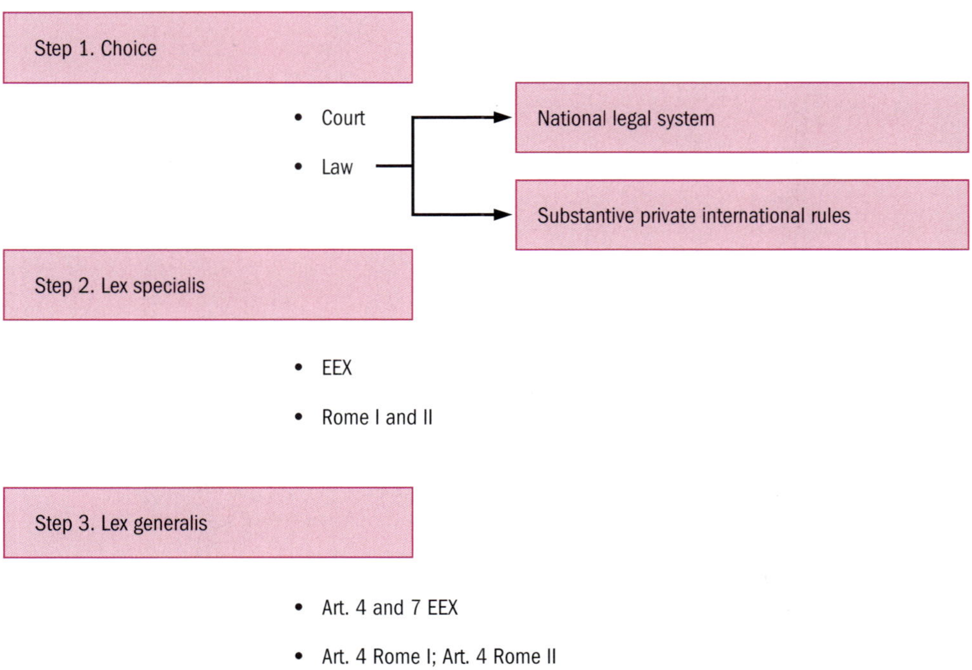

Rome I and the CISG

It needs to be noted here that as a result of the Rome I, the CISG can be applicable in a B to B setting. This would be the case when the two contracting parties, that did not make a legal choice in their contract, would be situated in two countries that are a member of the CISG, or when Rome I would lead to the application of the law of a country that is a member of the CISG.

Summary

- In an international legal dispute between two private parties, the following questions need to be answered:
  - What court has jurisdiction on the matter.
  - What law should be applied by this court.
  - How can the verdict of the court can be executed.

- The law then answering these questions is called 'private international law', and is different in each legal system. This might cause conflicting rules in similar cases. To solve this, international instruments are adopted to harmonize such rules.

- It is generally recognized that the contracting parties have a free choice to determine what they agree upon.

- This means that private parties who close a contract may determine the court that will have jurisdiction, and the applicable law when a legal dispute will occur based on their contract.

- Such a choice is only about private law, and should not lead to a violation of fundamental principles that are recognized in the country where the verdict will have effect.

- On an international level, countries have adopted instruments of private international substantive and objective law.

- Private international substantive law creates new rules that are internationally applicable in private legal relations;
  - Examples are the CISG, INCOTERMS and the Inter-American Specialized uniform through bill of lading for the international carriage of goods by road.

- Private international objective law creates reference rules and determines the jurisdiction and applicable national law in private legal relations.
  - Examples are the EEX, and ROME I and I Regulations in the European Union. These instruments can be applied using a three step-approach:
    - If the conflicting parties made a choice regarding the jurisdiction and applicable law, this will be leading.
    - In the absence of a choice, one needs to look for a *lex specialis* in the EEX and the Rome Regulations to find the court which has jurisdiction and the applicable law.
    - When there is no *lex specialis*, the *lex generalis* in the EEX and Rome I and II Regulation should be used.

Practice questions

Open questions

14.1 Jacob has an account for the website ‘Marketplace’. Marketplace is a French company. Jacob finds out that his profile picture, address, phone number and information about frequently visited products are not only published in a general database, but also sold to third-parties. Jacob regularly (but also secretly) orders second hand DVDs with a very explicit content. He is therefore unpleasantly surprised when a sex shop calls him on his cell phone offering certain products. To make matters worse, it is actually his girlfriend who answered the phone. Jacobs decides to claim compensation due to unfair contract terms. He therefore sues the French company.

For the following question, take these conditions into consideration:

Article 9 General Terms:
‘By creating an account and accepting the contract you automatically accept these general terms.’

Article 12 General Terms:
‘By creating an account you accept that all data on your account can be used by Marketplace for all purposes.’

Article 1 General Terms
‘By creating an account and accepting the contract you accept that French law is exclusively applicable.’

Article 6:231 of the Dutch Civil Code explicitly mentions that General Terms must be accepted by the consumer by signing or another active act of approval.

Assume that according to French law general terms do not have to be approved of by consumers, but merely have to be available to them by general publication.

Do you think Jacob’s claim based on unfair contract terms can be successful? Please explain thoroughly. Refer to the relevant legislation using the Rome I regulation.

14.2 Could you also figure out what court of law would have jurisdiction in the case of question 14.1, using the EEX Regulation? Please note that Jacob wants to sue the French company, and not the other way around.

14.3 An Italian company orders equipment from a German company. The equipment arrives, but is malfunctioning, while the Italian company already paid. The Italian company wants to sue the German company. In their contract, no choice of jurisdiction or applicable law was made.

Considering the EEX, what court would have jurisdiction over this case?

14.4 Consider the case in question 14.3, solely using the Rome I regulation, what law will be applied?

Essay question

Private international substantive law and private international objective law are two different ways to deal with private international disputes. Write an essay in which you explain what approach you prefer and why it relates to the applicable law (the second question in private international law).

Multiple choice questions

14.1 INCOTERMS regulate:
a only the liability between sender and receiver
b only the liability of the carrier
c both the liability between sender and receiver and the liability of the carrier

14.2 The CISG automatically applies to:
a international B to B contracts within Member States
b international and national B to B contracts within Member States
c international B to B and B to C contracts within Member States

14.3 The application of the CISG:
a cannot be excluded contractually
b can be partially excluded contractually
c can be excluded contractually

14.4 The Inter-American Specialized Uniform through Bill of Lading for the International Carriage of Goods by road is an example of:
a private international substantive law
b private international objective law
c private international formal law

Index